WHICH ARE THE WORLD'S SMARTEST ANIMALS?

CAN ANIMALS ... KEEPING THEM IN ZOOS?

WHAT CREATES A RAINBOW?

WHY DID PEOPLE GO EXPLORING?

WHERE WOULD YOU FIND THE WORLD'S TALLEST CACTUS?

MAGNETIC? ARE THERE MANY ASTEROIDS IN THE SOL... IS THE SUN YELLOW? WHAT IS THE MILKY WAY? WHI... WHICH HAVE BEEN THE MOST DESTRUCTIVE VOLCANOE... WHY DOES THE WIND BLOW? WHAT DOES A TORNADO LOOK LI... ...GRASS? ARE A... KINDS OF ANIMALS IN RAINFORESTS? ... WHAT ... A... AND LAKES DISAPPEAR? WHICH IS ... THE BIGGE... ...'S EDGE? WHAT'S THE DIFFERENCE ... B E T W E E ... METALS? WHERE DID THE GASES ON EARTH COME FROM? WHICH WERE THE FIRST ANIMALS TO LI... ...S THE FASTEST DINOSAUR? ARE THERE ANY DINOSAURS AROUND TODAY? WHERE ARE THE BEST PLAC... ...NMALS? HOW LIVING THINGS ARE CLASSIFIED? ARE THERE INVISIBLE CREATURES LIVING IN WATER? CA... ...BROKEN PARTS OF PLANTS STILL GROW? WHY DO SOME TREES SHED THEIR LEAVES? HOW DO ANIMA... ...? WHAT KINDS OF CAMOUFLAGE DO ANIMALS USE? DO ALL ANIMALS HAVE EARS? WHAT ARE ANTLE... ...GRATING ANIMALS FIND THEIR WAY? DO ANIMALS ALWAYS HAVE TWO PARENTS? WHY DO MARSUPIA... ...HE BIGGEST FISH IN THE SEA? WHICH ... IS THE WORLD'S BIGGEST SNAKE... ...THINGS HELP ONE OTHER? WHICH ARE ... THE SMELLIEST SUBSTANCES? HO... ...AIN DO? WHAT MAKES MUSCLES ACHE? ... HOW DOES THE BRAIN CONTRO... ...EZE? ARE ALL FINGERPRINTS DIFFERENT? DO WE ALL SEE THE SAME COLOURS? WHAT DOES EARWA... ...GLANDS? WHY DO WE BURP AND FART? WHY DOES FEELING NERVOU... ...HAVE TWINS? WHERE ARE GENES STORED? HOW MUCH DO PEOPLE EAT ... ...DETECT WITH A STETHOSCOPE? HOW DO YOU MEND A BROKEN BONE... ...WHO HAS THE WORLD'S LONGEST HAIR? IS THERE ANYTHING SMALLER THAN ... ...BECOME? HOW DOES AN ELECTRON MICROSCOPE WORK? WHAT IS A SONIC ... ...E EFFICIENT? HOW DO TOUCHSCREENS WORK? WHAT IS CLOUD COMPUTING? ... ...K? WHAT'S THE DIFFERENCE BETWEEN PLASMA, LCD AND LED SCREENS? WHAT IS 3D PRINTING? CA... ...WER A CAR? HOW WILL TRAIN TRAVEL CHANGE IN THE FUTURE? WHEN WERE SAILS FIRST USED? HO... ...PEOPLE DO ON THE INTERNATIONAL SPACE STATION? HOW ARE TUNNELS MADE? WHAT IS THE WORLD... ...E TURN WASTE INTO ENERGY? HOW ARE HUMANS RELATED TO OTHER APES? WHY DID PEOPLE BUI... ...DID PEOPLE START BUILDING FORTS AND CASTLES? WHO WAS THE FIRST PERSON TO SAIL AROUND TH... ...E ANCIENT ... GREEK MYTHS ABOUT? ARE SOM... ...TEN FOOD? ... HOW ARE FIZZY DRINKS MADE? HO... ...OF? WHY ... ARE GLASS BUILDINGS SAFE? WHI...

READER'S DIGEST

ULTIMATE BOOK OF

KNOWLEDGE

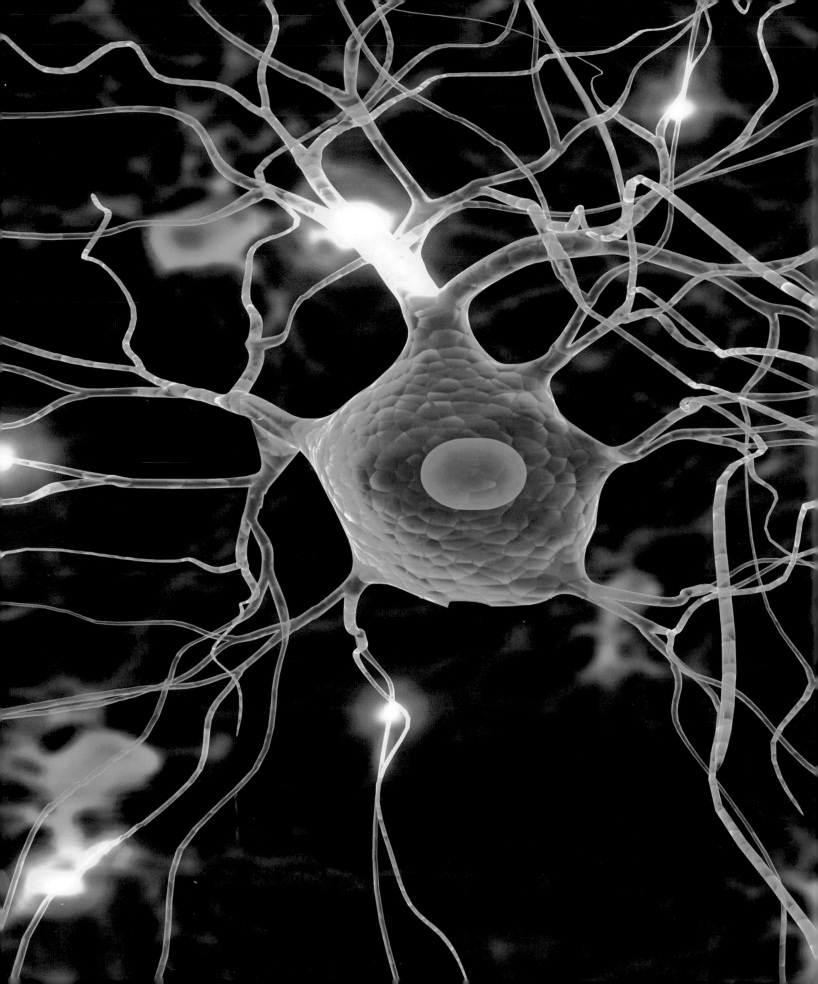

READER'S DIGEST
ULTIMATE
BOOK OF
KNOWLEDGE

FACTS · FIGURES · FUN

Reader's
Digest

EARTH AND SPACE 6

THE HUMAN BODY 140

HISTORY AND CULTURE 250

CONTENTS

EARTH AND SPACE

HOW THE UNIVERSE BEGAN

If you look into the night sky, what you see is the Universe – or at least part of it. The groups of stars known as galaxies, the planets and their moons, the floating lumps of rock called asteroids, even the cold empty spaces between them – all this began to form about 13.8 billion years ago, following an event called the 'Big Bang'.

WHAT WAS THE BIG BANG?

About 13.8 billion years ago, all the matter and energy in the Universe today was packed into a tiny, superhot ball smaller than a pinhead. The Universe began when this ball expanded rapidly. Within a minute, it was billions of kilometres wide.

WHAT HAPPENED AFTER THE BIG BANG?

As the superhot ball expanded, it started to cool. Then tiny particles of matter called protons and neutrons began to form and join to create the first atomic nuclei. These are the cores of atoms, the building blocks of the Universe (▶186). The expansion continued, but within the next 1 billion years the force of gravity began pulling matter into slightly denser clouds, which in turn gave rise to the first stars and galaxies (▶10).

❶ **FLYING START** Tiny, superhot ball of energy and matter expands rapidly.

❷ **WITHIN MINUTES** Particles begin bonding. The first gases – hydrogen and helium – appear.

❸ **NOT SO SMOOTH** Gravity forms denser areas in the smooth early Universe.

❹ **STAR BIRTH** About 500 million years after the Big Bang, the denser areas of matter form stars and galaxies.

![Cosmic microwave background map]

COSMIC MAP *Scientists have used special satellites to map thermal radiation – known as the cosmic microwave background – emitted just 370,000 years after the Big Bang. Tiny variations in temperature, shown here as different colours, gave rise to early galaxies.*

Is the Universe still expanding?

The Universe has been expanding ever since the Big Bang and continues to do so today. We know because, using powerful telescopes, astronomers can see that almost all the galaxies are moving away from us. Furthermore, we can still detect the energy from the Big Bang. This was first noticed in 1964 by two American scientists, Arno Penzias and Robert Wilson. Using a radio telescope, they picked up a microwave 'hiss' coming from all parts of the sky and eventually realised that it could only be heat radiation from the Big Bang spread across the Universe.

fast fact

Using the Hubble Space Telescope, astronomers have located a group of galaxies beyond the constellation Fornax that are thought to be 13.3 billion years old – the oldest objects ever discovered.

WILL THE UNIVERSE END?

Until recently it was thought that the expansion of the Universe would eventually slow down under the influence of gravity. But now we know that it is actually speeding up. What does this mean for the future of the Universe? According to the so-called Big Chill theory, the Universe will continue to expand until the stars run out of energy, leading to the extinction of all life – albeit in the very, very distant future. The more extreme Big Rip theory suggests that the expansion of the universe will eventually overwhelm the force of gravity everywhere and tear apart galaxies, planets and even atoms.

Can we see into the Universe's past?

Though light is the fastest thing in the Universe, it still takes time to travel across space. For example, light from the Moon takes just over a second to reach us, and light from the Sun about eight minutes. Light from visible stars may have taken thousands of years to reach us. So when you see these objects, you are not seeing the present but the past. Using modern telescopes, astronomers can see distant galaxies, including some of the first to form. Their light has been travelling towards us for 13 billion years, so we are seeing them as they were soon after the Big Bang.

DEEP SPACE *The smallest of the many galaxies in this Hubble Space Telescope image are billions of light years away.*

OUR PLACE IN SPACE

Less than 500 years ago, people thought that Earth was the centre of the Universe. It is only within the last few hundred years that we have learned that Earth is just one of eight planets revolving around the Sun. What's more, the Sun is just one of more than 200 billion stars in our galaxy, the Milky Way; and the Milky Way is one of countless billions of galaxies within the Universe.

WHAT IS THE MILKY WAY?

The Milky Way is the name of our galaxy, which derives from its misty appearance in the sky. The Milky Way and the Andromeda galaxy are the largest galaxies in the Local Group. The Milky Way has more than 200 billion stars, and Andromeda has more than 1 trillion. Situated about 2.5 million light years away from us, Andromeda is the most distant object visible to the naked eye – most of the other 50 or so members of the Local Group are too small and faint to see without a telescope.

Andromeda

M33

And I

And II

And III

NGC 5087

NGC 4995

Sombrero

NGC 4697

NGC 6822

DDO 210

IC 1613

NGC 205

Virgo

WLM

M51

M96
Centaurus

Coma 1

NGC 4151

NGC 3998

Ursa Major

Virgo W

M81

M94

NGC 3813

Sculptor

Local Group

NGC 3613

CAN WE SEE THE ENTIRE UNIVERSE?

Evidence suggests that over 95 per cent of the Universe is invisible. The presence of this mysterious 'dark matter' and 'dark energy' is inferred from observations of the behaviour of matter that we can see.

WHERE ARE WE IN THE UNIVERSE?

Galaxies tend to form groups, known as clusters, and these in turn are drawn to other clusters, forming superclusters – vast strings of galaxy clusters many millions of light years wide. The galaxy cluster we live in is known as the Local Group and it is part of a supercluster that is dominated by the Virgo cluster, which includes more than 2000 galaxies.

Neptune

Uranus

Saturn

WHAT IS A LIGHT YEAR?

The Universe has expanded to an almost unimaginable size, and distances between galaxies are vast. To measure such huge distances, scientists use a unit called a light year. That's the equivalent of the distance that light travels in one year: 9,460,700 million (or almost 10 trillion) km (6 trillion miles).

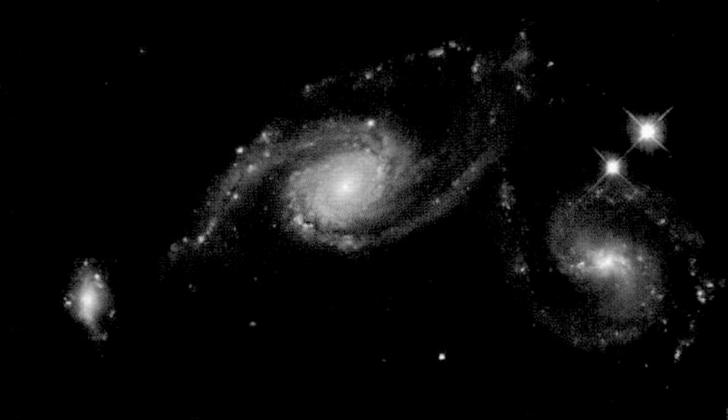

WHERE IS OUR STAR?

While the Milky Way looks like a band from our perspective, it is actually a wide, flat disc with spiralling arms. Our star, the Sun, is located in the so-called Orion Arm, about halfway out from the centre.

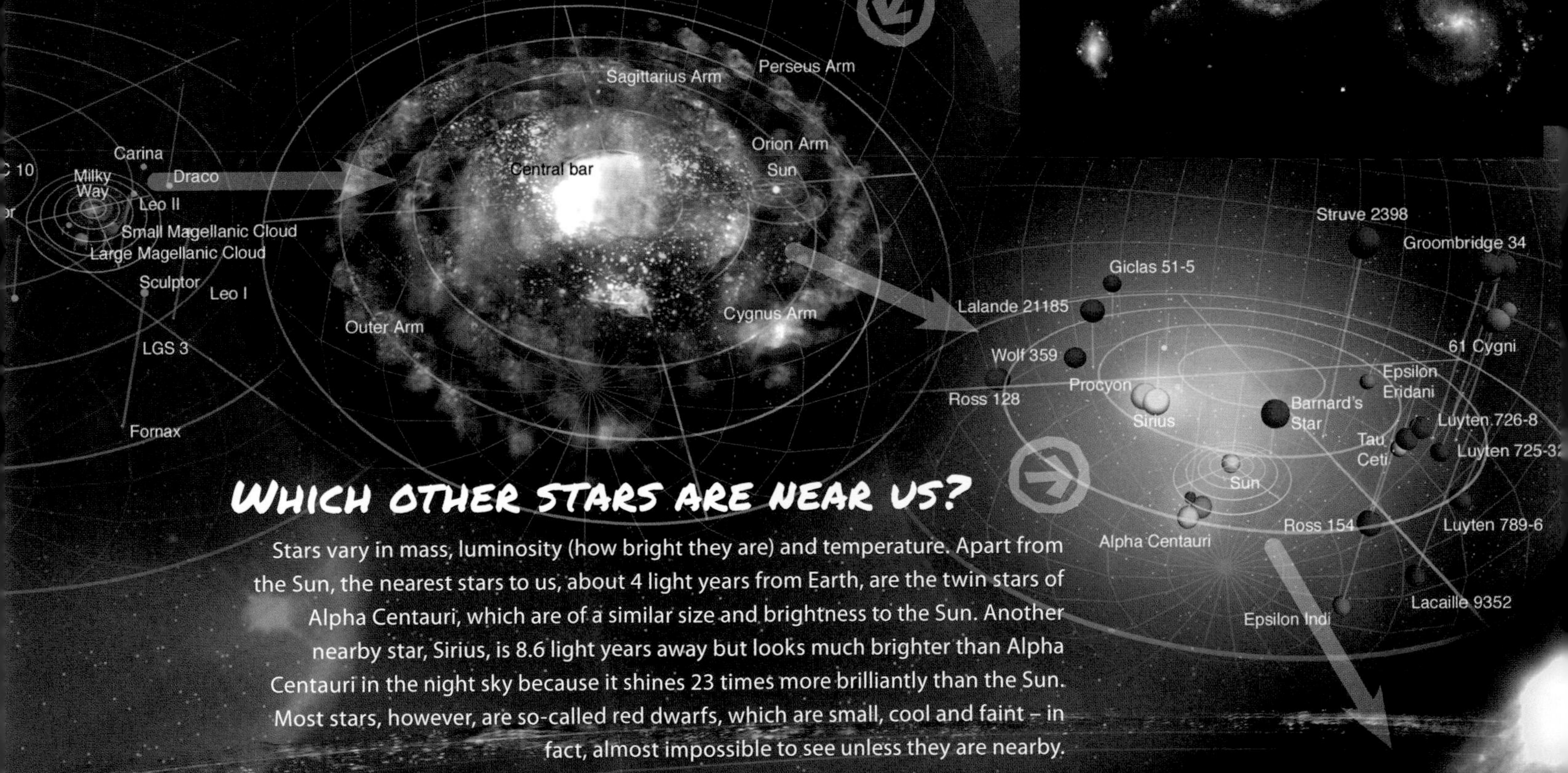

Sagittarius Arm

Perseus Arm

Orion Arm
Sun

Central bar

Carina

C 10

Milky Way

Draco

Leo II

Small Magellanic Cloud

Large Magellanic Cloud

Sculptor

Leo I

Cygnus Arm

LGS 3

Outer Arm

Fornax

Struve 2398

Groombridge 34

Giclas 51-5

Lalande 21185

61 Cygni

Wolf 359

Epsilon Eridani

Ross 128

Procyon

Barnard's Star

Luyten 726-8

Sirius

Tau Ceti

Luyten 725-32

Sun

Ross 154

Luyten 789-6

Alpha Centauri

Lacaille 9352

Epsilon Indi

WHICH OTHER STARS ARE NEAR US?

Stars vary in mass, luminosity (how bright they are) and temperature. Apart from the Sun, the nearest stars to us, about 4 light years from Earth, are the twin stars of Alpha Centauri, which are of a similar size and brightness to the Sun. Another nearby star, Sirius, is 8.6 light years away but looks much brighter than Alpha Centauri in the night sky because it shines 23 times more brilliantly than the Sun. Most stars, however, are so-called red dwarfs, which are small, cool and faint – in fact, almost impossible to see unless they are nearby.

HOW CLOSE ARE WE TO THE SUN?

Like many stars, the Sun is orbited by a solar system: a group of planets, moons and asteroids. Our Solar System includes eight planets, and our home, Earth, is the third planet from the Sun, orbiting at an average distance of 150 million km (93 million miles).

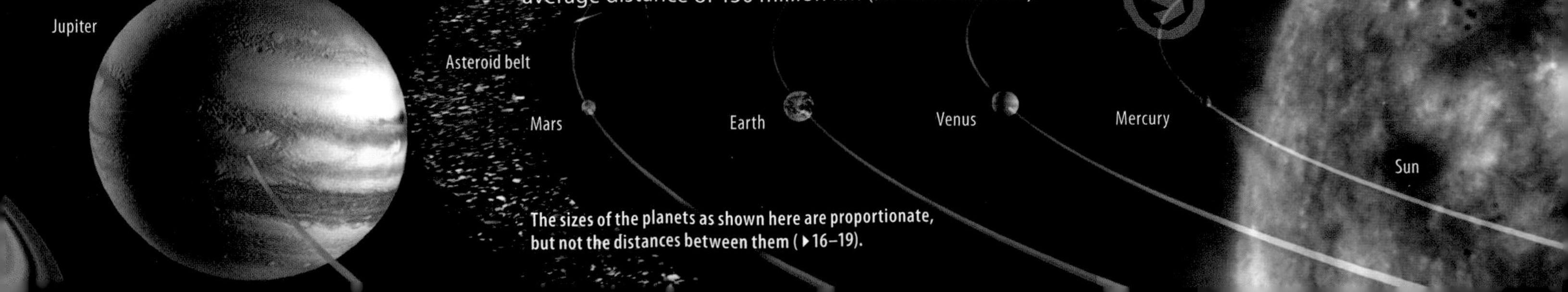

Jupiter

Asteroid belt

Mars

Earth

Venus

Mercury

Sun

The sizes of the planets as shown here are proportionate, but not the distances between them (▶16–19).

OUR STAR, THE SUN

The Sun, a glowing globe of hot gas thousands of times bigger than Earth, lies at the heart of our Solar System.

Scientists estimate that the Sun is less than halfway through its life, having formed, along with Earth and the other planets, around 4.6 billion years ago. Although it is 1,392,000 km (865,000 miles) wide, it is an average weight in star terms and of only medium brightness – a fairly ordinary star, in other words.

HOW DID OUR SUN FORM?

Billions of years after the Big Bang, the Milky Way galaxy was full of stars, as it is today, but also many clouds of gas and dust, known as nebulae (singular: nebula). Nebulae are where stars form and, about 5 billion years ago, one of these nebulae began to make a new star – our Sun.

Nebula

❶ IN A SPIN *About 5 billion years ago a cloud of gas began to collapse under its own weight and spin. As a result, it flattened into a disc and its centre began to heat up.*

❷ LIGHTING UP *When the temperature at the centre of the embryo star reached about 5 million°C (9 million°F), it triggered nuclear reactions. These turned hydrogen gas into helium and released enormous amounts of energy. A star was born.*

WILL THE SUN LAST FOREVER?

Stars last a long time, but not forever. The Sun has slowly increased in brightness since it settled into its long, stable life. It will continue to slowly grow in brightness and size for another 6 billion years. When it has burned up the fuel at its centre and is running out of energy, it will expand rapidly and cool down, becoming a red giant. Then it will shed its outer layers to reveal its core as a tiny, white star – known as a white dwarf – which will live on for further tens of billions of years.

❸ SHINING BRIGHTLY *Today the fully formed Sun continues to generate colossal amounts of energy. In this way it provides the warmth and light necessary for life on Earth.*

fast fact
The Sun consumes 500 million tonnes (550 million tons) of hydrogen per second.

WILL THE SUN BECOME A BLACK HOLE?

No, only a giant star – at least eight times the size of the Sun – can form a black hole. That happens when, nearing the end of its life, a giant star explodes – an event called a Supernova. The explosion blows away much of the matter of the star, but the core collapses in on itself, creating an area of intense gravitational pull, from which even light cannot escape – a black hole.

A black hole (at left) in a binary star system

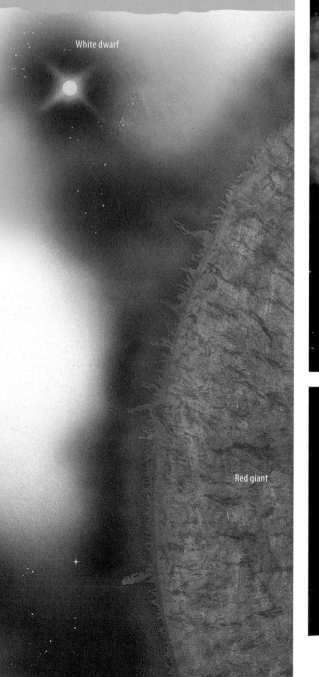

White dwarf

Red giant

APPROACHING THE END *Late in its life cycle, a star like the Sun will gently puff off its outer layers.*

WHY IS THE SUN YELLOW?

The colour of a star depends on how hot it is, and this, in turn, depends on its size and age. Fully formed, average-size stars, such as our Sun, look yellow. But as they get older, they expand and their surface temperature drops, with the result that they appear orange or red. When a Sun-like star has exhausted its energy, it lives out its life as a faint, pale point of light.

COLOUR CODE *Very hot stars look bluish-white (left); cooler ones look yellow; and the coolest ones look red.*

THE BIRTH OF THE SOLAR SYSTEM

WHERE DID THE PLANETS COME FROM?

In the swirling cloud of gas and dust around the newly formed Sun – the nebula – dust and debris collided and merged, slowly growing bigger until they formed planets. Nearer the Sun, the heat allowed only rocky materials to solidify, but in the outer Solar System the rocky objects also accumulated large amounts of ice and gas, resulting in much bigger planets.

Our Solar System has eight planets, all of which orbit the Sun, moving in the same direction and on a similar plane. It also includes several dwarf planets such as Pluto, at least 90 moons, dozens of comets and countless lumps of rock known as asteroids. All began to take shape about 4.6 billion years ago, as the Sun formed (▶12).

DISC WORLDS An artist's impression of the major stages in the formation of the Solar System

HARD RAIN As they formed, all the planets were bombarded by meteorites.

IS THERE LIFE ON OTHER PLANETS?

Life depends on about two dozen chemical elements, of which carbon, hydrogen, oxygen, nitrogen, sulfur and phosphorus are the most vital. For life to continue, water, light and warmth are also needed. Mars has the right chemical ingredients and may once have had the right conditions – for example, it shows many signs of having once had liquid water on its surface. However, conditions on Mars now, which include a thin atmosphere and subzero temperatures, are not suitable for life as we know it. They may, however, be kinder on Europa, one of Jupiter's moons. There, spacecraft have photographed an icy surface that is thought to lie on top of a deep ocean of water.

MOON WATER? Long cracks crisscross the ice floes forming the surface of Europa.

TODAY Even now, Earth is not a static body. Deep inside our planet, temperatures are still 4500°C (8100°F). Hot molten rock, or magma, rises towards the surface, bursting through cracks and holes to form volcanoes, and jolting sections of Earth's crust – movements we feel as earthquakes (▶34).

4.6 BILLION YEARS AGO Earth was a molten ball of rock. The surface cooled quickly, but it was constantly broken and melted by meteorites bombarding the planet. Heavier metals, such as iron, sank towards the core, while lighter materials rose to the surface. Gases began forming the atmosphere.

4.5 BILLION YEARS AGO Earth crashed into a smaller planet, roughly the size of Mars. The chunks of debris thrown out by the collision began circling Earth and gradually merged to form the Moon. Meanwhile, Earth's surface cooled to form a hard crust over its semi-liquid interior. The intense heat inside the planet caused regular eruptions that flooded the surface with lava and filled the air with carbon dioxide and water vapour.

HOW DID EARTH AND THE MOON FORM?

Gradually, each planet assumed distinct characteristics according to its composition and distance from the Sun (▶16–19). Soon after Earth took shape, a collision with a smaller planet resulted in the formation of the Moon.

4.3–3.5 BILLION YEARS AGO A thicker, more permanent continental crust formed on Earth's surface. The water vapour in the atmosphere began to condense, slowly forming the first rivers, lakes and oceans. The first oxygen-producing life forms appeared in the oceans – primitive bacteria. Clouds of water vapour began blocking the Sun's radiation, and surface temperatures fell while oxygen levels rose.

fast fact
The Sun weighs almost 1000 times as much as the rest of the Solar System put together.

THE INNER PLANETS

The four inner planets are all rocky on the surface and much smaller than the four outer planets. They also orbit relatively close to the Sun and are all visible at times in our night sky (▶26).

MERCURY

Distance from the Sun (minimum) 45,900,000 km (28,520,000 miles)
Distance from the Sun (maximum) 69,700,000 km (43,300,000 miles)
Period of orbit around the Sun 87.97 days
Diameter (at Equator) 4878 km (3031 miles)
Diameter x Earth 0.38
Mass x Earth 0.055
Spin period (at Equator) 58 days 15 hours 28 minutes
Average surface temperature 350°C (662°F) by day; −170°C (−274°F) at night
Atmosphere Very thin; some helium
Number of moons 0

WHICH PLANET IS CLOSEST TO THE SUN?

Mercury orbits nearest the Sun and is also the smallest and fastest-moving planet. Because it orbits so quickly, a year on Mercury lasts just three months in Earth time; in contrast, the planet spins very slowly on its axis, so that a day on Mercury lasts for two-thirds of a Mercury year. With no atmosphere to deflect or trap heat, surface temperatures on Mercury are extreme – scorching hot by day and intensely cold at night.

WHAT IS THE LANDSCAPE OF MERCURY LIKE?

Mercury has clear skies and is barren, rugged and pockmarked with craters – very like our Moon, in other words. Among the most intriguing land features are huge cliffs called rupes, which in places run unbroken for hundreds of kilometres.

RAISED UP Mercury's rupes may have formed as the planet cooled and shrank after formation.

VENUS

Distance from the Sun (minimum) 107,400,000 km (66,740,000 miles)
Distance from the Sun (maximum) 109,000,000 km (67,730,000 miles)
Period of orbit around the Sun 224.7 days
Diameter (at Equator) 12,104 km (7521 miles)
Diameter x Earth 0.95
Mass x Earth 0.815
Spin period (at Equator) 243 days 3 hours 50 minutes
Average surface temperature 480°C (896°F)
Atmosphere Dense; mainly carbon dioxide
Number of moons 0

WHY IS VENUS SO HOT?

Venus is further from the Sun than Mercury but experiences higher temperatures. The reason for this is that Venus has a dense, cloudy atmosphere made up mainly of carbon dioxide. Daytime heat from the Sun is trapped by this atmosphere and cannot escape at night, as it does on Mercury. As a result, Venus is extremely hot, all the time.

HIDDEN FROM SIGHT Venus's dense atmosphere obscures its landforms, but radar can be used to map the terrain. This image distinguishes low land (blue and green) from higher areas (brown).

WHAT IS THE SURFACE OF VENUS LIKE?

Venus is barren and rocky and studded with volcanoes, some of which may have erupted as recently as 800 million years ago. Vast lava flows are visible across much of the planet's surface.

SHORT VISIT This close-up of Venus's surface was taken by the Russian **Venera 13** space probe in 1982. The conditions were so extreme that the probe survived for only two hours after landing. Part of the probe is visible at bottom right.

Mercury

Venus

Earth

Mars

Planets shown to scale

MARS

Distance from the Sun (minimum) 206,700,000 km (128,440,000 miles)
Distance from the Sun (maximum) 249,000,000 km (154,730,000 miles)
Period of orbit around the Sun 687 days
Diameter (at Equator) 6794 km (4222 miles)
Diameter x Earth 0.53
Mass x Earth 0.11
Spin period (at Equator) 24 hours 37 minutes
Average surface temperature −63°C (−81°F)
Atmosphere Thin; mainly carbon dioxide
Number of moons 2
Names of main moons Phobos, Deimos

REMOTE CONTROL *The Mars rover* Curiosity *landed on the planet on 6 August 2012.*

IS THERE LIFE ON MARS?

Mars is in many ways like Earth: it has the same length of day, a similar tilt to its axis, and there are icecaps at its poles. Because of this, scientists thought it was the planet most likely to also have life. In recent years, space probes have landed on Mars and remote-controlled vehicles have explored, photographed and tested its surface. But so far no clear evidence of life has been found.

WHAT IS IT LIKE ON THE SURFACE OF MARS?

Most of the planet is covered in red rock and is dry and dusty. There are enormous volcanoes, including Olympus Mons, the highest volcanic mountain in the Solar System, rising 25 km (15 miles) from the planet's surface, and there is a vast canyon, the Valles Marineris, which is as long as the United States is wide. Massive dust storms sometimes blow up and can cover the whole surface of the planet.

EARTH

Distance from the Sun (minimum)
147,000,000 km (91,340,000 miles)
Distance from the Sun (maximum)
152,000,000 km (94,450,000 miles)
Period of orbit around the Sun 365.3 days
Diameter (at Equator) 12,756 km (7926 miles)
Diameter x Earth 1
Mass x Earth 1
Spin period (at Equator) 23 hours 56 mins
Average surface temperature 22°C (72°F)
Atmosphere Mainly nitrogen and oxygen
Number of moons 1
Names of main moons Moon

WHAT'S SPECIAL ABOUT EARTH?

Earth is the only planet known to support abundant life. This is partly due to its location – it orbits close enough to the Sun to stay warm, yet far enough away not to be too hot – but also to its oxygen-rich atmosphere and abundance of water. Only on Earth is water present in three forms – solid (ice), liquid (in rivers, lakes and seas) and vapour (in the air) – all of which are clearly visible from an orbiting spacecraft.

HIGH POINT *As this artist's impression shows, Olympus Mons is almost three times the height of Mount Everest.*

THE OUTER PLANETS

Mercury
Venus
Earth
Mars

Separated from the inner planets by the asteroid belt (▸23), the outer planets are much larger and, being much further from the Sun, colder than the inner planets.

They are sometimes referred to as the 'gas giants' because they consist mainly of hydrogen and other gases, though Uranus and Neptune are also known as the 'ice giants' because beneath their blue-hued, hydrogen-rich atmospheres lie layers of ice.

JUPITER

Distance from the Sun (minimum) 741,000,000 km (460,000,000 miles)
Distance from the Sun (maximum) 816,000,000 km (507,000,000 miles)
Period of orbit around the Sun 11 years 314 days
Diameter (at Equator) 142,800 km (88,732 miles)
Diameter x Earth 11.2
Mass x Earth 317.9
Spin period (at Equator) 9 hours 55.5 minutes
Average surface temperature −150°C (−238°F)
Atmosphere Mainly hydrogen and helium
Number of moons 50, and 17 awaiting names
Names of main moons Io, Europa, Ganymede, Callisto

JUST HOW BIG IS JUPITER?

Jupiter is by far the biggest planet. More than 11 times the diameter, 300 times the mass and 1300 times the volume of Earth, it is also more than twice as heavy as all the other planets in the Solar System combined. However, it consists mainly of gas and has only a small, rocky core.

WHAT IS THAT BIG RED SPOT ON JUPITER?

The Great Red Spot is a huge storm system in the planet's atmosphere. Four times the size of Earth, it has been present at least since it was first observed, in 1664, by English scientist Robert Hooke, but it shifts position and varies in shape and in the intensity of its colour, depending on weather patterns.

SKY HIGH *The Red Spot system rises 8 km (5 miles) above adjacent clouds.*

SATURN'S RINGS *One of the planet's moons is visible here at the edge of the rings.* | Moon

SATURN

Distance from the Sun (minimum) 1,350,000,000 km (839,000,000 miles)
Distance from the Sun (maximum) 1,504,000,000 km (934,500,000 miles)
Period of orbit around the Sun 29 years 168 days
Diameter (at Equator) 120,660 km (74,975 miles)
Diameter x Earth 9.46
Mass x Earth 95.2
Spin period (at Equator) 10 hours 12 minutes
Average surface temperature −180°C (−292°F)
Atmosphere Mainly hydrogen and helium
Number of moons 53, plus 9 awaiting names
Names of main moons Titan, Rhea, Tethys

WHAT ARE SATURN'S RINGS MADE OF?

The rings are made of chunks of ice that are orbiting the planet. There are three broad rings, extending to a diameter of 270,000 km (168,000 miles) but only about 30 m (100 ft) thick. Rings were once thought to be unique to Saturn, but fainter rings have been found around Jupiter, Uranus and Neptune.

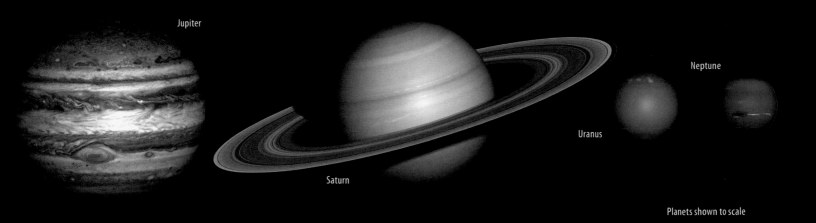

Jupiter

Neptune

Uranus

Saturn

Planets shown to scale

URANUS

Distance from the Sun (minimum) 2,749,000,000 km (1,708,000,000 miles)
Distance from the Sun (maximum) 3,004,000,000 km (1,867,000,000 miles)
Period of orbit around the Sun 84 years
Diameter (at Equator) 51,118 km (31,764 miles)
Diameter x Earth 4.01
Mass x Earth 14.5
Spin period (at Equator) 17 hours 14 minutes
Average surface temperature −214°C (−353°F)
Atmosphere Mainly hydrogen and helium
Number of moons 27
Names of main moons Titania, Oberon, Umbriel

WHY IS URANUS CALLED THE 'SIDEWAYS PLANET'?

Earth's axis tilts 23.5 degrees off the vertical, but Uranus tilts a whopping 98 degrees, so that it lies on its side and spins like a rolling wheel. The cause of this unusual position may have been a collision with another planet or an asteroid when Uranus was forming.

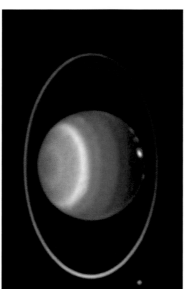

NEW LIGHT This near-infrared image reveals Uranus's rings, cloud bands and moons.

fast fact

The average surface temperature on Uranus is −214°C (−353°F). But down at the core it's a different story. There it's thought to be as hot as 5000°C (9000°F).

NEPTUNE

Distance from the Sun (minimum) 4,554,000,000 km (2,830,000,000 miles)
Distance from the Sun (maximum) 4,453,000,000 km (2,767,000,000 miles)
Period of orbit around the Sun 164 years 292 days
Diameter (at Equator) 49,528 km (30,775 miles)
Diameter x Earth 3.96
Mass x Earth 17.2
Spin period (at Equator) 16 hours 7 minutes
Average surface temperature −220°C (−364°F)
Atmosphere Mainly hydrogen and helium
Number of moons 13
Names of main moons Triton, Proteus

WHY ARE URANUS AND NEPTUNE BLUE?

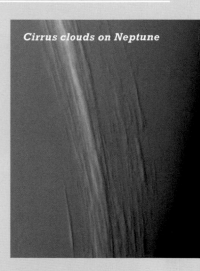

Cirrus clouds on Neptune

The blue colour is due to the presence of methane in their deep atmospheres. Methane absorbs red light from the Sun and reflects its blue light back into space. Due to differences in the quantity of methane, Uranus is more of a greenish blue, whereas Neptune is a brighter, deeper blue. The atmosphere of Uranus is feature-less, but Neptune often bears streaks of white cloud, including one fast-moving cloud in its southern hemisphere nicknamed the Scooter, as well as large dark spots.

WHICH PLANET HAS THE LONGEST YEAR?

Neptune's long, slow orbit means that a year on the planet lasts for approximately 165 years on Earth. After the planet was first identified in 1846, it did not complete a full orbit of the Sun until 2011.

DWARF PLANETS AND MOONS

As well as the planets, there are many other planet-like bodies in the Solar System. In a similar way to planets, dwarf planets orbit the Sun, but, unlike true planets, they have not yet cleared a path in their orbital zones, which may still be cluttered with other dwarf planets or smaller bodies. Moons, also known as natural satellites, are bodies that orbit around planets and dwarf planets. Mercury and Venus have no moons, while other planets have many. Earth has just one, which is clearly visible to us, and has a powerful influence on our world (▶64).

WHERE DO YOU FIND DWARF PLANETS?

Five dwarf planets have been officially identified: Pluto, Ceres, Eris, Makemake and Haumea. Ceres circles between Mars and Jupiter, while the others orbit beyond Neptune. Scientists believe that there could be hundreds of other dwarf planets in the Solar System, most yet to be discovered.

CERES First spotted in 1801, Ceres is about 1000 km (600 miles) across, with a rocky core and icy outer layers.

WASN'T PLUTO ONCE A PLANET?

Soon after it was discovered in 1930 Pluto was classified as the ninth planet, a status it retained for more than 75 years. However, in 2006, following the discovery of other, similar bodies in the outer Solar System, it was recategorised as a dwarf planet.

SMALL SATELLITES Dwarf planets may have their own moons. Egg-shaped Haumea has two, Hi'aka and Namaka, as shown in this artist's impression.

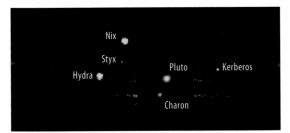

Nix
Styx
Hydra
Pluto
Kerberos
Charon

BARELY VISIBLE Pluto is so far away that only faint images of it and its five known moons have been captured.

MOON VIEW In this artist's rendering, Pluto is viewed from one of its moons. To its right is another moon, Charon. Charon is about half the size of Pluto, while the other moons are much smaller.

fast fact

Pluto follows an elliptical orbit, so its distance from the Sun varies considerably. When it is further away from the Sun, the dwarf planet's thin atmosphere freezes, forming a frost on its surface. When it is closer to the Sun, the atmosphere warms up and starts to circulate.

Io   Europa   Ganymede   Callisto

WHICH PLANET HAS THE MOST MOONS?

Both Jupiter and Saturn have large numbers of moons, and new ones are discovered regularly. Currently, Saturn has 53 named moons and another 9 awaiting confirmation and naming. Jupiter has 50 named moons and 17 awaiting confirmation, so it could have at least 67.

THE MOON

Diameter 3476 km (2160 miles)
Distance from Earth 384,400 km (238,828 miles)
Time to orbit Earth 27.32 days
Time to spin on axis 27.32 days
Time between new moons 29 days 12 hours 44 minutes 3 seconds

WHAT ARE THE DARK AREAS ON THE MOON?

The lighter areas on the surface of the Moon are rugged uplands. These are pitted with craters formed by meteorite impacts, so many that they overlap and obliterate each other. The dark patches are low-lying areas known as 'maria' (singular: mare) or 'seas'. They formed when very large meteorites struck the Moon soon after its formation. This cracked the surface and caused lava to flood out over a wide area, covering existing craters. The lava then cooled and solidified.

Surface of the Moon

WHAT IS IT LIKE ON THE MOON?

Our Moon is a dry and dusty place, pockmarked with craters and with no plants or water. It has no atmosphere to protect it from the Sun's rays or trap heat, so by day it is baking hot and at night it is freezing cold. The force of gravity (▸188) is only a sixth as strong on the Moon as it is on Earth, which is why the astronauts who landed there walked with a 'bouncing' gait.

ARE ALL THE MOONS DEAD AND BARREN?

No. Some moons show signs of volcanic activity, most notably Io, one of Jupiter's moons, which has approximately 400 active volcanoes that sometimes shoot ash and gases 200 km (120 miles) above its surface. On another of Jupiter's moons, Europa, a crust of ice may conceal an ocean with its own life forms (▸14). And the surface of one of Neptune's moons, Triton, is dotted with geysers.

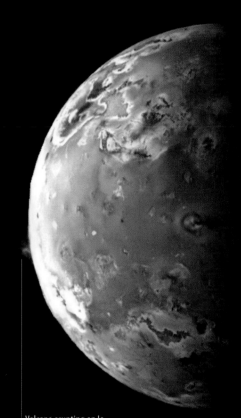
Volcano erupting on Io

Ice
Water
Rock
Iron and nickel

Possible structure of Europa

COMETS, ASTEROIDS AND METEORS

Debris left over after the formation of the planets still litters the Solar System. Rocky lumps that circle the Sun are called asteroids, while lumps of ice and dust that typically orbit further away from the Sun are known as comets. Fragments of rock or metal that enter Earth's atmosphere are referred to as meteors. Usually meteors burn up before hitting the ground, but those that reach Earth's surface become known as meteorites.

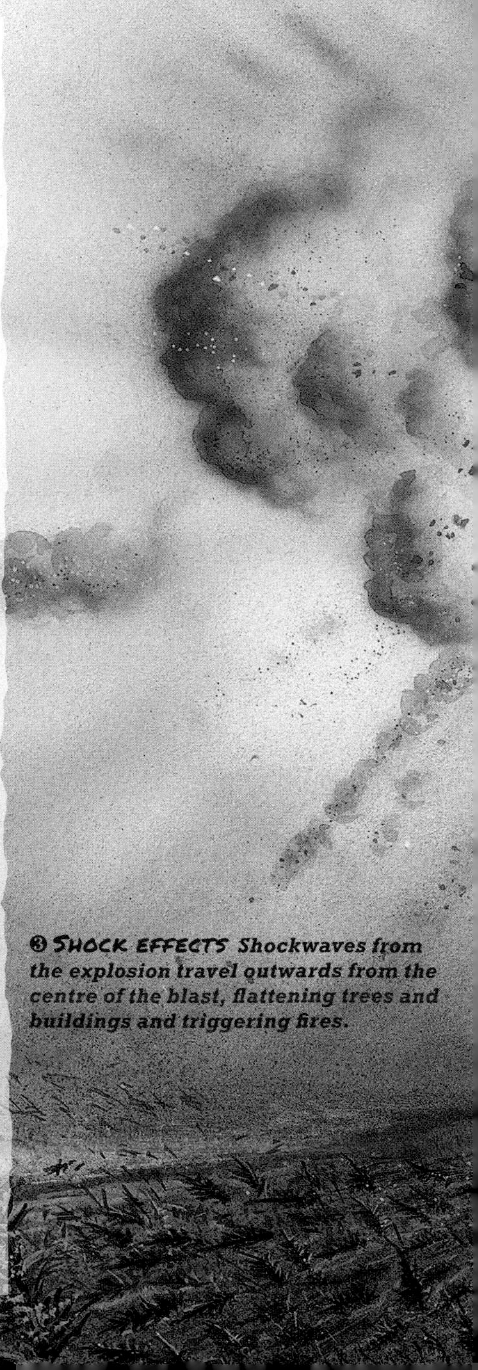

❶ HIGH-SPEED DELIVERY
A comet plummets through Earth's atmosphere, causing the air around it to heat up.

HOW OFTEN DO COMETS PASS NEAR EARTH?

So-called short-period comets orbit the Sun in less than 200 years. Long-period comets may take much longer to orbit or even never return. There are approximately 5000 known comets, but this is only a tiny fraction of the comet-like objects orbiting in the Solar System.

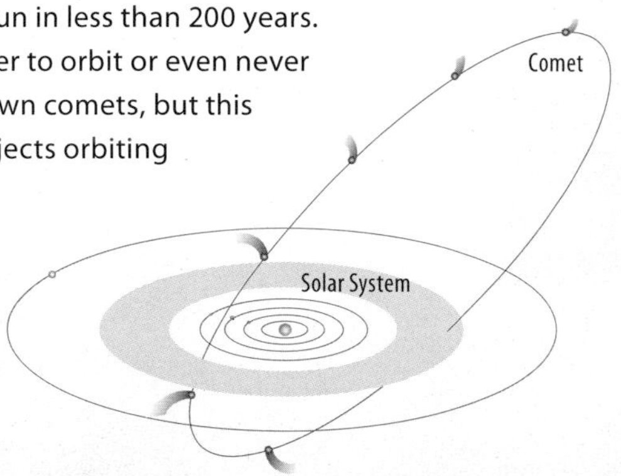

Comet

Solar System

WHAT'S INSIDE A COMET?

Resembling a large, dirty snowball, a comet consists of a mix of rock and ice.
Most comets remain invisible until they come close to the Sun, when they may shine spectacularly as some of the ice melts and forms a bright cloud, known as a coma, as well as a glowing trail up to 300 million km (200 million miles) long.

COMING CLOSE *Seen here over California in 1997, Comet Hale-Bopp was one of the brightest comets of the twentieth century.*

❸ SHOCK EFFECTS *Shockwaves from the explosion travel outwards from the centre of the blast, flattening trees and buildings and triggering fires.*

ARE THERE MANY ASTEROIDS IN THE SOLAR SYSTEM?

There are estimated to be around 1 million asteroids measuring at least 1 km (3/5 mile) across. Most orbit in a wide belt between the paths of Mars and Jupiter. Scientists estimate that Earth (and the other three inner planets, Mercury, Venus and Mars) is struck by an asteroid 1 km (3/5 mile) across every 500,000 years or so.

NEAR THING Discovered in 1898, the 433 Eros asteroid orbits between Earth and Mars. It is 34 km (21 miles) long.

WHAT MIGHT HAPPEN IF A COMET OR METEOR STRUCK EARTH?

If a meteor or comet made it through Earth's atmosphere, it could have a devastating impact. A small comet might break apart and vaporise in mid-air, as shown here. Larger comets and meteors could strike the ground with tremendous impact, forming a massive crater and triggering even more extensive devastation.

❷ *EXPLOSION IN THE SKY* The comet explodes 10 km (6 miles) above Earth's surface. The heat vaporises much of the comet, so there is no large impact crater on the ground.

Meteor Crater, Arizona, USA

HOW OFTEN DO METEORS ENTER EARTH'S ATMOSPHERE?

About 50 tonnes (55 tons) of meteors enter Earth's atmosphere every day – mainly dust-sized particles but sometimes much larger rocks. Most of this material is burned up as it hurtles through the atmosphere at speeds of between 30 and 90 km per second (20–60 miles per second): the blaze can be seen from Earth as a 'shooting' or 'falling' star. But about 500 meteors a year – about 1 tonne (1.1 tons) of material a day – reach the surface. Most are too small to be noticed, but every so often larger ones strike.

fast fact

The medieval town of Nordlingen in Germany is built inside a meteor crater 25 km (15 miles) in diameter. The crater formed 14.5 million years ago when a meteorite about 1.6 km (1 mile) across hit the ground. Stone walls in the town contain tiny diamonds formed by the impact.

THE END OF THE DINOSAURS?

About 66 million years ago, a missile from outer space – probably an asteroid about 10 km (6 miles) in diameter – struck the Yucatan Peninsula in Mexico. The impact formed a crater 180 km (110 miles) wide and 20 km (12 miles) deep, set off huge firestorms, created towering tsunamis and sent up a dust cloud that blotted out the Sun. These conditions may have caused the demise of the dinosaurs (▶82).

LOOKING AT THE NIGHT SKY

In all, about 5800 stars are bright enough to be seen with the naked eye in perfect conditions – on a clear, moonless night. With binoculars or a small telescope, you can see many more. The stars seem to move in a circle around the North and South poles. But it is of course Earth that moves, not the stars.

WHERE IS THE MILKY WAY?

All the stars we can see in the sky are part of our galaxy, the Milky Way. If you could see the Milky Way from outside, it would look like a huge, bright disc with spiralling arms (▶11). We are, however, inside this disc, so looking through it we see a dense band of stars. This band is the source of our galaxy's name.

BAND OF STARS *The Milky Way as it appears from Earth in clear conditions*

HOW DO YOU IDENTIFY STARS?

People have long recognised patterns of stars, called constellations. Thousands of years ago, they gave names to them and made up stories, or myths, about them. Astronomers still use the names to identify stars. There are 88 constellations covering the whole sky. Once you can recognise some of them, you will more easily find your way around the night sky.

NEAREST GALAXY *The Andromeda Galaxy, seen here at left, is the only galaxy visible to the naked eye in the Northern Hemisphere.*

WHY DO SOME STARS LOOK FUZZY?

Stars that look fuzzy are often other kinds of objects. One example appears in the middle of Orion's 'sword'. Through binoculars, you can see that it is not actually a single star but a number of stars embedded in a glowing cloud of dust and gas, called a nebula (▶12). It is known as the Great Nebula. Other fuzzy objects may turn out to be huge swirling masses of billions of stars – galaxies, in other words (▶10).

WHICH CONSTELLATIONS CAN YOU SEE IN THE NORTHERN HEMISPHERE?

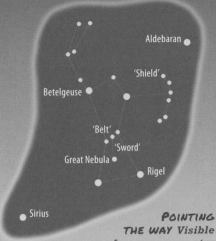

Aldebaran

'Shield'

Betelgeuse

'Belt'

'Sword'

Great Nebula

Rigel

Sirius

POINTING THE WAY Visible from every country in the world, Orion is a good guide to the night sky. The three stars in the belt point south-east to Sirius and north-west to Aldebaran.

Among the most distinct constellations in the Northern Hemisphere are the Big Dipper (or Plough), which is actually part of a bigger constellation called Ursa Major (Great Bear), and Cassiopeia, which forms a 'W' or 'M' shape in the sky. Both can be used like a compass to find north (see right). The constellation Orion is visible for part of the year. It was thought to resemble a hunter in Greek mythology and has a distinctive 'belt', 'sword' and 'shield'.

WHICH CONSTELLATIONS CAN YOU SEE IN THE SOUTHERN HEMISPHERE?

Orion is also visible for part of the year in the Southern Hemisphere. But the best known constellation of the southern sky is Crux, or the Southern Cross, which looks like a cross or a diamond-shaped kite. It can be used to find south (see right). Other prominent constellations include Scorpio, the scorpion, and Centaurus, the centaur.

HOW DO YOU NAVIGATE BY THE STARS?

Certain stars point you in the direction of the poles, so they can help you work out directions. In the Northern Hemisphere, the Pole Star, or Polaris, marks the North Celestial Pole in the sky, above the north point on the horizon. You can find Polaris by following the line of the two 'pointer' stars of the Big Dipper or Plough, Merak and Dubhe. The 'W' or 'M' of Cassiopeia also faces towards Polaris. In the Southern Hemisphere there is no bright star marking the South Pole, so you have to imagine a line drawn from the longest 'arm' of the Southern Cross. If you extend it by about three and a half times, that spot marks the approximate position of the South Pole.

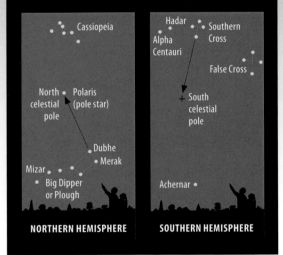

Cassiopeia

North celestial pole • Polaris (pole star)

Mizar

Dubhe • Merak

Big Dipper or Plough

NORTHERN HEMISPHERE

Hadar • Southern Cross
Alpha Centauri

False Cross

+ South celestial pole

Achernar

SOUTHERN HEMISPHERE

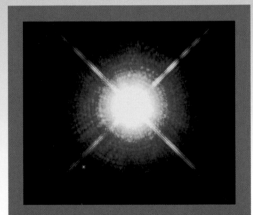

DOUBLE STAR The much brighter Sirius A star outshines the smaller Sirius B star, just visible at bottom left.

WHICH ARE THE BRIGHTEST STARS?

Viewed from Earth, the brightest star in the sky is a nearby star called Sirius. The second brightest star, Canopus, in the constellation Carina, is over 30 times further away. The third brightest, Alpha Centauri, in the constellation Centaurus, is actually a double star, consisting of Alpha Centauri A and Alpha Centauri B. Its immediate neighbour, Proxima Centauri, is the closest star to our Sun, about 4.25 light years away but is so small and faint that it can't be seen with the naked eye.

WHICH IS THE BIGGEST STAR?

A red supergiant in Orion, Betelgeuse, is the biggest of the bright stars. It varies in size and brightness, swelling and shrinking regularly. It is estimated to be 1 billion km (600 million miles) across on average – more than 700 times bigger than the Sun. If placed inside our Solar System, its diameter would enclose Jupiter's orbit.

LOOKING AT THE NIGHT SKY CONTINUED

WHICH PLANETS CAN WE SEE?

The planets Mercury, Venus, Mars, Jupiter and Saturn can all be seen in the night sky with the naked eye. Often, indeed, the planets are the brightest objects apart from the Sun and Moon. Mars and Venus are the closest visible planets to the Sun and can sometimes be seen together shining brightly in the western sky soon after sunset. Whereas stars twinkle, planets usually shine with a bright, steady light. From week to week, the planets can be seen to move among the stars, as they circle the Sun.

PLANETARY PATHS The tracks at the centre of this time-lapse image are those of (from left to right) Jupiter, Venus and Mercury.

WHICH FEATURES CAN YOU SEE ON THE MOON?

Even through ordinary binoculars, you can see the Moon's major topographical features, including many craters and seas, or maria (▶21). Although the Moon appears to be by far the biggest and brightest object in the night sky, that is only because it is much closer to Earth than any other object; it is actually quite small compared to stars and planets. As the Moon orbits Earth, the proportion of the visible surface lit by the Sun varies (▶29).

Mare Frigoris
Plato
Posidonius
Mare Imbrium
Mare Serenitas
Mare Crisium
Aristarchus
Apennine Mountains
Mare Tranquillitatis
Oceanus Procellarum
Copernicus
Kepler
Mare Fecunditatis
Langrenus
Ptolemeus
Theophilus
Grimaldi
Alphonsus
Cyrillus
Mare Nectaris
Catharina
Gassendi
Mare Nibium
Byrgius
Stevinus
Tycho

fast fact

The Moon rotates once in the same time that it orbits Earth, so we only ever see one side of it. The far side of the Moon was not viewed by humans until October 1959, when the Soviet spacecraft *Luna 3* beamed images of its cratered surface back to Earth.

WHAT IS A TRANSIT?

A transit occurs when one of the two planets between Earth and the Sun – Mercury or Venus – passes directly in front of the Sun, appearing as a tiny black disc. Transits of Mercury occur about 13 or 14 times every hundred years. Transits of Venus are less frequent: two transits, eight years apart, take place every 100 years or so. The last ones were in 2004 and 2012 and, before that, in 1874 and 1882.

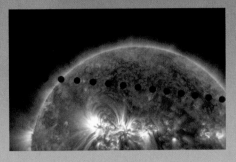

IN TRANSIT This image shows the most recent transit of Venus, in June 2012.

STREAK OF LIGHT A comet can look spectacular – a small bright 'head' or 'coma' with a long 'tail' behind it.

CAN YOU SEE COMETS IN THE NIGHT SKY?

Comets (▶22) are seen in the night sky relatively rarely. Most have been named and their arrival is anticipated – comet schedules can be found online. One of the most famous comets is Halley's Comet, which passes near the Earth and Sun every 76 years (next visit: 2061). Some large comets appear much less regularly: Comet Hyakutake was seen in 1996 for the first time in 17,000 years, and Comet Hale-Bopp in 1997 for the first time in 4000 years.

WHAT ARE THE NORTHERN LIGHTS?

The northern lights, or aurora borealis, are brightly coloured lights that sometimes appear in the far northern sky. They occur when electrically charged particles thrown out by the Sun interact with Earth's upper atmosphere. Similar lights – the southern lights, or aurora australis – occur in the Southern Hemisphere. Though rarely seen from densely inhabited areas, they can sometimes be viewed from southern New Zealand, Tasmania in southern Australia, Argentina and Chile, as well as Antarctica.

WHAT ARE SHOOTING STARS?

We refer to bright, fast-moving streaks of light across the sky as shooting stars, but they are more properly called meteors (▶22). These are particles of dust or lumps of rock that have entered Earth's atmosphere, where they usually ignite and burn. (In contrast, if you see a steadily moving 'star' crossing the night sky, it is probably an artificial satellite or part of an old rocket circling Earth.) At certain times of year meteors are common, forming 'meteor showers'. These showers seem to come from a particular point in the sky, and are named after the constellation covering that area. They are thought to be the result of Earth passing through debris left by a comet.

Watch out for meteor showers at these times of year:

NAME	DATE	NAME	DATE
Quadrantids	3–4 Jan	Orionids	21–22 Oct
Lyrids	16–26 Apr	Leonids	17 Nov
Eta Aquarids	5–6 May	Geminids	13–14 Dec
Perseids	11–13 Aug	Ursids	22–23 Dec

SPINNING EARTH

As it orbits the Sun, Earth also spins on its axis, taking 24 hours to complete each full rotation. This spinning action creates day and night. Earth's orbit around the Sun takes 365¼ days, an Earth year. And while Earth orbits the Sun, the Moon orbits Earth, taking 29½ days – a lunar month – to complete a full circuit, from one new Moon to the next.

JUNE *The top half of the globe – the Northern Hemisphere – is tilted towards the Sun and enjoys more of the Sun's light and warmth. While it is summer in the north, it is winter in the south, which is tilted away from the Sun.*

SEPTEMBER *The autumn days in the north gradually become shorter and cooler, while the spring days in the south become longer and warmer.*

WHY DOES THE LENGTH OF A DAY CHANGE THROUGH THE YEAR?

Earth's tilt is responsible for changing day-length as well as the seasons. In the middle of the year, when the North Pole tilts towards the Sun, the Northern Hemisphere experiences longer days and shorter nights and the Sun is higher in the sky during the day. At the same time, the Southern Hemisphere has shorter days and longer nights. At the end of the year, around Christmas, the situation is reversed.

MIDNIGHT SUN *At the North Pole in midsummer, the Sun never sinks below the horizon. The same is true at the South Pole during its summer.*

WHAT CREATES THE FOUR SEASONS?

Earth's axis is tilted at an angle of 23.5 degrees relative to the plane of Earth's orbit. This tilt results in warm summers and cold winters, and, for most parts of the world, two seasons of change, spring and autumn.

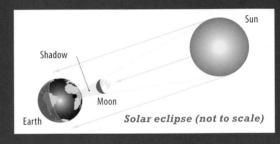

STRONG PULL *The motion of the Moon creates our tides (▶64).*

MARCH *The spring days in the north gradually become longer and warmer, while the autumn days in the south become shorter and cooler.*

DECEMBER *The countries of the Northern Hemisphere are tilted away from the Sun and receive the least light and warmth. While it is winter in the north, it is summer in the south, which is now tilted towards the Sun.*

WHAT IS A SOLAR ECLIPSE?

On rare occasions the Sun, Moon and Earth are in line with each other. The Moon blocks the light from the Sun, casting a shadow, typically around 160 km (100 miles) wide, and plunging that part of Earth into darkness for up to about seven minutes. A lunar eclipse takes place when Earth casts a shadow on the Moon.

Shadow

Sun

Moon

Earth

Solar eclipse (not to scale)

fast fact

We are barely aware of it, but Earth is travelling through space at an average speed of 107,180 km/h (66,600 mph) and spinning at 1674 km/h (1040 mph).

WHY DOES THE MOON CHANGE SHAPE?

The Moon does not generate light; moonlight is light from the Sun being reflected off the Moon's surface. Half of the Moon is always lit by the Sun, but the portion of this light that we see on Earth changes as Earth and the Moon move around the Sun. When the Moon is between Earth and the Sun, we don't see the Moon at all because the sunlight is on the other side (this is called the new Moon). But as the Moon moves away from the Sun, the sunlit area grows, or waxes, first into a sliver or crescent, then into a half then gibbous Moon, curved on both sides, and finally into a round full Moon. As the Moon moves back towards the Sun, the sunlit area grows smaller, or wanes, in a reversal of the process.

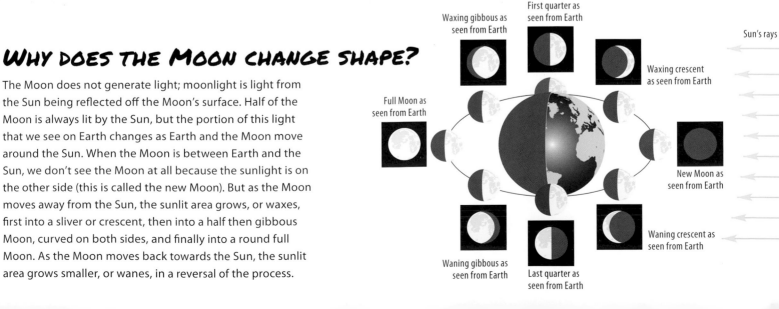

Waxing gibbous as seen from Earth

First quarter as seen from Earth

Waxing crescent as seen from Earth

Full Moon as seen from Earth

Sun's rays

New Moon as seen from Earth

Waning crescent as seen from Earth

Waning gibbous as seen from Earth

Last quarter as seen from Earth

INSIDE EARTH

Earth is not one solid ball of rock. Instead its interior has separated into layers, each with its own characteristics. Heat coming from Earth's core causes semisolid rock in the layer above, known as the mantle, to circulate. This movement pushes and pulls at Earth's hard crust, giving rise to earthquakes and volcanoes and, over long periods of time, reshaping the surface of our planet.

WHAT IS EARTH MADE OF?

Earth has a metallic core, with a diameter of about 6900 km (4300 miles). It consists mainly of iron and small amounts of nickel and sulfur, and is divided into a solid inner core and a liquid outer core. Above the outer core is the mantle, which is about 2900 km (1800 miles) thick. The mantle is composed of soft rock, made mostly of the gemstone peridot. A thin, brittle crust floats on top of the mantle.

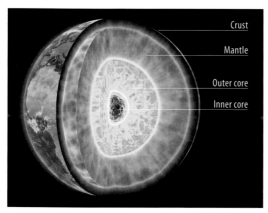

Crust

Mantle

Outer core

Inner core

FIRE BELOW
Temperatures rise as you descend through the crust. The world's deepest mine, TauTona in South Africa, is 3.9 km (2.4 miles) deep and the temperature at the bottom is 55°C (131°F).

IS EARTH MAGNETIC?

Earth's rotation generates electricity in the planet's outer core. This in turn creates a magnetic field inside Earth, like a huge bar magnet, producing opposite poles, north and south, at the top and bottom of the planet. The North Pole attracts a magnetised needle, allowing us to navigate with a compass.

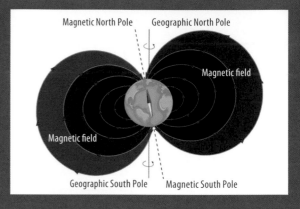

Magnetic North Pole   Geographic North Pole

Magnetic field

Magnetic field

Geographic South Pole   Magnetic South Pole

HOW DOES EARTH'S CRUST MOVE?

The crust of our planet is not one continuous layer of rock but is instead broken into large pieces, or tectonic plates. As hot, soft rock rises to the top of the mantle, it spreads out under the crust, cools off and sinks, forming convection currents that move the plates.

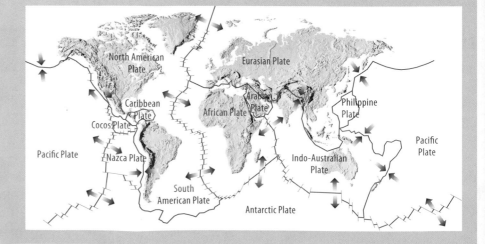

North American Plate

Eurasian Plate

Caribbean Plate

Arabian Plate

Philippine Plate

African Plate

Cocos Plate

Pacific Plate

Pacific Plate

Nazca Plate

Indo-Australian Plate

South American Plate

Antarctic Plate

PLATE SHAPES *The map shows Earth's plates and their directions of movement.*

WHAT HAPPENS WHEN PLATES MOVE?

Plate movements have a range of effects, depending on the direction of movement and the thickness of the crust. Sudden movements along plate boundaries are the main source of earthquakes.

PULLED APART
Where two areas of thin oceanic crust are pulled apart, hot liquid rock, or magma, rises through the crack then cools and solidifies to form new crust.

RUNNING HOT *Magma that reaches the surface is called lava. It cools to form volcanic rock.*

UP AND UNDER
Where thin crust meets thicker crust, the thinner crust is forced down into the mantle. Magma may then rise through cracks, forming volcanoes along the plate boundary.

CRASHING TOGETHER
Where two plates of thick continental crust collide, the land buckles and pushes upwards to form mountains.

HIGH LAND *The Himalayas are still rising today as a result of two plates colliding.*

SLIDING PAST
Where two plates are moving past each other in opposite directions, they form a transform fault. Earthquakes occur often along such faults.

HAVE THE CONTINENTS CHANGED SHAPE?

Plate movements constantly shift and reshape Earth's landmasses. Over millions of years this has altered the outlines and positions of the continents.

Panthalassa

Pangaea

Laurasia

Tethys Ocean

Gondwana

250 MILLION YEARS AGO
The continents were joined in one huge landmass called Pangaea and there was just one ocean, Panthalassa.

135 MILLION YEARS AGO
Pangaea split into two major continents, Laurasia in the north and Gondwana in the south, separated by the Tethys Ocean.

TODAY *Earth has six main landmasses: North America, South America, Eurasia (Europe and Asia), Africa, Australia and Antarctica.*

IN THE FUTURE *The Atlantic Ocean will get wider and the Pacific Ocean smaller. Africa will collide with Europe, and Australia may join South-East Asia.*

EARTH'S HISTORY

People studying the long-term history of Earth divide its 4.6 billion years into units of time known as aeons, eras, periods and epochs. These units reflect major changes in rock formation, which in turn are usually linked with major events, such as volcanic eruptions and mass extinctions.

HOW MANY AEONS ARE THERE?

The history of Earth is divided into four aeons. The earliest, called the Hadean, includes the formation of Earth before any life began. The next is the Archaean, which began 4 billion years ago (bya). It is marked by the origin of primitive life and lasted 1.5 billion years. The Proterozoic ('earlier life') began 2.5 billion years ago, and saw the evolution of more complex life. These three aeons are sometimes referred to as the Precambrian. The fourth aeon is the Phanerozoic ('abundant life'), which began 541 million years ago (mya), during which life as we know it today evolved.

HOW MANY ERAS DOES THE CURRENT AEON HAVE?

The Phanerozoic Aeon is divided into three eras. The first, called the Palaeozoic ('ancient life') era, began 541 million years ago. At first, life was largely confined to the seas. The later Palaeozoic era, from about 354 million years ago, saw the growth of the first forests and the reptiles and amphibians that lived in them. The second era, called the Mesozoic ('middle life'), began 252 million years ago and was the time of the dinosaurs. The most recent era is the current one, which is called the Cenozoic ('recent life'). It began 66 million years ago and is dominated by mammals and flowering plants.

WHAT ARE PERIODS AND EPOCHS?

Because so much has taken place during the Phanerozoic, its eras are divided into shorter timeframes called periods, which are in turn subdivided into yet smaller units called epochs. The Phanerozoic encompasses 12 periods, the current one being the Quaternary, which is split into the Pleistocene and Holocene epochs.

310 mya First vertebrates independent of w

360 mya First four-legged animals with backbones

325 mya First forests – their remains later form coal deposits

470 mya First fish appear; first land plants appear

450 mya First land animals appear

545 mya Earliest fossil shells

530 mya Earliest vertebrate ancestor: *Pikaia*, a small, eel-like creature

580 mya Jellyfish and flatworm-like organisms appear

2.5 bya First animal fossi burrow traces, made by worm-li organisms

Palaeozoic · Carbonifero · Devonian · Silurian · Ordovician · Cambrian · PHANEROZOIC · PROTEROZOIC · ARCHAEAN

359 mya · 419 mya · 443 mya · 485 mya · 541 mya

fast fact

If you translated the whole of geological time into one calendar year, Earth would commence its life as a Hadean ball of molten rock on 1 January. The reign of the dinosaurs would not commence till 11 December, and it would end on Christmas Day. And humans would only appear at 11.37 pm – 23 minutes to midnight – on the last day of the year!

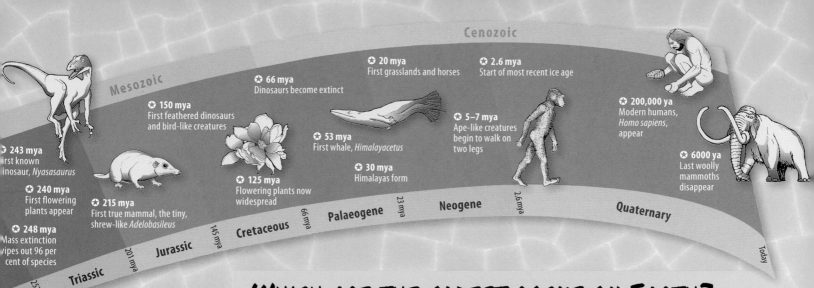

Cenozoic

Mesozoic

☼ 20 mya
First grasslands and horses

☼ 2.6 mya
Start of most recent ice age

☼ 66 mya
Dinosaurs become extinct

☼ 150 mya
First feathered dinosaurs
and bird-like creatures

☼ 200,000 ya
Modern humans,
Homo sapiens,
appear

☼ 243 mya
First known
dinosaur, *Nyasasaurus*

☼ 53 mya
First whale, *Himalayacetus*

☼ 5–7 mya
Ape-like creatures
begin to walk on
two legs

☼ 6000 ya
Last woolly
mammoths
disappear

☼ 240 mya
First flowering
plants appear

☼ 215 mya
First true mammal, the tiny,
shrew-like *Adelobasileus*

☼ 125 mya
Flowering plants now
widespread

☼ 30 mya
Himalayas form

☼ 248 mya
Mass extinction
wipes out 96 per
cent of species

23 mya

Neogene

2.6 mya

66 mya

Palaeogene

Quaternary

145 mya

Cretaceous

201 mya

Jurassic

Triassic

252 mya

nian

Today

ARCHAEAN

ARCHAEAN

HADEAN

HADEAN

ARCHAEAN

HADEAN

☼ 4 bya
First evidence of life

HADEAN

☼ 4.6 bya
Formation
of Earth

WHICH ARE THE OLDEST ROCKS ON EARTH?

The oldest-known rocks date
from 4.28 billion years ago,
when much of Earth's surface
was covered with active
volcanoes. They were found
in northern Canada in 2008.

ROCK OF AGES *Earth's
oldest rocks are part of the
Nuvvuagittuq greenstone
belt, north of Quebec.*

WHAT ARE THE OLDEST SIGNS OF LIFE ON LAND?

The oldest fossils of land plants yet found are those
of 472-million-year-old liverwort plants, found in
Argentina in 2010. Footprints of the first centipede-
like animals were found in sediments of similar
age in the Lake District of Britain.

LIVING ON *The Argentinian fossils
of liverworts (left) and their present-
day relatives (far left)*

WHEN DID HUMANS APPEAR?

Ape-like ancestors of humans began walking on
two legs about 5–7 million years ago. Modern
humans did not evolve until about 200,000 years
ago, but by 40,000 years ago our species, *Homo
sapiens*, had spread around the world (▶252).

ANCIENT ANCESTOR *The Omo
fossils, from Ethiopia, are the oldest-
known evidence of modern humans.*

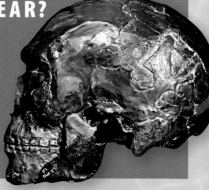

EARTHQUAKES AND TSUNAMIS

Earthquakes are caused by the movement of Earth's plates – the large segments into which its crust is broken (▸30). These plates are always moving and usually they move slowly and fairly smoothly. But sometimes they shift suddenly, causing a jolt that sends shockwaves, or seismic waves, through the crust – an earthquake. This may also occur underwater, which creates giant waves called tsunamis. Earthquakes and tsunamis are most common at plate boundaries, with about 70 per cent occurring along the so-called Ring of Fire, the plate boundaries that encircle the Pacific Ocean.

TUMBLING DOWN This house in Christchurch, New Zealand, was destroyed by a magnitude 6.3 earthquake in 2011.

HOW DOES AN EARTHQUAKE HAPPEN?

Where rocks at plate edges are being pulled apart, they may suddenly snap. Or rocks pushing against each other may suddenly give way after a long build-up of pressure. This can release a large amount of energy in the form of shockwaves, which pass through surrounding crust, buildings and ocean. Earthquakes can also be caused by volcanoes (▸36), meteorite impacts (▸22) and human activities such as bomb explosions, deep drilling and the filling of reservoirs.

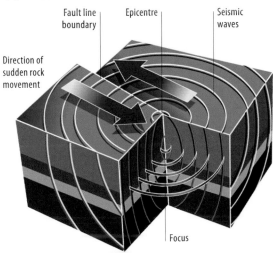

Fault line boundary   Epicentre   Seismic waves

Direction of sudden rock movement

Focus

HOW DO WE MEASURE EARTHQUAKES?

Instruments called seismometers detect earth movements and record the amount of energy released – the earthquake's magnitude. The result is usually presented as a number on the Richter scale, which was developed in 1935 by Charles F Richter. Each whole number on the scale, from 0 upwards, represents a release of energy 31 times greater than the previous number. The highest Richter-scale measurement ever recorded is 9.5, for the 1960 Valdivia earthquake in Chile.

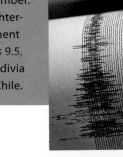

CAN WE PREDICT EARTHQUAKES?

We can't prevent earthquakes happening, but we can learn to recognise the danger signs. Using seismometers, scientists monitor earth tremors; an increase in tremor activity may indicate that a large earthquake is about to take place. People living in the area can then be alerted and, if appropriate, moved to a place of safety.

WHICH WERE THE WORST EARTHQUAKES IN HISTORY?

Mass destruction and terrible loss of life can result from earthquakes, usually in relation to the magnitude of the earthquake and how close its epicentre is to large cities or towns. The deadliest earthquake in history took place in 1556 in Shaanxi, China, killing 830,000 people. The strongest earthquake ever measured, at 9.5 magnitude, occurred in Valdivia, Chile, in 1960, and killed 1655 people.

fast fact

About 8000 microquakes (below 2.5 magnitude) take place daily. Each year, about 7000 quakes of magnitude 4 or more occur and, on average, one of magnitude 8 or more.

KILLER WAVES On 11 March 2011, a magnitude 9 earthquake off the coast of Japan – the fifth strongest ever recorded – triggered tsunamis up to 40.5 m (133 ft) high. Almost 16,000 people died and the tsunamis caused dangerous nuclear meltdowns at the Fukushima Daiichi Nuclear Power Plant.

WHAT IS A TSUNAMI?

A tsunami is a huge ocean wave. It is usually caused by an earthquake under the sea, though it may also be triggered by an undersea volcanic eruption, a coastal landslide or a meteorite impact. In all cases the event displaces a vast amount of seawater, which in turn forms the wave. When a tsunami enters shallow water along a coastline, it is pushed upwards, becoming even taller. It may then swamp coastal communities, destroying buildings and drowning people and animals. The tallest tsunami ever measured, at Lituya Bay, Alaska, was 524 m (1720 ft) high.

UNDERWATER EARTHQUAKE
Movement of the seabed causes the displacement of a large block of water.

LANDSLIDE The sudden collapse of a cliff into the sea triggers a wave.

UNDERWATER VOLCANO
An explosive eruption from a submarine volcano displaces a large volume of water.

DEADLY EFFECT Though measuring just 7 on the Richter scale, Haiti's 2010 earthquake devastated the small, poor, populous island nation.

TOP FIVE DEADLIEST EARTHQUAKES SINCE 1900

1 Haiyuan, China, 1920: 273,400 deaths; magnitude 7.8

2 Tangshan, China, 1976: 242,769 deaths (official total; some estimates as high as 655,000); magnitude 7.5

3 Sumatra, Indonesia, 2004: 230,210 deaths; magnitude 9.1

4 Haiti, 2010: 222,570 deaths (UN figure; estimates vary from 46,000 to 316,000); magnitude 7

5 Messina, Italy, 1920: 123,000 deaths; magnitude 7.2

VOLCANOES

Volcanoes are vents or fissures in Earth's crust, through which hot, molten rock, dust, ash and gases are ejected. They occur all over the world but mainly along plate boundaries (▶30). There are about 1500 active volcanoes and their eruptions can cause widespread destruction, loss of life and temporary changes in global weather patterns.

Volcanic activity on Mauna Loa, Hawaii

ASH CLOUD *The eruption of Eyjafjallajökull, Iceland, 2010*

WHICH PARTS OF THE WORLD HAVE THE MOST VOLCANOES?

Volcanoes are particularly numerous where two plates are pulling away from one another, as in Iceland, or where one plate is pushing under the other, as on the west coast of the Americas and in Japan and Indonesia. Some volcanoes do, however, form in the middle of plates; these are known as hotspot volcanoes and examples include the volcanoes of the Hawaiian Islands.

HOW DOES A VOLCANO ERUPT?

Currents and pressure inside Earth force magma up through weak spots in the crust. At the surface, the rapid expansion of gas bubbles in the magma causes it to swell and pour out of the volcano as lava, which cools and hardens to form rock. Some eruptions are small and may consist of little more than a belch of gas and hot rock. But others, particularly where pressure has been building for some time, may be colossally violent, spouting fountains of lava and firing rocks, dust and huge quantities of ash and gases high into the air.

WHAT'S INSIDE A VOLCANO?

Deep beneath a volcano there is usually a magma chamber that is the main source of its lava. Above ground level are domed layers of rock built up by successive eruptions. A main vent rises up from the magma chamber to the top of the volcano. Side vents and fissures may branch off this vent through cracks in the volcano's flanks. At the top of the volcano is a crater, sometimes filled with hot lava. Eruptions on the side of the volcano may form secondary cones.

ASH CLOUD

CRATER Lava erupts through opening

PYROCLASTIC FLOW A torrent of hot ash and gas

SECONDARY CONE Also called a parasitic cone

LAVA FLOW

DYKE Vertical channel containing magma

CENTRAL VENT Main outlet for magma

LACCOLITH Mass of magma that pushes rock layers upwards

MAGMA CHAMBER Underground reservoir of molten rock

ARE THERE DIFFERENT KINDS OF VOLCANOES?

Volcanoes vary significantly in terms of their size and shape, but there are four main kinds.

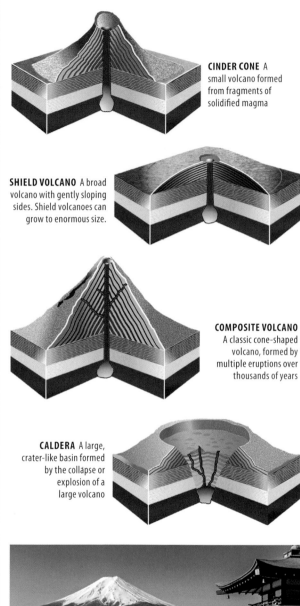

CINDER CONE A small volcano formed from fragments of solidified magma

SHIELD VOLCANO A broad volcano with gently sloping sides. Shield volcanoes can grow to enormous size.

COMPOSITE VOLCANO A classic cone-shaped volcano, formed by multiple eruptions over thousands of years

CALDERA A large, crater-like basin formed by the collapse or explosion of a large volcano

STANDING OUT About 60 per cent of volcanoes on Earth are composites, such as Japan's Mount Fuji.

WHAT IS A DORMANT VOLCANO?

A volcano that is still erupting is said to be active. After it has stopped erupting, it may still emit gases and vapour for some time, and even as it cools it may still emit sufficient heat to boil ground water and create hot springs, such as those found in Yellowstone, USA, and New Zealand's North Island. Once volcanic activity ceases altogether, a volcano is referred to as dormant. After it has been dormant for a long time and seems unlikely to erupt ever again, it is said to be extinct.

PRIME SITE Edinburgh Castle in Scotland sits atop an extinct volcano.

fast fact
Stromboli, a volcano in Italy's Aeolian Islands, has been erupting steadily for more than 2000 years.

FINAL FORM This cast is of a person buried in ash during the Pompeii eruption.

WHICH HAVE BEEN THE MOST DESTRUCTIVE VOLCANOES?

The eruption of Tambora in Indonesia in 1815 triggered tsunamis and filled the sky with ash, blocking the sun, lowering temperatures and causing crops to fail; at least 90,000 people died. When the Indonesian volcano Krakatoa blew up in 1883, the explosion was so loud that people over 4800 km (3000 miles) away heard it; associated tsunamis killed 36,000 people. The sudden explosion of Mount Pelée on the Caribbean island of Martinique, in 1902, rained hot rock and ash on the nearby town of St-Pierre, killing 29,000 people almost instantly. Most famously, the eruption in 79 AD of Vesuvius near present-day Naples, Italy, buried the Roman cities of Pompeii and Herculaneum.

EARTH'S ATMOSPHERE

The atmosphere is an envelope of gases that surrounds Earth and is held in place by gravity.

Most of the atmosphere lies within the first 16 km (10 miles) above the ground, a very thin layer compared to the size of the planet. The atmosphere regulates Earth's surface temperature and limits space debris and damaging rays from the Sun from reaching the ground. Crucially, it also contains oxygen and water vapour, both essentials for life as we know it.

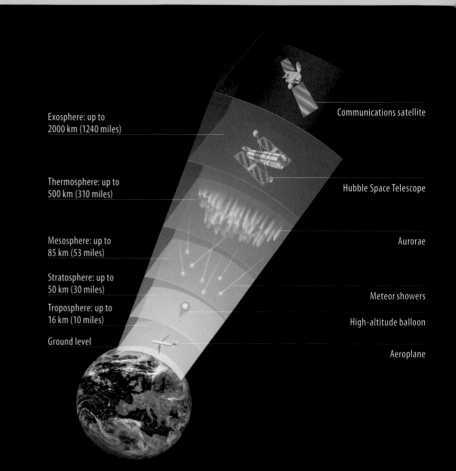

Exosphere: up to 2000 km (1240 miles)

Thermosphere: up to 500 km (310 miles)

Mesosphere: up to 85 km (53 miles)

Stratosphere: up to 50 km (30 miles)

Troposphere: up to 16 km (10 miles)

Ground level

Communications satellite

Hubble Space Telescope

Aurorae

Meteor showers

High-altitude balloon

Aeroplane

WHY DO WE NEED AN ATMOSPHERE?

Without its atmosphere, Earth would be uninhabitable. There would be no oxygen for living things to breathe. All surface water would evaporate and temperatures would fluctuate between extremes of heat by day and cold by night. The planet's surface would also be bombarded by rocks and harmful rays from the Sun that can cause sunburn and cancer.

IS THE ATMOSPHERE THE SAME AT THE TOP AND BOTTOM?

The atmosphere has five layers, each with different characteristics. The bottom layer, the troposphere, contains most of the atmosphere's gases, including enough oxygen for us to breathe, and is warm enough for us to live in; this is where most of our weather takes place. The much colder second layer, the stratosphere, is where the ozone layer is located. In the mesosphere, the third layer, temperatures can be as low as –100°C (–148°F). In contrast, gas particles in the next layer, the thermosphere, absorb heat, raising temperatures to more than 2000°C (3600°F); the effects known as aurorae (▸27) take place here. Gases other than hydrogen gradually become sparser in the highest layer, the exosphere, which merges with outer space.

WHY DOES THE SKY CHANGE COLOUR?

Light rays from the Sun are made up of violet, indigo, blue, green, yellow, orange and red rays. As sunlight passes through the atmosphere, water vapour, gas molecules and dust particles scatter these colours in different directions, beginning with the colours at the violet end of the spectrum. By day, when the Sun is high, the blue light is scattered more than other colours, making the sky look blue. Towards evening, the Sun shines at a lower angle and therefore passes through a greater depth of atmosphere, scattering the blue light even more. This allows the red and yellow to emerge, so the sky appears to change colour.

IS THERE A HOLE IN THE OZONE LAYER?

A layer of ozone gas in the stratosphere helps protect Earth from harmful solar radiation. In 1979 a hole was detected in this layer over Antarctica, which gradually grew bigger over the next decade. Most scientists believe this was caused by increasing human use of chemicals called chlorofluorocarbons or CFCs, found mainly in refrigerators and aerosol cans, which react with and destroy ozone. Strict controls of CFC production and use have since helped stabilise the hole.

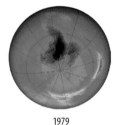  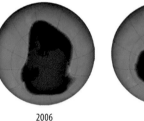 

| 1979 | 1989 | 2006 | 2010 |

DO ANY OTHER PLANETS HAVE AN ATMOSPHERE?

A number of other planets have an atmosphere. But no other planet's atmosphere that we know of can support life. For example, the atmosphere of Venus (▶16) consists mainly of carbon dioxide and the planet's surface temperature is around 480°C (896°F).

WHAT IS THE GREENHOUSE EFFECT?

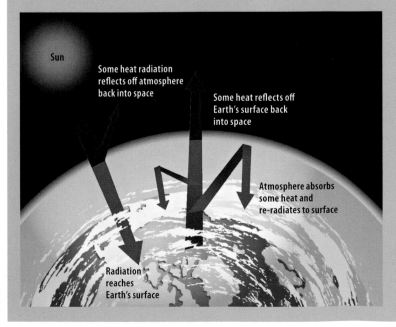

Sun

Some heat radiation reflects off atmosphere back into space

Some heat reflects off Earth's surface back into space

Atmosphere absorbs some heat and re-radiates to surface

Radiation reaches Earth's surface

Like a greenhouse, our atmosphere allows heat from the Sun to pass through and reach the ground but also prevents some of that heat escaping again. This is mainly due to the presence of the gases carbon dioxide and methane in the atmosphere, which absorb the reflected heat. Humans, however, are raising levels of carbon dioxide and methane, mainly by burning fossil fuels. This, in turn, is raising temperatures – a phenomenon known as anthropogenic or human-induced global warming.

fast fact

Air is heavy. In fact, as you read this you have around 1000 kg (2200 lb) of air pressing down on you, and this is about the same weight as a small car. Fortunately our bodies are designed to withstand this pressure.

WEATHER AND CLIMATE

Earth's atmosphere is always on the move. As Earth orbits the Sun and spins on its axis, air masses heat up and cool down, which in turn causes them to shift, dry out or become water-laden and produce rain and snow. These movements and changes are what we call weather. In most places, weather changes continuously, from day to day and even from hour to hour. Climate, on the other hand, refers to the long-term average of the weather and changes much less noticeably.

WHAT INFLUENCES CLIMATE?

CLIMATE ZONES — Polar — Subarctic — Cool temperate — Warm temperate — Arid — Tropical — High altitude

The main influence on climate is distance from the Equator. The Sun is at its hottest at the Equator, while it provides little warmth at the poles. In turn, this affects not only the amount of heat a place receives, but also how much rainfall there is. Wind patterns, ocean currents and altitude also affect climate. Broadly similar climates can be found in different parts of the world and are known as climate zones. Climate influences all aspects of people's lives, from the clothes they wear to the way they build their houses.

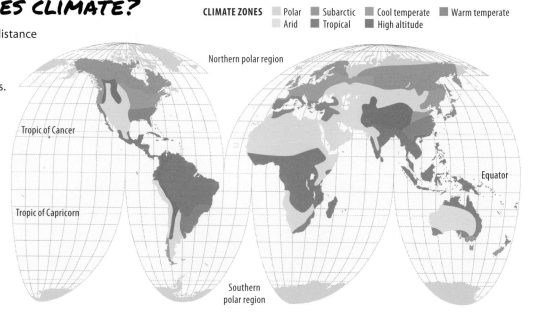

Northern polar region

Tropic of Cancer

Tropic of Capricorn

Equator

Southern polar region

WHY DOES THE WIND BLOW?

When air passes over warm ground, it is heated and becomes lighter. As a result it rises, creating an area of low pressure beneath it. Air is drawn into this low-pressure zone from surrounding areas where the pressure is higher. The movement of air between zones of different pressure is what we call wind. The bigger the difference in pressure, the faster the movement and the stronger the wind. In the Northern Hemisphere, air moves clockwise around high pressure and anticlockwise around low pressure (pictured below). The opposite occurs in the Southern Hemisphere.

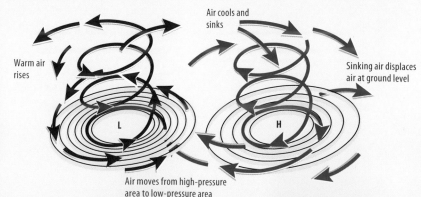

Air cools and sinks

Warm air rises

Sinking air displaces air at ground level

Air moves from high-pressure area to low-pressure area

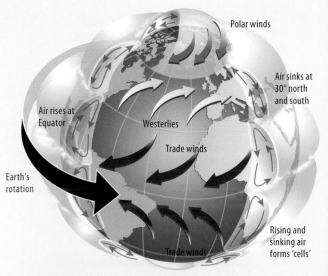

Polar winds

Air sinks at 30° north and south

Air rises at Equator

Westerlies

Trade winds

Earth's rotation

Rising and sinking air forms 'cells'

Trade winds

WORLD WINDS *Differences in pressure create global wind patterns, including easterly winds blowing towards the Equator (trade winds) and westerlies at higher latitudes.*

WHAT ARE CLOUDS MADE OF?

Air can hold moisture in the form of water vapour, and the warmer the air the more water vapour it can hold. When warm, moist air starts to cool, it can no longer hold as much moisture and the water vapour begins to condense, forming tiny water droplets. Clouds develop through this process of cooling and condensation. The resulting droplets are so light and small – less than 0.05 mm (¹/₆₄ in) wide – that they float in the sky. If the air temperature is below freezing, as is usually the case at higher altitudes, the droplets will turn into ice crystals. Water droplets and ice crystals are easily blown about by the wind, so the shapes of clouds are constantly changing.

CIRRUS *Cirrus is Latin for 'lock of hair' and this describes the wispy, streaky appearance of these high clouds. Temperatures at their level are well below freezing, so cirrus clouds are composed of ice crystals.*

CUMULUS *Cumulus is Latin for 'heap' and this describes the lumpy, puffy look of these clouds. They can grow to considerable heights and become thunderstorm or cumulonimbus clouds. The lower layers are usually composed of water droplets but upper levels may be ice crystals.*

STRATUS *Stratus is Latin for 'layer' and this type of cloud forms wide bands across the sky. Stratus clouds can be very low, sometimes obscuring the tops of hills and tall buildings.*

HOW DO RAIN AND SNOW HAPPEN?

Rain occurs when water droplets in clouds grow large and heavy enough to fall to the ground. This may occur when droplets attach themselves to particles in the air and grow bigger, or when droplets collide and coalesce to form larger droplets. If this takes place in temperatures below freezing, the water droplets may turn into ice crystals, which, in suitable conditions, can join to form snowflakes.

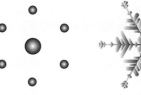

RAIN *Water droplets in a cloud grow until they are big and heavy enough to fall to the ground as rain.*

SNOW *In subzero temperatures, moisture droplets in clouds can freeze to form snowflakes.*

HAIL *Water droplets may freeze inside storm clouds to form hailstones.*

HOW DOES HAIL FORM?

Hailstones usually start to form inside thunderclouds as water droplets are carried high into the sky by powerful rising air currents, then freeze. Once heavy enough, they may fall and start to melt, only to be carried aloft again. The cycle of freezing and thawing builds up layers of ice, until the hailstone is heavy enough to fall to earth.

WATCHING THE WEATHER

You can observe weather patterns around you and learn to recognise particular phenomena as they develop.

Looking further afield and using a variety of modern technologies, weather forecasters, or meteorologists as they are known, gather a wide range of information to help them predict the weather.

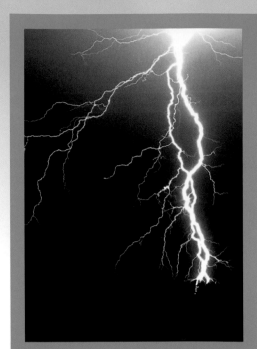

WHAT ARE FRONTS?

A front is the boundary between two air masses of different temperatures. When warm air moves into cold air, the boundary is called a warm front. When cold air moves into warm air, it is called a cold front. Fronts usually bring rain because both forms of interaction push warm air upwards, causing it to condense. This lifting process tends to be more vigorous with a cold front, often triggering thunderstorms.

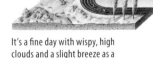 *WARM FRONT When a warm front arrives, clouds tend to form gradually, often producing large areas of stratiform or layered cloud, light rain or snow.*

It's a fine day with wispy, high clouds and a slight breeze as a warm front approaches.

Warm air at ground level begins rising slowly. Clouds build up and the breeze gets stronger.

As the warm air rises, it cools. Water droplets then condense and start to fall as light rain.

COLD FRONT A cold front usually produces more vigorous lifting, often resulting in heavy rain and thunderstorms.

The fast-rising air cools rapidly and its moisture condenses abundantly, yielding heavy rain. Strong rising air currents generate storm clouds.

The air currents inside the cloud carry water droplets up and down between freezing and warmer altitudes, forming hail (▶41).

As the cold front moves away, the thunderstorm runs out of warm, rising air, the clouds dissipate and the sky gradually clears.

WHAT CAUSES LIGHTNING?

Rising and falling air currents generate a positive electrical charge at the top of a cloud, a negative charge at the bottom and another positive charge on the ground below. As these charges build up, electrical discharges jump between the opposite charges, producing the bright flashes we call lightning.

fast fact

Worldwide, on average, there are 44 lightning flashes every second.

WHAT IS THUNDER?

A bolt of lightning heats the air around it extremely quickly, causing the air to expand. This sudden expansion creates the explosive blast we hear as thunder. Because sound travels more slowly than light, we don't hear the sound until after we see the lightning flash. The further away we are from the lightning, the longer the delay.

WHAT IS A HURRICANE?

Also known as a typhoon or tropical cyclone, a hurricane is a massive storm system that forms over warm tropical oceans and begins to spin under the influence of Earth's rotation. As it spins faster and grows bigger, it produces destructive winds and torrential rain, and as it nears land it may generate abnormally high water levels, known as a storm surge. The combined impact of winds, rain and storm surge can devastate coastal communities.

WHAT DOES A TORNADO LOOK LIKE?

A tornado is a violently rotating funnel of air generated by a severe thunderstorm. The funnel is made visible when it picks up dust and debris and moisture inside it condenses. Though a tornado may move fairly slowly, wind speeds within its funnel can top 450 km/h (280 mph).

UNDER WATER *When Hurricane Katrina struck the southeastern United States in 2005, it flooded the city of New Orleans, killed more than 1800 people and caused US$81 billion of damage, making it the costliest disaster in US history.*

HOW DO FORECASTERS MONITOR THE WEATHER?

Meteorologists use a range of traditional instruments and modern technologies to track and forecast the weather. Human observers and automated recording devices log temperature, humidity and wind speed over a wide area, while weather balloons take readings at high altitude; this data is fed into sophisticated computer models. Radar is used to track precipitation, and satellites provide regularly updated images of cloud patterns over large areas.

DATA SET *Automatic weather stations, such as this unit in Antarctica, record temperature, wind speed, humidity and air pressure and transmit the data to collection points for processing.*

COLOUR GUIDE *Radar is useful for tracking rainfall. The colours indicate its intensity, ranging from light (blue) through moderate (yellow) to heavy rain or hail (dark red).*

BIG PICTURE *Satellite images help forecasters track major weather systems, such as hurricanes.*

LIVING ZONES

Differences in climate and vegetation create distinct living zones, or biomes, on Earth. Each has particular plant and animal communities. Some plants and animals can survive only in zones such as tropical forests, where it is warm and damp, while others can cope with zones where drought is common. Yet others prefer zones with bitter cold for many months each year.

WHAT ARE OUR PLANET'S MAJOR LIVING ZONES?

The major biomes are forests, grasslands, deserts, mountains and polar regions. Forests are so varied, however, that they are usually divided into smaller categories, starting with tropical, temperate and boreal forests. The Arctic is rimmed by treeless, frozen land called tundra.

MAP KEY

	Boreal forest		Mountains
	Temperate forest		Tundra
	Tropical forest		Coral reef
	Grasslands		Polar regions
	Desert		

WHERE DO YOU FIND TROPICAL FORESTS?

Tropical forests run in a belt around the Equator, where the climate is warm and wet. Once, they occupied about one-fifth of Earth's land surface, but large parts have since been cut down. Most tropical forest is rainforest, which receives abundant rain year-round. But away from the Equator, in places such as north-eastern Australia, West Africa and parts of India, tropical rainforest turns into monsoon forest. Unlike rainforests, monsoon forests receive very little rain for several months each year.

WHAT IS A TEMPERATE FOREST?

Temperate regions have mild summers and cold winters. Most of the trees in these regions shed their leaves in winter. However, in some particularly wet temperate zones, such as the north-west coast of North America and western Tasmania, Australia, the trees stay green year-round. These forests are known as temperate rainforests.

AUTUMN GLOW Most trees in temperate forests begin to drop their leaves in autumn.

SNOWBOUND *In the boreal forest, winters are long and cold, and many animals hibernate.*

ARE ALL DESERTS DRY AND HOT?

Deserts (▶50) form where little rain falls, so all are dry. Many are among the hottest places on Earth; in one of the largest deserts, for example, the Sahara, daytime temperatures can reach 50°C (122°F). However, some deserts have cold winters – in Central Asia's Gobi Desert, for instance, winter temperatures may drop to –20°C (–4°F).

WHAT DOES 'BOREAL' MEAN?

Boreal essentially means 'of the north', so boreal forests are those that grow in the northern reaches of the Northern Hemisphere. The only trees that can survive in these cold zones are evergreen conifers, such as firs. The boreal forest is the biggest forest in the world, stretching in a wide band across Scandinavia, northern Russia and northern North America.

WHERE DO YOU FIND CORAL REEFS?

Coral reefs (▶65) can be found in tropical waters, fringing coastlines and islands of the Caribbean Sea and the Indian and Pacific oceans. The world's largest coral reef is Australia's Great Barrier Reef, which extends for more than 3200 km (2000 miles).

LIVING BARRIER *Like all coral reefs, the Great Barrier Reef teems with life.*

WHICH ARE THE HIGHEST MOUNTAIN RANGES?

The world's highest mountain ranges are in Asia and include the Himalayas in China, India and Nepal; the Karakoram in Pakistan; and the Hindu Kush in Afghanistan. The Himalayas have 96 of the world's highest mountains, including Mount Everest, at 8848 m (29,029 ft) the tallest of the lot. Mountains usually have several different temperature and vegetation zones between their base and summit (▶53), and some mountaintops may be covered in snow year-round.

WHICH ARE THE COLDEST ENVIRONMENTS?

SEE THROUGH *Only on the fringes of Antarctica is its landmass visible through its coating of ice and snow.*

The regions around the North and South poles (▶54) are the coldest places on Earth. The South Pole is in the middle of the continent of Antarctica, which is almost entirely covered with a very thick layer of ice and snow. The North Pole, on the other hand, is in the middle of a partially frozen ocean, the Arctic Sea; there is no land under this ice. Along the lands that border the Arctic Ocean, the ground below the surface is permanently frozen; this type of land is known as tundra.

ARE THERE DIFFERENT KINDS OF GRASSLANDS?

Grasslands (▶48) are found on every continent except Antarctica, but they have different characteristics from region to region, and often different names – for example they are known as prairies in North America, pampas in Argentina, veld in South Africa and steppes in Russia. Grasslands of tropical regions are referred to as savannah.

FORESTS

Trees can grow singly, out in the open, but more often they are crowded together in woodlands and forests. While some may be only knee-high, others provide high-rise homes for hundreds of different kinds of animals.

WHY ARE FORESTS IMPORTANT?

Forests are home to many animal species, but they are also valuable in other ways. Tree roots help bind the soil together and stop it being washed away when it rains. The leaves of trees absorb carbon dioxide and release oxygen, keeping the atmosphere fit for humans and other creatures to breathe. And, in mountains, forests also act as living crash barriers against avalanches.

Avalanche slowed by forest

WHICH PLANTS AND ANIMALS DO THE DIFFERENT FORESTS SUPPORT?

Particular kinds of trees are common to each kind of forest and, in turn, these support distinctive animal communities.

BOREAL FOREST *Nearly all the trees in this kind of forest are conifers, which include firs, pines and spruces. They grow for just a few weeks each year, and they have tough leaves that can survive frost, wind and snow. The forest floor tends to be dark and sparsely vegetated, and dotted with fungi. Common creatures of the boreal forest include deer, squirrels and owls.*

TEMPERATE FOREST *Most of the trees of temperate regions are broadleaved, deciduous trees. These trees lose their leaves in autumn and grow a new set in spring. Among the most common deciduous trees are ash, maple, oak and birch. Temperate forests are usually home to small birds and mammals such as deer and badgers.*

MONSOON FOREST *In this kind of tropical forest, trees lose their leaves during the annual dry season, when many animals survive on seeds. Typical plants include teak trees, bamboo and orchids. Among the animal inhabitants are monkeys, snakes, tigers and large birds such as parrots.*

TROPICAL RAINFOREST *Rainforest is the tallest and lushest kind of forest. Trees can be over 75 m (250 ft) high and usually have large, evergreen leaves. Vines wrap around the trees, and ferns grow in the shade. Rainforests support a vast array of animals, ranging from jaguars and panthers to parrots, frogs and a myriad of insects.*

How many kinds of trees grow in forests?

This depends on where the forest is, because more tree species live in warmer places than in colder ones. An area of tropical rainforest the size of a football pitch may contain more than 200 different kinds of trees, but in an area of boreal forest 1000 times bigger the total may be as low as six different sorts.

fast fact

The tallest trees alive today are California redwoods, which grow in northern California. Some reach 110 m (360 ft) high. In Australia in the nineteenth century, mountain ash trees, or giant gums, reached over 150 m (500 ft).

What's the difference between forest and woodland?

In forest, the trees grow thickly and the canopy is almost continuous and blocks out most of the light. In woodland, the trees are more widely spaced and more sunlight reaches the ground.

LIGHT FUELLED *Woodland's open canopy allows forest-floor flowers to flourish.*

FOSSILISED WOOD *One of the most famous petrified forests can be seen in Arizona, USA.*

WHAT IS A PETRIFIED FOREST?

Some prehistoric forests that were long ago buried by sediments have slowly turned to stone underground, as a result of their organic matter being replaced by minerals. This process is called petrifaction and the common outcome – a cluster of what look like fallen stone tree trunks – is known as a petrified forest. These fossilised trees are usually revealed when water and wind erode surrounding rock, or when geologists dig them up.

Orangutan

Scarlet macaws

Why are there so many kinds of animals in rainforests?

Well-watered rainforest trees produce a huge amount of food for animals, all year round. This allows many different species to survive side by side. Rainforests have existed for a long time, and animals living in them have developed many varied ways of life.

Madagascar day gecko

Tarsier

TROPICAL BOUNTY *The rainforests contain around 1.5 million species of plants and animals – over half the known total for the world.*

GRASSLANDS

Grasslands form where the climate is too dry for forests but there is enough rain to prevent the land turning into desert.

They often extend across vast, relatively flat or gently rolling areas, and consist of various types of grasses as well as other plants with soft stems.

HOW DOES GRASS GROW?

Most plants grow by stretching out the tips of their stems. Grass plants are different, because their stems grow from near the ground. This means that they can survive being nibbled, chewed and trampled by animals. Grass plants have another useful trick: they can spread sideways, which helps them extend across large areas of open ground and increases their chances of survival.

WHAT KINDS OF ANIMALS LIVE IN GRASSLANDS?

Common inhabitants of grasslands include large plant-eaters, or herbivores, such as bison, deer and antelopes, which often travel in large groups or herds, and their predators, such as wolves, lions and cheetahs. Grasslands are also home to many smaller creatures that eat plants and seeds and can conceal their burrows and nests in the grasses, including ground squirrels and birds, as well as countless types of insects and worms that live in the rich soil.

Temperate grassland

Prairie flowers, USA

WHY DO MANY GRASSLAND ANIMALS LIVE IN HERDS?

Grasslands sometimes have scattered clumps of trees, but otherwise they are very open and offer few places where animals can hide. By herding together, grassland animals deter predators and improve their chances of survival if they are attacked. Usually, while most members of the herd feed, others keep watch and raise the alarm if they become aware of threats.

SAFETY IN NUMBERS A herd of red lechwe antelopes in Botswana. Africa's grasslands are the world's most extensive and home to the largest herds of animals anywhere on Earth.

fast fact
A single grass plant can have over 100 km (60 miles) of roots. The roots make up a dense mat close to the surface, which helps keep the grassland soil in place.

WHY CAN'T WE EAT GRASS?

Grass contains cellulose, a tough substance that humans cannot digest. Many mammals that eat grass have a four-chambered stomach. One of the chambers contains microbes (minute living organisms) that break down the grass so that it can be digested.

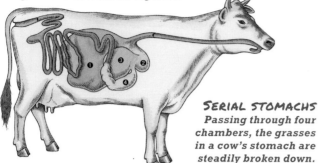

SERIAL STOMACHS *Passing through four chambers, the grasses in a cow's stomach are steadily broken down.*

ARE GRASSLANDS PRONE TO FIRE?

Dry grasslands often catch fire naturally as a result of lightning strikes. Such fires can spread rapidly but are not always as disastrous as they may seem. Many grassland plants are adapted to fire and quickly regrow, whereas invasive non-grassland species, such as trees and shrubs, are wiped out. Indeed, fires probably played a major part in creating and extending many of the world's grasslands, and many early human communities deliberately set fires to maintain open grasslands for hunting.

RESTORATION *Fire is used by ecologists to restore grasslands.*

PRAIRIE HERD *The American bison was once abundant on the tallgrass prairies of North America.*

SHORT SUPPLIES *In the dry season, African grassland animals gather at waterholes.*

WHY DO SOME GRASSES GROW HIGHER THAN OTHERS?

The types of grasses that grow, and their height, depend on how much and for how long it rains each year. In North America, rainfall patterns create three distinct north–south bands of grasslands in the middle of the continent: tallgrass prairie in the wetter east, shortgrass prairie in the drier west and midgrass prairie in between. Other grasslands, such as those in Africa, have a wet season, when the grass grows fast and tall, and a dry season, when it shrivels and turns brown.

WHAT DO HUMANS USE GRASSLANDS FOR?

CROP FIELDS *Grassland in South Africa replanted with rapeseed*

SPARSE PASTURE *Herders grazing sheep on semiarid grasslands in Afghanistan*

Early humans found grasslands ideal for hunting, and since ancient times people have used grasslands to graze domestic cattle, sheep and goats. More recently, large areas of grasslands have been ploughed up for agriculture, which has resulted in the reduction or disappearance of natural grasslands in many parts of the world.

DESERTS

Deserts are areas that receive very little rain. They can be intensely hot but may not be hot all the time; some deserts even have bitterly cold winters. In all types of desert, however, the lack of water makes it difficult for living things to survive, and the animals and plants that inhabit deserts have all had to develop a range of adaptations to help them endure drought.

WHY ARE DESERTS SO DRY?

Most large deserts are in the subtropics, which lie north and south of the tropical zone along the Equator. In these zones, warm, dry air flowing from the Equator (▶40) steadily sinks to the ground, creating a climate marked by clear skies and low rainfall. Other deserts formed because they lie far from the sea, where moist air seldom reaches – such deserts include the Gobi Desert in Asia. Yet others are the result of what is known as the rain-shadow effect: where air passes over mountains, almost all of its moisture tends to fall on the mountains as rain, so areas on the far, or lee, side of the mountains stay dry.

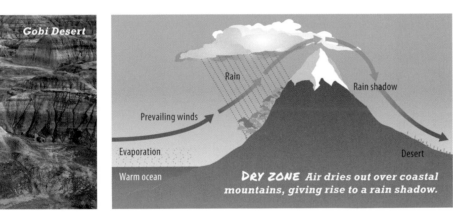

Gobi Desert

Rain

Rain shadow

Prevailing winds

Evaporation

Desert

Warm ocean

DRY ZONE *Air dries out over coastal mountains, giving rise to a rain shadow.*

WHICH IS THE DRIEST DESERT?

South America's Atacama Desert is the driest desert in the world. In some parts of this desert, which spans southern Peru and northern Chile, rain has never been recorded, and the records that do exist show that there was no significant rain in the area for 400 years – between 1571 and 1971. Today, people who live in the Atacama drink water brought in by tanker or piped in from the Andes Mountains.

DO ALL DESERTS HAVE SAND DUNES?

In all deserts, winds, temperature changes and occasional rains wear away rock, forming countless grains of sand. In some deserts this sand is blown by prevailing winds into huge piles, or dunes, which may stretch for hundreds of kilometres. In other deserts, however, the sand may be blown away entirely, leaving bare rock, or plains littered with large stones. Deserts that receive some rainfall may have expanses of tough grasses and shrubs.

HARD GOING *In Australia, stony deserts are called gibber plains.*

How do living things survive in deserts?

Plants and animals that live in deserts have adapted to the extreme conditions in a number of ways. Most can survive without water for long periods. Plants usually have tough stems and leaves and may have long roots that reach far underground to find water. Many creatures rest during the hottest times of the day and are active only at night. And some plants and animals remain dormant almost all the time, only coming to life in times of rain (▶120).

DESERT GIANT *The giant saguaro cactus grows to 15 m (50 ft) high. Like other cactuses, it can soak up and store rainwater. Its spines help protect it against plant-eating animals, but birds often nest inside it.*

How long can desert animals go without drinking?

Even at the hottest time of year, camels can survive for over a week without water. When they do find water, they can drink up to 50 litres (11 gallons) in one go, even if the water is salty. Some desert animals, such as kangaroo rats, never drink at all. They get all the water they need from their food.

Kangaroo rat

fast fact

The highest temperature ever recorded was measured on 10 July 1913, at Furnace Creek Ranch in Death Valley, part of North America's Mojave Desert. It was 56.7°C (134°F).

What is an oasis?

Even in the driest deserts, there is water deep underground. This water comes from rain that fell long ago, often far away. An oasis is a place where the ground is low enough for this water to reach the surface. Oases are important places for desert animals and also for people who travel or live in deserts.

LIFE LINE *A palm-fringed oasis in a deep depression in the Sahara Desert, Libya*

MOUNTAINS

The mountains we see today were formed over millions of years by the movements of Earth's plates (▶30).

Subsequently, they were shaped by the action of wind, water and temperature changes on rock. Some mountain ranges are many thousands of metres high and huge differences in climate and temperature occur as you climb from their bases to their highest peaks.

fast fact
The Himalayas are still growing, by about 5 mm (¼ in) a year, as the Indo-Australian Plate continues to push against the Eurasian Plate.

LIFTED AND FOLDED Crumpled sedimentary rock layers on the coast of Montenegro

WHAT ARE MOUNTAINS MADE OF?

On land, mountains are mainly formed from layers of sediment – particles of sand and mud deposited by ancient oceans and rivers. These layers have been squashed down then hardened into rock, before being uplifted by plate movements. However, some individual mountains and small ranges, including many under the sea, consist of volcanic rock, which formed when lava poured out of a volcano then hardened as it cooled.

HOW DO MOUNTAINS FORM?

Mountains form where two of Earth's plates are pushing together (▶30). Under the intense pressure, the rock slowly crumples and rises upwards. As more crust pushes together, the land rises higher and the mountains grow wider.

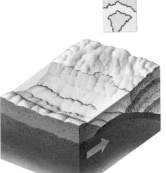

ON THE MOVE Around 40 million years ago, the Indo-Australian Plate carrying India was moving north towards the Eurasian Plate at a speed of 10 cm (4 in) a year. The movement pushed up the seafloor between the two plates.

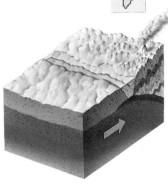

IN THE MAKING When the two landmasses collided, layers of rock crumpled into huge folds. These folds were pushed upwards, forming the beginnings of the Himalayas. Volcanoes formed and lava poured out.

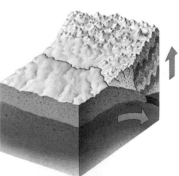

FULLY GROWN Over millennia, the layers of rock were forced higher and higher. Some rock that had been on the seafloor ended up on the mountaintops. Erosion then began to shape the mountains further.

HIGH SEAS Marine fossils from the summits of the Himalayas are evidence that its rocks were once part of the seafloor.

CARVED PILLARS *Weathering formed these dramatic sandstone pillars in Bryce Canyon, USA.*

WILL NEW MOUNTAINS FORM IN THE FUTURE?

Continents are constantly on the move, and where they meet, new mountains will be created. For example, when Australia eventually crashes into southern Asia, and Africa into southern Europe, mountain ranges will be formed as the rocks between the continents crumple and rise.

HOW ARE MOUNTAINS SHAPED BY THE ELEMENTS?

The folding process that creates mountains forms the main ridges and valleys. But the mountains are further fashioned by weathering and erosion. Water freezing and expanding in cracks causes pieces of rock to break off. Water falling as rain or snow pours down mountainsides, slowly wearing away rock and cutting deep river valleys (▶56). And wind blows sand against rock faces, gradually wearing parts away and forming new shapes.

WHAT CHANGES AS YOU CLIMB A MOUNTAIN RANGE?

It usually becomes colder as you climb a mountain range because the air temperature in Earth's lower atmosphere, or troposphere (▶38), falls on average by 6.5°C (12°F) for every 1000 m (3300 ft) of altitude. Oxygen levels also fall gradually, making it harder to breathe on high peaks. Vegetation normally becomes sparser too, as it is more difficult for most plants to survive in the cold, exposed conditions on mountaintops.

SOUTHERN PEAKS *The spine of the Andes mountains extends the length of South America, down to Patagonia.*

5000 m (16,500 ft) A freezing climate of snow and ice. Some algae, mosses and lichen are all that can survive.

4600 m (15,000 ft) A cold desert with only a few hardy plants growing in crevices. The ground is often frozen.

4000 m (13,000 ft) Cold and dry with patchy grasses and low oxygen levels. Only hardy animals, such as vicuñas and viscachas, live here.

3000 m (10,000 ft) Forest gives way to grasses, shrubs and giant leafy plants, some as big as trees.

1200 m (4000 ft) Cooler climate produces temperate forest. People grow potatoes and maize.

SEA LEVEL Hot and humid, teeming with wildlife, many farms and homes

GOING UP *The Andes mountains of South America rise from hot, wet tropics at sea level through high grasslands to bare rock and ice above 6000 m (20,000 ft).*

POLAR REGIONS

The North and South poles are by far the coldest places on Earth. Temperatures in these regions can drop to –80°C (–112°F). Biting winds blow for much of the year, and midwinter brings many days of complete darkness while the Sun remains below the horizon (▶28). But despite these severe conditions, the Arctic in the north and the Antarctic in the south are full of life. Most of this life is based in the sea, which in these realms is warmer than the air.

fast fact
Antarctica is covered by about 25 million km³ (6 million cu. miles) of ice. If all this ice melted, sea levels would rise by about 50 m (165 ft).

RESEARCH HUB At the South Pole's Amundsen–Scott Station, scientists study their surroundings and Earth's atmosphere and weather.

DOES ANYONE LIVE AT THE POLES?

The polar regions are generally too cold and inhospitable for people, although traditional peoples, including the Inuit, have long lived around the fringes of the Arctic Circle. Nobody had visited the poles until the first decade of the twentieth century, when Norwegian Roald Amundsen reached the South Pole in 1911 (▶263). Today the North Pole remains entirely uninhabited, but there are now permanent research centres in Antarctica, including the Amundsen–Scott Station at the South Pole.

HOW LARGE IS THE ARCTIC ICE SHEET?

The ice sheet that covers the Arctic Sea is frozen seawater; on average it is about 4 m (13 ft) thick. The ice spreads south in winter when the weather gets colder and contracts north again in summer. At its maximum extent it covers about 15.6 million km² (6 million sq. miles); in summer it is about half that size. Most likely as a result of global warming, the Arctic ice sheet has been shrinking steadily over the past 30 years. If it continues to shrink at the same rate, all the ice could disappear as early as 2040.

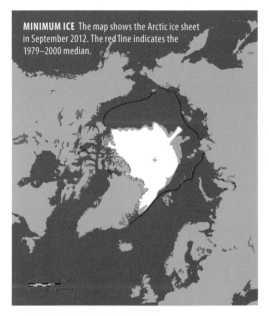

MINIMUM ICE The map shows the Arctic ice sheet in September 2012. The red line indicates the 1979–2000 median.

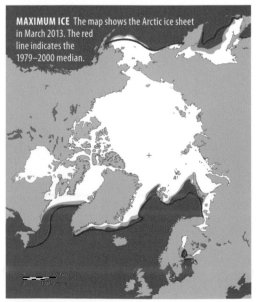

MAXIMUM ICE The map shows the Arctic ice sheet in March 2013. The red line indicates the 1979–2000 median.

WHAT IS ANTARCTICA LIKE?

Antarctica is Earth's fifth-largest landmass – about twice the size of Australia or the mainland United States. About 98 per cent of this landmass is covered with ice, which on average is 1.6 km (1 mile) thick and in places more than 3 km (2 miles) thick. Only at the edges of the continent can you see geological features such as mountains. Antarctica is also Earth's windiest place and – partly because its surface is so high – its coldest. The lowest temperature ever recorded was registered at Russia's Vostok Station on 21 July 1983: −89.2°C (−128.6°F).

BURIED CONTINENT *Ice conceals the enormous landmass of Antarctica.*

WHAT KINDS OF ANIMALS LIVE IN POLAR REGIONS?

If you parachuted down near one of the poles, you would be able to tell where you were by looking at the animals. Polar bears and walruses live only in the Arctic, while penguins and leopard seals live only in the Antarctic. The Arctic tern, a migratory bird, is one of the few creatures that is found near both poles.

WAITING GAME *Polar bears may wait by holes in the ice to ambush seals or dive into the water to catch fish.*

KEEPING WARM *Thick blubber protects walruses from the cold. Both males and females have tusks.*

WHERE DO ICEBERGS COME FROM?

Icebergs do not form from frozen seawater. They are produced by glaciers – rivers of frozen fresh water that move very slowly down mountains (▶56). At the coast, glaciers flow into the sea and break up into huge chunks of ice, which float on the water. Giant icebergs can be over 600 m (2000 ft) thick and many kilometres across, and even small ones can be dangerous to ships. Icebergs float low in the water, and only one-ninth, on average, shows above the surface.

HIDDEN HAZARD *Leopard seals lurk close to the ice and catch penguins as they feed.*

COLD START *Emperor penguins breed in large groups on the ice, huddling together for warmth.*

RIVERS AND LAKES

As rainwater hits the ground, gravity pulls it downhill. At first, the water flows in tiny trickles, but the trickles soon join up to form streams, and streams merge to form rivers. A river usually flows to a coastline, at which point it may be many kilometres wide. Lakes form where water from streams or underground springs collects in craters or hollows on Earth's surface, or sometimes where a river changes its course, leaving some water behind.

JOURNEY TO THE SEA

Water will follow the steepest and quickest path downhill that it can find. The terrain and force of its flow will determine its path.

1 As well as from rain and snowfalls, river water may come from melting snowfields and glaciers in high mountain areas.

2 Water races quickly down steep mountain slopes, forming streams that merge to form rivers.

3 Waterfalls form where a river tumbles over a sharp edge of extra-hard rock. At the bottom of the fall, the water carves out a deep pool.

4 Water pouring down into a hollow in the landscape may form a lake.

5 When a river reaches flatter ground, it slows down. The water in the middle of the river moves faster than the water near the banks.

6 Where the ground is almost flat, a river may flow first one way then the other, forming a series of wide bends, called meanders.

7 Sometimes, a river creates a new, more direct path for itself, which cuts off a loop. The resulting lake is called an oxbow lake (known in Australia as a billabong).

8 When a river arrives at the sea it may deposit sediments, forming a fan-shaped landform called a delta.

HOW FAST DO RIVERS FLOW?

This depends on what kind of terrain they are travelling down and how much water is flowing. A river may have a long, slow journey to the sea if the landscape is fairly flat and it isn't fuelled by much water; or it may rush down quickly if rainfall is abundant and the terrain is steep. Some rivers flow more than 40 km (25 miles) a day; in contrast, water that is seeping through the ground may move just a few metres each year.

ARE THERE LAKES UNDERGROUND?

Water flows through underground channels and may sometimes fill hollow chambers or caves, forming underground lakes. The largest underground lake so far discovered is the Dragon's Breath Cave in Namibia, which covers 2 ha (5 acres). Scientists have also discovered lakes far beneath the Antarctic ice cap. Cut off from the outside world ever since the ice cap first formed millions of years ago, they could contain life that exists nowhere else on Earth.

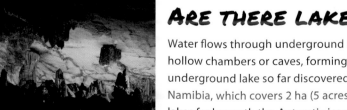
Reed Flute Cave, Guilin, China

WHY ARE SOME RIVER VALLEYS SO DEEP?

DIGGING DEEP *At the Grand Canyon, in the United States, the Colorado River has cut deep into the ground, revealing ancient sedimentary layers.*

When a river is moving fast, it picks up little pieces of grit, which scrape against the ground as they are carried along by the water. This constant scraping cuts into rock like a saw. If the river has been following the same course for thousands of years and the land is slowly rising, a deep valley or gorge will form. Moving at a much slower speed, glaciers have a similar effect, but cut distinctive U-shaped rather than V-shaped valleys.

WHAT GIVES A RIVER OR LAKE ITS COLOUR?

Some rivers and lakes are crystal clear, but most are not. This is because their waters carry sediment (tiny particles of rock and soil) and substances that dissolved out of the soil as rainwater seeped through it. Sediment can make a river or lake look brown, green, blue or even yellow, depending on the type of sediment.

ROCK FLOUR *Rivers or lakes formed below a glacier may contain rock flour, fine particles of rock rubbed off a mountain by the glacier. Rock flour can make the water a bright turquoise colour.*

WHAT CAUSES A FLOOD?

Floods usually happen when far more rain or snow than usual falls in a short period, causing rivers to overflow and inundate surrounding land, though they can also be caused by a dam collapsing or a storm surge from a hurricane (▶43). In central China in 1931, torrential rains caused the country's major rivers, the Yangtze and Yellow rivers, to burst their banks repeatedly. The resulting floods are considered the worst in history, killing up to 4 million people.

FLOOD PRONE *An overflowing river brought down this bridge in Sichuan, China, in 2010.*

HIGH AND DRY *A stranded boat on the Aral Sea bed*

CAN RIVERS AND LAKES DISAPPEAR?

In times of low rainfall, rivers and lakes may dry out. Lakes may also shrink when humans disrupt their supply of water. Since the 1960s, people have been diverting water from Central Asia's Aral Sea to irrigate surrounding farmland. As a result, the lake has shrunk dramatically, to just 10 per cent of its original size.

LANDSCAPE RECORDS

The surface area of our planet is about 510 million km² (nearly 200 million sq. miles).

Approximately 29 per cent of this is land. Earth's landforms are highly diverse, encompassing towering mountain ranges, deep valleys and hidden subterranean chambers. Despite the many high mountains, however, the average height of the continental landmasses is only about 300 m (1000 ft) above present sea level. In comparison, the average depth of all the oceans is some 4000 m (13,000 ft) below present sea level.

WHICH IS THE BIGGEST CONTINENT?

The biggest continuous landmass is Eurasia, which covers 54 million km² (21 million sq. miles), but it is usually regarded as two separate continents, Europe and Asia. Even so, Asia is still the biggest continent, at 43,820,000 km² (16,920,000 sq. miles), or 29.5 per cent of Earth's land. Africa is next largest with 30,370,000 km² (11,730,000 sq. miles), or 20.4 per cent, followed by North America (16.5 per cent), South America (12 per cent), Antarctica (9.2 per cent) and Australia (5.9 per cent).

BIGGEST ISLAND Greenland is by far the biggest island. With an area of 2,175,600 km² (839,780 sq. miles), it is nearly 10 times the size of the British Isles. The next largest is New Guinea at 808,510 km² (312,085 sq. miles).

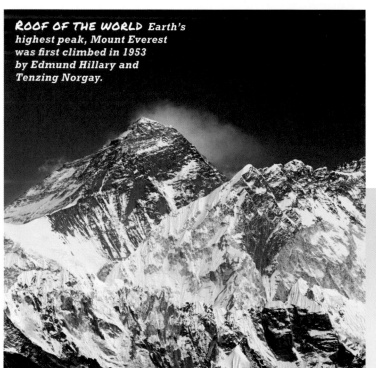

ROOF OF THE WORLD Earth's highest peak, Mount Everest was first climbed in 1953 by Edmund Hillary and Tenzing Norgay.

WHERE ARE THE HIGHEST MOUNTAINS?

The Himalaya mountain range, on the border between India, Nepal and China, is the highest area on Earth, rising to the world's highest point of 8848 m (29,029 ft) at Mount Everest. The Himalayas and the Tibetan Plateau to the north are often referred to as the 'Roof of the World', and the Tibetan Plateau is the most extensive uplifted area on Earth. It covers more than 5 million km² (2 million sq. miles) and has an average height of 5 km (3 miles).

HIGH POINTS Some of the world's tallest and most renowned mountains are compared here.

K2, Pakistan–China
8611 m (28,251 ft)

Mount Everest, Nepal–China
8848 m (29,029 ft)

Mount McKinley, USA
6168 m (20,237 ft)

Aconcagua, Argentina
6961 m (22,837 ft)

Mount Kilimanjaro, Tanzania
5899 m (19,340 ft)

Mont Blanc, France
4810 m (15,781 ft)

Popocatépetl, Mexico
5426 m (17,802 ft)

Mount Kosciuszko, Australia
2228 m (7310 ft)

Aoraki/Mount Cook, New Zealand
3754 m (12,316 ft)

Vinson Massif, Antarctica
4892 m (16,050 ft)

HIGHEST VOLCANO *As well as being South America's highest point, Aconcagua in Argentina is the world's highest volcano, reaching some 6961 m (22,837 ft) above sea level. The highest active volcano is Popocatépetl, near Mexico City, which rises 5426 m (17,802 ft).*

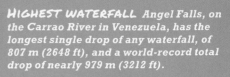

LARGEST CAVE *Discovered in 2009, Soon Dong in Vietnam is the world's largest known cave. At 9 km (5.5 miles) long, 200 m wide (650 ft) and 150 m (500 ft) tall, it could hold a city street.*

HIGHEST WATERFALL *Angel Falls, on the Carrao River in Venezuela, has the longest single drop of any waterfall, of 807 m (2648 ft), and a world-record total drop of nearly 979 m (3212 ft).*

ON LAND, WHICH IS THE LOWEST PART OF EARTH'S SURFACE?

The lowest point on any landmass is the bottom of the Bentley Trench in Antarctica. It is 2538 m (8327 ft) below sea level, far deeper than anywhere on any other continent. You can't go there, however, because the valley is buried deep below the Antarctic ice cap, the weight of which is responsible for its great depth.

fast fact

Though it rises just 4170 m (13,795 ft) above sea level, the volcano Mauna Kea on the Big Island of Hawaii extends about 6000 m (20,000 ft) down to the ocean floor. That gives it a total height of over 10,200 m (33,500 ft), making it both the tallest mountain and the biggest volcano on Earth.

WHERE ARE THE BIGGEST AND DEEPEST LAKES?

The Caspian Sea in south-western Asia is by far the biggest lake, being 370,998 km² (143,243 sq. miles) in area and up to 995 m (3264 ft) deep. In fact it is an inland sea with salty water. Lake Baikal in Russia is the deepest lake, reaching a maximum depth of 1620 m (5315 ft). It contains 20 per cent of the world's fresh surface water.

WHICH IS THE LONGEST RIVER?

Two river systems compete to be the world's longest: the Nile in North Africa and the Amazon in South America. Rivers are difficult to measure precisely and are constantly changing course. The Nile seems to have the edge at present. Its length is measured at about 6700 km (4100 miles), whereas the Amazon is 6400 km (4000 miles) long. However, the flow (the quantity of moving water per second) of the Amazon is roughly 60 times that of the Nile.

LIT UP *The nightlights of human settlements outline the Nile and its delta in this satellite image.*

THE OCEANS

The oceans cover more than 70 per cent of Earth's surface and contain 97 per cent of Earth's surface water.

At the bottom of the oceans, hidden from view, are mountain ridges, volcanoes, deep canyons, plains and plateaus.

fast fact
Earth's mid-ocean ridges form the longest mountain range on Earth, more than 50,000 km (30,000 miles) long.

HOW MANY OCEANS ARE THERE?

There are five named oceans, which are all connected to each other. The largest, the Pacific Ocean, covers one-third of Earth's surface.

PACIFIC OCEAN
Location: Extends from Asia and Australia east to the Americas
Area: 165,250,000 km² (63,800,000 sq. miles)
Average depth: 4100 m (13,500 ft)

ATLANTIC OCEAN
Location: Stretches eastwards from the Americas to Europe and Africa
Area: 106,400,000 km² (41,100,000 sq. miles)
Average depth: 3340 m (10,950 ft)

INDIAN OCEAN
Location: Bounded by Asia to the north, Africa in the west and Australia in the east
Area: 73,550,000 km² (28,400,000 sq. miles)
Average depth: 3890 m (12,760 ft)

SOUTHERN OCEAN
Location: Surrounds Antarctica and extends north to 60°S latitude
Area: 20,327,000 km² (7,848,000 sq. miles)
Average depth: 4500 m (14,800 ft)

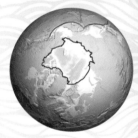

ARCTIC OCEAN
Location: Surrounds the North Pole (and is partially covered by pack ice)
Area: 14,000,000 km² (5,400,000 sq. miles)
Average depth: 1038 m (3406 ft)

HOW MOUNTAINOUS IS THE SEAFLOOR?

A continuous chain of undersea mountains, or oceanic ridges, winds its way around the globe. These mountains have formed where Earth's plates (▶30) are pulling away from each other under the ocean, allowing lava to seep up through the crack, harden and form ridges. Away from these ridges, however, large areas of the seafloor are flat, relatively featureless plains.

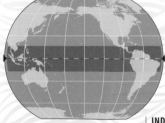

DOWN UNDER *The cross-section below shows the Pacific Ocean floor between Indonesia and South America, as also indicated above.*

INDONESIA

MARIANA TRENCH This is the deepest part of the ocean floor, dropping 10,911 m (35,797 ft) below the sea surface.

MELANESIAN BASIN The basin is rimmed by seamounts, including the Marshalls to the north and the Gilberts to the east. Some of the seamounts rise above the surface to form islands.

WESTERN PACIFIC This half of the ocean is generally deeper than the eastern half, with several basins, especially in the north, reaching depths of more than 6000 m (20,000 ft).

Mediterranean Sea

WHAT ARE SEAS?

Seas are smaller areas of salt water – often parts of the oceans – that are wholly or partially enclosed by land. Major seas include the Coral Sea off the north-east coast of Australia; the China Sea, south of China; the Caribbean Sea, off the west coast of the Americas; and the Mediterranean Sea, between Europe and Africa.

HOW DEEP ARE THE OCEANS?

In some places the oceans are more than 10 km (6 miles) deep – deep enough to submerge a mountain the height of Mount Everest. If you threw a coin into water this deep, it would take more than an hour to reach the bottom. The deepest point of all is the Mariana Trench, near the Mariana Islands in the western Pacific Ocean, which is 10,911 m (35,797 ft) deep.

HOW DO OCEAN CURRENTS FORM?

Surface currents are generally warm because the top of the sea is heated by the Sun; they form when the water is pushed along by the wind. Where surface currents are diverted north and south by the continents, they form huge loops. Deep-water currents form where cold, dense water sinks (the colder the seawater, the greater its density), and warm water moves in to take its place. Deep-water currents move cold water away from the poles extremely slowly. On average, it takes about 275 years for cold water to travel across the floor of the Atlantic, and over 500 years to travel across the floor of the Pacific. Ocean currents can have a significant effect on climate by warming or cooling the air above.

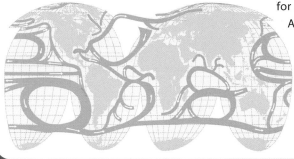

FLOW CHART *The map shows the major ocean currents, with warm currents in pink and cold ones in blue.*

HOW OLD ARE THE ROCKS ON THE SEAFLOOR?

No part of the seafloor is more than 200 million years old. That's because the seafloor is constantly forming along mid-ocean ridges and being drawn back down into the mantle along continental boundaries (▶30).

AGE OLD The map shows the approximate ages of seafloor rocks. The red areas correspond with the mid-ocean ridges.

- 0.5 million years
- 5–21 million years
- 21–38 million years
- 38–65 million years
- 65–140 million years
- 140–180 million years

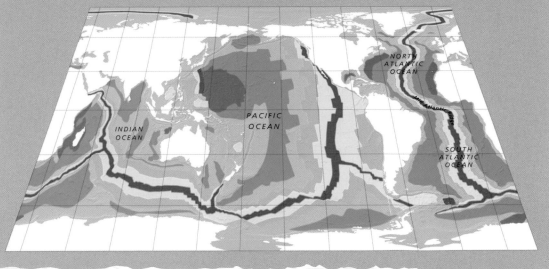

ABYSSAL PLAINS The eastern side of the Pacific Ocean floor is characterised by vast, relatively featureless plains.

EAST PACIFIC RISE Molten rock welling up through this mid-ocean ridge forms the Pacific Ocean floor.

PERU–CHILE TRENCH This deep trench formed where the Nazca Plate is subducting under the South American Plate. The trench reaches its maximum depth of 8065 m (26,460 ft) at Richards Deep.

SOUTH AMERICA

UNDER THE OCEANS

The oceans form the world's largest habitable environment and they brim with life. The most densely inhabited areas are the coastal intertidal zones and the shallow shelves that stretch from the continent's edge to the abyssal zone – the deepest, darkest level of the ocean.

WHAT LIVES IN SHALLOW OCEAN?

The continental shelf is home to thousands of different kinds of animals, including most of the fish we eat. Seaweeds live in shallow water, where the light is brightest. They form underwater gardens that are nurseries for young fish.

Lobster

Eel grass

Crab

Dogfish

Whelks

Plaice

Cod

Sand eels

WHY IS SEAWATER SALTY?

The oceans have been around for hundreds of millions of years. Over that time, rain seeping through the ground and rivers running to the seas have carried minerals, including salts, to the oceans. Heat from the Sun is constantly causing some seawater to evaporate, but the salts are left behind in the ocean and steadily build up. So the water vapour in the air and, consequently, the rain that falls from the sky, are low in salt – which is why rivers and lakes are not salty. Most of the salt in the sea is sodium chloride, the kind we use on our food – every litre (2 pints) of seawater contains about 35 g (1¼ oz) of salt. If all the salt was extracted from the oceans and spread across Earth, it would form a layer 150 m (500 ft) deep.

WHY AREN'T DEEP-SEA ANIMALS SQUASHED BY THE WATER ABOVE?

The deeper you go, the greater the pressure of the water on top of you. At a depth of 9000 m (30,000 ft), the pressure is the equivalent of a tonne weight resting on your thumb. This weight would quickly crush a human, but deep-sea creatures have evolved to cope with it. In most cases, their bodies contain little or no air, so they are quite solid and can resist the intense pressure. The difference between them and us is a bit like the difference between a solid rubber ball and an air-filled one – the solid one is much harder to squash out of shape.

Gulper eel

WHAT ARE BLACK SMOKERS?

Along mid-ocean ridges where oceanic plates are pulling apart, mineral-laden water in the crust meets hot rock below and gushes out through vents or fissures. The minerals harden and form chimneys, or smokers. The plumes of hot water are often dark and murky, hence the name 'black smoker', but they can sometimes be paler, forming so-called white smokers. Specialised communities thrive around smokers in total darkness, including unusual clams, tubeworms and shrimps.

Cock-eye squid

Deep-sea jellyfish

Scaleless black dragonfish

WHAT KINDS OF CREATURES LIVE IN DEEP OCEAN?

The deepest part of the oceans, the abyssal zone, is thousands of metres beneath the surface. Here it is always dark and cold. Strange fish hunt each other in the darkness. Most have giant mouths to scoop up potential food, and some have lures that light up to attract prey. Other animals sift through the ooze on the ocean floor, feeding on particles of food that have drifted down from above.

fast fact

About 20,000 years ago, the ice age was at its peak. The sea level was over 100 m (330 ft) lower than today because a huge amount of water was locked up in ice. As a result, people could walk across what is now the seabed from mainland Europe to Britain and from Asia to Alaska.

WHAT WOULD IT BE LIKE TO WALK ON THE SEAFLOOR?

In many places you would disappear, because you would sink into a deep layer of soft and slimy ooze. This ooze forms from the decomposing skeletons of tiny plants and animals that drift down to the seabed after they die. This build-up occurs at a very slow rate – just a few millimetres a century – but it has been going on for so long that in some places the ooze is several metres deep.

Submersible exploring the ocean floor

NAUTILE

Tripod fish

Sea cucumber

Sea spider

Brittle stars

AROUND THE COAST

Coastlines change as the tide rises and falls and the sea pounds away at the land. Shorelines teem with life, but the nonstop battering means that plants and animals have to be tough to survive. Many shore animals are protected by hard shells, and many seaweeds have rubbery stalks that are difficult to break. On sandy shores, most animals live buried beneath the surface, safe from the push and pull of the waves.

WHICH CREATURES LIVE AT THE SEA'S EDGE?

The shore between the high- and low-tide marks is called the 'intertidal zone'. Plants and animals living here have to survive both under water and in air. Barnacles and limpets fastened to the rocks show where the intertidal zone begins.

HIGH TIDE *Fish swim close to the shore to eat food stirred up by the waves. Limpets creep over the rocks, scraping off tiny plants. Seaweeds spread out in the water to catch the light.*

Sea lettuce

Bladderwrack

Seaweeds

Sea anemone

Sea urchin

Crab

LOW TIDE *Seaweeds lie on rocks. A jelly-like coating helps protect them from water loss. Small animals, such as periwinkles and tiny crabs, hide in the seaweed to avoid the Sun. Limpets clamp their shells to the rocks, trapping moisture and protecting themselves from predators.*

Seaweeds

Sea anemones

Starfish

Sea urchin

WHAT MAKES THE TIDES?

Tides are produced by the gravity of the Moon and Sun. This force tugs at the oceans as the Earth spins round (▶28), pulling the water in one direction, then another. The Moon is much closer to Earth than the Sun is, so, even though it is quite small, its gravity has the bigger effect. When the Sun and Moon are in line, their combined gravitational pull causes high spring tides.

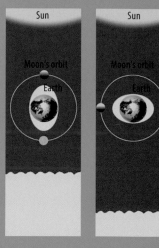

Sun | Sun
Moon's orbit | Moon's orbit
Earth | Earth

SPRING TIDE *At the new and full Moon, the Sun and Moon are in line. The blue area around the Earth illustrates the tidal bulge.*

NEAP TIDE *During the Moon's first and third quarters, the pull of the Moon and the Sun are at right angles to each other.*

WHAT IS A CORAL REEF?

Found mainly in tropical regions (44), coral reefs are hard structures made by tiny animals called coral polyps. The polyps have soft bodies and protect themselves by building hard cases around themselves, called exoskeletons. They do this by extracting calcium carbonate from the seawater and turning it into a solid form of the same compound, called aragonite. The corals attach their cases to those of older polyps and the cases build up to form reefs. Coral reefs are the biggest structures made by living things. The world's largest reef system – the Great Barrier Reef, off the north-east coast of Australia – covers 348,000 km² (134,000 sq. miles). It has taken more than 8000 years to form. Corals cannot survive in temperatures below 20°C (68°F).

CORAL REEF Most corals grow only a few centimetres each year.

HOW DO WAVES FORM?

Waves are normally produced by wind as it blows across the surface of the open sea. In deep water, waves are shallow and wide apart. As waves approach the coast, they become higher and closer together because the seabed rises and slows their progress. Eventually, a wave becomes top-heavy and topples over, forming a breaker that crashes against the shore. Much bigger waves, known as tsunamis, can be caused by undersea earthquakes or landslides (▶35).

DEEP WATER The waves are far apart.

INSHORE The seabed rises and the waves bunch together.

ROCKS AND MINERALS

Wherever you are on Earth's landmasses, you will be standing on a layer of solid rock between 12 and 60 km (8 and 37 miles) deep. Although rock seems firmly fixed in place, the tremendous heat of Earth's interior keeps it moving slowly. Over millions of years, new rock is built up and then gradually worn away. This has formed all the different features, such as mountain peaks, gorges and valleys, that we see on the surface.

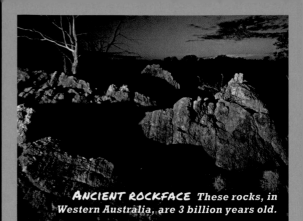
ANCIENT ROCKFACE These rocks, in Western Australia, are 3 billion years old.

WHAT IS ROCK?

Rock is a solid material that forms the surface of Earth on land and under the sea. In places rock can be very young: near volcanoes, for example, rock may have formed just thousands or hundreds of years ago, or may even form before your eyes as lava cools. However, in most places rock is very old. The oldest rocks found so far are in northern Canada. They date back more than 4 billion years, to a time when Earth's crust had only recently formed (▶32).

fast fact

Pumice is an igneous rock full of gas bubbles, which can make it light enough to float on water. In 1883, an Indonesian volcano called Krakatoa erupted and produced so much floating pumice that boats had trouble getting through it.

TOUGH STUFF Granite, an igneous rock, is hard and resists erosion. Granite domes and boulders often rise above other, softer rocks.

WHAT ARE THE MAIN TYPES OF ROCK?

Most of the rocks in Earth's crust – up to 95 per cent – formed when molten rock cooled and hardened. Such rocks are known as igneous rocks. Some, such as granite, formed underground, while others, notably basalt, formed on the surface as lava from a volcano cooled. As much as three-quarters of the rock on Earth's surface, however, is sedimentary rock. It originally formed when sediments such as sand, silt and mud – often laid down by seas – were compressed under other layers and gradually hardened to form rock. Types of sedimentary rock include sandstone and limestone. The third main type of rock, metamorphic rock, formed when either igneous or sedimentary rock was squeezed by intense pressure or heated by molten rock. Examples include marble and slate.

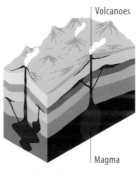
IGNEOUS ROCK Molten rock cools and hardens, either underground or on Earth's surface.

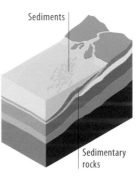
SEDIMENTARY ROCK Sediments are deposited under water. Layers build up and are compressed to form rock.

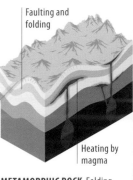
METAMORPHIC ROCK Folding, squeezing or heating of rock changes its composition.

WHY ARE SOME ROCKS HARDER THAN OTHERS?

The hardness of a rock depends partly on the minerals it contains. Some minerals are very hard, but a few are quite soft. You can test a mineral's hardness by seeing what will scratch it. For example, a sharp piece of glass will scratch fluorite and apatite but not quartz. No natural substance can scratch diamond because it is the hardest mineral of all.

SCALE OF HARDNESS *The Mohs scale arranges common minerals in order of scratch resistance or hardness, from softest (far left) to hardest (right).*

 Talc

 Gypsum

 Calcite

 Fluorite

 Apatite

 Feldspar

Quartz

Beryl

Corundum

 Diamond

WHAT'S THE DIFFERENCE BETWEEN ROCKS AND MINERALS?

Minerals are the chemical ingredients that make up rocks. Minerals often form crystals, and sometimes one type is found on its own. More often, though, different minerals or crystals are mixed or grow together, forming rock. Granite, for example, is made up of three different minerals: quartz, feldspar and mica.

IN THE MIX *Crystals of different kinds of minerals are visible in this block of granite.*

LAYERED UP *Distinct layers of different types of rock are often visible in sedimentary formations.*

ANOTHER FORM *In metamorphic rock such as marble, recrystallisation and realignment of minerals creates distinctive patterns.*

HOW DO CAVES FORM?

Large cave systems often form in limestone, a porous sedimentary rock. When water seeps through limestone, it slowly dissolves the rock, creating a cavity. As the water continues to drip into the cavity, it leaves behind mineral deposits that gradually build into hard formations that taper down from the ceiling, called stalactites. On the ground beneath, mounds grow where the mineral-laden water falls, called stalagmites. Sometimes stalactites and stalagmites meet, forming pillars.

GEMS AND PRECIOUS METALS

Gemstones are rocks or mineral crystals of many shapes and colours that have special qualities.

To be called 'precious', gems must be beautiful, durable and rare. Precious metals sometimes turn up as pure lumps, called nuggets. More often, they are found in the form of an ore – that is, mixed in with other minerals. Some gems and metals have special uses in industry and electronics, but many are valuable simply because they are beautiful and rare.

WHAT IS SO SPECIAL ABOUT PRECIOUS METALS?

Precious metals are in demand for their beauty but also for particular properties. For example, platinum is useful as a catalyst – a substance that speeds up chemical reactions. Gold and silver are about 10 times better than steel at conducting heat; they are also good at conducting electricity and are used in electronics. Gold is quite soft, so it can be hammered very thin, and never rusts or tarnishes.

BIT PART Every mobile phone contains gold worth about 50 US cents.

FOR SHOW Gold is not absorbed by the body, so it can be used to decorate food.

68

WHICH ARE THE MOST VALUABLE GEMS AND METALS?

The most valuable minerals are known as precious stones, or gems, and precious metals. The precious gems are diamond, ruby, emerald, sapphire and opal. Precious metals include gold, silver and platinum. Gemstones that are a little more common and less valuable, such as malachite and turquoise, are known as semiprecious stones.

Diamond

Ruby in rock

Sapphire

Opal

Emerald

Amethyst

Malachite

Tourmaline

Gold

Silver

Platinum

① **NORTH AMERICA** Precious metals, including gold, silver and platinum

② **COLOMBIA** The best emeralds and the largest single diamond crystal

③ **BRAZIL** The biggest aquamarine crystal ever found, and the largest emerald

④ **SOUTH AFRICA** The deepest gold mines in the world and many diamond mines

⑤ **SRI LANKA** Some of the world's biggest sapphires

⑥ **RUSSIA** The Ural Mountains are a source of large emeralds and diamonds.

⑦ **MYANMAR (BURMA)** The largest and best-quality rubies

⑧ **AUSTRALIA** The largest cut sapphire, the largest gold nugget, and famous for its opals

⑨ **NEW ZEALAND** Famous for its green jade

WHERE ARE THE BEST PLACES TO FIND PRECIOUS GEMS AND METALS?

Certain parts of the world have large, or the only, deposits of particular gems and minerals.

fast fact

Gold can be beaten to gold leaf less than a 10,000th of a millimetre thick, and 1 g (0.04 oz) can be drawn into a wire thread as long as 2.4 km (1½ miles).

HOW DO YOU CUT A DIAMOND?

Diamond is the hardest substance on Earth, so the only thing that can cut it is a diamond-bladed saw. The person cutting a rough diamond first marks where the blade should go, so that as little as possible is wasted. Each piece is cut into a shape that has lots of flat faces, called facets, arranged at precise angles to each other to reflect light in all directions.

WHY ARE SOME GEMS SO RARE?

Rare gems form in unusual underground conditions that do not occur in many places. Once these gems have formed, they can be difficult to find. For example, diamonds are made of carbon, which is one of the commonest elements on Earth. But carbon turns into diamond only when it is squeezed and heated deep below Earth's crust, then rapidly propelled upwards to the surface by an explosive eruption – something that happens only rarely.

WHAT IS A GOLD RUSH?

A gold rush is a mass migration of people to an area where gold has been discovered. Gold rushes transformed the fortunes and history of many parts of the world. After the discovery of gold in California in 1848, more than 300,000 people migrated to the region to search for the precious metal, resulting in the rapid growth of cities such as San Francisco and Sacramento. Much the same happened in Australia, where gold was found in New South Wales and Victoria. Between 1851 and 1861, the country's population doubled, mainly due to the discovery of gold.

NATURAL AND SYNTHETIC MATERIALS

Over thousands of years, humans have identified useful qualities in various kinds of natural materials. They have also worked out how to modify some of those materials to make them even more effective, and combine them in various forms to create new, or synthetic, materials.

WHAT IS AN ELEMENT?

An element is the pure form of a natural material, consisting of only one kind of atom. About 90 elements occur naturally. They include metals, such as iron, aluminium, copper and gold, and nonmetals, such as carbon and silicon, as well as substances that are usually gases, such as hydrogen and helium.

TOUGH STUFF
A tungsten carbide drill bit, used to drill oil wells

WHAT ARE ALLOYS?

Alloys are mixtures of elements, including at least one metal. The most widely used alloys are forms of steel. There are many types of steel, all based on iron with small amounts of carbon, manganese and other elements. Stainless steel, which resists rust, contains chromium and often nickel. The various types of tool steel, which are very hard, contain elements such as tungsten, cobalt or molybdenum. The most widely used lightweight alloys are those made with aluminium, one of the most common metallic elements in Earth's crust; aluminium alloys are, however, expensive to make.

LINING UP *Steel rods being made in a factory in Russia*

WHICH ARE THE TOUGHEST METALS?

Tungsten is the metal with the highest tensile strength – the ability to resist being pulled apart – and the highest melting point of any metal, 3410°C (6170°F). It is often found naturally as tungsten carbide, a substance that can be pressed into hard forms and, as such, is twice as stiff as steel. It is widely used for drills, saws and other cutting tools. Iridium is the metal that resists rusting and other kinds of corrosion best; it is also extremely hard and resists scratching. Gold and platinum also resist attack by almost all chemicals and stay bright and shiny, which is why they are used for jewellery.

WHICH METALS ARE USED FOR WIRING?

The best conductor of heat and electricity is silver, but copper is almost as good and is much cheaper than silver. So copper is generally used for electrical wires.

fast fact

The synthetic fibre known as Kevlar is five times stronger than steel. It is used to make bullet-proof vests.

WHICH ARE THE OLDEST HUMAN-MADE MATERIALS?

Ceramics are the most ancient human-made materials. Pottery was first made in prehistoric times, about 13,000 years ago. Today, ceramics are also important in industry and engineering. Ceramics are among the most heat-resistant of all materials and are often used where metals would melt or become weak. For example, some spacecraft are covered with ceramic tiles or pads made of woven fibres of silica (purified sand) to resist the heat generated when they re-enter Earth's atmosphere.

HEAT SHIELD *Ceramic tiles, in the lower central panel, protect instruments on the Orion space craft.*

WHAT IS SILICON?

Silicon is by far the most common solid element in Earth's crust, making up 28 per cent of the planet's weight. Sand is mainly silica, a compound of silicon and oxygen. Silicon is a metalloid – a substance that acts in some ways like a metal and in other ways like a nonmetal. It is also a semiconductor: it conducts electricity better than most nonmetals but not as well as metals. A widespread use of silicon is to make computer chips (▶204).

HOW ARE PLASTICS MADE?

Plastics are polymers – substances made of long chains of atoms – and they are usually made with chemicals derived from petroleum (▶72). The earliest plastic material, parkesine, was produced by Alexander Parkes of Birmingham, England, in 1856. There are two main types of modern plastics. Thermoplastics can be reshaped when heated; they include nylon, polyethylene, polystyrene and synthetic rubbers. Thermosetting plastics, on the other hand, cannot be reshaped after they have first hardened; they include melamine and polyurethane, as well as Bakelite, which was invented in 1909 and long used to make telephones.

WHAT ARE COMPOSITE MATERIALS?

Composite materials are two or more different materials that are combined to make something that is better than either on its own. The earliest composite material dates from over 2000 years ago, when the ancient Greeks used metal bars to strengthen marble. Today, reinforced concrete – concrete containing steel (or sometimes plastic) rods – is widely used for buildings, bridges and roads. Other widely used composite materials include plastics reinforced with fibres of glass or graphite (carbon).

PLASTIC COMPOSITES *Carbon-fibre plastics are widely used for car bodies, baths, parts of aircraft and sports equipment, such as bicycles, tennis rackets and snowboards.*

FOSSIL FUELS

In prehistoric times, people learned how to burn wood to keep themselves warm. Less than 3000 years ago, they discovered that coal, oil and natural gas also burn, and that they give off a lot more heat than wood. Since then, these three fuels have become an essential part of daily life. We use them for heat and light, and for powering all kinds of machines. They are called 'fossil fuels' because they formed from the buried (fossilised) remains of living things.

WHAT IS COAL?

If you look at a piece of coal through a magnifying glass, you may be able to spot pieces of fossilised wood and bark, and even the outlines of leaves. These show that coal is made from plants – mostly large tree ferns – and that it formed long ago. The plants grew in huge swampy forests in warm parts of the world. As they died, their remains piled up on the ground, but the swamp water stopped them rotting away. Instead, they were buried under mud and silt until they lay deep underground. Then, over millions of years, the pressure of the rock above squeezed the remains of the trees, turning them into the black, shiny rock we call coal.

FERN FOSSIL Fossilised fern leaves from plants that grew in prehistoric times can be seen preserved in this piece of coal.

❶ RAW MATERIAL The remains of microscopic plants and animals settle on the seabed.

❷ SLOW CONVERSION Warmth from Earth's interior, combined with pressure from the sediment above, converts the rotting remains into oil droplets and minute bubbles of gas.

❸ COMING WITHIN REACH Over millions of years, the layers of rock buckle and bend. The oil droplets and gas bubbles squeeze upwards through the rock until they are trapped by a layer of dense rock.

HOW DO OIL AND GAS FORM?

Today's stores of oil and natural gas were produced from microscopic plants and animals in the sea. These may have contained natural oils when alive. When they died, their remains settled on the seabed and became buried by sediment. Once buried, the pressure of the sea and sediment pressing down from above slowly turned them into these fossil fuels.

❹ EXTRACTING OIL Oil rigs drill down to the rock layers where the oil droplets and gas bubbles have become trapped. Pressure underground forces the oil or gas up the drill pipe to the surface.

HOW DO WE FIND OIL?

To find oil, geologists look for the kinds of sedimentary rock most likely to contain it – sandstone or limestone – and rocks that can trap it – usually shale. Then they set off shockwaves and measure the time they take to reflect off different rock layers. Using this data, they create a map. Domes and other structures that can hold oil will show up, and certain patterns can even directly indicate the presence of oil or gas.

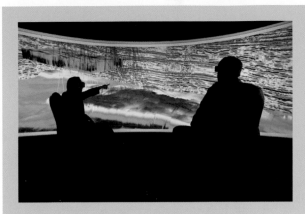

OUT OF SIGHT Geologists studying a 3D model of subterranean rock layers. The different colours indicate different kinds of rock.

fast fact

In a car engine, nearly half the energy provided by petrol is wasted making heat and noise.

WHEN WILL WE RUN OUT OF FOSSIL FUELS?

Earth contains finite resources of fossil fuels. That means they will eventually be used up. How quickly this will happen depends on the size of the reserves, how much we can find and how quickly we consume them. Our known coal reserves will last for at least another 100 years, and proven gas reserves are likely to last about 60 years at current rates of consumption. Debate rages over when oil production is likely to peak (after which supplies will start to run out), with some experts saying this could happen in the next 10 years and others arguing it will take much longer.

FILLING UP Ocean-going oil tankers taking on cargo at an oil rig in the North Sea.

ARE FOSSIL FUELS DAMAGING THE ATMOSPHERE?

The burning of fossil fuels – at power plants, in cars and in homes – releases poisonous gases into the air. Especially around large cities, this causes dangerous air pollution. When sulfur dioxide from fossil fuels combines with water in the atmosphere, it forms so-called acid rain, which damages plants and buildings. Furthermore, the burning of fossil fuels increases the amount of carbon dioxide in the atmosphere; this in turn appears to be intensifying Earth's natural greenhouse effect and resulting in global warming (▶39). As a result, many nations are seeking to increase their use of renewable forms of energy (▶242).

MELTING ICE In recent years, the ice sheet that covers Greenland has been melting at the fastest rate ever recorded, which may be due to global warming.

NATURAL HISTORY

HOW LIFE BEGAN

If you could travel back 4 billion years in time, you would find Earth a very different place. You would not be able to breathe because the air would be filled with poisonous gases, and you would not be able to eat because there would be no plants or animals. Most of the ground would be bare rock. But out in the oceans, the first signs of life would be stirring.

HOW DID LIFE GET STARTED?

Life probably began as a series of chemical reactions between substances in the sea and atmosphere. Scientists have tested this idea by re-creating the conditions of early Earth. In one experiment, they put water in a glass container to imitate the sea and replaced the air above it with the gases they think were in the atmosphere 4 billion years ago. Then they passed electric sparks through the gases, to imitate lightning. Afterwards, the water was found to contain some of the complex chemicals that make up living things.

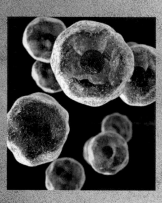

WHAT WERE THE FIRST LIFE FORMS?

The first life forms almost certainly appeared in the oceans and were a type of microscopic bacteria, each consisting of just a single cell (your body, on the other hand, is made up of trillions of cells). Critically, these bacteria were able to reproduce themselves.

Artist's impression of single-celled bacteria

WHERE DID THE GASES ON EARTH COME FROM?

Most of the gases, including methane, hydrogen and ammonia, came from inside Earth and were released through volcanoes. Four billion years ago, there were many more volcanoes on Earth than there are now, and they were erupting all the time because the centre of the planet was intensely hot.

WHAT IS THE EARLIEST EVIDENCE OF LIFE ON EARTH?

The earliest evidence of life – traces of bacteria in ancient rocks found in Western Australia – dates from about 3.5 billion years ago – about 800,000 years after Earth formed. However, some scientists think life may have emerged even earlier, perhaps around 4.3 billion years ago, soon after Earth's atmosphere began to form.

FIRST UP These Western Australian rock-like forms are stromatolites, structures built by primitive bacteria about 3.5 billion years ago.

HOW DID THE FIRST LIFE FORMS DEVELOP?

The first bacteria grew by using chemicals in the sea. As those chemicals ran out, it became harder for them to survive. But another kind of bacteria then appeared, which learned to develop in a different way, by photosynthesis. This involves using the energy in sunlight to make food (▶96), and it produces oxygen as a waste product. So, as this new gas began to build up, Earth's atmosphere changed, forming the kind of air we breathe today and creating opportunities for other life forms to develop.

IN BLOOM *Many bacteria still derive energy from sunlight, such as the cyanobacteria on this pond.*

fast fact

About 2.4 billion years ago, rising oxygen levels created the ozone layer. It protects all life forms by blocking out 99 per cent of harmful ultraviolet radiation.

WHY DIDN'T LIFE START THIS WAY ON OTHER PLANETS?

It may have done, but so far we don't know of such a planet. In our Solar System, Earth is the only planet suited to life. The main thing that makes it so is water. No other planet we know of has the huge oceans we have, nor the many lakes and rivers. Water is a very important ingredient of all living things because it has many properties that no other substance has. All the important reactions that occur inside our cells require water, and all the organs in our bodies, such as the heart and lungs and liver, rely on being surrounded by water. Without water, life as we know it could not go on. It's possible that there could be a type of life form that doesn't depend on water, but so far scientists have not worked out what that could be.

THE FIRST ANIMALS AND PLANTS

WHAT DID THE FIRST MULTICELLED CREATURES LOOK LIKE?

Some early bacteria evolved into green algae, while other multicelled life forms gradually emerged that resembled seaweeds and sponges. These were eventually joined by creatures rather like modern jellyfish and squid. This all happened very slowly, but about 550 million years ago the oceans were suddenly teeming with life. Among the most common animals of this era were hard-shelled sea creatures called trilobites.

SMALL FRY *Dating from about 550 million years ago, Spriggina measured up to 5 cm (2 in), had a segmented body and possibly eyes and antennae.*

IN ABUNDANCE *Fossils of trilobites, which ranged in size from 1 mm (¹/₂₅ in) to 70 cm (28 in) across, are abundant.*

Life existed only as seaborne single-celled bacteria for more than 3 billion years. Then about 1 billion years ago the first multicelled life forms appeared and gradually began to assume a wide variety of forms, eventually leading to the first recognisable animals and plants.

WHEN DID THE FIRST FISH APPEAR?

Evidence for the first fish-like creatures dates back to about 470 million years ago. These were also the first creatures with a backbone – they were the first vertebrates, in other words. The earliest fish were jawless forms, such as the eel-like conodonts and the armoured ostracoderms. Appearing about 420 million years ago, the earliest known jawed fishes were the placoderms, another kind of armoured fish.

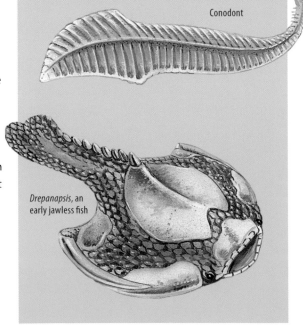

Conodont

Drepanapsis, an early jawless fish

HOW DID PLANTS START GROWING ON LAND?

It's likely that about 475 million years ago, some algae began living on the edge of the land and then developed tiny shoots to fix themselves in the ground. This, in turn, began to break up soil and make it more accommodating for other life forms. By about 400 million years ago, plants had developed stalks, leaves and seeds. Among the earliest plants that are still around today were ferns.

FOSSILISED FERN *About 300 million years ago, ferns dominated Earth's vegetation.*

WHY DID SOME ANIMALS AND PLANTS DISAPPEAR?

Every so often in the fossil record, large numbers of plants and animals disappear abruptly. Such mass extinctions were usually the result of massive volcanic eruptions, ice ages, asteroid impacts or other sudden environmental changes. Major extinctions have occurred several times in Earth's history. About 445–440 million years ago, for example, about three-quarters of all species on Earth vanished, probably as a result of falling temperatures and sea levels associated with the onset of an ice age. Similar events took place about 365 million years ago; about 245 million years ago, just before the first dinosaurs; about 208 million years ago, wiping out many of the dinosaurs' rivals; and 66 million years ago, killing off the dinosaurs themselves.

DIVIDING LINE *The white band in these rock layers was formed by deposits laid down during the extinction event that killed the dinosaurs 66 million years ago.*

Hylonomus

WHICH WERE THE FIRST ANIMALS TO LIVE ON LAND?

Among the first animals to appear on land, about 450 million years ago, were primitive insects, spiders, centipedes and millipedes. About 370 million years ago, some fish developed legs and began to live partly on land and partly in the sea – they were amphibious, in other words. The earliest creatures of this type, such as *Hylonomus*, probably resembled modern salamanders.

fast fact
About 350 million years ago, animal life included 2 m (6 ft) millipedes and giant dragonflies with a wingspan of more than 1 m (3¹/₃ ft).

WHAT WERE THE FIRST FORESTS LIKE?

The first true tree species, with a thick trunk and branches, was called *Archaeopteris*. Soon after it appeared, about 360 million years ago, it spread quickly around the world and formed many of the world's first forests. These forests were succeeded, around 250 million years ago, by forests characterised by tall conifer trees, including the monkey puzzle, which is still around today, as well as ginkgo trees, small palm trees (cycads), and tree ferns.

WELL PROTECTED *The tough, spiky leaves of monkey puzzles protect them from plant-eating animals.*

IN FLOWER *Fossils of flowers belonging to the magnolia family date back 100 million years.*

WHEN DID THE FIRST FLOWERS APPEAR?

Recent discoveries suggest that the first flowering plants may have appeared as early as 240 million years ago, but they do not seem to have been widespread until about 120 million years ago. Some of the first common flowering species included magnolias and water lilies.

HOW LIVING THINGS EVOLVE

Every living thing on Earth is descended from one common ancestor that lived long ago. We know this because, although living things have different genes, they have all inherited the same genetic code to make those genes work. That ancestor was probably a creature similar to a bacterium. But how could a bacterium produce descendants as different as sharks, daisies, cucumbers and camels? The answer is that living things slowly change, or evolve, and over millions of years, tiny differences have built up to produce millions of completely new species.

WHY DO LIVING THINGS EVOLVE?

Evolution has produced all the different creatures found on Earth. The evidence for this comes from fossils, and from comparing the structure and chemistry of living creatures. But what makes evolution happen? Scientists believe that the answer is something called 'natural selection'. Most adult animals and plants produce more than enough young to replace themselves. Some of these offspring die without breeding, while others go on to produce young of their own. It is usually the ones best suited to their environment that survive, while the weakest die out. Because the best adapted survive and are most likely to pass on their genes to the next generation, a successful species will gradually become more and more suited to its environment.

ON PAPER *English scientist Charles Darwin was the first person to widely publish theories about evolution and natural selection.*

HORSE ANCESTOR
Hyracotherium had feet with four toes.

Anchitherium

Hipparion

Merychippus

Equus

Hypohippus

Hyracotherium

Mesohippus

Pliohippus

HOW DO SPECIES CHANGE OVER TIME?

Gradually a species develops features or abilities that are especially suited to its environment. Horses belong to a family of animals 50 million years old. Their earliest known ancestor, called *Hyracotherium*, was the size of a dog and had four-toed feet. Its descendants grew bigger and evolved longer legs with fewer toes, to help them run faster and cover more ground on the open grasslands they usually inhabited – today's horses have just one toe or hoof on each foot. Then populations in particular types of grasslands developed characteristics that helped them survive in that habitat, such as stripes for camouflage on zebras living in the East African savannah.

EVOLVING SPECIES *The illustration shows how horses have evolved over 50 million years.*

DO SPECIES SOMETIMES BECOME EXTINCT NATURALLY?

It is part of the process of evolution that, while some creatures will flourish, others will die out. And sometimes this results in the loss of an entire species. Successful species tend to be ones that are not only suited to their environment but can also adapt to change – perhaps by moving to other areas or starting to eat different food or learning to cope with a different climate. In turn, they may eventually evolve into new forms of a species or even an entirely new species. One of the major changes living things have to cope with is the impact of humans on environments through such activities as forest clearance, building and hunting. Sometimes this happens too quickly for animals to adjust, resulting in rapid extinctions.

GONE FOREVER *The dodo was hunted to extinction by humans in the late seventeenth century.*

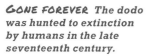

fast fact

If current rates of human-influenced extinctions continue, we can expect half of the world's presently known species to disappear by the end of the twenty-first century.

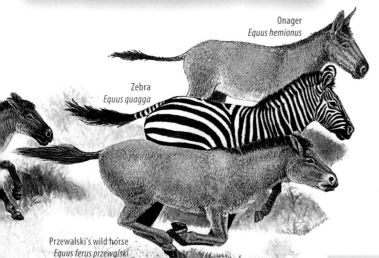

Onager
Equus hemionus

Zebra
Equus quagga

Przewalski's wild horse
Equus ferus przewalski

TODAY
Horses now have feet with just one toe.

SAME APPROACH
The Cape pangolin, or scaly anteater (above), from Africa and the armadillo (right) from the Americas have evolved in similar ways.

DO SOME UNRELATED ANIMALS EVOLVE IN THE SAME WAY?

Yes, if two or more animals live in a similar way and eat the same kinds of food, they may evolve to look like each other, even if they are unrelated and live in different parts of the world. This is called convergent evolution. The armadillos of the Americas and the pangolins of Africa have evolved to look similar because both families feed on insects in open areas: so both need long snouts to ferret out insects and armour to protect them from predators.

CAN ONE SPECIES EVOLVE INTO MANY DIFFERENT SPECIES?

Yes, this is called divergent evolution. It usually happens when separate groups of one species are able to take advantage of different niches – ways of living and eating. A famous example is that of the finches of the Galápagos Islands, which was first noted by Charles Darwin during a visit in 1835. Originally just one species from South America took up residence in the Galápagos. But as they spread across the islands, local populations of the birds found different sources of food and different ways to feed on them. So they eventually developed different beak shapes, each suited to the food available – larger beaks for breaking seeds or pointed beaks for probing bark for insects, and so on.

Some of the finches that evolved in the Galápagos

Common cactus finch   Small tree finch   Vegetarian finch   Warbler finch   Woodpecker finch

THE AGE OF THE DINOSAURS

The dinosaurs were a large group of reptiles that lived between about 243 million years ago and 66 million years ago. During that time, they came to dominate the animal kingdom. There were a great many different kinds of dinosaur. They included harmless plant-eaters, which often fed in herds, but also some of the biggest, fastest and most dangerous meat-eating animals ever to inhabit our planet.

HOW BIG WERE THE DINOSAURS?

Dinosaurs were all different shapes and sizes. The largest were the sauropods, colossal long-necked plant-eaters that thrived during the Jurassic period (201 to 145 million years ago). The biggest sauropod for which there is firm fossil evidence is *Argentinosaurus*, which could have been up to 35 m (115 ft) long; however, another sauropod, *Amphicoelias*, for which only descriptions of a nineteenth-century fossil exist, could have been up to 60 m (200 ft) long. At the other end of the scale, *Microceratus*, despite being related to the much larger *Triceratops*, was only about 60 cm (2 ft) high, and the feathered, bird-like *Anchiornis*, found in China, was as small as a pigeon – just 40 cm (16 in) long.

LINING UP *This illustration of six common dinosaurs shows them to scale.*

Ornitholestes
2 m (6²/₃ ft)

Compsognathus
1 m (3¹/₃ ft)

Dilophosaurus
7 m (23 ft)

Torosaurus
8 m (26 ft)

Giganotosaurus
13 m (43 ft)

WHICH WERE THE MOST TERRIFYING PREDATORS?

Different predators existed in different periods and in different parts of the world. Probably the most fearsome were the meat-eaters of the late Cretaceous period (145 to 66 million years ago). The most famous of these is *Tyrannosaurus rex*, which stood up to 12 m (39 ft) long and weighed 6.8 tonnes (7.5 tons). But it was more than matched by less well-known predators on other continents, including *Giganotosaurus* from South America (13 m [43 ft] long) and *Carcharodontosaurus* (13.5 m [44 ft] long) and *Spinosaurus* (up to 15 m [49 ft] long) from Africa.

Carcharodontosaurus

SURPRISE ATTACK *A Tyrannosaurus launches itself at two Gallimimus.*

Camarasaurus
18 m (60 ft)

Struthiomimus

WHICH WAS THE FASTEST DINOSAUR?

Going full tilt, *Tyrannosaurus rex* could probably run at about 30 km/h (20 mph). But many smaller dinosaurs could run a lot faster. *Velociraptor*, a small predator of the Cretaceous, could reach 40 km/h (25 mph). However, the speediest dinosaurs were the ostrich-like dinosaurs, such as *Gallimimus*, which could run at about 65 km/h (40 mph), and *Struthiomimus*, which may have reached speeds of 80 km/h (50 mph).

fast fact

A large feathered dinosaur found in China called *Therizinosaurus* had the longest claws of any animal, measuring more than 1 m (3⅓ ft). It was, however, a herbivore and used them only to reach high branches.

DID DINOSAURS LAY EGGS?

All dinosaurs reproduced by laying eggs and many fossilised eggs have been found, including some with fossilised baby dinosaurs inside them. Until the 1970s, scientists thought dinosaurs probably just laid their eggs then left them to hatch on their own. But evidence unearthed since then suggests that many species not only guarded their eggs until they hatched, but also fed and looked after their young.

Fossilised dinosaur eggs

Ankylosaurus

Triceratops

HOW DID OTHER DINOSAURS DEFEND THEMSELVES?

Many large plant-eaters of the Cretaceous, such as the ceratopsians – *Triceratops* and its relatives – had long, sharp horns, and wide, bony frills that shielded their necks. Another group, the ankylosaurs, had armoured plates and large, bony spines on their backs; many also had spikes or clubs at the ends of their tails, which could deliver a fearsome blow.

ARE THERE ANY DINOSAURS AROUND TODAY?

You might imagine that creatures like crocodiles are the closest living relatives of the dinosaurs. But while they are distantly related, the most direct descendants of the dinosaurs that are still around today are birds. They evolved directly from the meat-eating theropod dinosaurs, which include *Tyrannosaurus rex* and *Velociraptor*.

WHAT HAPPENED TO THE DINOSAURS?

Most scientists now believe that the dinosaurs were wiped out as a result of a huge meteor striking Earth 66 million years ago (▶23). This created huge tsunamis and widespread fires and filled the air with smoke, blocking out the Sun and forming acid rain that destroyed much plant life. An enormous meteor crater dating from this time lies off the south-east coast of Mexico. Other possible causes of the dinosaurs' demise include huge volcanic eruptions and climate change.

FOSSIL EVIDENCE

Almost all our knowledge about prehistoric plants and animals comes from fossils. These are traces of living things that have been preserved in rock layers and then exposed by movement of Earth's crust, erosion or excavation. Most fossils are bones, teeth or (less often) eggs or droppings that have turned into a type of rock as a result of a natural chemical process. Others are imprints in rock of plants, bones, teeth, feet – even skin, fur and feathers. The sum total of all the fossils found is known as the fossil record.

PLANTS PRESERVED *Fossilised traces of ancient forests, such as bark and leaves, can be found in rocks, especially coal deposits.*

FINE DEPOSITS
If a creature dies in water, this helps keep scavenging animals away. Water is also likely to deposit fine sediments on top of the remains.

BARE BONES *As the sediments build up, the soft parts of the body rot away, leaving only bones.*

HOW DO FOSSILS FORM?

Fossils form when animal or plant remains are covered by fine sediments, and the sediments and remains slowly turn into rock.

COVERED UP
Eventually the remains are completely buried by sediments. But water continues to slowly seep into the bones, leaving behind minerals that will help turn the bones into fossils.

FINISHED FOSSIL
As other layers of sediment build up, the original sediments turn into rock. And inside those rocks, the mineralised bones turn into another kind of rock and form fossils.

DO ALL DEAD ANIMALS TURN INTO FOSSILS?

Far from it. Fossils only form where a plant or dead animal is buried quickly by sediments. Otherwise it is likely to be eaten, scattered by the rain and wind, or bleached and broken down to dust by the Sun. Even if a life form is preserved in rock layers, those layers may later be twisted, crushed or melted by movements of Earth's crust before the remains turn into a fossil. Of all the animals that have ever lived, no more than one in a million has survived as a fossil.

fast fact
Fossils are sometimes found inside other fossils. A skeleton of *Compsognathus*, a small dinosaur, found in Germany, contains a fossil of its last meal: a lizard.

WHERE ARE THE BEST PLACES TO FIND FOSSILS?

Fossils are almost always found in rocks such as chalk, limestone, shale and sandstone. Known as sedimentary rocks (▶66), these kinds of rocks form over millions of years as sediments build up on a seafloor or lake bed. You can find fossils where sedimentary rocks are being cut away by erosion, such as in sea cliffs or river gorges. Fossils are not found inside igneous or metamorphic rocks (▶66), as the intense heat and pressure involved in the formation of these rocks would destroy any remains.

HOW DO FOSSILISED FOOTPRINTS FORM?

If an animal walks across soft mud and the prints are then filled and covered over by another kind of dirt or sand, the layers may eventually turn into rock. If those layers are unearthed much later and the types of rock are separated, the prints may be once more revealed.

WALK WAYS *Palaeontologists study sauropod tracks at Purgatoire River, Colorado, USA.*

HOW DO YOU IDENTIFY A FOSSIL?

Identification is usually a matter of comparing the fossil to other finds. Most teeth and bones, especially skulls, are quite distinctive of particular groups of creatures or even individual species. If an incomplete skeleton is found, it can be completed by making casts of bones from other skeletons of the same type.

MADE UP *This skeleton of a Diprotodon, a giant prehistoric marsupial, is based on various fossils.*

THE RISE OF MAMMALS

Mammals were around throughout the age of the dinosaurs, but they kept a low profile. At that time, most were small and nocturnal and confined themselves to forests and woodlands. After the dinosaurs were wiped out 66 million years ago, however, mammals moved into many of the habitats and niches the dinosaurs had left vacant. Thereafter, they flourished, growing larger, stronger and steadily more intelligent.

WHAT WERE THE EARLIEST MAMMALS LIKE?

The earliest mammals, which appeared around 230 million years ago, were small, furry creatures, rather like today's shrews, which foraged mostly at night, usually for insects. Some may have laid eggs, like modern platypuses and echidnas, but gradually most evolved to give birth to live young and feed them on milk. They also became warm-blooded, meaning that they could use their internal body systems to control their body temperature.

STARTING SMALL *A nocturnal insectivore, Megazostrodon was about 13 cm (5 in) long. The species was around from the late Triassic period to the early Jurassic.*

WHY DID MAMMALS FLOURISH?

With the demise of the dinosaurs, mammals could move into and occupy all sorts of habitats, notably open grasslands, which at that time were spreading and diversifying. Their warm-bloodedness and intelligence allowed them to adapt to a wide range of temperatures and environments. Gradually, thousands of new mammal species evolved.

WHEN DID MAMMALS GET BIGGER?

As mammals diversified and took advantage of the more extensive habitats and food supplies at their disposal, they evolved to become much arger. Their average body mass grew rapidly, reaching a peak about 30 million years ago with animals such as *Indricotherium* and other enormous herbivores. Large carnivores also evolved to prey on these herbivores. Many of these very large mammals, sometimes referred to as megafauna, were still around when the first humans evolved more than 200,000 years ago (▶252), and hunting by humans may have played a part in their disappearance.

KILLER CANINES *The best-known of the so-called saber-toothed tigers, which lived all over the world, Smilodon inhabited the Americas from about 2.5 million years ago until just 10,000 years ago. Its huge canine teeth were up to 18 cm (7 in) long.*

HOW CAN WHALES AND DOLPHINS BE MAMMALS?

Though they now spend their entire lives in the seas, whales, dolphins and porpoises evolved from smaller, land-dwelling mammals. For example, the first whales are thought to have evolved from land-based carnivores such as *Pakicetus*, which lived about 54 million years ago and probably spent part of its time in water. As the descendants of these carnivores became more aquatic, they developed flipper-like limbs, and an amphibious creature called *Ambulocetus* appeared. This in turn led to the evolution of water-based species more akin to modern whales.

Pakicetus

Minke whale
Balaenoptera acutorostrata

Aetiocetus

Ambulocetus

TITANIC TUSKS An ancestor of today's elephants, Amebelodon lived in North America between about 9 and 6 million years ago. It stood about 3 m (10 ft) tall and had massive, flattened tusks projecting from its lower jaw, which helped it dig up aquatic plants, its main food.

HEIGHT ADVANTAGE The largest land mammal that ever lived, Indricotherium was up to 8 m (26 ft) long and weighed up to 20 tonnes (22 tons). It browsed on leaves, rather like a modern giraffe.

TUCKED AWAY Female echidnas carry their eggs in their pouch.

WHAT ARE THE MAIN KINDS OF MAMMALS?

Modern mammals are divided into three main groups:
- **Placental mammals** give birth to fully developed live young and feed them on milk. By far the largest group, placentals include humans.
- **Marsupials** are mammals that give birth to immature young, which then develop further inside a pouch on the mother's body. Kangaroos and wallabies are among the best-known modern marsupials.
- **Monotremes** are mammals that lay eggs. The platypus and the echidnas, which are confined to Australia and New Guinea, are the only modern monotremes.

HOW LIVING THINGS ARE CLASSIFIED

BACTERIA

WHAT ARE BACTERIA?

Bacteria are the simplest living things on Earth, often consisting of just one cell. They are too small to be seen with the naked eye, yet they outnumber all other living things put together.

WHERE DO THEY LIVE?

Bacteria live in all kinds of places. They are found in soil, in milk, and even inside other living creatures. Some bacteria help us to digest the food we eat, but others can cause illnesses, such as cholera, tetanus and food poisoning.

HOW MANY SPECIES ARE THERE?

At least 35,000 but possibly millions.

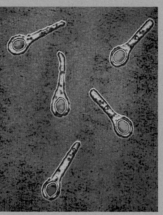

TINY GERMS *These bacteria are responsible for causing the disease tetanus.*

Recent estimates indicate that there are at least 8 million kinds of living things on Earth, of which about 1.7 million have been identified. Scientists classify living things in five major groups, known as kingdoms: bacteria, protists, fungi, plants and animals.

PROTISTS

SAFE HOME *Single-celled protists live inside these microscopic shells.*

WHAT ARE PROTISTS?

These tiny creatures are bigger and more complex than bacteria but are still too small to be visible to the naked eye. Some protists eat food, as if they were animals; others live like plants, obtaining their energy from sunshine.

WHERE DO THEY LIVE?

Most protists live in water or damp places on land. Some live inside larger animals and can cause diseases, such as malaria.

HOW MANY SPECIES ARE THERE?

Approximately 200,000 different species of protists have been identified, but there are probably many more.

PLANTS

WHAT ARE PLANTS?

Plants are multicellular living things whose cell walls are made chiefly of cellulose and which survive by converting sunlight into energy – a process known as photosynthesis. Plants contain a substance called chlorophyll, which gives them their typical green colour and plays a major role in photosynthesis. One of the byproducts of photosynthesis is oxygen, and it is by means of this process that plants provide most of the world's oxygen. They are also the source of most of the world's staple foods and a wide range of medicines.

WHERE DO THEY LIVE?

Plants live almost everywhere on land, except places where it is very cold or dry. They also live in fresh water, but only a few grow in the sea. They range enormously in size, from minuscule buds to colossal trees like the sequoia (▶102), which is among the largest living things on Earth.

HOW MANY SPECIES ARE THERE?

It is estimated that more than 400,000 plant species have been identified.

FUNGI

WHAT ARE FUNGI?

Fungi (▶94) are single-celled or multicelled organisms that sometimes resemble plants but live in a very different way. They do not need sunlight but feed off a host organism, such as rotting plant matter, and develop by sending out slender threads that break down and absorb any food that they touch. Many fungi, such as yeasts and moulds, are microscopic. However, some grow large 'fruiting bodies' in order to reproduce, such as mushrooms and toadstools.

WHERE DO THEY LIVE?

Almost all fungi live on land. Some dwell in the soil, but many grow inside the remains of dead plants and animals, helping to break them down.

HOW MANY SPECIES ARE THERE?

About 100,000 different fungi have been described but there may be more than 1.5 million species.

TOADSTOOLS These are the fruiting bodies of the fly agaric fungus. The rest of the fungus lives underground.

WHICH ARE THE MAIN GROUPS OF PLANTS?

Plants are divided into a variety of groups depending on systems of classification. Four of the major groups are:

SIMPLE PLANTS

Simple plants, such as mosses and liverworts, do not have true roots or leaves. They tend to live in damp places and usually reproduce by scattering spores rather than seeds – spores work like seeds, but are smaller and simpler. There are about 16,000 species of simple plants.

SOFT FLOOR Mosses thrive in dark, damp environments.

FERNS

Ferns have roots and leaves, but, like simple plants, they reproduce by scattering spores, not seeds. In the tropics, some ferns grow to more than 15 m (50 ft) high. There are about 13,000 species of ferns.

CONIFERS

These plants have long, needle-like leaves and they reproduce by growing seeds inside cones. Most conifers keep their leaves year-round – they are evergreens, in other words. There are more than 600 species.

PIN SHARP The tough, narrow leaves of conifers are often called 'needles'.

FLOWERING PLANTS

As their name suggests, flowering plants reproduce by growing flowers. Some have tiny flowers that are difficult to see, but others have huge blooms, which are impossible to miss. This giant group of plants includes grasses, cacti and orchids, as well as all the world's broadleaved trees. There are estimated to be around 280,000 species in all.

FERN FRONDS Most ferns have so-called fiddleheads that open into fronds.

SHOWING OFF The sunflower has one of the largest flower heads of any plant.

HOW LIVING THINGS ARE CLASSIFIED

ANIMALS

WHAT ARE ANIMALS?

Like plants, animals have cells, each with a nucleus. In contrast to plants, however, animals are generally mobile for at least part of their life cycle; cannot manufacture their own food but have to seek it out and eat it; have sense organs that tell them about their surroundings; and do not grow from a specific point in the ground or elsewhere – instead growth takes place throughout the body and usually stops at adulthood.

WHERE DO THEY LIVE?

Animals live almost everywhere on Earth. Many species have learned to survive in extreme environments, such as deserts, the icecaps of the poles, dark caves far below the ground – even inside other animals.

HOW MANY SPECIES ARE THERE?

The number of animal species that have so far been identified and named is about 1.3 million, but undoubtedly many more species still await discovery.

WHAT ARE THE MAIN KINDS OF ANIMALS?

There are two broad groups of animals: invertebrates, which do not have a backbone, and vertebrates, which do. In turn, these are usually divided into other subgroups.

SIMPLE SENSE *A network of nerves helps jellyfish detect what's around them.*

LAND MOLLUSC *Snails are related to mussels as well as squid.*

STAR ATTRACTION *Many starfish species are brightly coloured.*

INVERTEBRATES

Invertebrates include a vast range of animals, from simple sponges to complex creatures such as crustaceans and insects.

SPONGES

These are among the world's simplest animals. They live by sucking in water, and filtering it for small particles of food. There are about 5000 known species.

CORALS, JELLYFISH AND SEA ANEMONES

There are about 9000 species in this category. Jellyfish can move through the water, but sea anemones and corals remain static, in one location, for most of their lives. All have stinging cells, which they use to catch their food.

ROUNDWORMS

The worms of this group have thin, rounded bodies that are pointed at both ends. They live in an amazing variety of habitats, including inside plants and other animals. They include at least 15,000 species – perhaps many more.

FLATWORMS

Numbering at least 20,000 species, flatworms often live in water or damp places. Some, however, are parasites that live inside other animals; these include tapeworms, which sometimes live in people.

MOLLUSCS

Among the 85,000 or so species of molluscs, there are several distinct subgroups, including snails, mussels and clams, octopuses and squid. Most are soft-bodied animals and often they are protected by a hard shell.

SEGMENTED WORMS

As their name indicates, segmented worms have bodies that are made up of long chains of segments, or rings. They include earthworms, leeches and many worms that live in the sea. There are more than 9000 species.

STARFISH, SEA URCHINS AND SEA CUCUMBERS

This group of about 6500 species includes many, notably starfish, whose bodies are divided into five equal parts. They all live in the sea – some along the shore, others on the deep seabed.

CRUSTACEANS

Crabs, lobsters, shrimps and woodlice are among the 47,000 or so species of crustaceans. These creatures generally have antennae, or 'feelers', like insects. Most live in salt water, but there are also many freshwater species, and a few – such as woodlice – live on land. Most crustaceans have eight or ten legs, unlike insects, which have only six.

SPIDERS, MITES AND SCORPIONS

Arachnids, the animals of this group, walk on eight legs. They are similar to insects, but do not have antennae. Instead, they have bristles on their bodies for sensing what is happening around them. Most are hunters, catching their prey by biting, crushing or stinging it. About 100,000 species belong to the group.

CENTIPEDES AND MILLIPEDES

These long-bodied animals are famous for having lots of legs. They are easy to tell apart: centipedes have two legs on each body segment, while millipedes have four. Another important difference is that centipedes are hunters, with a poisonous bite, while millipedes feed only on decaying plants or animals. There are about 13,000 different species.

INSECTS

Insects live almost everywhere on land and in fresh water, but very few are found in the sea. Most insects have wings when they are adults, making them the only invertebrates capable of flight. With few exceptions, their bodies are divided into three main sections: a head, thorax and abdomen. There are more species of insects than all other types of animals put together – at least 1 million.

LEFT, RIGHT A millipede's legs extend along the full length of its body.

FEASTING IN FLIGHT The colourful European bee-eater catches insects – mainly honeybees – on the wing.

LONG HAUL Slow-moving on land, green sea turtles swim swiftly and cover vast distances in the open sea.

VERTEBRATES

Although they make up less than 3 per cent of the world's animal species, vertebrates include the strongest, fastest and most intelligent creatures on Earth.

MAMMALS

Mammals – including humans – generally feed their young on milk and live on land, though there are notable exceptions: whales and dolphins, for example, spend all their lives at sea. With the exception of the monotremes (four species of echidna and the platypus), mammals do not lay eggs but give birth to live young. About 5500 species have been identified.

BIRDS

Of all the world's animals, only birds, of which there are about 10,000 species, have feathers. All birds lay eggs and most can fly, although some have lost this ability, including penguins, emus and ostriches.

REPTILES

Of the 9000 or so reptile species, the best known include types of snakes, lizards, crocodiles, turtles and tortoises. They generally have a tough skin covered with hard scales and, though a few give birth to live young, most lay eggs.

AMPHIBIANS

As the name indicates, amphibians can live both in water and on land; usually they are born in water and develop an ability to live on land as they grow up. Familiar groups among the 6400 or so species are frogs, toads, salamanders and newts.

FISH

All fish have streamlined bodies that make it easy to move about in water. Most of them breed by laying eggs, but some – notably sharks – give birth to live young. There are approximately 31,300 species of fish.

MICROSCOPIC LIFE

A large proportion of living things are too small to be seen with the naked eye and are only revealed when observed through a microscope (▶194). Some of these microscopic creatures are parasites, organisms that live on and feed off a host, often harming it in the process. But some are especially useful to humans, such as the yeasts that help us make bread, and the bacteria that make yogurt and cheese.

DO OTHER MICROSCOPIC LIFE FORMS SHARE OUR HOMES?

As well as noticeable small creatures, such as flies, spiders and woodlice, your house is likely to be full of other microscopic animals and plants, no matter how clean it is. Carpets, armchairs and mattresses are usually full of tiny animals called house dust mites, which feed on the flakes of skin that you shed every day. Before the mites get to them, these bits of skin provide food for microscopic moulds, and the mites eat the moulds along with the skin. As long as you are not allergic to moulds or dust mites, neither will do you any harm.

ARE THERE TINY CREATURES LIVING ON OUR BODIES?

A large, warm-blooded creature such as a human being is like a walking restaurant to smaller forms of life, and the meals are all free. While most animals – and our human ancestors – tend to tolerate fleas, lice and other parasites, we use soaps and other chemicals to get rid of them. Nevertheless, our bodies still carry many microscopic life forms, most of which do us no harm at all. Some are even beneficial, such as the bacteria that live on our skin and in our intestines.

UNWELCOME GUEST *This microscope image shows a head louse clinging to a strand of human hair.*

MICROSCOPIC OCCUPANT *Dust mites are related to spiders. They collect food using their pincers and usually feed at night.*

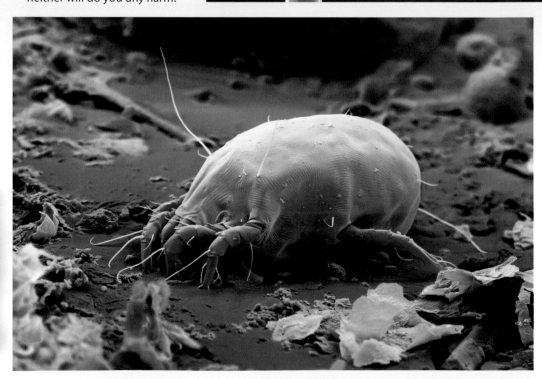

fast fact
Blue whales feed on very small animals called krill, which in turn feed on microscopic animals called plankton. So the world's largest animals are dependent on some of the world's smallest for their food!

WHICH MICROSCOPIC CREATURES ARE ESPECIALLY DANGEROUS?

Many of the most devastating diseases are caused by parasites. Malaria, for example, results from a bite from a mosquito carrying a single-celled parasite called *Plasmodium*. The parasite gets into the blood, where it feeds on red blood cells and also attacks the liver. Malaria kills up to 1 million people a year.

UNDER ATTACK
This red blood cell is infected with malarial parasites.

WHAT IS THE SMALLEST LIVING THING?

The smallest living things may be viruses, though there's much debate about whether they can be defined as 'alive'. They are like car engines without any wheels or bodywork: they have no way of moving and no cell wall, unlike other living things. Nor do they have any way of reproducing themselves: to produce more viruses, they have to invade other cells and take them over. This is why viruses cause diseases. When you catch a cold, the cells in your nose have been taken over by viruses so that they can reproduce.

ARE THERE INVISIBLE CREATURES LIVING IN WATER?

Most drinking water has been treated to remove living organisms. However, a drop of pond water can be full of the most astonishing animals and plants, visible only with a microscope.

VORTICELLA Each **Vorticella** consists of a single cell with a cup on a long stalk. Tiny beating hairs (cilia) drive food particles into the 'cup', where they are absorbed.

CHLAMYDOMONAS These tiny organisms live near the surface of lakes and ponds. Like plants, they need sunlight to survive.

ROTIFERS Rotifers are thought to be related to roundworms (nematodes) and arthropods (the group that includes insects and spiders). There are about 2000 species.

CYCLOPS Relatives of crabs and shrimps, Cyclops are named for the fact that they have only one 'eye', like the Cyclops of Greek legend. This female has eggs attached to its tail.

PARAMECIUM These single-celled creatures are called ciliates because they are covered with tiny hairs known as cilia, which propel them through the water.

DAPHNIA Related to crabs and shrimps, Daphnia swim by beating their brush-like antennae.

HELIOZOANS Heliozoans live mainly in ponds and lakes. Their spiky skeletons are made of silica – the same substance that makes glass.

EUGLENA Each **Euglena** moves around by beating a hair-like growth called a flagellum. Euglena live like plants – by harnessing energy from sunshine.

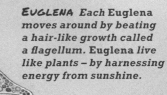

FUNGI

Fungi are living things that are neither plants nor animals.

Although they appear to grow like plants, they cannot use photosynthesis to make their own food as plants do (▶88). Instead, they mostly feed off other organisms, usually breaking down dead organic matter into nutrients, which they then absorb. Fungi spread by scattering spores, dust-like particles that are much simpler than seeds.

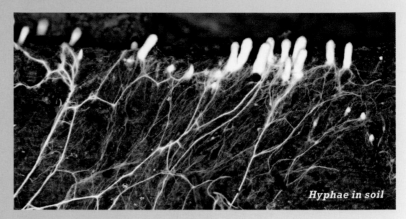

Hyphae in soil

HOW DO FUNGI GROW?

Most fungi grow by sending out slender threads or tubes, called hyphae. These break down organic matter and absorb nutrients. Some fungi, such as yeasts, are simple single-celled organisms that cannot be seen with the naked eye. But others grow a huge clump of hyphae – known as a mycelium – that can cover an enormous area.

WHAT ARE MUSHROOMS AND TOADSTOOLS?

Many species of fungi produce so-called fruiting bodies. These generate and disperse spores above ground. We usually refer to them as mushrooms or toadstools and they are most commonly found in forests and woodlands, where they feed on wood and fallen leaves.

fast fact

The largest fruiting body of a fungus ever found belonged to the species *Phellinus ellipsoideus*. Found on Hainan Island, China, it was 11 m (36 ft) long by 88 cm (35 in) wide and about 5 cm (2 in) thick.

HONEY FUNGUS *An enemy of trees, this fungus feeds on living and dead wood.*

JELLY ANTLER *This grows on the ground, sprouting from old pieces of rotting wood.*

TRUFFLE *This delicious fungus lives underground on the roots of oak trees.*

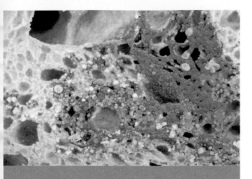

ARE FUNGI POISONOUS?

Some mushrooms and toadstools are very poisonous. You would only have to touch them and lick your fingers for them to make you ill. People have died from eating just a few of them. In 1534, Pope Clement VII was killed by eating the death cap mushroom, the world's most poisonous fungus. There are many delicious wild fungi, but you need to be an expert to distinguish them from the poisonous ones.

KEEP CLEAR! *The death cap grows in woodland in Europe and North America. Some edible fungi look quite like it.*

CAN FUNGUS GROW ON FOOD?

Moulds are types of fungi. As fungi spores are everywhere in the air, they may land on food such as bread and start growing. Long before you see any furry mould on the bread, moulds may be growing in it. However, in small amounts, moulds do us no harm.

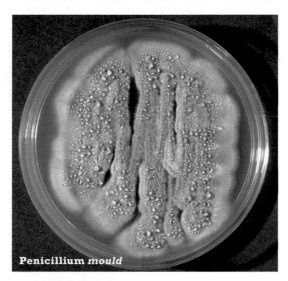

Penicillium *mould*

CAN FUNGI BE USEFUL?

Fungi have been the source of many important modern medicines. The antibiotic penicillin was made from a *Penicillium* fungus after scientist Alexander Fleming noticed in 1928 that a *Penicillium* mould in a petri dish had killed bacteria. Introduced in the 1980s, the first statins – medicines used to lower cholesterol – were derived from an *Aspergillus* fungus, which grows in soil and plant matter.

FLY AGARIC *Beautiful but highly poisonous, this brilliantly coloured fungus usually lives close to birch or spruce trees.*

OYSTER FUNGUS *This edible fungus grows on dead or dying trees.*

RED CAGE FUNGUS *Inside the cage of this golf-ball-sized fungus are slimy spores that are spread by flies.*

LEMON DISC *This fungus feeds on dead wood, growing in dense clusters on old fallen branches.*

IN WHAT OTHER WAYS ARE FUNGI SPREAD?

Some fungi are spread in unusual ways. One form of sac fungus is spread by a beetle, the elm bark beetle. The beetle carries the fungal spores into the bark of elm trees, causing them to wither and die. Dutch elm disease, as this affliction is known, has killed most mature elms in western Europe, including 25 million in Britain alone. Many other fungi are spread by animals, such as birds and mice, inhaling the spores and then distributing them in their droppings.

Elm trees killed by Dutch elm disease

HOW PLANTS LIVE

Look at trees and other plants, and what colour do you see?

The answer, almost always, is various shades of green. That green colour is produced by a chemical called chlorophyll, which is found in the leaves of plants. Chlorophyll is one of the most important substances on Earth, because it absorbs energy from sunlight and enables plants to grow. Without it, plants could not survive and animals would have nothing to eat.

Bamboo forest

fast fact

The world's fastest-growing plants are certain species of bamboo. They can grow at a rate of about 90 cm (35 in) in a single day!

HOW DO PLANTS FEED?

Unlike animals, plants do not need to find food. Instead, they make food 'out of thin air' with the help of chlorophyll. The chlorophyll in a plant's leaves absorbs energy from sunshine. The plant then uses this energy to combine water with carbon dioxide, making a sugary food substance called glucose. This process is called photosynthesis. Plants use glucose to grow. They also use it to form sweet-tasting fruits and to make nectar, a syrupy liquid that attracts insects to flowers. Any spare sugar is stored in the plant's seeds or roots. Without light, plants cannot make glucose. This is why plants always grow towards light and, if shut up in a dark place, will turn pale as the chlorophyll breaks down, and die.

Energy from Sun

Glucose for energy

SUGAR FROM THE SUN *Plants make glucose in their leaves, using energy from the Sun.*

Water from roots

Carbon dioxide from air

Oxygen released into air

HOW DO PLANTS DRINK?

Although plants can absorb a little water through their leaves, they get most of the water they need by drawing it up from the ground through their roots. The roots are in close contact with the particles of soil around them. Tiny rootlets connected to the roots extend into the soil, and these draw in moisture. If you pull up a plant, you can see the delicate white roots, but you cannot see the microscopic rootlets that absorb water because they break off and remain in the soil. And as soon as they stop working, the plant starts to wilt.

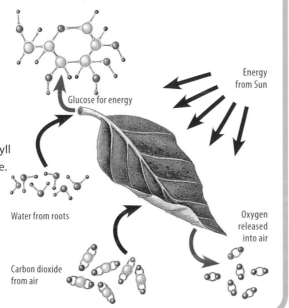

ABOVE AND BELOW *The branches and stems of a plant that you can see above the ground are sometimes much less extensive than the network of roots below the ground.*

HOW DO SEEDS GROW INTO PLANTS?

Most plants – including the maize plants we eat as 'sweetcorn' – start life as seeds. However tiny, they contain all the genetic 'instructions' needed to make a new plant. At first, a plant lives on a store of food packed inside the seed. But, after a few days, it grows its first leaves and starts to make its own food. Eventually, the plant flowers and grows seeds of its own.

❶ GERMINATION *The seed absorbs moisture from the soil and starts to grow.*

❷ SPROUTING *The shoot grows up, while the roots grow down.*

❸ GROWTH *More roots grow below ground, and more leaves above ground.*

❹ FLOWERING *Finally, the maize plant flowers and then sets seed, producing a new cob of corn.*

❶   ❷   ❸   ❹

COULD ANIMALS SURVIVE WITHOUT PLANTS?

All animals depend on plants, even animals that eat only meat, for it is plants that feed most of their prey and without prey they would not survive. In the same way, our supplies of milk and other dairy products depend on grass, for without grass there would be no cows to give us milk. The link from grass to cows to humans, or from grass to plant-eater to meat-eater, is called a food chain (▸137).

DO SOME PLANTS EAT ANIMALS?

Some plants that grow in poor soil obtain the nutrients they need by trapping and digesting passing insects. Most produce an attractive scent or glistening drops that look like nectar to lure insects to their doom. Sticky glue or a pool of liquid keeps an insect in the trap while the plant closes and begins to digest it.

A Venus flytrap closes on its victim.

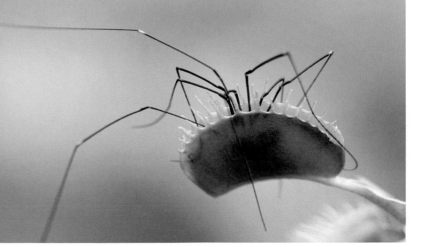

HOW PLANTS REPRODUCE

Plants have to reproduce, just as animals do. First of all, most develop flowers, which are then fertilised, or pollinated, to produce seeds. The seeds ripen and are scattered far and wide, eventually growing into new plants. Ferns and mosses reproduce in a different way. They do not have flowers. Instead of making seeds, they make microscopic spores, which drift through the air.

ON THE WIND When fern spores are ripe, the pads in which they have formed split open and the spores drift away on the wind.

HOW ARE FLOWERS POLLINATED?

Flowers contain male parts, which produce a fine dust called pollen, and female parts, which produce seeds when they receive pollen from another flower. Some plants rely on the wind to spread their pollen, but most depend on animals. Insects, birds and bats visit flowers to feed on their sugary nectar. As they travel from bloom to bloom, they carry pollen with them, pollinating or fertilising the flowers they visit.

BUSY BEE In a day, a honeybee pollinates thousands of flowers.

fast fact
Some plants, such as Australian banksias, depend on fire and smoke to trigger the release and germination of their seeds.

HOW ARE SEEDS SCATTERED?

Seeds need to move away from the plants that produced them, so that they don't compete with them for space or nutrients. Some seeds are shaped so that they are easily propelled by the wind: dandelion seeds, for example, have a shape at one end like a parachute; sycamore seeds spin like propellers. Other seeds, like those of burdock, have tiny hooks that catch in the fur of passing animals (or the clothes of humans). Coconut seeds are covered with thick fibres so that they float and will drift with the tides to another landmass. The liquid inside a coconut gives the young coconut plant some fresh water, which it needs when it lands on a sandy beach and starts to grow.

Sycamore

Burdock

Coconut

Dandelion

IN WHAT OTHER WAYS DO PLANTS SPREAD?

Some plants, such as wild strawberries, develop flowers and grow 'mini-plants' on long stalks, called runners. Ferns and mosses make spores in tiny pads on the undersides of their leaves, or in special containers called capsules.

MOSS LIFE CYCLE *Mosses spread by shedding spores. Before spores can be made, a tiny male cell has to swim over the surface of the moss to fertilise a female cell.*

Spores spreading in air

Capsule releases spores

Male cell

Female cell

Adult moss plant

Adult moss plant with spore capsule

STRAWBERRY RUNNER *This young plant will soon take up life on its own.*

WHAT HAPPENS TO SEEDS WHEN BIRDS EAT THEM?

When birds eat many small fruits, they also swallow the seeds inside them. They digest the fruit, but the seeds usually survive and come out in the bird's droppings. The seeds can then germinate and grow, with the droppings providing the fertiliser they need for a good start in life.

SPREADING SEED *Birds often drop seeds while trying to eat them.*

CAN BROKEN PARTS OF PLANTS STILL GROW?

When a storm breaks branches from willow trees growing by a river, these fall in the water, float downstream and can get stuck in the bank. The broken-off branches may make roots in the mud and grow into new trees. Many plants can grow in this way, and gardeners also 'take cuttings' to grow new plants.

TAKING A CUTTING *Gardeners cut off a small stem or twig and push it into a pot of soil. The cutting develops roots and grows into a new plant.*

TREE LIFE

A tree is like other, smaller plants, except that it can grow very tall.

To keep upright, it has a thick, strong central stem, called a trunk. Water from the roots travels up the trunk to the leaves. Glucose made in the leaves (▶96) moves down the trunk to the roots, where it is stored until needed. So the tree trunk is rather like a vertical motorway, connecting the leaves with the roots.

WHY DO SOME TREES HAVE NEEDLES?

Coniferous trees, such as pines and spruces, have needles instead of leaves. One advantage of needles is that they are hard, and difficult for insects to chew. They are also useful for keeping in moisture, so the pine trees grow well in hot, dry places, such as Greece or California. And where there is heavy snow in winter, the snow slides off without harming them.

PINE NEEDLES *Most conifers are evergreen. Their tough leaves last for several years.*

HOW MIGHT A TREE DEVELOP OVER HUNDREDS OF YEARS?

If you see a large, gnarled tree, such as an English oak, still alive today, it could be many hundreds of years old and have passed through several long stages of growth.

1200s *A small sapling sprouts from an acorn.*

1500s *After 300 years, the oak is a sturdy young tree.*

1800s *By the time the first railway lines appear in the nineteenth century, the oak is already an old tree.*

EARLY 2000s *The oak is still alive, while the world around it has changed beyond recognition.*

WHY DO SOME TREES SHED THEIR LEAVES?

AUTUMN COLOUR *Leaves turn a range of yellows, golds and reds as they die in autumn.*

Some trees shed all their leaves at about the same time each year, before the onset of particularly cold or dry weather, and enter a kind of hibernation, just as some animals do. These trees are known as deciduous trees and they do this to conserve energy and water, so that they can survive harsh environmental conditions. Nutrients are reabsorbed from the leaves before they are shed, for storage in the roots until they are needed for new growth in the following season. Trees that don't lose their leaves all at once are known as evergreens.

HOW CAN YOU TELL A TREE'S AGE?

When a tree has been cut down, you can count the rings in the cross-section of the trunk. Each ring marks one year of growth. The light part of the ring is the fast growth that occurs in the spring, while the dark part of the ring is the slower summer growth. The rings also reveal what the weather was like at the time: wide rings show a good year, with plenty of rainfall and sunshine producing rapid growth; thin rings show a bad year, when growth was slow. Scientists can tell the age of trees without cutting them down. They use a tube-like instrument with a sharp end to bore into the trunk from the side, and pull out a long, thin sample of wood that shows all the rings.

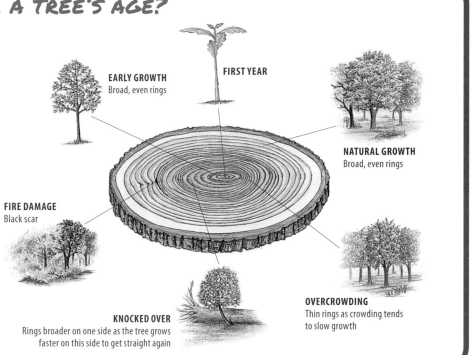

FIRST YEAR

EARLY GROWTH
Broad, even rings

NATURAL GROWTH
Broad, even rings

FIRE DAMAGE
Black scar

KNOCKED OVER
Rings broader on one side as the tree grows faster on this side to get straight again

OVERCROWDING
Thin rings as crowding tends to slow growth

fast fact

The roots of a spruce tree in Sweden were found to have been growing for 9500 years. In that time they had given rise to at least four separate trees.

ON THE HOP *A tree frog pounces on a fly from a high branch.*

WHAT KINDS OF ANIMALS MIGHT ALL LIVE IN ONE TREE?

Thousands of different animals can live in a single tree. There will be insects feeding on the leaves or nectar from the flowers, boring into the wood and laying eggs. Birds will come to feed on the insects. Small mammals, such as squirrels, may also feed in the tree, while larger mammals may browse on the ground beneath it for fallen seeds and fruit.

RECORD-BREAKING PLANTS AND FUNGI

As they have evolved, plants and fungi have taken on a bewildering range of forms. But some species stand out as record-breakers of the natural world.

WHICH IS THE TALLEST TREE?

The tallest living plant is a redwood tree known as Hyperion, in Redwood National Park, California. It is just over 115 m (377 ft) high – about twice the wingspan of a jumbo jet. In the past, some trees were even bigger than this. An Australian *Eucalyptus regnans*, which was measured in 1872 at Watts River, Victoria, was 132 m (433 ft) high. Its top had broken off, so it had probably reached over 152 m (500 ft) before it was damaged.

FOREST GIANT *The enormous Californian sequoia tree known as the General Sherman is thought to be about 2100 years old.*

WHICH IS THE WORLD'S BIGGEST PLANT?

The biggest plants are trees, and the biggest tree is the General Sherman, a giant sequoia growing in California. It stands 82.6 m (271 ft) tall, has a diameter of 8.2 m (27 ft) and is thought to have a volume of 1530 m³ (54,000 cu. ft). It's estimated weight of 1814 tonnes (2000 tons) is the equivalent of the weight of almost 330 African elephants.

ROTTEN MEAT *The giant flower of the* Rafflesia *plant gives off a smell similar to rotting meat to attract flies, which then pollinate it.*

WHICH PLANT HAS THE BIGGEST FLOWER?

The biggest single flowers are those of a plant called *Rafflesia arnoldii*, which grows in the rainforests of South-East Asia. The flowers grow on the ground, and measure up to 90 cm (3 ft) across and weigh up to 11 kg (24 lb).

WHICH IS THE SMALLEST PLANT?

The smallest flowering plants are duckweeds of the genus *Wolffia*, which float on the surface of ponds. One species from Australia measures about 0.35 mm (1/70 in) across, which is about one-third as wide as a pinhead. Despite being so tiny, duckweeds can cover ponds completely, turning them bright green.

WHICH IS THE MOST VALUABLE FUNGUS?

Many fungi are valued for their flavour, but truffles are the most prized of all. They grow underground and the only way to find them is to use a dog or a pig to sniff them out. Currently, the most valuable truffle is the white truffle (*Tuber magnum pico*), which grows in Croatia and northern and central Italy and normally sells for around US$3000 per kilo. In 2007, however, a Macau casino owner paid US$330,000 for one of the largest-ever white truffles, weighing 1.5 kg (3¹/₃ lb).

A white truffle

WHICH PLANT HAS THE BIGGEST SEEDS?

A rare palm tree called the coco-de-mer, or Maldive coconut, has by far the biggest seeds in the world. Each one weighs up to 30 kg (66 lb) and takes about seven years to ripen. In ancient times, sailors thought that these trees grew at the bottom of the sea. In fact, they grow in the Seychelles, in the Indian Ocean.

Cardon cactus

WHICH PLANT HAS THE LARGEST LEAVES?

The raffia palm, which grows around the Indian Ocean, has the biggest leaves of any plant, sometimes reaching more than 20 m (65 ft) in length.

WHICH IS THE WORLD'S OLDEST PLANT?

Bristlecone pine trees growing in the White Mountains of California, USA, are the oldest living trees, being at least 4600 years old. This means that they started growing when the first of the pyramids was being built in ancient Egypt.

WHICH IS THE WORLD'S BIGGEST FUNGUS?

A honey fungus found in the Blue Mountains of Oregon in the United States covers 965 ha (2384 acres). However, it's not clear if it's one single organism or numerous interconnected ones. It is thought to be at least 2400 years old.

WHERE WOULD YOU FIND THE WORLD'S TALLEST CACTUS?

The tallest cactus species is the cardon cactus, which grows in the deserts of north-western Mexico and can reach a height of 63 m (206 ft). The plant has a wide main stem, up to 1 m (3¹/₃ ft) across, and several broad side branches. Cardon cactuses are known to live for hundreds of years.

HOW ANIMALS MOVE

Running, jumping, slithering, swimming – over hundreds of millions of years, animals have developed amazingly varied ways of moving. The form of locomotion is often dictated by the environment an animal lives in and how quickly it needs to move to catch prey or escape predators.

WHAT ARE THE MAIN WAYS ANIMALS MOVE ON LAND AND IN WATER?

These Australian creatures demonstrate the main ways that animals get around on land and in water. Kangaroos, emus and frilled lizards all race along on two legs, but dingoes, marsupial mice and rabbit-eared bandicoots use four. Snakes slither across the ground or through water by curving their bodies; fish swim by using fins. Geckoes have toe pads that help them cling to smooth surfaces, and bell frogs have sucker-like toes to aid climbing. The marsupial mole has powerful claws that help it tunnel underground and pull itself through the dirt.

Gecko

Kangaroo

Rabbit-eared bandicoot

Frilled lizard

Spotted water snake

Murray cod

HOW DO ANIMALS MOVE WITHOUT LEGS?

If you lie face down, with your arms by your side and legs together, you may be surprised how far you get by wriggling. Snakes evolved from lizard-like animals with four legs by learning to wriggle. By moving like this, they can slither through vegetation, go down burrows after mice or bury themselves in sand.

WRIGGLING ALONG A viper slithers forwards and sideways across the desert sand.

Dingo

Emu

Bell frog

Hopping mouse

Marsupial mouse

Marsupial mole

fast fact

A red kangaroo can jump a height of 3 m (10 ft) and a length of 9 m (30 ft) with one leap. Bounding along at top speed, it can travel at up to 60 km/h (37 mph).

WHY DO SOME ANIMALS HOP AND OTHERS RUN?

Hopping is a good idea if the ground is hot, because both feet come off the ground for a moment and into the air where they can cool down. That is probably why hopping first evolved in animals such as kangaroos and hopping mice, which live in hot, dry places. Once hopping is perfected, it is a fast way of getting around. And it can confuse a predator in close pursuit: the hopper can suddenly change direction, leaving the predator going the wrong way.

HOW DO ANIMALS MOVE IN WATER?

Most aquatic animals swim by moving their body from side to side – something humans cannot do. A very flexible spine is needed, and powerful muscles in just the right places. Fish and whales have large, paddle-like tails that they use to push against the water. Even snakes, which have no 'paddles', can swim well simply by swinging from side to side. Few animals use their limbs to swim, in the way humans do, but frogs are an exception. They kick with their legs like someone swimming breaststroke.

JET POWER Cuttlefish swim by squirting water backwards through a nozzle. The force of the jet pushes them in the opposite direction.

HOW ANIMALS MOVE CONTINUED

GIANT FLIER *Meganeura was one of the huge dragonfly-like insects that dominated the skies 300 million years ago.*

fast fact

Hummingbirds can flap their wings at up to 80 beats a second. This allows them to not only move fast – up to 54 km/h (34 mph) – but also hover in one spot. Hummingbirds are the only birds that can fly backwards.

WHICH WERE THE FIRST ANIMALS TO FLY?

The first animals to fly were insects much like modern dragonflies, which took to the air about 350 million years ago. Earth was then covered with dense forests, and flying probably made it easier for these insects to reach distant sources of food. Because there were no other flying animals at that time, they had no predators. Consequently, some grew to enormous sizes, gaining wingspans of up to 70 cm (28 in). With these tasty morsels flapping about, it was not long before larger animals evolved the power of flight too. The ancestors of birds and bats quickly wiped out the giant dragonflies, which were easy prey. Smaller, faster-flying insects then evolved to replace them.

HOW DO ANIMALS FLY?

Animals fly in a completely different way from aeroplanes. Planes have fixed wings that create lift when air flows past them, and they move forwards by pushing air very fast through a jet engine or around a propeller. The wings of animals do both these jobs at once. When the wings flap downwards, they push the bird or bat or insect forwards, as well as keeping it aloft and stabilising its flight.

SMOOTH SHAPE A swallow's body is streamlined to help it fly at speed.

FOUR WINGS Ladybirds have two pairs of wings; the hindwings do most of the work.

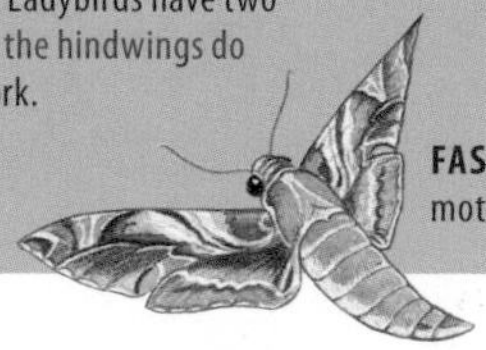

FAST FLIGHT Compared to most moths, hawkmoths are powerful fliers.

WHEN DID BIRDS FIRST TAKE TO THE AIR?

Birds evolved from the dinosaurs, which began to develop bird-like features, such as feathers and wings, about 150 million years ago. One of the first fossils to show these features was the famous *Archaeopteryx* fossil found in Germany in 1861. *Archaeopteryx* may have glided or flapped clumsily from tree to tree. More recently, other fossils have been found of feathered, flying dinosaurs that are more closely related to modern birds. These include *Microraptor*, which is thought to have first glided through the air on four feathered limbs about 125 million years ago and may have been capable of powered flight. Around the same time, the first true birds emerged, including *Confuciusornis*, a competent flyer with large wing feathers and two long tail feathers.

BIRD In most birds, powerful flight muscles are anchored to a bony flap on its chest. The flap is called a keel.

Keel

FLAT CHESTED *Archaeopteryx* was flat-chested – it did not have a keel.

ON THE WING *Microraptor* probably had to launch itself into the air from a high perch.

NATURAL FLYERS *Young puffins know how to fly without being taught by their parents.*

HOW DO BIRDS LEARN TO FLY?

Though some birds learn by watching their parents, the skills involved in flying are mainly inherited and instinctive: a young bird has the knowledge in its brain, even before it hatches. This is borne out by the behaviour of puffins. These birds nest in burrows in cliffs beside the sea. The adult puffins feed their chicks until they are very fat, but then leave them. The puffin chick stays in its burrow without food, but after a week it becomes hungry. Emerging at night, the chick flies out over the waves – never having flown before but knowing exactly what to do.

DO FLYING SQUIRRELS REALLY FLY?

Flying squirrels and other flying furry creatures, such as the Australian gliders, are not true flyers; instead, they glide on flaps of skin that stretch between their arms and legs. To take off, a flying squirrel or glider gives a sudden kick. Once it is airborne, it opens out its flaps and it travels up to 50 m (165 ft) through the air, dropping all the time. Meanwhile, it uses its tail like a rudder, to steer safely towards another tree. Some snakes, too, are able to glide by flattening their bodies till they are wide and ribbon-like.

GIANT LEAP *A flying squirrel glides towards a tree trunk, a small pine cone in its mouth.*

ANIMAL SENSES

All animals need senses to find out what is happening in the world around them. They use their senses to help them find their way around, to keep out of danger and, most important of all, to track down food. Many animals have much keener senses than humans do, and many can detect things that we cannot.

Tympanal organ on frog

DO ALL ANIMALS HAVE EARS?

Vertebrates usually have a pair of ears, with one on either side of the head. In mammals the outer ear is usually visible as a flap of tissue, but in other animals it may be harder to spot. For example, lizards and birds have small ear openings behind their eyes, and in birds these are hidden by feathers. Invertebrates normally have different kinds of sense organs. Many insects and frogs, for example, have external tympanal organs, each consisting of a membrane that (like our eardrum) vibrates in response to sound. In insects these may be on the abdomen or legs. Other invertebrates, such as worms, have no hearing organs and only sense vibrations, not sounds.

DO SOME ANIMALS HAVE MORE THAN TWO EYES?

Some kinds of spiders have several eyes, which gives them superb eyesight. The jumping spider, for example, has eight eyes: two large ones facing forwards and six smaller ones that look sideways. Keeping still, it uses its eyesight to spot prey, then pounces onto it with pinpoint accuracy. Although flies are good at spotting movement (which is why they are so hard to swat), they are not so good at noticing things that keep still, so the jumping spider's strategy works well.

Main eye

Sideways-facing eye

Sensitive hairs

HOW DO INSECT EYES WORK?

Each of your eyes has a single lens, so it produces a single picture of what it sees. Insect eyes are built in a different way. They are divided into lots of compartments, which work like separate eyes side by side. Each compartment sees just a small part of the view around an insect's head, but the insect's brain adds together the pictures from all the compartments to build up an all-round image. Some insects have only a few dozen compartments in each eye, but others have thousands.

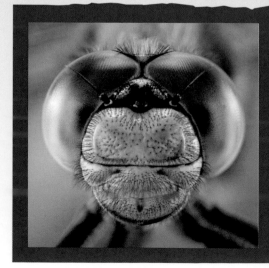

DRAGONFLY EYE *A dragonfly has more than 20,000 compartments in each eye.*

INSIDE VIEW
A cutaway diagram of the inside of an insect's eye. The part sticking out is a compartment magnified hundreds of times.

HOW DO ANIMALS FIND THEIR WAY IN THE DARK?

Animals that are active at night usually have suitably adapted senses. Cats and owls, for example, have eyesight that works in dim light. Other, often smaller hunters find their way by touch or by smell. Bats, on the other hand, have a quite different navigation system, called echolocation. Using their larynx, they create high frequency pulses; by interpreting how the pulses are reflected, or echoed, back to them, they create an accurate image of what is around them and take appropriate action.

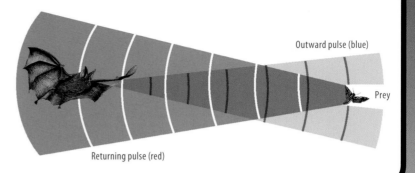

Outward pulse (blue)

Prey

Returning pulse (red)

SNIFFER MOTH Male moths have feathery antennae like these. The females' antennae are smaller, because they do not need such a good sense of smell.

WHICH ANIMALS HAVE THE KEENEST SENSE OF SMELL?

Polar bears and albatrosses can smell food up to 30 km (18 miles) away, but they can do this only when the food is rotting, and very smelly indeed. The true best-smellers in the animal world are moths, because they can sense smells in much tinier amounts. Male moths often track down females by scent alone. Using their sensitive feathery antennae, they pick up faint traces of a female's scent, and then work their way upwind towards her. Some male moths can do this when the female is 10 km (6 miles) away.

DO ANIMALS SENSE THINGS IN OTHER WAYS TOO?

Some creatures have other kinds of senses that help them monitor their surroundings. Sharks and many other kinds of fish can sense the electrical field created by other creatures – this is known as electroreception.

PREDATORS AND PREY

Animals that catch other animals for food are called predators. These hunters use a wide variety of clever tricks to capture their prey, such as camouflage, stalking and pouncing. Some animals hunt in packs, but many search for food on their own.

WHY DO SOME ANIMALS HUNT IN PACKS?

Hunting in packs allows smaller animals to hunt larger prey. For example, wolves often work together in packs of up to 20 animals to hunt large animals, such as deer, caribou and wild horses. Usually the pack will target young, old or sick animals that tire easily. The wolves take it in turns to chase their victim until it becomes exhausted, then they all encircle it for the kill.

HUNTERS' FEAST Members of a wolf pack surround an isolated deer.

LONE HUNTER Tigers and leopards usually hunt alone, while lions often stalk in coordinated groups.

WHICH ANIMALS STALK THEIR PREY?

Many animals will patiently stalk prey before suddenly pouncing on it. Most big cats, including tigers and leopards, adopt this strategy, using their camouflaged coats to conceal themselves while creeping along silently behind or around a target. They then leap suddenly onto the animal and use a swift, powerful bite to the neck to kill it. Not all hunts are successful, however; indeed, tigers make a successful kill only one time out of every twenty attempts on average.

FEEDING FRENZY A Nile crocodile lunges at the legs of a wildebeest to drag it into the water.

HOW DOES A CROCODILE CATCH FAST-MOVING PREY?

A crocodile lies motionless in the water like a harmless log. Only its eyes and nostrils stick up above the water as it watches for large mammals and birds coming to drink. If any animal comes too close to the edge, the crocodile quickly grabs it in its powerful jaws and drags it under the water until it drowns. The crocodile then twists about in the water to pull the animal to pieces before devouring it.

SWOOPING DOWN *As the African fish eagle closes in, it swings its feet forwards, ready to make a catch. It uses its tail like a rudder to stay on course.*

HOW DOES AN EAGLE CATCH A FISH?

Most eagles live on mammals, such as hares and rabbits, but some, including the osprey and the African fish eagle, prey on fish. The African fish eagle uses dead trees as lookout posts, and when it spots a telltale ripple it immediately takes off. After climbing into the sky, the eagle swoops down over the water, catching the fish in its needle-sharp claws, called talons.

READY TO ATTACK *As the eagle nears the water, its wings work like brakes, slowing it down.*

IN FOR THE KILL *As it reaches the surface of the water, the eagle snatches its prey, often using just one of its feet to hold the catch. Rough scales on the soles of its feet help it grip the slippery fish.*

fast fact

Creatures such as snakes and spiders use venom to kill or immobilise prey. The most poisonous snake of all is the inland taipan of Australia. One bite transmits enough poison to kill up to 100 people.

WHAT OTHER WEAPONS DO ANIMALS HAVE?

The range of techniques, strategies and weapons used by animals to catch prey is vast and amazing. Many species of anglerfish have a long fin attached to their snout, at the end of which is a glowing lure (bait) that attracts fish close enough to be sucked into their huge, gaping mouth. Some snakes have so-called pit organs at the front of their heads that allow them to 'see' heat (infrared radiation) emitted by other animals. This allows them to spot prey in the dark, while the victim remains unaware of the lurking snake.

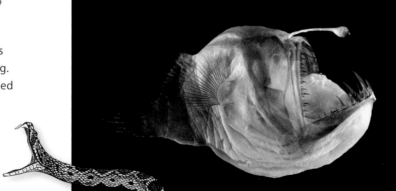

POWER SUPPLY *The light in an anglerfish's lure is generated by bacteria.*

ON TARGET *A rattlesnake can detect heat given off by prey. It kills with its venomous bite.*

ANIMAL DEFENCES

For animals, the world is a dangerous place. Every time they venture out to find food, they risk becoming a meal for another animal. To survive, they rely on their defences. Some animals specialise in making a quick getaway, while others use armour or weapons to make themselves difficult to attack.

WHAT ARE ANTLERS AND HORNS USED FOR?

Antlers and horns are grown by plant-eating animals, such as deer, antelope and rhinos. Antlers are solid and are made of bone. Horns are hollow and are made of keratin, the same substance as hooves and fingernails. Antlers and horns are mainly used during courtship for fighting rivals, but they are also useful for fighting off predators.

DEFENSIVE WALL Musk oxen form a circle around their calves to fend off wolves with their horns.

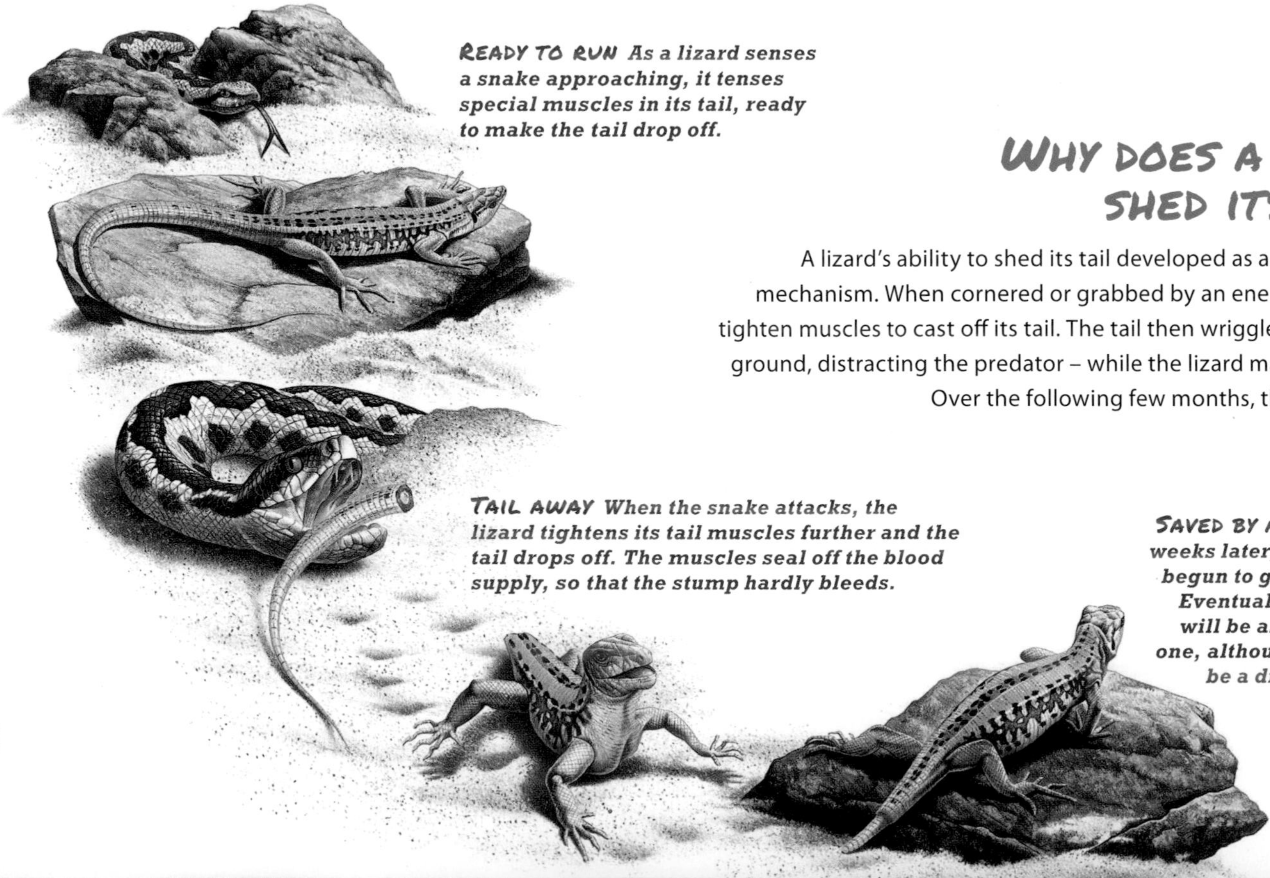

READY TO RUN As a lizard senses a snake approaching, it tenses special muscles in its tail, ready to make the tail drop off.

WHY DOES A LIZARD SHED ITS TAIL?

A lizard's ability to shed its tail developed as a useful defence mechanism. When cornered or grabbed by an enemy, a lizard can tighten muscles to cast off its tail. The tail then wriggles about on the ground, distracting the predator – while the lizard makes its escape. Over the following few months, the tail regrows.

TAIL AWAY When the snake attacks, the lizard tightens its tail muscles further and the tail drops off. The muscles seal off the blood supply, so that the stump hardly bleeds.

SAVED BY A TAIL Several weeks later, the lizard has begun to grow a new tail. Eventually, the new tail will be as big as the old one, although it will often be a different colour.

The well-named bombardier beetle can mix chemicals inside its body that cause an explosion, firing stinging gas at an attacker from a hole in its rear end.

DEFENSIVE POSTURE *A hedgehog rolls in a ball.*

MOST DEADLY *The golden poison-dart frog is found in Colombia.*

RED FLAG *The colour of the strawberry poison-dart frog is a warning to predators.*

HOW DO SPINES AND PRICKLES HELP WITH DEFENCE?

Animals such as hedgehogs, echidnas and porcupines have sharp spines to protect them. When threatened, hedgehogs roll themselves into a ball with only the spines showing, so that they are hard to pick up. Echidnas dig their bodies into the ground leaving only the sharp spines above the surface. If a porcupine is threatened, it makes its quills stand on end pointing backwards, then rattles its quills and stamps its feet to show that it is dangerous. If this does not work, it may reverse into its enemy, jabbing the quills into its skin.

ARE POISONS USED FOR DEFENCE?

Many animals use poisons or venoms to protect themselves. Often predators will know that an animal is poisonous and steer clear. In Central and South America, tiny frogs known as poison-dart or poison-arrow frogs store deadly poisons in their bodies, and have brilliant colours to show other animals that they are dangerous to eat. Central and South American Indians used these frogs to make poison-tipped arrows, hence their name. The most toxic species, the golden poison-dart frog, carries enough poison to kill up to 20 people or 10,000 mice!

STINGING ACTION *A bee holds tight with its legs and forces its sting through the skin. Once it has lost its sting, it dies.*

Venom sac

Sting

HOW DO STINGS WORK?

A sting works by injecting poison into an animal's skin. Wasps usually make a quick jab with their stings and then pull them out, but honeybees often leave their stings behind. Honeybees' stings have backward-pointing spines, which make them difficult to remove once they have been implanted in the skin. The deadliest stingers are scorpions: they kill over 3000 people every year.

CAMOUFLAGE AND MIMICRY

POLAR PREDATOR *Only a polar bear's nose and eyes show up against the snow.*

Many animals that don't have other defences or can't run fast enough to escape predators rely on another strategy to protect themselves: camouflage. This means blending in with the surrounding environment so that they become almost invisible. As long as they keep still, they are likely to go unnoticed. However, some predators also have camouflage, giving them the element of surprise in many encounters.

WHY IS COLOUR IMPORTANT?

If an animal is the same colour as its environment, it will be hard to spot. That will help it hide – or creep up on prey. For example, the polar bear's white fur helps it blend in with the snowy landscapes it usually inhabits. Keeping low to the ground, it is able to sneak up on animals, such as seals, before they notice it is there.

WHAT KINDS OF CAMOUFLAGE DO ANIMALS USE?

Many animals have colours or patterns that resemble those of a particular type of foliage or bark in their normal environment. All are also experts at keeping still, as a single move would quickly give them away.

HIDING OUT *Concealed in this illustration are 10 different animals that rely on camouflage as a means of defence.*

❶ Horned frog
❷ Leaf-tailed gecko
❸ Spider
❹ Nightjar
❺ Thorn bugs
❻ Stick insect
❼ Brimstone butterfly
❽ Bird-dropping spider
❾ Leaf insect
❿ Vine snake

HOW DO CHAMELEONS CHANGE COLOUR?

Chameleons can match the colour and pattern of almost any leafy background using chemical colours, or pigments, which are stored in their skin. The chameleon's outer skin is basically yellow, but the creature can change this to green or brown by moving specks of dark pigment up into the yellow layer. Each part of the skin is controlled by separate nerves, so different parts can be different colours.

WHAT IS MIMICRY?

Mimicry means looking like something else. Some animals look like leaves or twigs so that they remain unnoticed. Other creatures have evolved to resemble other animal species, often ones that are poisonous, so that predators will shy away. For instance, birds and other predators will not attack hover flies because they have black and yellow stripes, just like wasps, which can of course sting.

DOUBLE TAKE *Most milk snakes (left), which are harmless, have patterns that resemble those of deadly coral snakes (above). This keeps predators at bay.*

fast fact

Chameleons can change colour completely in less than two minutes. Cuttlefish are even faster: they take less than one second to change their colour.

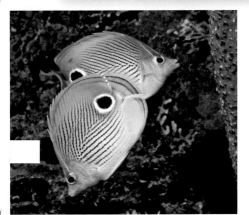

LOOK AGAIN *The foureye butterflyfish has a large eyespot near its tail, which confuses predators.*

DO SEA CREATURES USE CAMOUFLAGE AND MIMICRY?

Many fish species have silvery bodies that reflect light, making the fish hard to see side-on at middle levels of the ocean, and some jellyfish are almost transparent. On reefs and the seafloor, numerous creatures have developed extraordinary forms of camouflage and mimicry. Leafy sea dragons look just like drifting seaweed. Stonefish have pink-hued patterns that make them almost indistinguishable from surrounding rock and coral. Flounders move along the seafloor, changing colour to match their surroundings; if threatened they also dig themselves into the sand, leaving only their eyes protruding. And some reef fish have 'disruptive' patterns that break up their outlines and confuse predators, while others have bold markings, such as large eyespots, that make them look like larger species.

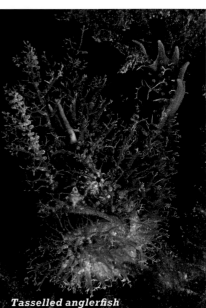

Tasselled anglerfish

4

ANIMAL HOMES

Some animals spend their whole lives on the move, and never have a place that could be called a home.

Others build homes so that they can protect their young or hide away from danger. Animals use many different types of building material, including wood, leaves, mud and even their own saliva, to make homes. Unlike us, they do not need any plans and they do not have to learn how to build: instead, they simply follow their instincts.

HOW DO BIRDS BUILD THEIR NESTS?

Birds that feed on the ground – such as pheasants and ostriches – are generally the least impressive builders. Many of them simply scratch a hollow in the earth or sand. Birds that nest in trees are usually more ingenious. Most make small cup-shaped nests from twigs, which they often line with moss or mud. The smallest tree-nests are made by hummingbirds, and are about the size of a thimble. The biggest are made by bald eagles, which live in North America. The largest bald eagle's nest ever recorded was found in Florida in 1963; it measured nearly 3 m (10 ft) across and 6 m (20 ft) deep and was thought to have weighed more than 2 tonnes (2.2 tons).

Mallee fowl

DIVERSE DESIGNS *Birds employ a wide range of materials to build nests. Mallee fowl create a huge mound of sand and leaf litter, storks pile up large sticks, and hummingbirds weave delicate bowls.*

WHY DO BEAVERS MAKE DAMS?

People sometimes think that beavers make dams to catch fish, but they actually feed on wood, and build dams to protect their homes. A beaver's home is called a lodge. It looks like a giant pile of sticks and it is surrounded by water. The lodge's entrances are hidden well below water level, so that the beavers can come and go without being seen. The dam controls the water level around the lodge.

Lucifer hummingbird

Stork nests

BUILDING BIG *Some beaver dams are over 250 m (820 ft) long, making beavers among the best engineers in the whole animal world.*

HOW DO WASPS BUILD NESTS?

Many kinds of wasps build their nests from a paper-like substance that they make by chewing tiny fibres of wood into a soft paste. They spread out the paste to make thin sheets and build these sheets up in layers. Inside the nest they also create six-sided compartments called cells, which house their eggs and larvae (newly hatched insects). The outside walls help to keep the nest warm.

MAKING SPACE *The cells inside a wasp nest are arranged in layers, like floors in a house. The entrance is at the bottom of the nest. This keeps warm air inside.*

BUILDING MATERIALS *Worker wasps scrape wood fibres from fence posts and tree trunks.*

RESTING PLACE *A young gorilla relaxes on a platform made out of branches and ferns.*

HOW OFTEN DO ANIMALS MOVE HOME?

Many animals build a home once a year, so they have somewhere to raise their young. But some make a new home every evening, and move on when the next day dawns. The biggest of these daily movers are gorillas. They make platform-shaped nests on the ground or in trees – a job that usually takes less than five minutes. In the sea, parrotfish protect themselves in a different way. As the sun begins to set, they make slimy 'sleeping bags' from mucus produced by glands in their skin, and settle down to sleep inside. At dawn, they eat up their overnight homes and swim off to feed.

SLEEPING BAG *Pacific parrotfish sleeping inside a bag of mucus*

LEAFY HIDEOUT *The tent-making bat of Central and South America fashions a daytime shelter out of a large leaf. It gnaws through the stem so that the end of the leaf flops down, creating a form of tent.*

fast fact

Cave swiftlets that live in South-East Asia make their delicate nests using their saliva, which turns white and rubbery when it dries. In China, these nests are expensive, sought-after delicacies, often served in soup.

ANIMAL BEHAVIOUR

For wild animals, there is no such thing as good or bad behaviour. All that matters is doing the right thing at the right time. Most animals start life with much of their behaviour built in. For example, they know from birth how to react to danger, how to find food and how to communicate. But animal behaviour is not always like this. Some animals – particularly mammals – acquire new kinds of behaviour and skills as they grow up.

WEB WEAVERS *Spiders instinctively know what shape their webs should be and how to make them, even though the designs are often highly intricate.*

WHAT IS INSTINCT?

An instinct is a pattern of behaviour that is built into an animal's nervous system, just like a program loaded into a computer. It does not have to be learned, and it is always ready for use. Spiders build their webs by instinct. Animals also use instinct when they hunt, breed and migrate. Because instincts are automatic, they can sometimes be triggered by mistake. Moths are instinctively drawn to bright lights, perhaps because they use the Sun and Moon to guide them; so if you switch on a bright light outside after dark, instinct makes moths fly towards it.

fast fact
Sea otters have a pouch on their chest in which they carry a rock. Lying on their back in the sea, they crack shellfish against the rock to open them.

WHY DO BIRDS SING?

Male birds sing to attract females and to keep rival males away. Birds are born with the instinct to sing, but at first they are not very good at it. They get better by listening to older birds and they can pick up a 'local accent' as they learn. Bird songs often contain lots of notes packed closely together – the notes follow each other so quickly that we can hear only the overall sound of the song. All birds also use calls to communicate with their flock or raise an alarm.

BIG SOUND *Male wrens are tiny, but they have amazingly loud voices. They sing from the tops of trees and fenceposts, so that their songs can be heard all around.*

EYE CATCHING *Many birds, like this greater bird of paradise, instinctively perform elaborate mating displays at breeding time.*

WHY DO ANIMALS FIGHT?

In nature, animals often have to fight off their enemies, but they sometimes fight among themselves. This happens most often during the breeding season, when males fight for the chance to mate. In most species, these fights rarely cause any harm, but in elephant seals they can result in serious injuries.

BLOODY FIGHT *Bull elephant seals often draw blood. The oldest males are usually covered with scars.*

UNSURE SHOT *Though instinct tells the Egyptian vulture to use a stone to crack an ostrich egg, the bird doesn't really understand the process in the way we do. Sometimes it will throw the stones onto the ground, instead of the egg.*

CAN SOME ANIMALS USE TOOLS?

Some creatures appear to know how to use objects as tools. For example, the Egyptian vulture cracks open an ostrich egg to get at the food inside by dropping a large stone on it. It repeats this until the egg cracks and it can get its meal. Studies show that the bird knows how to do this instinctively, rather than learning from a parent.

WHICH ARE THE WORLD'S SMARTEST ANIMALS?

Many animals can use stones or twigs to get at food, but only the cleverest animals can shape tools for particular tasks. We are the world experts at doing this, but chimpanzees come second on the list. They use leaves as scoops to collect water, and they snap off twigs and peel away the bark to make 'fishing sticks' for collecting termites. Young chimps learn this kind of behaviour by watching and copying adults.

WORKING IT OUT *A young chimp uses a fishing stick to dig into a termite mound.*

SURVIVING EXTREMES

It would be difficult for a human to survive a night on a mountaintop in subzero temperatures, or walk across the Sahara Desert without water. But certain animals do these things all the time. They achieve this through adaptations to their environment: body parts or systems that protect them from extreme cold, heat or drought. Some of these are obvious, such as thick fur for cold weather, while others are less visible but often highly sophisticated.

HOW DO ANIMALS SURVIVE THE COLD?

When there is snow on the ground, many small animals survive by burrowing underneath it; they may have a set of runways and grassy feeding spots on the ground below. They usually have a thick winter coat for extra warmth. Breathing cold air can damage the lungs, so some animals have special channels in their nostrils that warm up the incoming air by taking heat from the outgoing air.

GOOD INSULATION Thanks to their amazingly thick fur, Arctic foxes can survive temperatures as low as −50°C (−58°F).

HOW DO ANIMALS SURVIVE IN THE DESERT?

There are two big problems in the desert: keeping cool and saving water. Camels survive by using their fur like a sunshade, and by drinking huge amounts of water whenever they get the chance. Many other desert animals hide from the heat during daylight hours. Some desert frogs and toads have a different survival technique: they spend most of their lives underground, inside a coat of mucus that stops them drying out. When it rains, they dig their way to the surface to mate and lay eggs.

DRY WEATHER

LEAVES Many desert plants grow leaves only after it has rained. During dry times, they look almost dead.

LIZARD Reptiles, such as this black-headed monitor lizard, do well in deserts because they need relatively little moisture.

BURROWING FROG A thin coat of transparent mucus stops this frog drying out during many months underground.

GECKO Geckos are lizards that hunt insects. They come out mainly at night, when the air is cool.

SCORPION Like many desert animals, scorpions obtain moisture from their prey and do not have to drink.

ICE FISH *Thanks to antifreeze proteins, Antarctic icefish can survive in water with a temperature of −2°C (28.4°F).*

WHY DOESN'T BLOOD FREEZE IN SUBZERO TEMPERATURES?

Cold-environment animals keep their body temperature above freezing in a variety of ways. Some have the ability to raise their body temperature when required. Others, notably some fish, have so-called antifreeze proteins in their blood and their body fluids that prevent these liquids from freezing. Without the antifreeze, ice crystals would form inside their bodies and they would quickly die.

fast fact
Microscopic creatures called waterbears or tardigrades can survive in temperatures from −273°C (−460°F) to more than 151°C (304°F) and can go without food or water for more than 10 years.

AFTER HEAVY RAIN

AT REST *Kangaroos rest during the hottest part of the day, like many desert animals.*

READY TO GO *Rainwater dissolves the frog's jacket of mucus, and it scrabbles its way to the surface to breed.*

GERMINATION *Many seeds stay dormant while it is dry. Then, when rains come, they grow, flower and set seed themselves, all in the space of a few weeks.*

DEEP SLEEP *This hibernating dormouse is in such a deep sleep that it will not wake even if picked up.*

WHY DO ANIMALS HIBERNATE?

If there is not enough food to survive the winter, it makes sense for an animal to sleep through it, or to hibernate. During hibernation, an animal's breathing and heart rate slow right down, and its body temperature falls to just above the temperature of its surroundings. By going into this 'half-alive' state, the animal saves energy and can survive on fat reserves built up during late summer and autumn. If the temperature outside becomes so cold that the animal is in danger of freezing, a special mechanism in the brain wakes it, so that it can become active and warm itself up. Regular hibernators include bears, rodents, bats, turtles and snakes.

ANIMAL MIGRATIONS

Every year, billions of animals undertake remarkable long-distance journeys, known as migrations. They may make the journey to avoid a cold winter, or to take advantage of bountiful food sources in particular locations at particular times of year. Or, like salmon, they may travel in order to return to their birthplace to breed and, usually, die.

WHAT KINDS OF ANIMALS MIGRATE?

All sorts, ranging from birds to whales and turtles to geese. Some of the most famous and remarkable migrations are shown on this map.

WILDEBEEST *As the African rainy season begins, about 2 million of these large, plant-eating antelopes travel from the thorn woodlands to the open grasslands to feed on new grass.* ROUND TRIP: Up to 2900 km (1800 miles).

RED-BREASTED GOOSE *In summer, this goose breeds in the Siberian Arctic. To escape the cold, it flies to the wetlands around the Black and Caspian seas at the start of winter.* ROUND TRIP: Up to 13,000 km (8000 miles).

SHARP-TAILED SANDPIPER *From May to July, this shorebird raises its young on the tundra of north-eastern Siberia. To escape the winter, it flies as far south as Australia and New Zealand.* ROUND TRIP: Up to 26,000 km (16,000 miles).

SHORT-TAILED SHEARWATER *About 23 million of these birds breed in Australia from September to April. They then fly to the Arctic over the western Pacific, returning via the central Pacific.* ROUND TRIP: Up to 33,000 km (20,000 miles).

GREY WHALE *Grey whales feed in the northern Pacific Ocean. In October, as Arctic ice pushes south, they migrate to the coast of Mexico to breed, returning north the following March.* ROUND TRIP: Up to 20,000 km (12,500 miles).

AMERICAN GOLDEN PLOVER *At the start of winter, this shorebird migrates from the North American Arctic to Argentina, where it spends the northern winter before returning north in spring.* ROUND TRIP: Over 20,000 km (12,000 miles).

REINDEER *Reindeer (known as caribou in North America) spend the summer on the open Arctic tundra, then migrate south to the coniferous forests, where food is easier to find, for winter.* ROUND TRIP: Up to 1000 km (600 miles).

EUROPEAN EEL *When ready to lay eggs, these eels swim to breeding grounds in the Sargasso Sea, in the middle of the Atlantic Ocean. After hatching, the young eels make their way back to Europe.* ONE-WAY TRIP: Up to 4000 km (2500 miles).

GREEN TURTLE *Green turtles feed in open oceans but migrate long distances to islands to lay their eggs. One group feeds on the coast of South America and breeds on Ascension Island.* ROUND TRIP: Up to 6000 km (3700 miles).

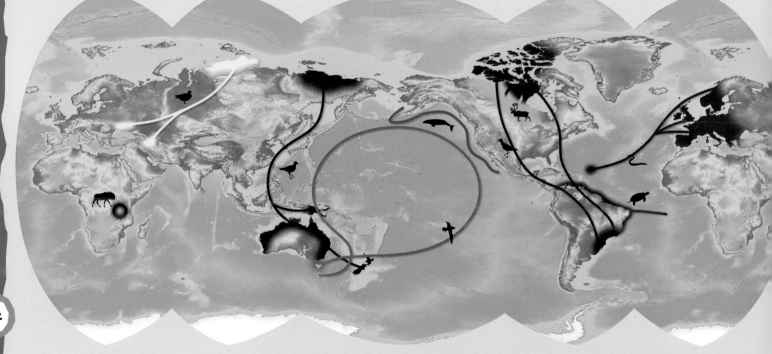

WHICH ANIMAL MIGRATES THE FURTHEST?

Birds are the greatest long-distance migrants, and the Arctic tern is the greatest of all. Every year, it flies from its wintering grounds around Antarctica to breeding grounds in the Arctic, and back again. Its meandering return journey over open ocean may cover more than 70,000 km (44,000 miles).

KEEPING UP *Fast movers, reindeer can cover up to 55 km (34 miles) a day while migrating.*

fast fact
During an average lifetime, a grey whale migrates about 800,000 km (500,000 miles) – roughly the distance to the Moon and back.

HOW DO MIGRATING ANIMALS KNOW WHEN TO START?

For migrating animals, setting off at the right time is just as important as ending up at the right place. Their timing is amazingly precise: cuckoos, for example, nearly always arrive in Britain during the second or third week of April. To do this, they use an inbuilt 'body clock', which keeps time by the changing length of the days. Other animals – such as spiny lobsters and wildebeest – set off when the temperature or weather changes.

NIGHT FLIGHT *Migrating geese pass across the evening sky in Canada.*

HOW DO MIGRATING ANIMALS FIND THEIR WAY?

Animals have a variety of navigation methods. Salmon find their way back to their breeding grounds by tasting the water where rivers meet the sea. If the taste is right, they head upstream. Whales usually stay close to coasts and use the shape of the shoreline as a guide, as do birds, which can follow rivers and mountain ranges as well. But birds also use other navigational aids, including the Sun and stars, to judge direction. They can even check their position by sensing the direction of Earth's magnetic field (▶30).

WHEN DO SALMON MIGRATE?

Most salmon are anadromous, meaning that they spend most of their adult lives in the ocean but return to the river where they were born to spawn and then die. The annual migration of such salmon back to their birthplaces is known as the salmon run.

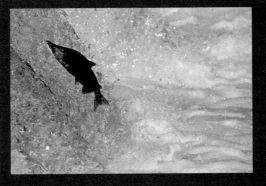

BREEDING SEASON *When they return to their spawning grounds, male sockeye salmon turn bright red to attract females.*

ANIMAL REPRODUCTION

MAKING MORE
Two scarlet lily beetles mating

After eating, reproducing is the most important task in any animal's life. Most animals have young every year, and their families vary in size from just one to a million or more. A smaller number of animals breed only once, after which they die.

WHY DO ANIMALS HAVE TO MATE?

Before most animals can reproduce, male sperm cells and female egg cells have to join together. This is called fertilisation. It can take place outside the body in water, but this does not work on land because the cells quickly dry out and die. To get around this problem, most land animals mate: the male puts his sperm cells directly into the female's body, and fertilisation takes place inside her.

INSECT BIRTH Female aphids can reproduce without mating. In summer, they give birth up to five times a day.

DO ANIMALS ALWAYS HAVE TWO PARENTS?

Some animals can produce families without needing a mate. These animals are mostly very small, like amoebas, but they also include some kinds of sea anemones, aphids and fish. These single parents have unusual families, because, like human identical twins, all their offspring are exactly the same – they are clones of the parent.

WHICH ANIMALS GIVE BIRTH TO LIVE YOUNG?

Animals whose babies develop inside the mother's body and are then born live are known as viviparous animals. They include most mammals and some fish. The only exceptions among mammals are the monotremes – the platypus and echidnas – which lay eggs.

BORN LIVE A two-week-old lion cub and its mother

WHICH ANIMALS LAY EGGS?

Animals that lay eggs are known as oviparous animals. Birds are the best-known egg-layers, but many other kinds of animals lay eggs too, from reptiles to insects and fish.

BIG CLUTCH
Some lizards, such as geckos, only ever lay two eggs at a time, whereas larger lizards, such as iguanas, lay large clutches of up to 40 eggs at once, as shown here.

fast fact

A female Atlantic cod fish can lay over 5 million eggs at one time. If all these survived to adulthood (instead of a tiny percentage, as actually happens), there would be enough cod within 10 years to fill the world's oceans.

DO ALL ANIMALS LOOK AFTER THEIR YOUNG?

In the animal world, parents behave in different ways. Birds and mammals have small families and usually look after their young well. Some fish and frogs are careful parents too, as are scorpions and crocodiles. But many more animals leave their young to fend for themselves; such animals can have thousands or even millions of young, most of which usually die before they can reproduce. Some newborns, such as those of certain birds and hoofed plant-eaters like deer and antelope, can immediately walk and feed by themselves – these are called precocial animals. Others, such as human babies, are helpless at birth – these are known as altricial animals.

READY TO GO *Soon after birth, a newborn springbok antelope will get up on its four legs and begin to walk around.*

WHERE DO SEA TURTLES LAY THEIR EGGS?

Sea (or marine) turtles spend almost all of their lives at sea, but once a year the females come ashore to lay their eggs. They haul their heavy bodies up sandy beaches and dig a nest hole with their back flippers. Once they have laid their eggs, they cover up the eggs and head back out to sea. By the time the baby turtles hatch – 10 weeks later – their mother is far away.

❶ COMING ASHORE *Turtles usually come ashore on dark, moonless nights. They have to clamber above the high-tide mark before they can begin to dig their nests.*

❷ TIME TO LAY *After digging her nest hole, the mother turtle lays about 100 eggs. The eggs drop into the hole, but they do not break because their shells are tough and leathery.*

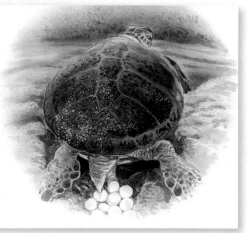

❸ DASH TO THE SEA *The baby turtles dig their way to the surface and then scurry towards the sea.*

GROWTH AND DEVELOPMENT

As living things get older, they get bigger and change shape. In mammals, these changes are usually quite small, so it is not too hard to imagine what a young mammal will look like when it is fully grown. But in other animals – such as ladybirds, frogs and some fish – the shape changes are much more dramatic, with the result that the young and the adults look completely different. This kind of development is called metamorphosis.

HOW DOES AN ANIMAL'S BODY START TO FORM?

Most animals start life as a single cell. Soon after fertilisation has taken place, the original cell divides many times, until thousands or even millions of new cells have formed. These cells move into different positions, and they start to work in different ways to form skin, bones, muscles and nerves.

BABY BIRD *A newly hatched herring gull chick sits beside two other incubated eggs.*

fast fact

By drinking about 190 litres (50 gallons) of its mother's milk each day, a young blue whale increases its weight by 3.6 kg (8 lb) per hour!

PUTTING ON A SHOW *A butterfly's often dazzling wing colours help it attract mates.*

WHY DO ANIMALS CHANGE SHAPE?

When animals are young, they concentrate on feeding and growing. When they are adult, they concentrate on reproducing. By changing shape, they make sure that they are equipped for these different tasks. If you watch caterpillars growing up, you can see how this double life works. Caterpillars spend most of each day feeding, but when they turn into butterflies feeding takes up much less of their time. Their bodies are then developed enough for reproduction, and they travel far and wide looking for a mate. Because butterflies have wings, it is easy for them to reach good places to lay their eggs.

TAIL END *A tadpole can transform into a frog within the space of a day. The last stage is the reabsorption of the tail.*

HOW DOES A LADYBIRD DEVELOP?

Like other beetles, a ladybird goes through metamorphosis. It starts life as a wingless grub, called a larva. Next comes a resting stage, when the larva turns into a pupa (or chrysalis). Two weeks later, a brand-new adult ladybird emerges, with working wings.

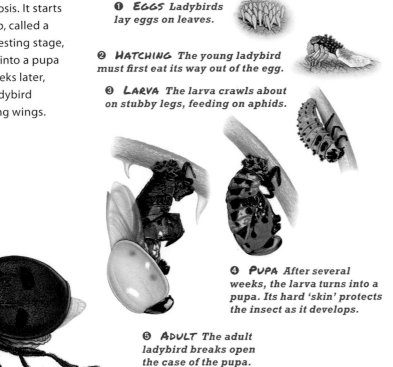

❶ **EGGS** *Ladybirds lay eggs on leaves.*

❷ **HATCHING** *The young ladybird must first eat its way out of the egg.*

❸ **LARVA** *The larva crawls about on stubby legs, feeding on aphids.*

❹ **PUPA** *After several weeks, the larva turns into a pupa. Its hard 'skin' protects the insect as it develops.*

❺ **ADULT** *The adult ladybird breaks open the case of the pupa.*

❻ **BREEDING** *The ladybird is now ready to find a mate.*

WHY DO MARSUPIALS HAVE POUCHES?

Most young mammals develop inside their mothers' bodies. Marsupials – which include kangaroos, wallabies and possums – are different, however: their young are born while they are still tiny and poorly developed. So they remain inside a pouch on the mother's body, feeding on her milk, for the first several months of their lives.

STAYING SAFE *Even after it has become mobile, a young kangaroo will get back in its mother's pouch if danger threatens.*

HOW LONG DO ANIMALS TAKE TO GROW UP?

The answer depends partly on an animal's size, and also on the way it lives. Small animals usually grow up more quickly than big ones. A housefly, for example, can develop from an egg to an adult in just two weeks. Most birds and mammals take much longer to grow up, but they also live much longer too. The prize for the longest 'childhood' probably goes to a North American insect called the periodical cicada. It takes 17 years to become adult, and then dies 2 months later.

		GROWING UP	TOTAL LIFE SPAN
Giant tortoise		10 years	150 years
African elephant		11 years	75 years
Royal albatross		9 years	60 years
Periodical cicada		17 years	17 years and 2 months
Starling		1 year	10 years
Housefly		2 weeks	8 weeks

AGE RANGE *Different animals take different lengths of time to grow into and then live as adults.*

ANIMAL RECORDS

From microscopic bacteria to the giant blue whale, animals have assumed a bewildering array of shapes and sizes. In the following pages you'll meet some of the biggest, smallest, fastest and most dangerous animals within each of the main animal groups.

INVERTEBRATES

Lion's mane jellyfish

Colossal squid

WHAT IS THE WORLD'S SIMPLEST ANIMAL?

The simplest animal in the world doesn't have a common name. Scientists call it *Trichoplax*. It is only about 2 mm (1/10 in) across, and is transparent and flat, without a head, eyes, mouth or legs. *Trichoplax* was first discovered in a seawater aquarium in 1883. Its natural habitat appears to be tidal zones of tropical and subtropical seas, but it has only rarely been found in the wild.

WHAT IS THE WORLD'S BIGGEST JELLYFISH?

The lion's mane jellyfish, which inhabits the cold seas of the Arctic, can grow to more than 2 m (6 2/3 ft) across. When its tentacles are stretched out, they may be more than 30 m (100 ft) long.

WHICH IS THE LONGEST WORM?

The bootlace worm, found on muddy shores around Britain, is not only the longest worm but also the longest creature in the world. A specimen found in Scotland in 1864 was 55 m (180 ft) long and 10 cm (4 in) wide.

WHICH IS THE BIGGEST INVERTEBRATE?

The biggest animal without a backbone is thought to be the colossal squid, which is probably also the world's largest mollusc. Colossal squids live in the deep sea and are so elusive that a complete specimen was not seen until 2003. However, based on examinations of specimens and body parts retrieved from the stomachs of sperm whales (which feed on the squid), it is thought that the species can grow to 14 m (46 ft).

WHICH MOLLUSC HAS THE HEAVIEST SHELL?

The giant clam, which lives in the warm waters around coral reefs, can weigh over 300 kg (660 lb). Most of this weight is made up by its shell, which can be 130 cm (50 in) long.

HOW BIG IS
THE BIGGEST STARFISH?

The sunflower sea star, found in the north-eastern Pacific Ocean, has an 'armspan' of up to 1 m (3¹/₃ ft), and can have up to 24 arms.

Sunflower sea star

WHICH CREATURES
HAVE THE MOST LEGS?

Millipedes and centipedes have more legs than any other animal. Centipedes can have more than 200 legs, but a rare species of millipede, *Illacme plenipes*, is the world's leggiest creature, with 750 legs.

Tropical stick insect

WHAT IS THE WORLD'S
BIGGEST INSECT?

Tropical stick insects are the world's longest insects. With their legs fully stretched out, some of them measure over 50 cm (20 in). However, because stick insects are so thin, they do not weigh much. The heaviest insect is the African goliath beetle, which can weigh up to 100 g (3½ oz) – about six times as much as a fully grown mouse. It is rivalled by the New Zealand weta, a cricket-like creature that can weigh over 70 g (2½ oz).

WHICH INSECT HAS
THE BIGGEST WINGS?

The Malaysian Atlas moth and the Queen Alexandra's birdwing, a rare butterfly from New Guinea, both have wings that can measure over 28 cm (11 in) across. The Brazilian white witch moth, or owlet moth, has an even wider wingspan, of 30 cm (12 in), though its wings are narrower and have a smaller overall area.

Malaysian Atlas moth

WHICH INSECT CAN
JUMP THE HIGHEST?

The insect world's highest jumper is a tiny creature called the froghopper, which can leap 70 cm (28 in). Given that the froghopper is just 6 mm (¼ in) long, this is like a 1.8 m (6 ft) person jumping 180 m (600 ft) in one bound.

HOW BIG IS THE
WORLD'S LARGEST SPIDER?

With females reaching weights of 120 g (4¼ oz) – about the same as a small bird – the goliath bird-eating spider of South America is the world's largest spider. Its leg length of 28 cm (11 in) is, however, beaten by that of the recently discovered giant huntsman of Cambodia – 30 cm (12 in).

Goliath bird-eating spider

ANIMAL RECORDS CONTINUED

FISH

Whale shark

Beluga sturgeon

Paedocypris progenetica *is only about 1 cm (½ in) when fully grown.*

Indo-Pacific sailfish

WHAT IS THE BIGGEST FISH IN THE SEA?

Whale sharks are the biggest fish of all. They can be over 12 m (40 ft) long, and weigh up to 20 tonnes (22 tons). Despite being so big, whale sharks are not dangerous. They feed by swallowing huge mouthfuls of tiny animals, which they sieve out of the water with their gills.

WHICH IS THE BIGGEST FRESHWATER FISH?

The largest freshwater fish are various kinds of catfish and sturgeon. The beluga sturgeon is the biggest fish to inhabit fresh water, with several specimens exceeding 5 m (16½ ft) in length. However, it spends part of its time in brackish or salt water. The biggest fish that lives exclusively in fresh water is the Mekong giant catfish, which regularly exceeds 3 m (10 ft) in length.

WHICH IS THE SMALLEST FISH?

The smallest fish species found so far has the scientific name of *Paedocypris progenetica*. It inhabits the wetlands and streams of Sumatra in Indonesia. Most fully grown specimens are about 1 cm (½ in) long, but one mature female was measured at just 7.9 mm (⅓ in).

WHICH ARE THE MOST NUMEROUS FISH?

Small fish are much more numerous than big ones. Many scientists believe that deep-sea bristlemouths, also known as lightfish, account for more individuals than any other fish group. They are only about 7.5 cm (3 in) long, and often fall apart when they are brought to the surface.

WHAT IS THE FASTEST A FISH CAN SWIM?

Over short stretches, the Indo-Pacific sailfish can swim at over 110 km/h (68 mph), which makes it faster than anything else in the sea. It has a sword-like beak, and a big sail-shaped fin on its back. When the fish is moving at full speed, this fin folds flat.

WHICH FISH LIVE THE LONGEST?

Rather like trees, many fish have growth rings in their scales that indicate their age. Based on a study of its growth rings, a koi carp named Hanako was said to have been 226 years old when it died in 1977.

REPTILES AND AMPHIBIANS

WHICH IS THE WORLD'S BIGGEST FROG?

Adult goliath frogs from West Africa often weigh more than 3 kg (6 lb) – as much as a fully grown rabbit – and can grow to 33 cm (13 in) in length.

HOW FAR CAN A FROG JUMP?

The prize for the record leap goes to the South African sharp-nosed frog, which can jump 5.35 m (17 ft). This frog is only about 6.6 cm (2½ in) long when its legs are tucked up. This means that it can jump more than 80 times its own length.

HOW LARGE IS THE WORLD'S LARGEST CROCODILE?

The saltwater crocodile is the biggest crocodile in the world, as well as the biggest living reptile. Adult males regularly exceed 5 m (16½ ft) and in the past they may have reached over 8 m (26 ft) – a specimen shot in northern Australia in 1957 was recorded as being 8.63 m (28 ft).

WHERE WOULD YOU FIND THE WORLD'S BIGGEST LIZARD?

The Komodo dragon is found only on a small group of islands in Indonesia, including the island of Komodo. Adult males average 2.6 m (8½ ft) in length and weigh up to 90 kg (200 lb). Komodo dragons scavenge on dead animals but also attack and kill creatures as large as pigs and deer.

WHICH IS THE WORLD'S BIGGEST SNAKE?

The longest is the reticulated python, which regularly exceeds 6 m (20 ft). A specimen called Medusa, held at the Full Moon Productions tourist attraction in Kansas City, USA, is the longest captive snake ever, at 7.67 m (25⅙ ft). The reticulated python does not kill its prey with poison; instead, it squeezes its victims to death, and then swallows them whole. The world's heaviest and second-longest snake is the green anaconda of northern South America, which can weigh almost 100 kg (220 lb).

WHICH ANIMALS LIVE THE LONGEST?

Big reptiles often live to a great age because they spend a lot of their time resting or basking in the sun. Crocodiles can live to be 80 years old, but giant tortoises often survive well past their 100th birthday. A radiated tortoise presented to the royal family of Tonga by Captain James Cook died in 1965 at the age of 188, while Adwaita, an Aldabra giant tortoise that died in its Indian zoo in 2006, is thought to have been 255 years old.

Goliath frog

Saltwater crocodile

Komodo dragon

Reticulated python

ANIMAL RECORDS CONTINUED

BIRDS

HOW BIG IS THE BIGGEST BIRD?

The biggest bird alive today is the ostrich, which is flightless and lives in Africa. Males can be up to 2.7 m (9 ft) tall, and can weigh over 150 kg (330 lb).

WHICH IS THE SMALLEST BIRD?

The bee hummingbird, which lives in Cuba, is just under 6 cm (2½ in) long. It weighs about 1.6 g (1/18 oz) – less than a sugar cube. Lots of moths and butterflies are much bigger than this tiny bird.

WHICH ARE THE MOST NUMEROUS BIRDS?

The most numerous bird in the world is a seed-eating finch called the red-billed quelea, which lives in Africa. A single flock can contain 10,000 birds, but up to a million queleas may come together to roost. Estimates for the total population range from 1.5 to 10 billion.

WHAT KIND OF BIRD HAS THE LARGEST WINGSPAN?

The wandering albatross, a sea bird, has a wingspan of over 3.5 m (11½ ft), giving it the widest wings of any bird alive today. Among land-based birds, those with the biggest wings are the African marabou stork and the Andean condor. Their wings can measure 3 m (10 ft) from tip to tip.

HOW HEAVY IS THE HEAVIEST FLYING BIRD?

Flying is difficult for heavy birds. The great bustard, which can weigh up to 21 kg (46 lb), is the heaviest flying bird, yet it is still only one-seventh as heavy as the flightless ostrich.

WHICH IS THE WORLD'S FASTEST ANIMAL?

During a dive, a peregrine falcon can reach speeds of 322 km/h (200 mph), making it not only the fastest-moving bird but also the fastest animal of all. Flying on the level, it probably reaches about 100 km/h (60 mph) in short bursts.

Ostrich

Bee hummingbird

Flock of red-billed queleas

Wandering albatross

WHICH BIRD HAS THE LONGEST BEAK?

The Australian pelican's beak can be over 45 cm (18 in) long, which makes it the biggest in the bird world. However, in proportion to its body, the sword-billed hummingbird's beak is even longer. Its beak measures about 10 cm (4 in) from base to tip, making it the only bird whose beak is longer than its body.

Sword-billed hummingbird

Australian pelican

WHICH BIRD HAS THE LONGEST FEATHERS?

Some pheasants have tail feathers that are 1.5 m (5 ft) long. But the bird with the longest feathers relative to its body is the ribbon-tailed astrapia, a bird of paradise found in Papua New Guinea, whose ornamental tail feathers are more than three times the length of its body – over 1 m (3⅓ ft) in some cases.

Ribbon-tailed astrapia

WHICH BIRDS HAVE THE LOUDEST CALLS?

Birds with very loud calls include the superb lyrebird of Australia, the three-wattled bellbird of Central America, and various kinds of bittern, whose booming calls can be heard up to 5 km (3 miles) away. The kakapo, a rare flightless parrot of New Zealand, emits its call while sitting in a bowl-shaped hollow that amplifies the sound. That helps it carry for up to 7 km (4 miles).

WHICH ARE THE SMALLEST AND LARGEST BIRDS' EGGS?

Some hummingbird eggs are less than 1 cm (½ in) long – not much bigger than a pea – while the eggs of the ostrich can be up to 20 cm (8 in) long and as large as 24 hens' eggs. The biggest bird's egg of all time was that of the now-extinct great elephant bird, a huge flightless bird that once lived in Madagascar. Its egg was up to 34 cm (13½ in) long, and had a volume of up to 9 litres (2.4 gallons).

Kakapo

WHICH BIRD DIVES THE DEEPEST UNDER WATER?

Emperor penguins can dive to at least 500 m (1640 ft). They are much aided in this by their ability to hold their breath for at least 15 minutes.

Elephant bird, ostrich and hummingbird eggs

WHICH BIRD LIVES THE LONGEST?

Albatrosses probably live longer than any other birds in the wild, surviving well into their fifties. But, in captivity, some parrots, notably macaws, have lived more than 75 years.

ANIMAL RECORDS CONTINUED

MAMMALS

Crabeater seals

Common dolphin

Sea otter

Blue whale

WHICH ARE THE MOST NUMEROUS SEA MAMMALS?

There are probably more crabeater seals than any other mammal in the sea. They live around Antarctica, which makes it difficult to count them, but estimates of their total population range from 7 to 15 million. Despite their name, they feed on shrimp-like animals called krill, not crabs. As well as being the most numerous mammals in the sea, crabeater seals are probably the most common large mammals on the entire planet, after humans.

WHICH SEA MAMMAL IS THE FASTEST?

Dolphins, porpoises and killer whales (orcas) are all hunters and flesh-eaters, and so can swim at high speeds to catch their prey. The fastest of all are thought to be common dolphins, which can power through the water at 64 km/h (40 mph). At this speed, they are easily able to overtake most boats and ships.

WHICH IS THE SMALLEST SEA MAMMAL?

The smallest mammal that frequents the ocean is the sea otter, which weighs up to 40 kg (90 lb) and measures about 1.4 m (4½ ft) in length. The vaquita – a rare porpoise that lives in the Gulf of California – is only 1.5 m (5 ft) long, making it the smallest member of the cetaceans (whales and dolphins).

WHICH IS THE BIGGEST MAMMAL OF ALL?

The blue whale is easily the biggest sea mammal, and also by far the largest animal on Earth. The largest blue whale ever measured was 33.5 m (110 ft) from head to tail, and probably weighed about 190 tonnes (210 tons) – more than 30 fully grown elephants. Whales can grow this large only because they live in water, which helps to support their huge bodies. No land animal could grow to this size, as its muscles would not be strong enough to move it.

WHICH SEA MAMMAL DIVES THE DEEPEST?

Cuvier's beaked whales have been recorded diving to a depth of 1900 m (6230 ft) and staying under water for up to 85 minutes without breathing.

On land, which is the biggest mammal?

The African elephant is the world's largest land mammal. Adult males often weigh more than 6 tonnes (6½ tons) and some individuals have topped 10 tonnes (11 tons). To keep themselves alive, these big males have to eat nearly a quarter of a tonne (550 lb) of food a day. They strip bark from trees with their tusks, and pluck down leaves with their trunks. They chew up their food with giant molars, each the size of three bricks put together.

Giraffe

How tall is the tallest land mammal?

For height, no other animal comes close to the giraffe, which can stand up to 6 m (20 ft) high. When they are feeding, giraffes can reach even farther than this, because their tongues are 45 cm (18 in) long – handy for reaching the highest leaves on a tree.

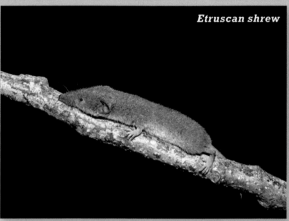

Etruscan shrew

Which is the world's smallest mammal?

The smallest mammal by mass is the Etruscan shrew, found in many parts of Eurasia, which weighs on average just 1.8 g (¹/₁₆ oz). Excluding its tail, it usually grows to about 4 cm (1½ in). The world's smallest mammal by length is the Kitti's hog-nosed bat, also known as the bumblebee bat, which lives in Thailand and reaches a maximum body length of about 3.3 cm (1¼ in).

What speed can the fastest land animal reach?

Over short distances, cheetahs can run at up to 120 km/h (75 mph) – faster than any other animal on land. After the cheetah, the next fastest is the pronghorn, a North American antelope, which can reach speeds of 88 km/h (55 mph).

Cheetah

Which mammal has the longest gestation period?

A mammal's gestation period is the time it takes for its young to develop before they are ready to be born. In elephants, this is about 22 months, compared with 9 months for humans.

Elephant

On average, which mammals live the longest?

Humans live longer than any other mammal, sometimes reaching the age of 100 or more. After us, those that live longest are large whales and elephants, which can live to be more than 70 years old.

ECOLOGY

On Earth, nothing can live entirely on its own. Living things are all connected to each other in complicated ways. Plants collect energy from the Sun, animals feed on plants, and some animals eat each other. When plants and animals die, their remains do not pile up. Instead, fungi and bacteria break them down, so that their components can be recycled and re-used. Ecology is the science that investigates all these different connections and the way they work.

SIGNS OF LIFE Even in the apparently barren Dry Valleys of Antarctica, microscopic life forms live in the rocks and soil.

WHAT IS THE BIOSPHERE?

The biosphere is all the parts of the world where living things can be found. It includes the land and the sea, and also the lower part of the atmosphere. Scientists have recently discovered that the biosphere also reaches far beneath our feet, because some bacteria live in rocks many hundreds of metres underground.

DO HUNTERS EVER RUN OUT OF PREY?

Hunting animals are often faster than their prey, but they never manage to catch them all. If they did, they would have no more food. Hunting is not an easy way of life. Each chase takes a lot of time and effort, and often fewer than one in ten ends with a successful kill.

IN PURSUIT Even in deep snow, a Canadian lynx can run fast. However, it still has to work hard to catch an Arctic hare.

fast fact

The brown rat is possibly the most abundant and widespread of all mammals. Originating in northern China, it has spread to all continents except Antarctica.

DO LIVING THINGS HELP ONE OTHER?

In nature, living things always look after themselves. However, it sometimes pays to team up with other forms of life. For example, flowering plants provide insects with sugary nectar; in return, insects help plants by spreading pollen from flower to flower. This type of partnership is called symbiosis, or a symbiotic relationship.

BIRD AND BEAST Oxpeckers help rhinos by eating the ticks that feed on their blood.

WHAT IS A FOOD CHAIN?

A food chain is the sequence of relationships between animals living in the same environment, based on what they eat. An illustration of a food chain, known as a food web, shows how food is passed from one living thing to another within a particular environment.

Fox

Weasel

Buzzard

Mole

Deer

Rabbit

Starling

Beetle

Oak leaves and acorns

Grasshopper

WEB OF LIFE *In this food web, the animal at the tip of each arrow eats whatever is at the base of the arrow.*

STRIPED INVADER *Native to Central Asia, the zebra mussel has spread to Western Europe and North America, where it not only displaces local species but also clogs waterways and water-treatment plants.*

OUT OF PLACE *The red fox was introduced to Australia in the 1800s so English settlers could enjoy their traditional pastime of fox hunting.*

WHAT IS AN INTRODUCED SPECIES?

In nature, each species lives in a particular part of the world. It is used to the other species around it, because they share a long history of living in the same place. When humans move from one part of the world to another, they may take plant or animal species with them. If these 'introduced' species can easily out-compete other animals, the native species may suffer, be forced out of their natural environment or even become extinct. For example, foxes and cats introduced into Australia by Europeans have devastated populations of native ground-dwelling rodents and marsupials, causing numerous extinctions.

WHAT IS BIODIVERSITY AND WHY IS IT IMPORTANT?

An environment's biodiversity is the variety of life within it. Because species are interdependent, it is vital to maintain biodiversity. The loss of just one species from an environment can have a dramatic effect. For example, the loss of a pollinator, such as a bee, can stop plants reproducing. In turn, the disappearance of a particular plant may leave some animals without an important food source, resulting in further extinctions.

WILDLIFE CONSERVATION

In today's world, wild places are hard to find. Roads, houses, farms and factories are all spreading. We use more water and wood than people did 50 years ago, and we produce far more waste. All this means that life is becoming more difficult for Earth's natural inhabitants. Without conservation, many of them could die out.

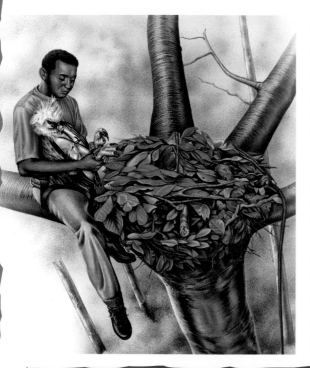

HOW DO WE LEARN HOW TO PROTECT ANIMALS?

Before endangered species can be properly protected, scientists need to find out where and how they live and how much space they need. Much of this knowledge is acquired through observation. One way to do this is to attach radio transmitters to animals, so that scientists can track them and monitor their lives and needs.

HIGH RISE This researcher is attaching a transmitter to a harpy eagle chick. Harpy eagles live in the rainforests of Central and South America, and build their nests in giant trees, sometimes more than 70 m (230 ft) above the ground. The transmitter beams a signal to a satellite, which the scientists can then monitor.

DOES IT MATTER IF FORESTS ARE CUT DOWN?

Tropical forests are home to more types of animals than any other habitat on land. When forests are cut down, most of these animals have nowhere else to go. Half of the world's tropical forests have already disappeared, and most of the remaining forests are now divided up into small, isolated tracts, where wildlife is more vulnerable. The only large areas left are in Central Africa and the Amazon Basin of South America.

WHICH ARE THE MOST ENDANGERED ANIMALS IN THE WORLD?

Until recently, the Pinta Island tortoise was one of the rarest animals in the world, for the subspecies consisted of just one known member, a male named Lonesome George, who lived in the Galápagos Islands off the coast of Ecuador. When George died on 24 June 2012, aged over 100, the subspecies became officially extinct. Other now-rare species include these animals.

BAIJI It looks like fishing, pollution and habitat disturbance have probably killed off this Chinese species, also known as the Yangtze River dolphin, as a live specimen has not been seen since 2007.

JAVAN RHINOCEROS Numbers have dwindled due to hunting and habitat loss. A population in Vietnam died out in 2011 and only about 40 individuals remain in a national park in Java, Indonesia.

Two of perhaps just 10 northern white rhinos left in the world live at San Diego Zoo, California, USA.

CAN ANIMALS BE SAVED BY KEEPING THEM IN ZOOS?

Zoos may help preserve a species by protecting some of the last surviving members and encouraging them to breed. Animals born in captivity can then be returned to the wild to boost populations.

fast fact

In 1952, the Nene or Hawaiian goose was on the point of extinction, with only 30 birds left alive. A handful of the birds were caught and encouraged to breed in captivity. Today, there are almost 2000 Hawaiian geese, and the species is considered more secure.

WHAT ELSE CAN BE DONE TO PROTECT ANIMALS?

As well as protecting habitats, conservationists and many governments take steps to prevent hunting and the capture of rare animals for selling as pets. Wildlife investigators help to track down people involved in the illegal wildlife trade. Customs officials search shipments and baggage for live animals and frequently smuggled animal products, such as rhino horn, tortoiseshell and ivory.

IMPOUNDED IVORY Customs officers examine 800 kg (1760 lb) of elephant tusks, which smugglers had attempted to bring from Africa to Thailand.

BROWN SPIDER MONKEY Poaching and habitat destruction in Colombia and Venezuela have drastically reduced populations, leaving only 50 or so in the wild. Captive breeding programs have had limited success.

IBERIAN LYNX Numbers of this wild cat native to southern Spain and Portugal dwindled to about 100 in 2005. Captive breeding programs and reintroductions have helped boost wild populations, but the species remains critically endangered.

SPIX'S MACAW A wild specimen of this Brazilian parrot hasn't been seen since 2000. A captive population of 96 has been bred from 7 wild birds and is the last hope for the species.

THE HUMAN BODY

BONES AND JOINTS

Bones support your body, and make up about one-fifth of your total weight. Without them, you would not be able to move, eat or even breathe. Bones change as the body grows, and they also become thicker and stronger if they have to do a lot of extra work or carry extra weight.

WHAT ARE THE MAJOR GROUPS OF BONES?

The human body contains many long, thin bones – some flat, some cylindrical and hollow – but also groups of much smaller bones. About one-tenth of all the bones in the body form the skull, while more than half make up the hands and feet.

HUMAN SKELETON *The main groups of bones are shown here. Most of the bones are connected by flexible joints.*

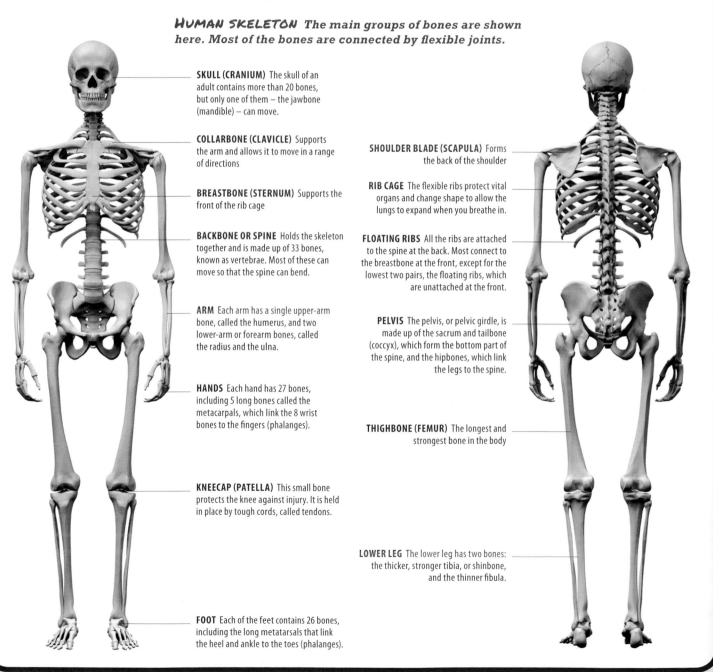

SKULL (CRANIUM) The skull of an adult contains more than 20 bones, but only one of them – the jawbone (mandible) – can move.

COLLARBONE (CLAVICLE) Supports the arm and allows it to move in a range of directions

BREASTBONE (STERNUM) Supports the front of the rib cage

BACKBONE OR SPINE Holds the skeleton together and is made up of 33 bones, known as vertebrae. Most of these can move so that the spine can bend.

ARM Each arm has a single upper-arm bone, called the humerus, and two lower-arm or forearm bones, called the radius and the ulna.

HANDS Each hand has 27 bones, including 5 long bones called the metacarpals, which link the 8 wrist bones to the fingers (phalanges).

KNEECAP (PATELLA) This small bone protects the knee against injury. It is held in place by tough cords, called tendons.

FOOT Each of the feet contains 26 bones, including the long metatarsals that link the heel and ankle to the toes (phalanges).

SHOULDER BLADE (SCAPULA) Forms the back of the shoulder

RIB CAGE The flexible ribs protect vital organs and change shape to allow the lungs to expand when you breathe in.

FLOATING RIBS All the ribs are attached to the spine at the back. Most connect to the breastbone at the front, except for the lowest two pairs, the floating ribs, which are unattached at the front.

PELVIS The pelvis, or pelvic girdle, is made up of the sacrum and tailbone (coccyx), which form the bottom part of the spine, and the hipbones, which link the legs to the spine.

THIGHBONE (FEMUR) The longest and strongest bone in the body

LOWER LEG The lower leg has two bones: the thicker, stronger tibia, or shinbone, and the thinner fibula.

HOW MANY BONES DO WE HAVE?

It depends how old you are. At birth, a lot of the skeleton is made of a rubbery substance called cartilage. As you grow, most of this turns to bone and some bones join up. In your mid-teens, for instance, five bones at the base of the spine fuse into a single bone, called the sacrum. By their twenties, most people have 206 bones. However, some people also have tiny bones inside some muscles, called sesamoids, which have no clear function.

BONY FINGERS These X-rays show the hands of a three-year-old (left) and a thirteen-year-old (right). In the three-year-old's hand, many bones have not yet formed.

WHAT ARE BONES MADE OF?

Nearly two-thirds of a bone's weight is made up of crystals of a mineral called calcium phosphate; the other third is made up of fibres of a substance known as collagen. The crystals and fibres are produced by bone cells, which are scattered throughout the bone. Tiny channels running through the bone allow blood to reach the bone cells. Most bones contain cavities filled with marrow, a jelly-like substance that makes blood cells. These cavities also make the bones lighter.

INSIDE A BONE In this magnified cross-section of a long bone, the rings are made up of mineral crystals. At the centre of each set of rings is a channel through which run blood vessels, lymph vessels and nerves.

WHICH IS THE SMALLEST BONE?

The smallest bone is the stirrup, inside the ear. It is just 5 mm (1/4 in) long and helps to carry sounds into the inner part of the ear. There are three bones in each ear, and they are so small that they would all fit inside a matchbox.

HOW ARE BONES CONNECTED?

Bones are connected by joints. There are two main kinds of joints: fixed joints, where the bones are fused and there is little movement, as in the skull; and synovial joints, which are lubricated and allow movement.

BONE TO BONE There are six kinds of synovial joints.

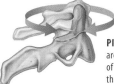

HINGE A hinge-like joint permits movement on one plane only, as at the elbow.

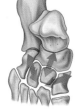

PIVOT One bone swivels around a projecting part of another bone, as with the vertebrae.

BALL AND SOCKET A ball-ended bone fits into a socket on another bone, allowing circular movement, as at the hips.

GLIDING Flat surfaces of bones glide over each other, as with the foot bones.

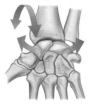

CONDYLOID (ELLIPSOIDAL) The egg-shaped end of one bone fits into an elliptical cavity on another, as at the wrist.

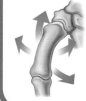

SADDLE The rounded end of one bone sits in a saddle-shaped socket to allow limited movement on two planes, as at the base of the thumb.

fast fact

Most people have 12 pairs of ribs, but about 1 person in 20 has 13 pairs.

MUSCLES AND MOVEMENT

Muscles are bundles of fibres that alternately contract and relax to make parts of the body move. They make up more than half your body's weight. Muscles enable you to walk, run, breathe and blink, and they keep your body in position when you sit or stand. Some muscles, such as the biceps in your arms, work only when you want them to. Others, such as your heart, never stop working.

WHAT ARE THE MAIN GROUPS OF MUSCLES IN THE BODY?

There are three kinds of muscles. Cardiac muscle is found only in the heart and is unique in being able to contract automatically. Smooth muscle controls many of our internal organs and contracts in response to messages from nerves, but without our being aware of it. Skeletal muscle connects bones and contracts mainly in response to conscious messages from the brain.

CLOSING UP *When bright light shines in your eyes, muscles inside your eyes automatically make your pupils smaller to reduce the amount of light getting in.*

MUSCLE GROUPS *The main groups of skeletal muscles are shown here. Cord-like extensions at the end of many of these muscles, known as tendons, attach them to the bones.*

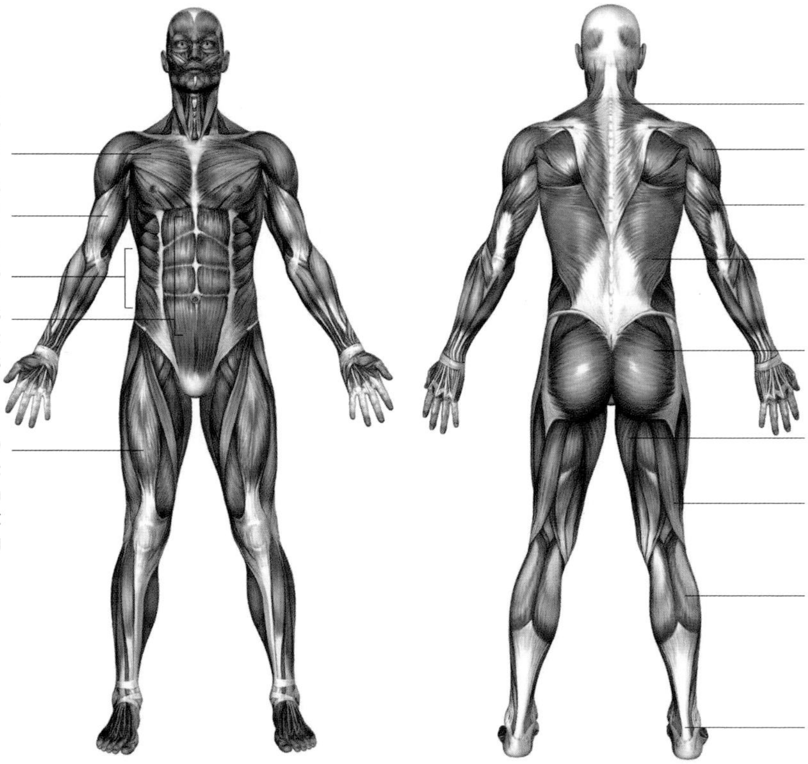

PECTORAL MUSCLES Fan-shaped muscles cover upper chest and connect to muscles in upper arm

BICEPS Controls upwards movement of lower arm

EXTERNAL OBLIQUES Contract, along with internal obliques, to twist torso forwards

RECTUS ABDOMINUS Four rows of muscles down front of abdomen; contract to bend body forwards

THIGH MUSCLE (QUADRICEPS) Group of four muscles (hence 'quad'); pulls the lower leg forwards when walking and holds leg straight when standing

TRAPEZIUS Large, diamond-shaped muscle; holds head straight and contracts to pull it backwards

DELTOID Raises arm outwards

TRICEPS Contracts to straighten arm

LATISSIMUS DORSI Large muscle, helps hold trunk upright

GLUTEUS MAXIMUS Largest muscle in the body, helps keep the trunk upright, pulls leg backwards when walking

ADDUCTOR MUSCLES Contract to pull leg inwards

HAMSTRING MUSCLES Contract to bend leg at knee

CALF MUSCLES Pair of muscles; contract to lift back of foot off ground

ACHILLES TENDON Tough cord; connects calf muscle to heel

HOW DOES THE BRAIN CONTROL MUSCLES?

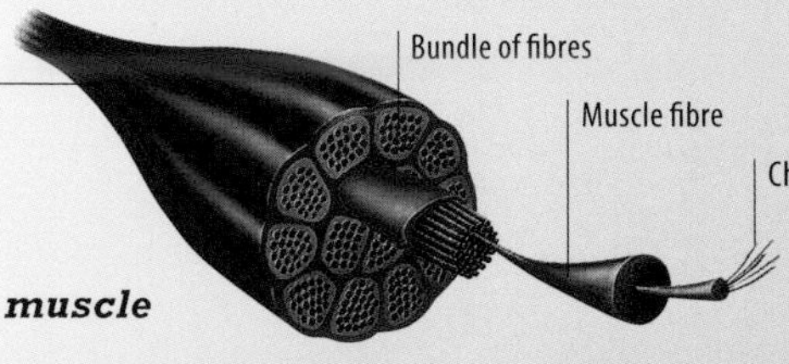

Muscle sheath

Bundle of fibres

Muscle fibre

Chemical threads

Inside a muscle

Muscles are made up of millions of cells, called muscle fibres, which contain overlapping chemical threads. When a muscle receives signals from the nervous system, the threads slide closer together, making the whole muscle shorten or contract. This moves the part of the body to which the muscle is attached.

WHAT ARE OPPOSING MUSCLES?

Many muscles are arranged in opposing pairs or groups that generate movement in opposite directions. For example, to raise your forearm you tighten the biceps muscle at the front of the upper arm, while relaxing the triceps muscle at the back of the upper arm. To straighten the arm again, the actions of the muscles are reversed. The biceps has to be larger and stronger because it is working against gravity.

Biceps contracts

Triceps contracts

HOW DO WE MAKE FACES?

You have more than 40 facial muscles. You use them all the time when you are awake, and sometimes when you are asleep. They help you to speak, eat and blink, and they also enable you to alter the expression on your face.

VISUAL SIGNS *Facial expressions can indicate a wide range of emotions.*

HOW DO MUSCLES WORK TOGETHER?

ALL TOGETHER *To do a cartwheel, you need to employ muscles in the legs, back, arms and abdomen.*

To make movements such as running and jumping you have to use many different skeletal muscles at the same time. Leg muscles push you along and lift your legs, arm muscles help you to stay balanced, and muscles in your back hold your body upright. Though you are barely aware of it, your brain coordinates these movements. Continual repetition of a movement develops your ability to make all the relevant muscles work together.

WHAT MAKES MUSCLES ACHE?

Muscles need energy to work. They obtain it by using oxygen to break down a chemical fuel called glucose, a form of sugar, which is delivered to them by the blood. If a muscle is working hard, it starts to run short of oxygen and it cannot break down glucose in the normal way. Instead, glucose is turned into lactic acid. The acid builds up inside the muscle and makes it ache. If the muscle is allowed to rest, the acid is broken down and the ache disappears.

TO THE LIMIT *After being pushed hard, muscles may take some time to stop aching.*

fast fact
You have about 650 muscles. Almost 40 connect the wrist, fingers and thumb alone.

BLOOD AND CIRCULATION

Blood is pumped to every part of your body by your heart. In an adult male, up to 5 litres (10½ pints) hurtle through arteries and veins, completing a double loop around the body in less than one minute. During this endless high-speed journey, blood delivers oxygen, collects waste and supplies the substances that your body's cells need to survive. Blood also helps the body to fight diseases and spreads warmth from one part of the body to another.

HOW DOES THE HEART WORK?

Your heart is made of muscle and has four chambers: two atria at the top and two ventricles at the bottom. About 100,000 times a day, the heart fills with blood then contracts to pump the blood out again. This contraction is called a heartbeat. Deoxygenated blood from your body flows into the right atrium and ventricle, and is pumped to the lungs, where it takes in oxygen. The oxygenated blood returns to the left atrium and ventricle, which pump the blood out through a large artery, the aorta, and around your body. Each side of your heart has two valves – flaps that stop blood flowing backwards after each beat.

HEART STRUCTURE This diagram shows the main components of the heart.

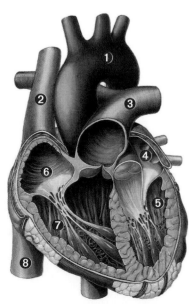

❶ **AORTA** Carries oxygenated blood away from the heart

❷ **SUPERIOR VENA CAVA** Drains deoxygenated blood from upper body

❸ **PULMONARY ARTERY** Takes deoxygenated blood to the lungs

❹ **LEFT ATRIUM** Oxygenated blood from the lungs enters here.

❺ **LEFT VENTRICLE** Oxygenated blood is pumped from here into the aorta.

❻ **RIGHT ATRIUM** Deoxygenated blood from the body enters here.

❼ **RIGHT VENTRICLE** Deoxygenated blood is pumped from here into the pulmonary artery.

❽ **INFERIOR VENA CAVA** Drains blood from the lower body and legs

WHERE DOES BLOOD GO?

Blood travels around your body via a network of pipes, called blood vessels. The blood vessels that carry blood away from the heart are called arteries; the ones that carry it back again are called veins. Arteries and veins are connected to each other by about 80,000 km (50,000 miles) of capillaries, tiny blood vessels much thinner than a hair. Arteries expand every time your heart beats. In places such as the wrist, this creates a 'pulse' that you can feel.

CIRCULATORY SYSTEM This diagram shows the body's major arteries (in red) and veins (in blue).

COMMON CAROTID ARTERY Supplies blood to the head

SUBCLAVIAN ARTERY Supplies blood to the arms

AORTA Directs oxygenated blood to the head and body, and is the largest blood vessel

CORONARY ARTERIES Supply oxygen to the heart

RENAL ARTERY Supplies oxygenated blood to the kidneys

INFERIOR VENA CAVA Carries deoxygenated blood from the lower body

COMMON ILIAC ARTERY Takes oxygenated blood to the legs

COMMON ILIAC VEIN Carries deoxygenated blood from the legs and feet

FEMORAL ARTERY Carries oxygenated blood to the thigh

FEMORAL VEIN Returns deoxygenated blood from the thigh

GREAT SAPHENOUS VEIN The longest vein in the body

ANTERIOR TIBIAL ARTERY Carries blood to the front of the lower leg

ANTERIOR TIBIAL VEIN Returns blood from the front of the lower leg

POSTERIOR TIBIAL ARTERY Carries blood to the back of the lower leg

POSTERIOR TIBIAL VEIN Returns blood from the back of the lower leg

WHAT IS BLOOD MADE OF?

Of a single drop of blood, just over half is a liquid called plasma. Plasma consists mainly of water, but it also contains many dissolved chemicals, including glucose, the substance that your body uses to make energy. The rest of a drop of blood consists of millions of microscopic cells. Most of these are red blood cells, which carry oxygen. Scattered among them are transparent cells, called white cells, which are involved in fighting disease, as well as cells called platelets, which aid the process of clotting.

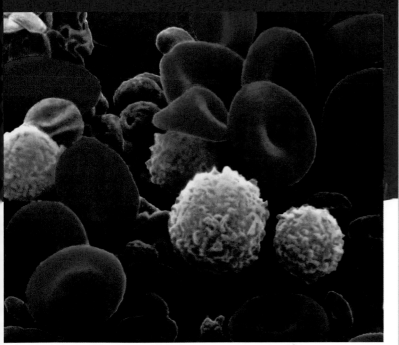

ASSORTED CELLS *This electron microscope image shows the coin-shaped red blood cells; the larger, more spherical white cells; and the smaller, pink-coloured platelets.*

WHY IS BLOOD RED?

Blood derives its colour from a red chemical called haemoglobin, which is stored in red blood cells. When blood flows through the lungs, the haemoglobin collects oxygen and carries it to other parts of the body. Haemoglobin that is carrying oxygen is bright red, but after it has released that oxygen into the body's cells as it flows past them, it becomes much darker. As a result, the blood flowing in your arteries is a brighter red than the blood flowing in your veins.

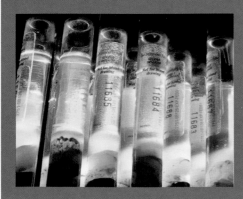

BLOOD SAMPLE *This sample has been separated into liquid plasma and dark red blood cells.*

HOW DOES BLOOD CLOT?

When a blood vessel is cut, cells called platelets rush to the site and attach to the walls of the affected vessel. At the same time, a chemical in the blood called fibrinogen turns into another chemical called fibrin, which creates a maze of sticky strands. These bind the platelets, forming a clot, which hardens to form a scab. Protected by the scab, the skin slowly heals, and, finally, the scab dries out and falls off.

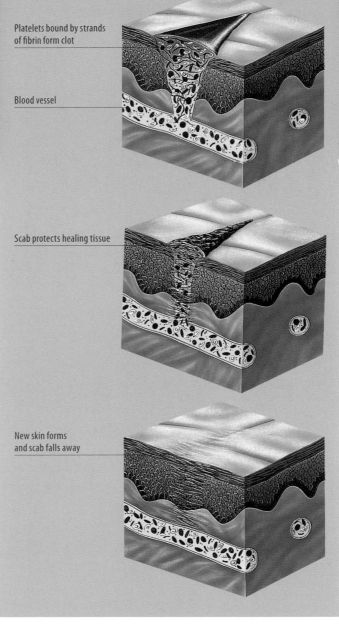

Platelets bound by strands of fibrin form clot

Blood vessel

Scab protects healing tissue

New skin forms and scab falls away

fast fact

Two or three drops of blood contain about 1 billion red blood cells, which outnumber white cells by 600 to 1. They wear out quickly, and every day the body makes about 2.5 billion new ones to replace them.

LUNGS AND BREATHING

Humans need oxygen to survive. Each time you take a breath, air rushes into your lungs and oxygen passes from the air into your blood. To get enough oxygen into your body, your lungs require a large surface area in contact with the air. If your lungs could be unpacked and laid out flat, they could wrap up your body at least 25 times.

HOW DO WE BREATHE?

Lungs do not have any muscles, so they cannot move air on their own. Instead, the diaphragm, a sheet of muscle that lies between the chest and abdominal cavities, and the intercostal muscles, which lie between the ribs, work together to expand and contract the chest cavity. As they expand the chest, the difference in pressure inside and outside the body causes air to rush into the lungs – you breathe in, in other words. As they contract, the opposite happens, and you breathe out.

INHALATION
The diaphragm contracts and flattens, increasing the volume of the chest cavity, and the intercostal muscles pull the ribs outwards. Air rushes in.

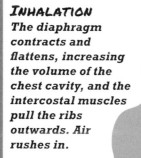

Diaphragm

EXHALATION
The diaphragm relaxes upwards, reducing the volume of the chest cavity. The intercostal muscles relax, moving the ribs downwards and inwards. Air is pushed out.

Diaphragm

WHAT HAPPENS INSIDE THE LUNGS?

Lungs are like air-filled sponges. Air flows into the lungs through a tube called the windpipe, or trachea. This tube divides into two slightly narrower tubes called bronchi (singular: bronchus), one going into each lung. Inside the lung, the bronchi subdivide into numerous smaller tubes called bronchioles. Each bronchiole ends in a cluster of tiny air pockets called alveoli. These pockets are surrounded by capillaries carrying blood. As the blood circulates around the air pockets, oxygen passes into the blood and carbon dioxide waste passes from the blood into the alveoli to then be breathed out.

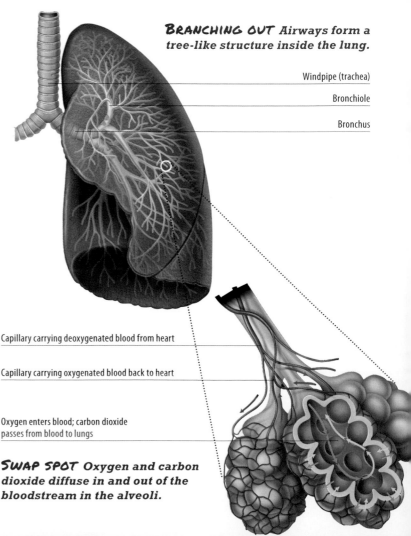

BRANCHING OUT *Airways form a tree-like structure inside the lung.*

Windpipe (trachea)

Bronchiole

Bronchus

Capillary carrying deoxygenated blood from heart

Capillary carrying oxygenated blood back to heart

Oxygen enters blood; carbon dioxide passes from blood to lungs

SWAP SPOT *Oxygen and carbon dioxide diffuse in and out of the bloodstream in the alveoli.*

WHY DO YOU GET OUT OF BREATH?

The amount of oxygen you need depends on how hard your body is working. If you are resting, you need only a small amount. If you are running or playing sport, you use up oxygen more quickly. Part of your brain automatically adjusts your breathing rate to make sure you get the oxygen you need, by breathing faster and more deeply.

0.25 litre
(½ pint)

1.75 litres
(3¾ pints)

2.5 litres
(5¼ pints)

GASPING FOR AIR *At rest, a 10-year-old takes in about 0.25 litres (½ pint) of air with each breath. Taking deep breaths consumes seven times more air. Working really hard forces more air out of the lungs and draws in 10 times more.*

WHY DO WE COUGH AND SNEEZE?

Coughs and sneezes are mechanisms that help clear out your airways. Coughs usually clear the windpipe and throat of irritants, such as dust and smoke, or germs – a recurring cough is often an indication of an infection. A sneeze is usually the result of irritation of the nasal mucous membrane. It expels air rapidly through the mouth and nose, ejecting the irritant. Although sneezing and coughing help keep you healthy, they also spread disease by spraying germs into the air.

CLEAR-OUT *Drops of moisture, dust and germs shoot into the air when you sneeze.*

WHAT CAUSES HICCUPS?

Hiccups happen when the diaphragm contracts suddenly, pushing air up into the lungs and out the windpipe. In response, the vocal cords – membranes lying across your trachea that you use to talk – close, creating the 'hic' sound. Possible causes of hiccups include intense excitement, eating too fast, coughing, laughing, and consuming carbonated drinks or spicy foods. Once hiccups are triggered, they may continue for some time, but they usually pass without any action being required. It has been suggested that the mechanism evolved to help infant mammals clear air from the stomach when feeding, and thereby ingest more milk.

fast fact

On average, an adult breathes about 15 times a minute, or 21,600 times a day, inhaling about 10,800 litres (2853 gallons) of air every 24 hours.

SKIN, HAIR AND NAILS

Skin grows in step with the rest of the body. Although it constantly wears away, it is also replacing itself all the time. Like hair and nails, skin helps to protect the body from the outside world. It can do this because its surface is made of dead cells. These are tough, and they form a barrier that shields the living cells underneath. Like the surface of skin, most of each hair is also made of dead cells.

WHAT IS SKIN MADE OF?

Skin is made of cells arranged in three main layers. The deepest layer, called the dermis, contains living cells, blood vessels, and nerve endings that sense pressure, heat, cold and pain. Above this is a thin layer, called the epidermis, which produces new cells all the time. The new cells die as they are slowly pushed towards the surface, where they form a protective outer layer. Then they fall away in small flakes.

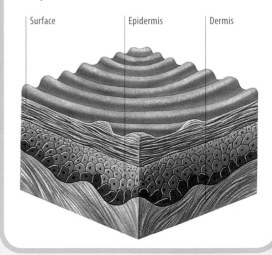

Surface   Epidermis   Dermis

WHY DO PEOPLE HAVE DIFFERENT COLOURED SKIN?

Skin colour is created by chemicals called pigments, which are present in skin cells. One pigment, melanin, makes skin brown or black. Another, carotene, gives skin a yellow colour. Pigments help to protect skin against sun damage, so people from warmer parts of the world tend to have darker skin than those from cooler climates.

DO I HAVE DIFFERENT KINDS OF SKIN?

Yes, different parts of the body have different kinds of skin. For example, the skin on the back of your arm is covered with hairs, which can range from fine to coarse. The skin on the palms of your hands and the inside of your fingers has no hair at all, but it does have lots of tiny ridges, which help hands and feet grip, and it is also extra thick for added protection.

WHY DO WE HAVE HAIR?

Hair protects the head and eyes from the sun. On other parts of the body, it helps you feel things brushing against your skin. And it helps to keep you warm. Most of a hair is made of dead cells.

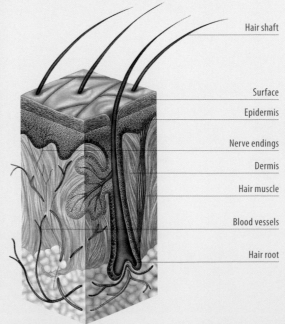

Hair shaft

Surface

Epidermis

Nerve endings

Dermis

Hair muscle

Blood vessels

Hair root

HAIR RAISING *Human hair is a robust and flexible substance, allowing it to be cut, coloured and shaped in a range of styles.*

WHY DO WE HAVE FINGERNAILS?

Nails protect your fingertips (and toenails your toes), and also help you to pick things up. They are made from keratin – the same substance that makes up hair. On average, a fingernail grows at a rate of about 1 mm (1/25 in) per week – four times faster than a toenail.

fast fact

Every year, the average person sheds about 3.6 kg (8 lb) of dead skin flakes, up to 30,000 hairs, and about 2.5 cm (1 in) of nail from each finger.

CAN HAIR REALLY STAND ON END?

If you are cold or frightened, your hair may feel as if it is standing on end. A tiny muscle pulls on the root of each hair, levering it into a more upright position. As each hair moves, it pushes against the skin, making a 'goosebump'. Long ago, humans had lots of body hair; warm air trapped in the little pits formed by the goosebumps helped keep people warm.

TEMPERATURE CONTROL
Sweating helps us stay cool during intense exercise.

WHY DO WE SWEAT?

Sweating helps keep your body cool. When you get hot, sweat is released from glands in the skin. As the sweat then evaporates from the surface of the skin, it draws off heat and, in turn, cools the blood circulating beneath the surface. The palms of your hands have more sweat glands than anywhere else – up to 500 per cm² (3250 per sq. in) of skin.

Pore

Sweat gland

ARE ALL FINGERPRINTS DIFFERENT?

Fingerprints are created by sweat and body oils, and match the patterns of ridges of skin on your fingertips. Each person has their own unique pattern. This allows police and other investigators to identify people from their fingerprints.

PRINT PATTERNS
Most fingerprints resemble one of these patterns. Investigators (far right) use powder to reveal prints.

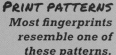

Arch   Loop   Whorl   Composite

COILED TUBES *Sweat is a watery fluid produced by skin glands.*

BRAIN AND NERVES

Every second, whether you are awake or fast asleep, your brain is busy processing information. It receives millions of signals from all parts of the body, and it sends out signals that control the way the body works. These signals travel along nerves – bundles of cells that conduct tiny bursts of electricity. The brain itself contains over 1000 billion nerve cells, and when they are busy these cells generate enough electrical energy to power a light bulb.

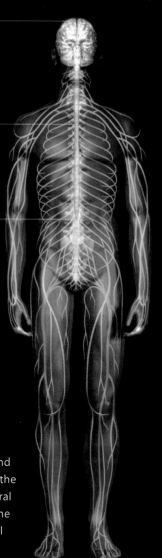

CRANIAL NERVES Twelve nerves emerge from the brain, branching to reach the eyes, ears, nose, mouth and facial muscles. One extends down, outside the spinal cord, to the heart, larynx, lungs and stomach. Two go to the neck: one controls the speech organs, the other contracts neck muscles.

SPINAL CORD The spinal cord is the central pathway of the nervous system, consisting of a thick bundle of nerves that runs from the brain stem down inside the spine to just below the twelfth rib.

SPINAL NERVES Thirty-one pairs of large nerves emerge from the spinal cord through gaps in the vertebrae. These divide and subdivide to reach every part of the body.

WHERE ARE THE MAJOR NERVES?

A network of nerves extends throughout our bodies, carrying sensory information to the brain and instructions from it. The brain and the spinal cord together form the central nervous system (CNS); the rest of the network is known as the peripheral nervous system.

HOW DO NERVES WORK?

The building blocks of the nervous system are nerve cells or neurons. Each neuron has a cell body with a nucleus. Extending from the cell body is a nerve cell fibre or axon, which in some cases is protected by a sheath of the protein myelin. Axons are microscopically thin, but can be up to 1 m ($3\frac{1}{3}$ ft) long. Their ends split to form branches called dendrites, which end in synapses. Brain signals travel along axons as electrical impulses and pass from neuron to neuron via the synapses. Each axon may end in several synapses, enabling it to link with more than one neuron.

WHAT ARE THE MAIN TYPES OF NERVE CELLS?

There are three main kinds of nerves: those that go out from the brain to muscles under voluntary control, sometimes referred to as motor neurons; others that run to parts of the body that are not under voluntary control, such as the intestines; and nerves that bring information back from the rest of the body to the brain.

MOVEMENT CONTROL *Motor neurons tell your muscles what to do and coordinate their movements.*

fast fact

Signals travel along nerves at over 50 m (165 ft) per second. So a message sent from head to toe arrives in about $\frac{1}{30}$ of a second.

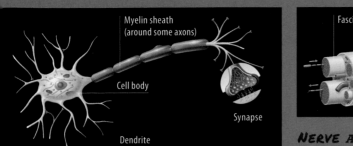

Myelin sheath
(around some axons)

Cell body

Synapse

Dendrite

NEURON *With their far-reaching axons, neurons are by far the longest cells in the body.*

Fascicle

NERVE *Axons form bundles that are called fascicles, which in turn bunch together to form a nerve.*

WHAT'S A REFLEX?

If you touch something very hot, your hand pulls away almost instantly, without waiting for your brain to tell it to. This is an example of a reflex – a rapid reaction that helps protect you from injury. A message flashes from your hand to your spinal cord. The message is then passed straight to motor nerves, which make your arm muscles contract.

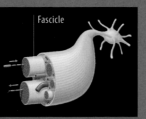

REACTION *Reflex actions happen automatically, and often do not involve signals from the brain.*

ACTION *Deliberate actions – such as picking up an apple – are triggered by brain signals.*

WHAT DO THE DIFFERENT PARTS OF THE BRAIN DO?

Your brain is divided into three main parts: the brain stem, cerebellum and cerebrum. The first two control essential processes, such as breathing, and keep all the parts of your body working together, while the cerebrum is associated with conscious activities and intelligence.

BRAIN BOX *The parts of the brain are enclosed by three different membranes, which are separated by layers of fluid. This allows the brain to float and protects it against knocks to the head.*

THALAMUS The top of the brain stem directs incoming nerve impulses to the appropriate parts of the brain.

CEREBELLUM This part of the brain coordinates movement and balance.

BRAIN STEM This connects the brain to the spinal cord.

CEREBRUM The largest part of the brain, it is divided into two hemispheres.

CORPUS CALLOSUM This joins the two hemispheres of the brain together.

MEDULLA OBLONGATA The lower half of the brain stem controls heart rate, breathing and other involuntary functions.

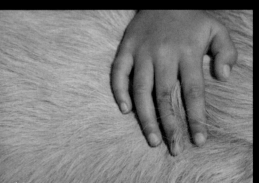

MAKING SENSE *Sensations such as texture and pressure are interpreted in the parietal lobe.*

CONTROL CENTRE *Different areas of the outer layer of the cerebrum, known as the cerebral cortex, control different functions and body parts.*

FRONTAL LOBE Problem-solving, planning, reasoning, controlling emotions

TEMPORAL LOBE Interpreting sounds, language comprehension, processing information, learning and memory

PARIETAL LOBE Spatial awareness, recognition of objects and sensations, sense of time

OCCIPITAL LOBE Interpreting and processing visual data, including patterns, colours and shapes

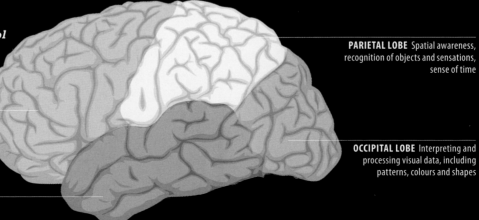

EYES AND EARS

Humans rely on vision and hearing more than any other senses. Our eyes can adjust to a huge variety of light levels, from brilliant sunshine to almost total darkness, and they can tell the difference between millions of shades of colour. Our ears can pick up the faintest whisper, but they can also cope with the roar of a jet engine 10 billion times as loud. Our eyes and ears work by producing nerve signals, which are then sent to the brain.

Optic nerve

Lens

Pupil

Cornea

Retina

HOW DO OUR EYES WORK?

Light enters your eye through a transparent outer covering, called the cornea, which provides the eye's focusing power, then through a hole called the pupil. Just behind the pupil, it passes through a lens. The lens focuses the light onto a curved screen at the back of the eye, called the retina. The retina contains millions of nerve cells, called rods and cones, that sense light according to its brightness and colour. Signals from these cells travel along the optic nerve to your brain, and the brain analyses these signals to piece together whatever you are looking at. The image on the retina is upside down, but the brain reassembles it the right way up.

Rods

Cones

HOW DO WE SEE IN THE DARK?

In the retina, the cones sense colours; however, they need bright light to work effectively. The rods distinguish between black and white. They continue to function well in dim light and provide a clear but grey view of our surroundings.

fast fact

Each retina contains about 125 million rod cells and about 7 million cone cells. Colour vision is so complicated that one-quarter of the brain is involved in processing it.

SENSES COMBINE *Each eye provides a slightly different view, which helps you judge distances, and the different sound patterns detected by each ear help you work out where sounds are coming from. At the same time, your sense of balance helps keep you upright.*

DO WE ALL SEE THE SAME COLOURS?

Most people see the same colours. But some people, mainly males, have an inherited condition that makes it difficult to tell some colours apart, known as colour deficiency or colour blindness. However, true colour blindness, when a person has no colour vision at all, is extremely rare.

SPOT CHECK *If you cannot make out a number in this pattern of dots, you may have a colour deficiency.*

HOW DO OUR EARS WORK?

The outer part of your ear gathers waves of sound and channels them through the ear canal deep inside your head. Here, the sound-waves strike your eardrum and make it vibrate – up to 40,000 times a second for the highest sounds we can hear. Three tiny bones – the anvil, hammer and stirrup – then transmit these vibrations to a spiral chamber, called the cochlea, where nerves detect the vibrations and send signals to the brain via the auditory nerve.

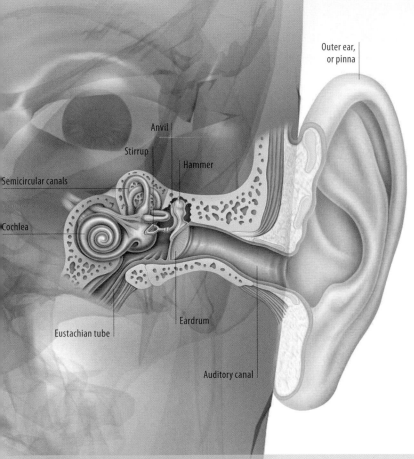

Outer ear, or pinna

Anvil

Stirrup

Hammer

Semicircular canals

Cochlea

Eustachian tube

Eardrum

Auditory canal

WHAT DOES EARWAX DO?

Earwax is a fatty secretion produced by glands in the outer ear canal. Its job is to clean the ear canal and protect it against infection. As the wax builds up, it carries dust, bacteria, fungal spores and dead skin cells out of the ear. It also contains antibacterial ingredients and bitter substances that deter small insects from entering the ear. Just one single gene determines whether earwax is wet or dry. In Europe and Africa, the wet variety is by far the more common.

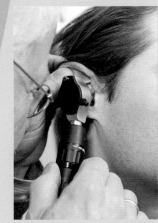

BLOCKED EAR *A build-up of earwax can block the ear canal, resulting in temporary hearing loss, and sometimes requires treatment.*

HOW DO OUR EARS HELP US BALANCE?

The fluid-filled semicircular canals of the inner ear lie at right angles to each other, which means that movement in any direction causes fluid to move in one or more canals. Nerve endings in the canals detect this movement and send signals to the brain. These tell you which way up you are and whether you are moving or still.

WHY DO OUR EARS 'POP'?

For your ears to work well, the air pressure on either side of the eardrum must be equal. The Eustachian tube, on the inside of the eardrum, is connected to the throat and nose and can let air in and out. If the pressure is unequal, air passes in or out of this tube (often when you swallow, yawn or blow your nose). As the pressure equalises, you hear a 'pop'.

SMELL, TASTE AND TOUCH

Along with vision, hearing and balance, our senses of smell, taste and touch tell us most of what we need to know about our surroundings – as well as the things we eat and drink. Our sense of smell detects odours from a wide range of sources and, in tandem with our tastebuds, helps us distinguish flavours. Our sense of touch allows us to evaluate the properties of objects, such as their temperature, texture, hardness and weight.

HOW DO WE DETECT ODOURS?

Smells are created by chemicals evaporating into the air. Different substances produce chemicals in different quantities – those that produce the most are the easiest to smell. Under each of our eyes lies a bundle of nerves called the olfactory bulb. Nerves extend from this into our nasal cavities. Receptor cells on these nerve endings detect chemicals in the air and pass messages to our brain.

Sinus

Nerve endings

Olfactory bulb

Nasal cavity

Teeth
Tongue

Salivary glands

WHICH ARE THE SMELLIEST SUBSTANCES?

The world's smelliest chemical is ethyl mercaptan, which contains carbon and sulfur – a few drops could be smelled throughout the world's biggest indoor stadium. It is often added to odourless gases, such as natural gas, to warn of leaks. One of the smelliest foods is vanilla, 100 times more potent than garlic oil and 15,000 times more pungent than citrus peel.

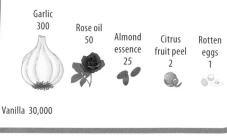

Garlic
300

Rose oil
50

Almond
essence
25

Citrus
fruit peel
2

Rotten
eggs
1

Vanilla 30,000

FLORAL FRAGRANCE *Oil glands in the petals produce the powerful scent of the rose.*

fast fact

Humans have about 5 million smell receptors in their noses and can distinguish about 10,000 different odours. Dogs have about 200 million smell receptors and, consequently, can detect many more scents than humans can.

HOW DO WE IDENTIFY FLAVOURS?

Small sense organs called tastebuds are found on the throat and palate and, in much greater number, on the tongue. These detect just five main tastes – sweet, sour, bitter, salty and savoury (sometimes referred to by the Japanese term 'umami'). However, in combination with our sense of smell they can identify a much wider range of flavours. When you have a cold, your sense of smell may not work as well and, as a result, your ability to identify flavours will be impaired too.

TASTE SENSATIONS *Saliva dissolves food, releasing chemicals into the mouth and nose.*

WHERE IS OUR SKIN MOST SENSITIVE?

All over the surface of the body are nerve endings that provide information about the things we touch. Instead of being spread out, they are concentrated in places where the sense of touch is most useful. The most sensitive parts are the mouth and fingertips, while the least sensitive are the backs of the arms and legs. You can test this by closing your eyes and asking someone to touch your skin gently in sensitive and less sensitive areas with a pencil or paintbrush.

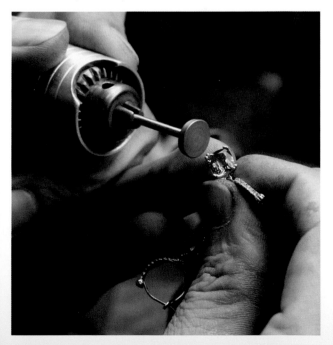

GENTLE TOUCH *Extra-sensitive hands and fingertips help us manipulate small items. Here, a jeweller is carefully repairing a ring.*

WHAT CREATES THE HOT TASTE OF SPICY FOODS?

The spicy taste of some foods, such as curries, is not a taste sensation but a feeling of pain. Capsaicin, the chemical compound that makes chillies (and some other members of the genus *Capsicum*) hot, binds to pain receptors in the mouth and nose. The nerve signals produced in this way travel to the brain and are registered as a painful, burning feeling. The same receptors also react to heat, so that when heavily spiced food is eaten hot the effect is even more intense.

GLANDS AND HORMONES

In different parts of the body, clusters of cells called glands produce substances called hormones, which help regulate body systems. Your glands make more than 20 different hormone types, and each one has a particular job to do. Some work like an accelerator, speeding up the rate at which your body works; others regulate growth, energy levels and the body's defences. Though they are usually produced in tiny amounts, hormones have important and long-lasting effects in the body.

BODY CLOCK *Production of melatonin in the pineal gland is triggered by darkness and inhibited by light.*

WHERE ARE OUR GLANDS?

Hormonal, or endocrine, glands are scattered all over the body and together make up what is known as the endocrine system. They are controlled by an area of the brain called the hypothalamus (▶160). Most glands release hormones into the blood, which transports them to their target, but some secrete hormones directly to their target via a duct.

PITUITARY GLAND Located just beneath your brain, this pea-sized gland releases hormones that trigger hormone production in other glands, controls bone growth, and produces prolactin for breastfeeding.

ADRENAL GLANDS Located above the kidneys, the adrenal glands make adrenaline, which gets your body ready to take emergency action.

OVARIES Located on either side of the bladder in females, the ovaries produce the female sex hormones, oestrogen and progesterone.

PINEAL GLAND This small gland at the back of the brain produces the hormone melatonin, which influences body temperature, sleep and appetite.

THYROID GLAND This controls the rate at which your body uses up the fuel provided by food.

PANCREAS The largest gland in the body, the pancreas releases hormones that control the amount of glucose in the blood.

TESTES In males, these two glands yield the male sex hormone, testosterone.

fast fact

Hormones are needed in only very small quantities. Thyroxine controls the rate at which the body uses energy. An adult's blood contains about 0.0005 g ($1/50,000$ oz) of the hormone, so 5000 people would only have a teaspoonful between them.

HOW DO HORMONES WORK?

Seconds after being released, a hormone is carried around the body, usually in the blood. When it reaches its target, it adjusts the way the cells there work. For example, as it gets dark at night, the pineal gland directs melatonin to the hypothalamus in the brain, causing us to feel sleepy. Hormones are very specific and work only on target cells; soon after release, they are broken down by the body.

WHY DO WE NEED ADRENALINE?

When your body senses danger, the adrenal glands release the hormone called adrenaline. It primes your body to take evasive or emergency action by preparing it to work harder and faster – this is sometimes known as the 'fight-or-flight response'. Your heart rate goes up, speeding up blood circulation so that oxygen is carried around the body more quickly; your lungs breathe more deeply; and your digestion slows down, diverting extra blood to the muscles so that they can work harder. The sensation can be exciting, which is partly why many people enjoy extreme activities, such as bungee jumping and sky-diving, as they usually generate an adrenaline rush.

THRILL SEEKER People who participate in extreme sports are often referred to as 'adrenaline junkies'.

DO SOME HORMONES COUNTERACT EACH OTHER?

Yes, some hormones have opposing effects. But they work together to balance chemicals inside your body. One of the most important things that has to be balanced is the amount of glucose in your blood. Two hormones, called glucagon and insulin, make sure that your glucose level stays just right. If the blood glucose level starts to fall, glucagon steps it up. When the glucose level is too high, it triggers the release of more insulin, which lowers the level again. As a result, the glucose level settles down at the correct point.

WHAT ARE SEX HORMONES?

Most hormones are at work from the moment you are born. Sex hormones are different, because they start to work later on. They gradually prepare the body for reproduction and give it an adult shape. These changes start between the ages of about 9 and 13, and they usually take at least five years to complete – the stage of life known as puberty. Men have one main sex hormone, called testosterone, but women have two, called oestrogen and progesterone. Female sex hormones prepare a woman's body for pregnancy.

CHANGING TIMES Hormones are responsible for the physical changes that everyone goes through in their teens.

EATING AND DIGESTION

As soon as we start eating, our digestive system begins processing the food, turning it into fuel for the body. Digestion takes place in the gut, or alimentary canal, essentially a long tube that runs from the mouth down through the body and is linked to several organs. Muscle action and proteins called enzymes break the food down into molecules that are then absorbed into the bloodstream.

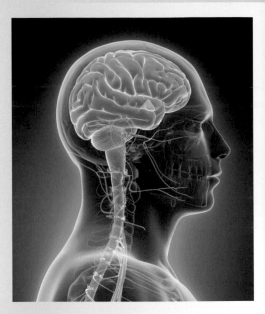

PIVOTAL POINT *In this MRI scan, the hypothalamus is highlighted in yellow. The size of an almond, it coordinates a wide range of body functions.*

WHAT MAKES US FEEL HUNGRY?

You start to feel hungry when the amount of glucose in your blood drops below a certain level. In response, a part of the brain called the hypothalamus sends signals to your stomach, telling it to prepare for the next meal. Your stomach may begin to make rumbling noises, and the sight and smell of food will make you feel even hungrier.

WHAT ARE OUR TEETH MADE OF?

Teeth break up food and begin the digestive process. Above the gum line, teeth are covered by a layer of hard enamel. Under that is a softer layer of calcified tissue, called dentine. Sheaths of another calcified material, cementum, cover the roots of the tooth and together with the dentine protect the pulp, which contains blood vessels and nerves. Humans have two sets of teeth: 20 milk teeth begin to appear at six months of age; from about six years old they are slowly pushed out by adult teeth. Most adults have 8 incisors, 4 canines, 8 premolars and 12 molars.

Crown
Enamel
Dentine
Pulp
Jawbone
Root
Nerves

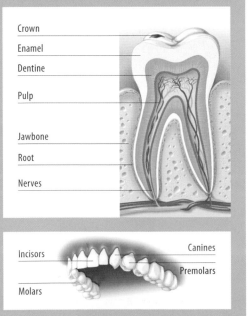

Incisors
Canines
Premolars
Molars

WHAT HAPPENS WHEN FOOD 'GOES DOWN THE WRONG WAY'?

When you swallow, a flap called the epiglottis closes off your windpipe (trachea). Sometimes it does not close quickly enough, and food goes down the wrong tube. This makes you cough, which dislodges the food from your windpipe and sends it back up.

fast fact

In adults, the alimentary canal is up to 9 m (30 ft) long. The small intestine alone is nearly 6 m (20 ft) long.

WHERE DOES OUR FOOD GO?

Food moves through your body inside the gut, or alimentary canal. Each section of the alimentary canal carries out particular tasks. In addition, the organs attached to the canal, such as the gall bladder and the pancreas, also play vital roles in digestion. The whole process usually takes at least 24 hours.

❶ TEETH, SALIVARY GLANDS AND TONGUE Teeth cut up and grind the food. Enzymes in saliva help break it down further. The tongue pushes chewed food to the back of the throat.

❷ OESOPHAGUS Rhythmic muscular contractions in the walls of this tube push food down into the stomach.

❸ STOMACH Cells in the stomach wall produce hydrochloric acid and the enzyme pepsin, which break down proteins, and the enzyme lipase, which breaks down fats. Mucus in the stomach lining stops these chemicals damaging the stomach itself.

❹ LIVER The liver produces bile, a thick green solution that breaks down fats.

❺ GALL BLADDER Bile from the liver is stored in this sac until needed.

❻ PANCREAS This small organ secretes enzymes that break down proteins, carbohydrates and fats, as well as sodium bicarbonate, which neutralises stomach acid.

❼ SMALL INTESTINE This long tube secretes enzymes that combine with bile and pancreatic juice to complete the digestive process. Most of the nutrients and water needed by the body are absorbed here.

❽ LARGE INTESTINE The large intestine, or colon, absorbs water and processes the remaining waste matter.

❾ RECTUM Waste matter remains here until muscular contractions prompt you to go to the toilet.

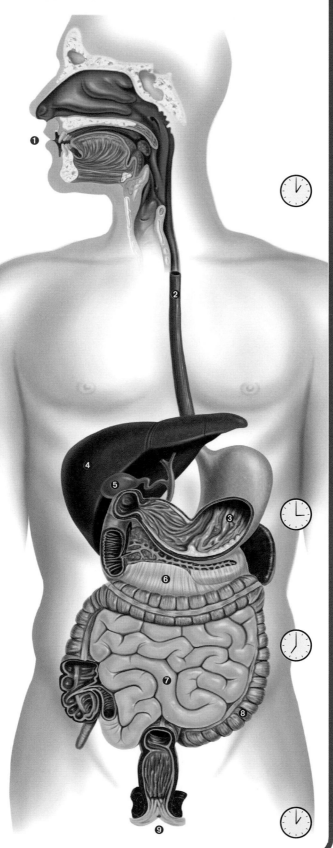

WHY DO WE BURP AND FART?

When you swallow food, you cannot help swallowing air as well. When you belch or burp, this air escapes. When food is digested in your intestines, it often produces gas as a waste product. These gases make food mumble and squeak as it works its way through your digestive system. Farting releases this gas.

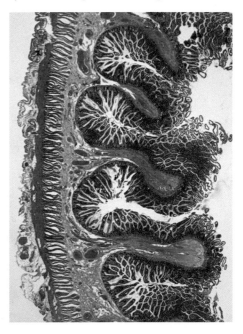

WAY OUT *The lining of the small intestine is covered with millions of finger-like projections, called villi, through which nutrients are absorbed. The process often produces gas.*

WATER WORKS

Water is essential for your well-being. Various organs and processes help maintain the correct proportions of water in the body, taking in and disposing of fluids and adjusting their concentration in the blood. The most notable are the two kidneys, which filter waste products out of the blood and reabsorb useful ones, then direct excess water to the bladder for disposal via the urethra.

RAGING THIRST *When the body is short of water, the brain produces a sensation of thirst, and also slows the excretion of water from the kidneys until levels are restored.*

WHY DO WE NEED WATER?

All the important chemical processes that take place in the body require water – our blood is 80 per cent water, our lungs are 90 per cent water and our brains are 70 per cent water. Water carries minerals and nutrients around the body and helps flush out toxins. It also keeps tissues moist and lubricates joints.

HOW DO WE TAKE IN WATER?

Most obviously, we take in water by drinking it. But we also obtain some of the water we need from foods, and a small amount is also produced by our body cells.

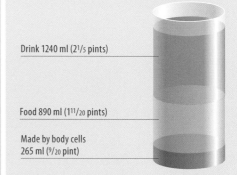

Drink 1240 ml (2^1/$_5$ pints)

Food 890 ml (1^{11}/$_{20}$ pints)

Made by body cells
265 ml (9/20 pint)

TOTAL WATER IN PER DAY 2395 ml (4^1/$_5$ pints)

HOW DO WE DISPOSE OF WATER?

We dispose of waste water regularly when we go to the toilet, and we breathe out a significant amount of water in the form of water vapour. Additionally, some water passes out through the skin as sweat (▶151) and then evaporates into the air.

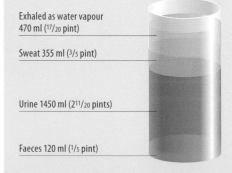

Exhaled as water vapour
470 ml (17/20 pint)

Sweat 355 ml (3/5 pint)

Urine 1450 ml (2^{11}/$_{20}$ pints)

Faeces 120 ml (1/5 pint)

TOTAL WATER OUT PER DAY 2395 ml (4^1/$_5$ pints)

WHAT DO OUR KIDNEYS DO?

Kidneys filter your blood, removing chemical waste that the blood has collected from the cells in your body. You have two kidneys, each containing more than a million microscopic tubes, called nephrons. As blood flows through the kidneys, the waste trickles into the tubes, making urine. The urine flows from the kidneys into an expandable bag, called the bladder. When your bladder is stretched, nerve endings there tell your brain that it is time to empty it.

URINARY SYSTEM *The organs that dispose of liquid make up the urinary system.*

KIDNEY FUNCTION *This cross-section shows the main components of the kidneys.*

RENAL PELVIS Urine collects here.

KIDNEYS These two organs filter out waste products, including urea, uric acid and excess water from the blood, to make urine.

RENAL ARTERY Feeds blood to the kidney

URETERS These long tubes carry urine from the kidneys to the bladder.

RENAL VEIN Carries blood out of the kidney

URETER Urine flows out to the bladder.

BLADDER A large muscular bag, the bladder stores urine until you go to the toilet.

URETHRA This tube leads from the bladder to an opening at the end of the penis in men and above the vagina in women.

RENAL MEDULLA Each one contains thousands of nephrons.

WHAT HAPPENS IF YOUR KIDNEYS STOP WORKING?

You can live quite healthily with just one kidney. But if both kidneys failed, you would need regular treatment, called dialysis, to clean your blood. Another option is to have a healthy kidney transplanted (▶181) into your body. This is now a relatively common procedure.

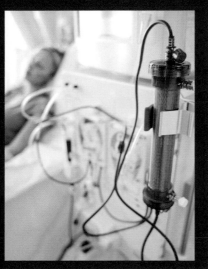

WHY DOES FEELING NERVOUS MAKE YOU WANT TO GO TO THE TOILET?

If something makes you anxious or frightened, your body prepares to cope with danger. Hormones and nerves make your heart beat faster and make your muscles tense. One of these muscles is in the lining of your bladder. When it tenses up, it makes you feel that you need to go to the toilet, even though your bladder may not be full.

fast fact

The two kidneys filter the whole bloodstream about once every 25 minutes. In an adult, this means that they filter over 11,000 litres (3000 gallons) of blood a year – all through tiny tubes that are thinner than a hair.

SELF-DEFENCE

The average person has more than 500,000 billion bacteria living on the surface of their body – a far greater number than they have cells. Most bacteria do no harm. But if bacteria and other microbes get inside the body, they can trigger disease. To stop this happening, the body is armed with a self-defence system, called the immune system, which recognises and destroys dangerous invaders.

HOW DOES THE BODY FIGHT INFECTION?

If bacteria get inside your body – for example, through a cut – the immune system attacks them with defensive cells. There are several kinds, but the most significant are phagocytes and antibodies. Phagocytes normally circulate in the blood but can also enter body tissues. When they find bacteria, they swallow and digest them, thereby rendering them harmless. Antibodies are protein molecules produced by lymphocytes. They attach themselves to the surface of invading bacteria, preventing them from functioning normally and also attracting phagocytes, which then mop up the bacteria.

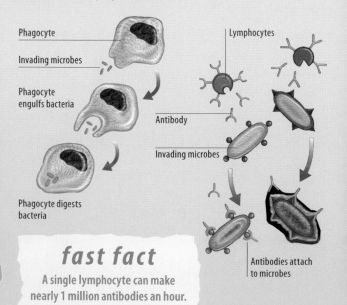

Phagocyte
Invading microbes
Phagocyte engulfs bacteria
Phagocyte digests bacteria
Lymphocytes
Antibody
Invading microbes
Antibodies attach to microbes

fast fact
A single lymphocyte can make nearly 1 million antibodies an hour.

WHERE IS THE IMMUNE SYSTEM?

The immune system depends on a network of vessels and nodes that extends throughout the body, known as the lymphatic system. This system drains surplus fluid (called lymph) from body tissues, filters out any impurities and then empties the fluid into the blood. It also makes cells called lymphocytes, which help defend the body against infection.

LYMPH NODES These swellings contain lymphocytes, which help filter out foreign cells.

RIGHT LYMPHATIC DUCT Drains lymph from the right upper body into the right subclavian vein

SUBCLAVIAN VEIN Here lymph mixes back into the blood.

THYMUS GLAND Matures some lymphocytes and distributes them to the lymphatic system; also makes hormones (▶158)

THORACIC DUCT Drains lymph from the left side of the head and upper body, and from the lower body, into the left subclavian vein

SPLEEN Filters blood and stores some types of immune cells

LEFT AND RIGHT LUMBAR TRUNKS Drain lymph from the abdomen and legs into the thoracic duct

LYMPH VESSELS Drain fluid from tissues all over the body

FLUSHING OUT *The illustration shows the main components of the lymphatic system.*

WHY DO WE GET SWOLLEN GLANDS?

What are often referred to as 'swollen glands' are not glands (▶158) but enlarged lymph nodes. The nodes expand as they become more active in fighting off infection and disease.

WHY DO WE CATCH SOME DISEASES ONLY ONCE?

The first time an invading germ appears, the immune system may take several days to produce antibodies, which build up slowly through cell division. This gives the disease time to take hold. But once your immune system fights off a disease, some of the lymphocytes turn into memory cells that will recognise the germ if it returns, even years later, and more quickly produce the appropriate antibodies to fight it off.

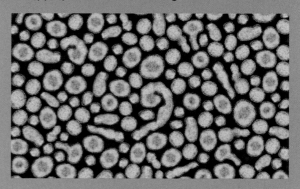

EVER CHANGING Flu viruses (orange) in an infected cell. You can catch flu more than once because the virus keeps changing.

WHY DO SOME ILLNESSES CAUSE A HIGH TEMPERATURE?

A high temperature of 38.5°C (101°F) and above is a sign that your body is fighting infection. It happens because immune-system cells reset your brain's 'thermostat', making your body heat up. At this higher temperature, the immune system can make antibodies more quickly, while bacteria find it harder to reproduce. Once the infection is under control, your temperature begins to fall.

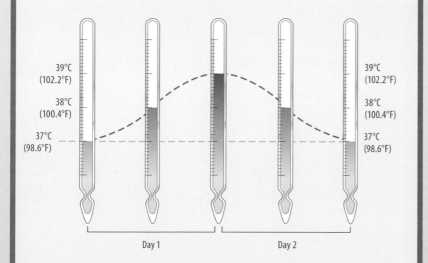

39°C (102.2°F)
38°C (100.4°F)
37°C (98.6°F)

39°C (102.2°F)
38°C (100.4°F)
37°C (98.6°F)

Day 1   Day 2

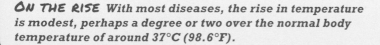

ON THE RISE With most diseases, the rise in temperature is modest, perhaps a degree or two over the normal body temperature of around 37°C (98.6°F).

WHAT ARE ALLERGIES?

If you are allergic to something, it means that your immune system attacks that substance, even though the substance is harmless. Allergies are triggered by many things, but the most common ones involve plant pollens, medicines and substances in food. Most allergies produce a mild reaction, although they can still make people feel unwell. But a few, such as an allergy to peanuts, can provoke a severe reaction, known as anaphylaxis, which can cause swelling of the tongue and throat, shortness of breath, dizziness and collapse, and even death.

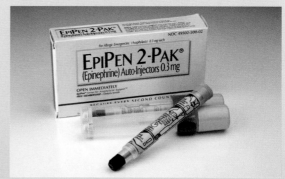

FIRST AID Injecting with adrenaline is the first response to anaphylaxis, so severe allergy sufferers usually carry an injection kit.

HUMAN REPRODUCTION

Everyone begins life as a single cell. These cells are called eggs, and each woman has a store of them inside her body. In order to develop, an egg cell has to join up with a sperm cell from a man. This process is called fertilisation and it takes place inside the woman's body during or shortly after sexual intercourse. Once an egg has been fertilised, it immediately starts to grow into a new human being. Nine months later, that new person is ready to be born.

WHERE ARE EGGS PRODUCED?

Eggs are made in a woman's ovaries. Each woman has two ovaries, and at her birth they contain a lifetime's supply of eggs. From about the age of 13, one egg is released every month. It passes along the fallopian tube to the womb (uterus), where an enriched blood supply has developed, ready to nourish it. If the egg is not fertilised, it is expelled with the uterine blood, a process called menstruation.

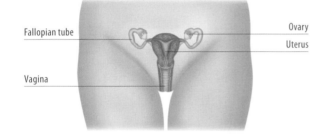

Fallopian tube — Ovary
Uterus
Vagina

WHERE DO SPERM COME FROM?

From about the age of 11 or 12, sperm are produced by two organs in the male body, called testes. Sperm mature in about two weeks and are stored in a long tube above each testis, called the epididymis. When the penis is erect, they move to the urethra, mixing with fluid to form semen. During sexual intercourse this is ejected into the woman's vagina, from where it passes into the uterus and fallopian tubes.

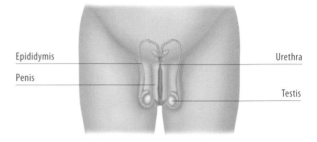

Epididymis — Urethra
Penis
Testis

WHAT HAPPENS IMMEDIATELY AFTER FERTILISATION?

Millions of sperm cells may reach the egg, but only one will gain entry to it and fertilise it, creating a single 'zygote' cell containing all the genetic information required to make a new person. This occurs high in the fallopian tube. The fertilised egg then makes its way down the tube, repeatedly subdividing itself into two then four then eight cells, and so on. After a week or so, the cluster of cells, now called a blastocyst, reaches the uterus and implants itself in the lining. Pregnancy then begins.

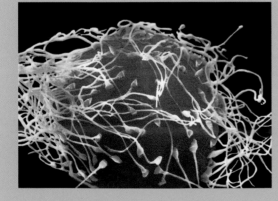

ALL FOR ONE *Sperm crowd onto the surface of an egg. Only one will make it inside.*

CONCEPTION A single sperm cell penetrates the egg.

PRODUCTION Eggs in ovary at various stages of development

CELL DIVISION Within 30 hours, the cell starts subdividing.

ON THE MOVE The zygote moves towards the uterus.

IN POSITION The blastocyst contains the embryo and will form the placenta and amniotic sac.

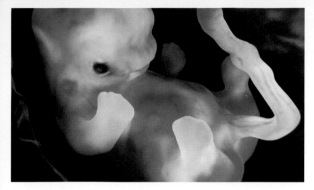

HOW DOES A BABY DEVELOP?

During the first several weeks of development the baby is known as an embryo; in the later stages until birth it is referred to as a foetus. As it grows, the amniotic sac and uterus grow with it. Nutrients and oxygen are delivered from the mother's blood via a spongy pad, called the placenta, which is in turn connected to the baby by the umbilical cord.

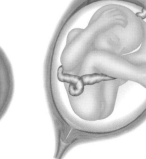

LIFE LINE The umbilical cord is highly flexible, so it is not a problem if it is twisted and turned by the baby.

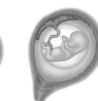

4 WEEKS Embryo is 5 mm (¼ in) long. Organs have begun to form, including the heart.

6 WEEKS Brain has begun to develop and limbs are starting to form.

8 WEEKS Foetus is now about 2.5 cm (1 in) long and has recognisable limbs.

12 WEEKS Foetus now has all major organs, tooth buds, eyelids and ears. It measures roughly 8–9 cm (3¼–3½ in) in length.

24 WEEKS All organs are now functioning. From this point on, the baby has at least a 50 per cent chance of survival if born early.

40 WEEKS Baby is fully formed, and has head positioned downwards, ready to be born. Muscles in the uterus now push it through the vagina, or birth canal, and into the outside world.

fast fact

Each year, the average man produces about 50 billion sperm cells – enough to replace Earth's entire human population seven times over.

WHY DO PEOPLE SOMETIMES HAVE TWINS?

Twins usually come about when a woman releases two eggs at the same time, and both are fertilised. Known as fraternal twins, they are born close together, but they grow up to be as different as ordinary brothers and sisters. Twins who look alike, called identical twins, are produced when a single fertilised egg splits into two.

WHAT IS IVF?

IVF stands for 'in vitro fertilisation', which means fertilisation outside the body. If, for some reason, a woman's eggs cannot be successfully fertilised inside her body, doctors may offer IVF. This involves removing some of the woman's eggs, fertilising them in a petri dish using her partner's sperm, growing them for approximately five days, and then replacing one blastocyst in the woman's uterus. If it implants successfully, it should then develop in the normal way.

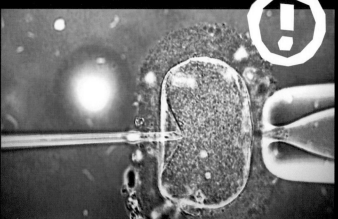

DIRECT TRANSFER In a special form of IVF called intracytoplasmic sperm injection, or ICSI, sperm are injected directly into the egg cell (centre).

CELLS AND GENES

Almost every feature of your body – from the colour of your eyes to the shape of your fingernails – is controlled by instructions called genes. These instructions are stored inside body cells in the form of a substance called DNA, and passed from parents to children.

WHAT ARE CELLS?

Cells are the smallest structural units in the body. There are various kinds of body cells, including blood, fat, muscle, skin and nerve cells, but all have a similar structure: a nucleus containing DNA and an outer layer, or cell membrane. Cells multiply by dividing themselves in two, over and over again.

fast fact
If all the DNA in one of your cells was stretched out, it would be about 2 m (6²/₃ ft) long – but so thin it would be invisible to the naked eye.

MICROVILLI Folds on the cell membrane that help absorb nutrients

RIBOSOME Assembles proteins from amino acids

CYTOPLASM Liquid part of cell, mainly water

MITOCHONDRION Breaks down sugars and starches (carbohydrates) to release energy

CELL MEMBRANE Skin made of proteins and fats

NUCLEUS Centre of cell

ENDOPLASMIC RETICULUM Flattened tubules that move proteins and other materials around the cell

VACUOLE Some of these bubbles carry nutrients to feed the cell; others carry waste matter out of the cell.

CENTRIOLES Two short bundles of hollow tubules that help a cell divide

GOLGI APPARATUS Packages proteins into vacuoles, ready for use by the cell

CHROMOSOME A duplicate pair of chromosomes coiled up prior to cell division

NUCLEOLUS The core of the nucleus. It is filled with a chemical called RNA, which acts as a messenger between the nucleus and the rest of the cell.

CELL STRUCTURE *In the cytoplasm, various specialised structures, called organelles, carry out the cell's tasks, including turning nutrients into energy and expelling waste.*

DATA PACKET *The nucleus contains the chromosomes. It is surrounded by a double-layered porous membrane, called the nuclear envelope.*

WHERE ARE GENES STORED?

Genes are stored in the cell nucleus, in thread-like structures called chromosomes. Each chromosome consists of a long molecule of DNA coiled around a protein core. Most of the time the chromosomes are unravelled inside the cell, so that their DNA can be accessed. But just before a cell divides, they coil up into bundles. Then each bundle replicates itself, forming two identical versions that pair up in an X shape. As the cell divides, each pair of chromosomes splits apart and one copy is drawn into each new cell.

HOW DO GENES WORK?

Genes work by telling cells how to make proteins, the materials from which all living matter is built. There are thousands of types of proteins, and each has a specific function in the body. For example, one gene instructs eye cells to make a protein that produces a pigment called melanin. If you have this gene, specks of melanin build up in your eyes, making them brown.

WHAT DETERMINES IF YOU ARE MALE OR FEMALE?

Your gender is determined by two special chromosomes, the X and Y chromosomes: females have two X chromosomes and males have an X and a Y. Unfertilised eggs contain only X chromosomes; sperm contain either X or Y chromosomes. After an egg has been fertilised by sperm, it has either two X chromosomes, in which case it develops into a female, or an X and a Y chromosome, in which case it becomes male.

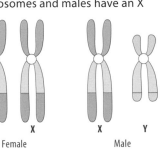

X X X Y
Female   Male

WHAT IS A GENOME?

A genome is the entire set of instructions encoded in the DNA of one living thing. Begun in 1990, the international Human Genome Project has mapped the sequence of all 3 billion base pair combinations in human DNA and thereby identified every one of our genes. Having this complete set of instructions for human DNA helps scientists understand the causes of illnesses and learn how to prevent hereditary diseases being passed on.

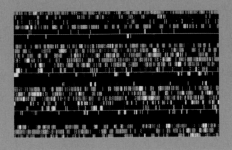

HOW ARE GENES PASSED ON?

All human cells have 46 chromosomes, except for sperm and egg cells, which have 23 chromosomes. When the sperm and egg cells combine, they join up 23 chromosomes from the father with 23 from the mother to create a complete cell, with a new combination of genes. This cell then begins dividing to create a new human (▶166). A person may inherit two forms of a gene for a particular trait, one from each parent. But some genes are dominant and are more likely to be expressed – show up, in other words – while others are recessive, meaning that they may be passed on without necessarily showing up in every generation.

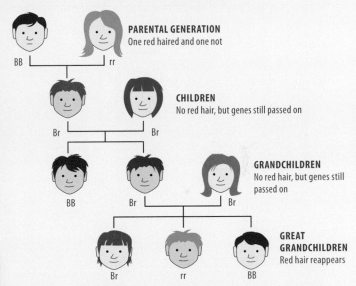

PARENTAL GENERATION
One red haired and one not

BB   rr

CHILDREN
No red hair, but genes still passed on

Br   Br

GRANDCHILDREN
No red hair, but genes still passed on

BB   Br   Br

GREAT GRANDCHILDREN
Red hair reappears

Br   rr   BB

IN THE BACKGROUND Red hair is a recessive trait. This diagram shows how it might be passed on and be expressed in one particular family. The letter 'r' stands for the red hair gene and 'B' for brown hair.

DNA When DNA unravels, it looks like a spiral ladder (called a double helix).

BASE PAIRS Four types of 'chemical bases' – adenine, cytosine, guanine and thymine – pair up to form the rungs of the ladder. The order in which the base pairs occur forms the genetic instructions, or code.

SUGAR STRING Molecules of a sugar called deoxyribose form the sides of the 'ladder'.

Cytosine

Adenine

Guanine

Thymine

GROWTH AND AGEING

Compared with other animals – even ones as big as elephants and whales – we humans take a long time to grow up. An elephant is fully grown by the time it is 15, but we keep growing until we are at least 18. Throughout childhood and our teenage years, our bodies get bigger and they also change shape in preparation for adult life. Fewer changes take place during our adult years, until our body systems and processes begin to deteriorate from our mid-forties onwards.

WHAT ARE THE MAIN STAGES OF GROWTH?

Humans go through several major stages of growth. The main changes in our brains occur between birth and the age of seven, during which time we develop from simple, almost instinctive behaviour patterns to a rounded and conscious understanding of the world. The most significant physical changes take place during infancy, puberty and early adulthood.

BIRTH Can see (but not clearly), hear and has primitive reflexes; recognises shape of human face and, after three days, mother's voice

0–2 MONTHS Learns to smile and focus eyes; memory limited to about 15 seconds

2–6 MONTHS Distinct emotions emerge, including fear, anger and satisfaction; learns to recognise objects and explore shapes

6–9 MONTHS Learns to recognise facial expressions and to sit up and crawl

9–12 MONTHS Begins to speak, imitate and walk

1–2 YEARS Becomes proficient walker, starts talking

2–3 YEARS Understands concept of sharing, can classify more objects

3–4 YEARS Speech and sense of balance improve

4–5 YEARS Develops friendships, starts writing; brain now two-thirds of full size

5–7 YEARS Becomes more sociable, aware of past and future

9–15 YEARS Start of puberty brings on physical and hormonal changes

15–20 YEARS Body reaches maximum height and brain is full size

20–30 YEARS Body increases in bulk and brain matures

30–40 YEARS Testosterone levels decline in men (from mid-thirties)

40–60 YEARS Body processes start to decline; hair thins and turns grey; female fertility declines

60–80 YEARS Skin wrinkles and sags, muscles waste; vision and hearing deteriorate

80 YEARS AND OVER Bones become brittle, structure of brain deteriorates

PERSONAL PACE Rates of growth and the changes that take place will vary in timing and degree according to a person's genetic make-up.

170

9 MONTHS   4 YEARS   7 YEARS   12 YEARS   19 YEARS   33 YEARS   58 YEARS   84 YEARS

WHAT HAPPENS DURING PUBERTY?

Puberty begins in girls between the ages of 9 and 13 and in boys from 10 to 15. Hormones trigger changes in growth and the development of the sex organs to prepare the body for reproduction. Rapid growth and weight increase occur, as well as psychological and emotional changes. In girls, the ovaries secrete the female hormones, oestrogen and progesterone, which cause breasts to develop, hips to broaden, pubic and underarm hair to appear, and menstruation to begin. In boys, the testes secrete the male hormone testosterone, which triggers the growth of facial, body and pubic hair; an increase in muscle bulk; a deepening of the voice; growth of the genital organs; and the production of sperm.

DO BOYS GROW FASTER THAN GIRLS?

No, but they grow for longer. Girls usually start a burst of growth at about the age of 10, and they reach their adult height by about 16. Boys begin their burst of growth at about 12, but many do not reach their adult height until they are 19 or 20.

GROWTH SPURT *At its fastest, growth in adolescent boys and girls can reach more than 8 cm (3 in) a year.*

HOW LONG CAN HUMANS LIVE?

How long a person lives is determined by a combination of variables, including their genes, nutrition, exercise regimen and other environmental factors. Currently, the maximum human age is about 125 years. This has not changed throughout history; however, thanks to medicines and improved living conditions, people are, on average, living much longer, especially in industrialised countries. And some scientists believe that the use of genetic modification and cutting-edge medicines could soon extend the maximum limit by 10 or even 15 years.

STAYING ALERT *Because exercise activates the brain and supplies it with oxygen, it can help maintain memory function in older people.*

IS IT HARDER FOR OLDER PEOPLE TO LEARN NEW THINGS?

Generally, our ability to learn decreases with age. People find it difficult to retain new information as they get older. This is due to a reduction in inhibition – the ability to ignore or forget unimportant information. Young people can better distinguish between important and unimportant facts. When this capacity diminishes, too many pieces of information jostle for a place in the memory and fresh information is more readily lost.

fast fact

The oldest person in modern history was a French woman called Jeanne Calment, who died in 1997 at the age of 122. She was still riding a bicycle when she was 100 years old.

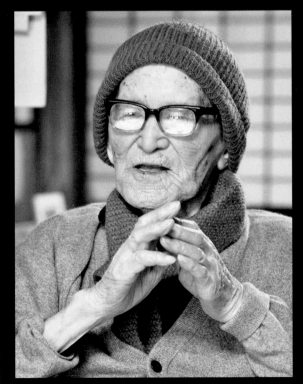

LIFE LONG *Japan's Jiroemon Kimura, the oldest man on record. He died in 2013, at 116.*

FOOD AND NUTRITION

Food is the fuel that makes the body work. Unlike the fuel that drives machines, however, it contains many different substances. Some foods provide energy, while others provide the raw materials used for growth and for replacing cells that have become worn out. To maintain good health, we need to eat a well-balanced diet that provides all these substances in appropriate amounts.

WHAT DO WE OBTAIN FROM FOOD?

The useful substances in food are known as nutrients. We need three types of nutrients in large amounts (the so-called macronutrients): carbohydrates, which provide us with energy; fats, which also provide energy; and proteins, which the body uses for growth and for replacing and repairing cells. We also require other nutrients in smaller amounts, called vitamins and minerals (the so-called micronutrients), to help build and maintain bones and teeth and regulate body processes. Food also provides the body with water and dietary fibre. Consisting of the tough parts of fruit, seeds and vegetables – such as skins and husks – dietary fibre helps the digestive system work efficiently.

NUTRIENT MIX *Different kinds of food provide different levels of the major nutrients.*

FISH

Fish contains a large proportion of protein, very little carbohydrate, and a moderate amount of fat. It is also a good source of minerals.

Protein	23%
Carbohydrate	Trace
Fat	7%
Fibre	None
Water	70%

BREAD

Bread is high in carbohydrate. Wholegrain bread, which includes the ground-up husks of grain, is high in dietary fibre.

Protein	10%
Carbohydrate	48%
Fat	3%
Fibre	9%
Water	30%

FRUIT

Oranges are rich in vitamin C. They contain almost no protein or fat, but include some energy-rich carbohydrates.

Protein	Trace
Carbohydrate	9%
Fat	Trace
Fibre	2%
Water	89%

HOW MUCH DO WE NEED OF EACH NUTRIENT?

For optimum health the body requires a diet with the following proportions of macronutrients:

- Carbohydrates: 58 per cent
- Proteins: 12 per cent
- Fats, unsaturated or polyunsaturated: 20 per cent
- Fats, saturated: 10 per cent

fast fact

The average American eats almost 900 kg (1 ton) of food every year. That's the equivalent of the weight of a small car.

HOW MUCH DO PEOPLE EAT IN DIFFERENT COUNTRIES?

Food energy – the energy our bodies derive from our food – is measured in kilojoules (kJ) or kilocalories. The average minimum daily requirement per person is 7500 kJ (1800 kilocalories), though many people require

SIMPLE FARE *A family in Ghana, West Africa, prepares the main meal of the day.*

WHAT'S A FOOD INTOLERANCE?

A food intolerance is an adverse reaction to a particular kind of food, possibly due to a lack of particular enzymes needed to digest the food, an inability to absorb certain foods, or a reaction to a chemical in the food. Common intolerances include lactose intolerance (an inability to digest lactose in dairy products), gluten intolerance (a sensitivity to gluten, a protein found in wheat and other grains) and salicylate intolerance (an adverse response to salicylate, a chemical that occurs naturally in some foods). A food intolerance is not the same as a food allergy (▶165), which provokes an adverse response of the immune system.

CUSTOM DIET *A wide range of gluten-free foodstuffs is now available for people who suffer from gluten intolerance.*

much more, notably active teenagers and those doing heavy manual labour. The actual intake of food varies significantly from person to person and around the world. People in Western nations generally consume more than 12,550 kJ (3000 kilocalories), whereas in some poor African countries the average daily intake is less than 6700 kJ (1600 kilocalories).

REGULAR FEAST *This US family's special dinner of many dishes is a sharp contrast.*

WHY DOES OVEREATING MAKE YOU FAT?

Your digestive system absorbs all the food that you eat. If you eat more than you need, your body stores the surplus as fat. It is useful to have some body fat, as it provides an extra source of energy, but too much will make you overweight and can lead to health problems, such as heart disease and type 2 diabetes. Today, more people are overweight than ever before, mainly because food is more readily available and people are generally less active than in the past.

DOES THE APPEARANCE OF FOOD MATTER?

Good food smells nice, but it has to look appetising, too. You can test this by dyeing a favourite food an unusual colour, such as blue (few natural foods are blue), and then trying to eat it. It's likely to be much less enjoyable – or even left untouched!

FOOD AND NUTRITION CONTINUED

GOOD GREEN
Spinach is rich in vitamin C and folic acid.

HOW MUCH DO WE NEED OF EACH VITAMIN AND MINERAL?

The daily consumption of vitamins and minerals advised by medical authorities is referred to as the RDI (recommended dietary intake) or AI (adequate intake). It is usually expressed in milligrams (mg) or micrograms (mcg) – a milligram is one-thousandth of a gram, and a microgram is one-thousandth of a milligram. Suitable intakes for older people will vary.

WHAT DO VITAMINS DO?

Vitamins are organic substances essential to health. With the exception of vitamin D and niacin, the body cannot manufacture vitamins, so it must obtain them from food. Fat-soluble vitamins can be stored by the body, but water-soluble ones cannot and therefore must be obtained daily.

VITAMIN DEFICIENCY Curved leg bones (rickets) are one side effect of not having enough vitamin D.

FAT-SOLUBLE VITAMINS

VITAMIN	SUITABLE INTAKE (MEN/WOMEN)	SOURCES	FUNCTIONS
A (retinol)	900 mcg/700 mcg	Fish liver oils, leafy greens, egg yolk, dairy products	Promotes bone growth, healthy skin; protects eyes
D	5 mcg/5 mcg	Dairy products, cereals, fish oil, egg yolk; made by skin when skin is exposed to sunlight	Strengthens bones and teeth, promotes healthy nerve and muscle function, assists blood clotting
E	10 mg/7 mg	Vegetable oils, leafy vegetables, wholegrain foods, eggs, fish, liver	Aids production of red blood cells, protects cells from damaging chemicals
K	70 mcg/60 mcg	Leafy greens, potatoes, wheat germ, egg yolk, pork, liver; bacteria in gut	Vital for healthy bones and blood clotting

WATER-SOLUBLE VITAMINS

VITAMIN	SUITABLE INTAKE (MEN/WOMEN)	SOURCES	FUNCTIONS
B1 (thiamine)	1.2 mg/1.1 mg	Bread, meat, peas, beans, nuts	Supports nerve and muscle function
B2 (riboflavin)	1.1 mg/1.1 mg	Dairy products, leafy vegetables, peas, beans, meat, eggs, milk, cheese	Maintains healthy mucous membranes and skin
B3 (niacin)	16 mg/14 mg	Fruits, meat, eggs, fish, nuts, peas, beans	Maintains nerves, digestive system, skin; aids production of sex hormones
Pantothenic acid	6 mg/4 mg	Green vegetables, peanuts, liver, wholegrain cereals; also made by bacteria in gut	Maintains skin and nervous system; aids production of sex hormones
B6 (pyridoxine)	1.3 mg/1.3 mg	Meat, fish, liver, dairy products, fruits, vegetables	Aids production of red blood cells and antibodies; maintains healthy skin
Biotin	30 mcg/25 mcg	Eggs, liver, kidneys; also made by bacteria in gut	Assists cell growth and function
Folate	400 mcg/400 mcg	Leafy vegetables, wholegrain foods, peas and beans, nuts	Aids DNA and red blood cell production; maintains nervous system
B12	2.4 mcg/2.4 mcg	Meat, fish, dairy products, eggs	Aids red blood cell production and maintains nervous system
Choline	550 mg/425 mg	Milk, liver, eggs, peanuts, cell membranes	Used by nervous system to make chemical messengers
C (ascorbic acid)	45 mg/45 mg	Citrus fruits, capsicums, potatoes, tomatoes, blackcurrants	Promotes growth and healthy bones and teeth; helps fight off infection

WHAT DO MINERALS DO?

Minerals are inorganic substances that are essential for good health. They cannot be made by the body, so they must be obtained from food. Minerals needed in tiny amounts are known as trace minerals.

BUILDING UP *Dairy products, such as cheeses, are a good source of calcium, which helps build strong bones and teeth.*

MINERALS

MINERAL	SUITABLE INTAKE (MEN/WOMEN)	SOURCES	FUNCTIONS
Calcium	1000 mg/1000 mg	Dairy products, green vegetables, nuts, fish, eggs	Helps build strong bones and teeth; assists with blood clotting
Magnesium	400 mg/215 mg	Green vegetables, meat, milk, fish, peas, beans, nuts, wholegrain foods	Essential for healthy teeth and bones, efficient muscle and nerve function
Phosphorus	1000 mg/1000 mg	Dairy products, meat, fish, eggs, green vegetables, fruits, nuts, wholegrain foods	Promotes strong bones and teeth; production of DNA, healthy cell, nerve and muscle function
Potassium	3800 mg/2800 mg	Bread and wholegrain cereals, green vegetables, beans, fruits	Vital for nerve function, muscle contraction
Sodium	460–920 mg/ 460–920 mg	Salt, many other foods	Maintains water balance in body, nerve function
Sulfur	No RDI/AI set	Meat, eggs, dairy products	Helps make proteins, including insulin

TRACE MINERALS

MINERAL	SUITABLE INTAKE (MEN/WOMEN)	SOURCES	FUNCTIONS
Chromium	35 mcg/25 mcg	Meat, liver, dairy products, wholegrain foods, yeast, fruits, nuts	Helps break down carbohydrates and adjust blood sugar
Copper	1.7 mg/1.2 mg	Meat, liver, fish, seafood, green vegetables, wholegrain cereals	Vital for many chemical reactions
Fluoride	4 mg/3 mg	Fish, seafood, tea, fluoridated water	Promotes strong bones and teeth; prevents tooth decay
Iodine	150 mcg/150 mcg	Sea fish, seafood, seaweed, iodised table salt	Used by thyroid gland to make hormones
Iron	8 mg/18 mg	Red meat, liver, green vegetables, nuts, eggs	Helps make oxygen-carrying molecules in red blood cells
Manganese	5.5 mg/5 mg	Meat, wholegrain foods, nuts, tea, coffee	Makes enzymes, which speed up chemical reactions
Molybdenum	45 mcg/45 mcg	Liver, barley, pulses, buckwheat	Important constituent of many enzymes
Selenium	70 mcg/60 mcg	Fish, seafood, dairy products, meat, Brazil nuts, wholegrain foods	Protects cells; aids sexual development
Zinc	14 mg/8 mg	Meat, liver, eggs, fish, cereals, beans, nuts	Supports cell growth, sperm production; constituent of many enzymes

DANGER SIGN *A bloated stomach can be caused by a lack of protein in the diet.*

WHAT IS MALNUTRITION?

Malnutrition is a medical condition caused by a diet that is lacking certain nutrients or contains nutrients in inappropriate proportions. Mostly it is a result of under-nutrition – a lack of food, in other words. Roughly 842 million people around the world, mainly in developing nations, do not get enough to eat and malnutrition causes the deaths of more than 3 million children under five each year. However, malnutrition is also a feature of Western diets and can be the result of an excess intake of some nutrients, such as sugars and fats – which causes obesity – or a lack of particular micronutrients, such as vitamins.

BOOSTING GROWTH *A major source of iron, red meat promotes the development of new cells.*

MEDICAL DIAGNOSIS

While it's easy to recognise the signs of a cold, most other illnesses are harder to identify. Doctors make use of a range of techniques and tests, as well as their own experience, to determine the source of an illness or condition. Some of these tests are simple and can be undertaken in the doctor's consulting rooms. Others require more complex equipment or a more detailed analysis, and, consequently, a visit to a specialist or a hospital.

WHAT DOES A DOCTOR DETECT WITH A STETHOSCOPE?

A stethoscope detects the sounds made by the heart, blood rushing through arteries, and air moving in and out of the lungs. Unusual sounds can help the doctor pinpoint medical problems. For example, when the heart beats, it makes two particular sounds a split-second apart. These sounds are produced by the closing of valves that prevent blood flowing the wrong way. If a person's heart is making other sounds, it may indicate that their heart valves are not working properly. If someone's lungs are making wheezing sounds when they breathe, it often indicates that they have a lung infection.

HEART SOUNDS *A graph of a single heartbeat. The first sound is made after the heart has filled with blood; the second when it empties.*

HOW DO DOCTORS SEE INSIDE THE BODY?

Doctors can see inside the body using various types of scans. X-rays travel straight through the soft parts of the body, but are blocked by hard substances, such as bone. A CT or CAT (computerised axial tomography) scanner takes a series of X-rays from different directions, which are then combined to provide a 3D image. An MRI (magnetic resonance imaging) scanner creates a magnetic field around the body then scans it with radio waves. An ultrasound scanner bombards the body with soundwaves, which bounce back to create a picture of what is inside. Nuclear medicine scans involve injecting radioactive material into the body, where it collects in diseased tissue and then gives off radiation that can be detected by a special camera.

WINDOWS ON THE BODY *Since the late 1800s, scientists have developed a range of ways of seeing inside the body.*

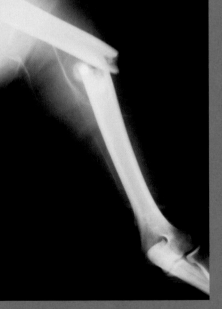

1895: X-RAYS First made by Austrian scientist Wilhelm Röntgen in 1895. X-rays can reveal fractures, bone disease and foreign bodies.

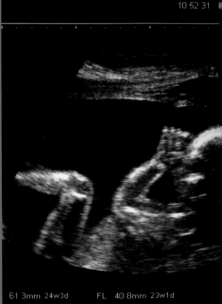

1950: ULTRASOUND Echoing soundwaves create two-dimensional images of soft internal tissue, including babies in their mothers' wombs.

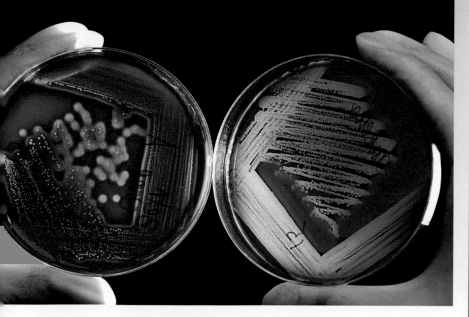

SPOTTING THE CULPRIT When grown in a petri dish, bacteria can be identified by the shape and colour of their colonies.

WHY DO DOCTORS TAP YOUR KNEES?

This test checks your reflexes. A tap against your knee stretches a tendon there, and the tendon pulls on a muscle in your thigh. If your reflexes are working, the thigh muscle reacts by contracting, which makes your leg give a kick. If your leg does not kick, there may be something wrong with your nervous system.

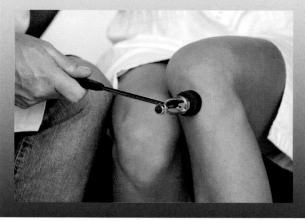

HOW DO DOCTORS DIAGNOSE AN INFECTION?

If a doctor thinks you have an infection, he or she can employ a range of tests to identify it. Suitable samples may include blood, urine, sputum, faeces or swabs of the skin, nose or throat. A sample can be examined in a variety of ways, including testing for bacterial or viral DNA (▶168) or attempting to grow any bacteria present in a petri dish, then studying the results under a microscope.

fast fact

One of the first diagnostic X-rays to be taken, in 1896, was of a child who had swallowed a tiny model bicycle. The X-ray showed the bicycle stuck in the child's throat.

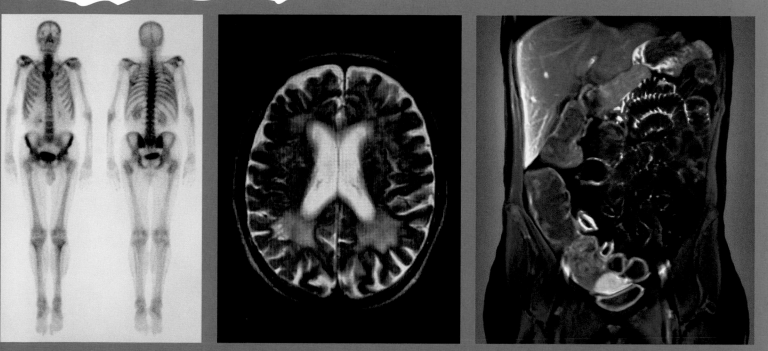

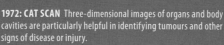

1950s: NUCLEAR MEDICINE SCAN These scans are especially useful for detecting bone ailments, including stress fractures, infections and cancers.

1972: CAT SCAN Three-dimensional images of organs and body cavities are particularly helpful in identifying tumours and other signs of disease or injury.

1980: MRI SCAN This type of scan distinguishes all types of tissue, from soft tissues to tooth enamel. This image has been artificially coloured to highlight particular organs.

MEDICAL TREATMENT

Once a doctor has made a diagnosis of an illness or injury, he or she can decide what kind of treatment is needed to deal with the problem.

Many illnesses can be cured with a course of drugs. Bruises, cuts and broken bones, on the other hand, are usually treated simply by helping the body repair itself.

HOW DO DRUGS REACH THEIR TARGET?

To do its job, a drug has to reach the parts of the body where it is needed. Many painkillers and antibiotics can travel through the lining of the stomach and into the blood, so they can be taken in the form of pills or medicine. If a drug needs to reach its target more quickly, it may be injected directly into that area. Other methods include using patches on the skin (as with nicotine patches) and inhalers to reach the lungs.

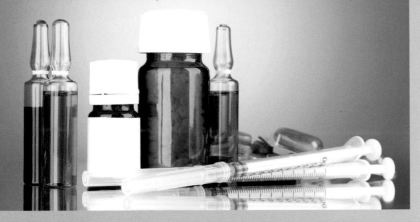

WHAT ARE ANTIBIOTICS?

An antibiotic is a drug that kills bacteria without damaging body cells. The first antibiotic to be used, called penicillin, was discovered in 1928. Most antibiotics work by preventing bacteria from building up their cell walls, so that they collapse and eventually die. Some antibiotics are effective against a small range of bacteria; others, notably penicillin, destroy many different kinds. Antibiotics cannot kill viruses, however, which is why they cannot cure a cold or flu.

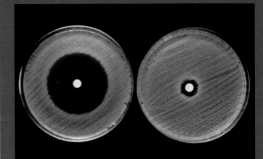

CAVING IN These bacteria cells have collapsed as a result of the action of antibiotics.

fast fact
One of the most useful antibiotics, called cephalosporin, was first discovered in fungi that were growing in water mixed with sewage.

HOW DOES IMMUNISATION WORK?

Immunisation, also known as vaccination, is a way of preventing the spread of infectious diseases. It works by triggering the immune system, so that it can stop a particular infection taking hold. To do this, the body has to be given a vaccine that makes the immune system react without actually allowing the disease to start. The most common way of doing this involves injecting dead or weakened viruses that have been altered to make them harmless. Once the immune system detects these cells in the blood, the immune system learns to identify them and can then fight off the harmful forms as well.

EARLY PREVENTION Young children are now routinely given a range of vaccinations to stop them contracting major diseases. Some immunisations are also vital for elderly people.

WHAT IS COMPLEMENTARY MEDICINE?

In addition to mainstream medical treatments, a wide range of traditional and alternative treatments are available, ranging from acupuncture to herbal remedies. When these are used in conjunction with conventional treatments, the overall approach is known as complementary medicine. Some alternative therapies, such as acupuncture, have been in use for hundreds of years. Others, such as osteopathy and chiropractic – which both involve making sure that bones and joints are in their correct positions – were developed more recently.

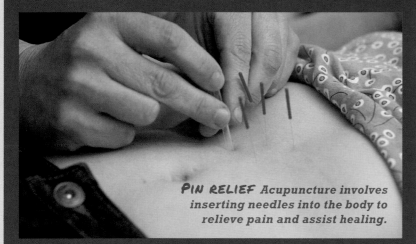

PIN RELIEF *Acupuncture involves inserting needles into the body to relieve pain and assist healing.*

HOW DO YOU TREAT A CUT?

The body has a remarkable ability to self-heal. When skin is cut, for example, cells and chemicals in the body immediately trigger blood clotting, which seals the wound and allows the cut to start healing almost immediately (▶147). But if a cut is long, deep or bleeding profusely, it may need to be more quickly sealed using stitches, or sutures. Some sutures have to be removed once the cut has healed, but many types are now absorbable, meaning that they are made of natural materials that slowly break down before being absorbed by the body.

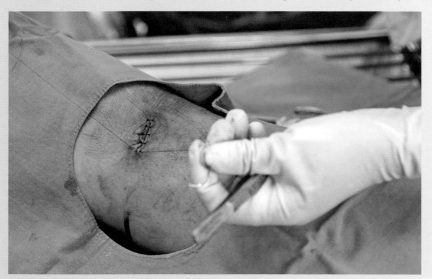

HOW DO YOU MEND A BROKEN BONE?

Bone fractures can generally repair themselves – immediately after the break, blood fills the fracture and is slowly replaced by cartilage, which is in turn replaced by bone. But to make sure the bone heals straight it is often encased in a plaster cast, especially if it is a limb bone.

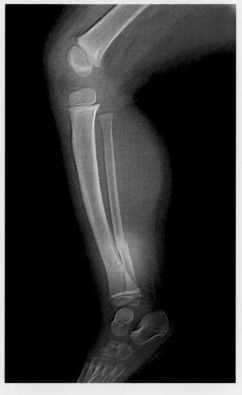

GREENSTICK FRACTURE *With this kind of fracture, which is common in children, one side of the bone is cracked and the other side is bent.*

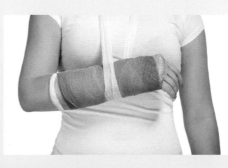

REPAIRED ARM *Plaster protects the arm until the damage is repaired, usually within about six weeks.*

MEDICAL TREATMENT CONTINUED

If an illness or injury is severe, a doctor may recommend surgery. Thanks to modern technology, such as lasers and surgical microscopes, surgeons can repair skin, bones and blood vessels, and even components, such as nerve endings, that are too small to be seen with the naked eye. They can also carry out surgery through tiny incisions, and replace a wide range of body parts.

WHAT GOES ON IN AN OPERATING THEATRE?

A number of people are always present in a theatre during major surgery. They include the surgeon and his or her surgical assistant; one or more theatre nurses to prepare instruments and hand them to the surgeon; an anaesthetist to administer the anaesthetic and then monitor the patient's breathing and heart rate during the operation; and, in the case of heart surgery, a perfusionist, who monitors the heart–lung machine that oxygenates and pumps the patient's blood during surgery.

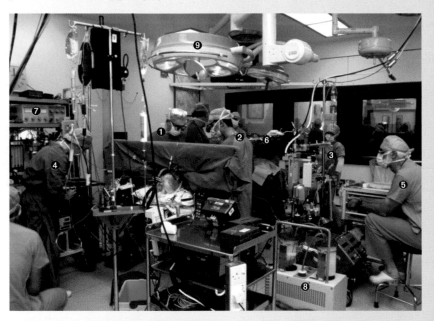

❶ Surgeon
❷ Surgical assistant
❸ Theatre nurse
❹ Anaesthetist
❺ Profusionist
❻ Instrument trolley
❼ Anaesthetic trolley
❽ Heart–lung machine
❾ Light source

HOW DO SURGEONS STOP BLEEDING?

When using traditional scalpels, surgeons prevent bleeding by fastening clamps to any cut arteries or veins. Before the operation is over, the cut ends are sewn together again so that blood can flow once more. If a patient does bleed during an operation, they can be given extra blood, called a blood transfusion, to make up for the blood they have lost.

LIGHT KNIFE *This surgeon is using a laser scalpel to operate on a patient's eye.*

HOW DO SURGEONS MAKE INCISIONS?

Surgeons still use traditional scalpels, with super-sharp metal or ceramic blades, for most operations. However, they also use high-tech versions for some procedures. Consisting of an intense beam of light, a laser scalpel cuts by generating heat in body tissues; at the same time the heat cauterises severed blood vessels, so it minimises bleeding. A laser scalpel can also be used to 'weld' delicate parts back together. A plasma knife creates intense miniature shockwaves that slice through tissue and also cauterise it at the same time. Such a cut is even easier to close than one formed by laser surgery, so plasma knives are increasingly used for complicated surgery on delicate tissue, such as the brain or eyes.

WHAT IS KEYHOLE SURGERY?

Modern instruments allow surgeons to operate on patients through holes not much bigger than a keyhole – hence the term 'keyhole surgery'. Normally this involves the use of an endoscope, a thin tube fitted with an eyepiece, lenses and a light, which together allow the surgeon to see inside a patient's body. Miniature tools, including tiny scalpels and tweezers, are passed down the centre of the endoscope and operated by remote control.

Endoscope

WHICH BODY PARTS CAN BE REPLACED WITH ARTIFICIAL ONES?

The list of artificial replacement body parts is always growing. It already includes teeth, hip joints, knee joints and heart valves, as well as the lenses in the eyes and entire prosthetic limbs. Sensors in artificial limbs can even pick up nerve impulses from the body and use them to trigger movement. Another remarkable recent development is the use of replacement body parts made by 3D printers – machines that lay down thin layers of a material, such as a plastic or metal alloy, which are then fused to create a three-dimensional object.

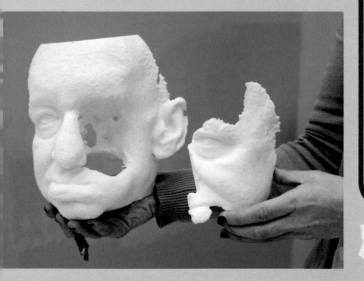

PROSTHETIC FACE *Using a 3D printer, doctors created this nylon-plastic replica of a section of a cancer patient's face to conceal a hole left by radical surgery.*

WHICH ORGANS AND TISSUES CAN BE TRANSPLANTED?

Many body parts, if damaged or functioning badly, can be replaced with healthy specimens from a donor. They include organs, such as the heart, lungs, liver, kidneys and pancreas, as well as arteries, tendons, bone, bone marrow, skin and corneas. A transplant operation involves connecting the blood vessels and nerves in the replacement body part to those in the patient's body. The more nerves and blood vessels there are, and the smaller they are, the harder they are to connect. Hearts are not the most difficult organs to transplant, because their arteries are large; livers are more complicated because they have numerous blood vessels that can be difficult for a surgeon to reach. Recent advances in this field of medicine have included the first successful transplants of hands, legs and arms, and even faces.

LIFE GIFT *Organs must be transplanted soon after their removal from the donor's body to limit time without a constant blood supply. They are kept at 4°C (39°F) in an ice-filled esky during that time.*

fast fact

Before the introduction of anaesthetics, surgeons had to be speedy. In the early 1800s, Scottish surgeon Robert Liston became famous for being able to amputate a limb in less than 30 seconds.

HUMAN BODY RECORDS

The human body is an amazing organism. All sorts of extraordinary things are going on inside your body and everyone else's every day. But, either as a result of chance or design, certain individuals stand out from the crowd for record-breaking body attributes.

WHICH ARE THE BIGGEST KINDS OF BODY CELLS?

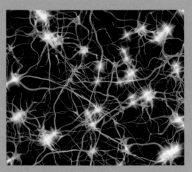

Your body is made up of about 75,000 billion (or 75 trillion) cells, and produces about 300 billion cells a day. The longest cells are nerve cells, some of which can stretch for 1 m (3$\frac{1}{3}$ ft); however, they are so slender that they are invisible to the naked eye. The bulkiest cells are egg cells, which develop into babies if fertilised. These are over 0.1 mm ($\frac{1}{250}$ in) across, just big enough to be visible.

CELL TO CELL *This artist's impression shows brain signals passing between nerve cells.*

WHICH CELLS LIVE THE SHORTEST AND LONGEST?

The shortest-lived cells are ones that make up the lining of the mouth, stomach and intestines. On average, these last for just three days before they wear out and are replaced. Nerve cells, on the other hand, are formed before we are even born and should last a whole lifetime.

WHICH ARE THE STRONGEST AND WEAKEST BONES?

The strongest bone in the human body is the thigh bone, or femur. Together with the tibia in the lower leg, it carries much of the body's weight when you are upright. Other strong bones include those that protect the brain – although thin, they are remarkably tough. The weakest bones are inside the head, around the air spaces behind the nose. These bones are paper-thin but are protected by the rest of the skull.

HARD HAT *A head X-ray reveals the bones of the face and cranium.*

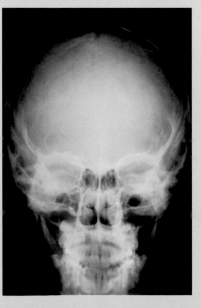

TWO EXTREMES *Sultan Kösen in 2010 with the then shortest man, He Pingping.*

WHAT IS THE TALLEST ANYONE HAS GROWN?

The tallest person ever was American Robert Wadlow (1918–40), who reached a height of just over 272 cm (8 ft 11 in). The tallest person alive today is Sultan Kösen of Turkey, who stands 251 cm (8 ft 3 in) tall.

WHICH ARE THE BUSIEST MUSCLES?

Your eye muscles are the busiest in your body. Even when you think your eyes are still, these muscles make them flicker dozens of times a second. This flickering constantly changes the pattern of light inside the eye and without this movement, the things you see would quickly fade.

fast fact
Your eyes blink more than 14,000 times a day and about 400 million times in an average lifetime.

WHAT IS THE LONGEST ANYONE HAS GROWN THEIR FINGERNAILS?

Melvin Boothe, who died in 2009, had fingernails with a total length of 9.85 m (32 ft 3¾ in). The longest nails on a woman belonged to American Lee Redmond. They measured a total of 8.65 m (28 ft 4½ in) – before they were unfortunately broken off in a car crash in 2009.

FROM SCRATCH Lee Redmond displays her record-breaking fingernails.

WHICH ARE THE BIGGEST MUSCLES?

Your biggest muscle is the gluteus maximus, a pair of which forms your bottom. The body's longest muscle is the sartorius, which runs from the outside edge of the hip to the inside of the knee. It can be over 300 times longer than the shortest muscle, the stapedius, which is attached to the stirrup bone (stapes) inside the ear.

WHAT IS THE HEAVIEST WEIGHT A HUMAN CAN LIFT?

At the 2000 Sydney Olympics, super heavyweight weightlifter Hossein Rezazadeh raised 212.5 kg (468 lb) in the snatch event and 260 kg (573 lb) in the clean and jerk, giving the highest combined total ever recorded in this sport, 472.5 kg (1042 lb).

GOING UP Hossein Rezazadeh during his world-record lift in Sydney

WHO HAS THE WORLD'S LONGEST HAIR?

The longest head hair ever recorded belongs to Xie Qiuping of China. When measured in 2004, it was 5.627 m (18 ft 5½ in). At that point, Xie had not cut her hair since 1973, when she was 13.

SCIENCE AND TECHNOLOGY

ATOMS AND MOLECULES

WHAT IS AN ATOM?

An atom is the smallest particle of an element that can take part in a chemical reaction. Atoms are so tiny that 10 million of them lined up would measure just 1 mm ($\frac{1}{25}$ in). All atoms consist of a nucleus made up of particles, called protons and neutrons. Protons have a positive electrical charge and neutrons have no charge, so the nucleus has a positive charge. Around the nucleus orbit much smaller particles, called electrons. These have a negative charge and are held in place by the attraction between their charge and the nucleus's positive charge. The numbers of protons and electrons are equal, so an atom has no overall charge.

ATOMIC IDENTITY *It is the number of protons in the nucleus that determines the type of element.*

CARBON ATOM The nucleus contains six protons and six neutrons; six electrons orbit in two layers, or shells.

SULFUR ATOM The nucleus contains 16 protons and 16 neutrons; 16 electrons orbit in 3 shells.

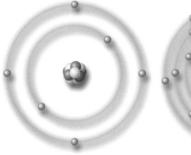

NATURAL SHADE *In one of its pure states, the element sulfur forms bright yellow crystals.*

The building blocks of all matter are called atoms. These are the smallest part of an element (▶70) – such as carbon or oxygen – that is recognisable as that element. Different kinds of atoms join to form molecules, in turn creating the vast variety of substances and materials around us, ranging from rocks to wood to water and plastics. Atoms themselves are made up of even smaller units called subatomic particles.

IS THERE ANYTHING SMALLER THAN AN ATOM?

Protons, neutrons and electrons are called 'subatomic particles', because they are smaller than atoms. In total, physicists have discovered more than 200 types of subatomic particles. Most, including protons and neutrons, are actually composite particles called hadrons, made up of pairs or triplets of particles called quarks. Many physicists believe that all particles are actually vibrations of line-like or loop-like units called strings.

DIGGING DEEPER *Just as the nucleus is composed of protons and neutrons, so those particles are themselves composed of even smaller particles.*

ELECTRONS Unlike protons and neutrons, electrons are fundamental, or elementary, particles. That means they are not made up of smaller particles.

NUCLEUS An atom's nucleus contains most of its mass.

PROTONS AND NEUTRONS The nucleus consists of both protons and neutrons.

QUARKS Each proton and neutron is in turn made up of three quarks. A neutron has two 'down' quarks and one 'up' quark; a proton has two 'up' quarks and one 'down' quark.

fast fact

Atoms consist mainly of empty space. If the protons and neutrons were the size of tennis balls, the electrons would be smaller than pinheads and the atom would be thousands of metres in diameter.

WHAT ARE MOLECULES?

Atoms of different elements readily bond together. The result is what we call a compound. Many compounds exist as small units called molecules. For example, if two hydrogen atoms bond with one oxygen atom, they form a water molecule. Any compound can be represented as a chemical formula that indicates the proportions of the atoms of the different elements. So the formula for water, H_2O, tells you that water contains two hydrogen atoms for every one oxygen atom. Likewise, the formula for sulfuric acid, H_2SO_4, indicates that this substance contains hydrogen, sulfur and oxygen in the proportions 2:1:4.

LINKING UP *Groups of atoms bond together to form molecules.*

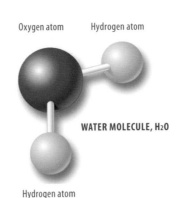

Oxygen atom   Hydrogen atom

WATER MOLECULE, H_2O

Hydrogen atom

SULFURIC ACID MOLECULE, H_2SO_4

Hydrogen atom

Oxygen atom

Sulfur atom

PURE FORM *Copper is one of the relatively few elements that is readily found in its pure state, rather than mixed with other elements.*

FLOWING METAL *Mercury is the only metal that forms a liquid at room temperature.*

WHY ARE SOME SUBSTANCES HEAVIER THAN OTHERS?

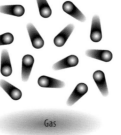

An object's mass depends on what kinds of atoms or molecules it consists of and how closely they are packed together. For example, polystyrene foam has light atoms and well-spaced molecules. Lead, on the other hand, has heavy atoms, tightly packed together. As a result, lead is much more dense than polystyrene, and weighs 2000 times as much as the same volume of polystyrene.

HOW CAN SUBSTANCES EXIST IN DIFFERENT STATES?

All elements, and many compounds, can exist as solids, liquids or gases, depending on temperature and pressure. Liquid water, for example, freezes to a solid (ice) and evaporates to form a gas (water vapour). In ice, there are bonds between the water molecules, which make the material hard. Heating ice weakens the bonds and the molecules start to drift apart, turning the ice into liquid water. If you keep heating the water, the molecules move faster and faster, until they escape from each other, into the air, forming vapour. As the vapour cools, water molecules collect together, forming a cloud of droplets called steam.

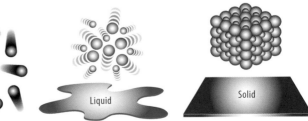

Gas   Liquid   Solid

DIFFERENT STATES *Cooling or heating water changes its state.*

FORCE AND MOTION

A force is an invisible push or pull, the effects of which can be seen or felt. Forces cause objects that are free to move to start or stop moving, or change their direction or speed. And they cause objects that are not free to move to stretch, bend, twist or change shape.

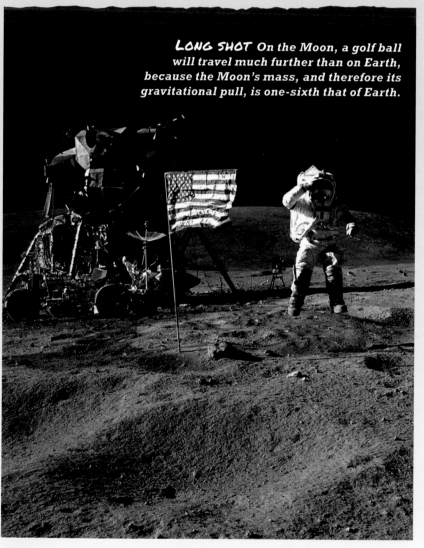

LONG SHOT *On the Moon, a golf ball will travel much further than on Earth, because the Moon's mass, and therefore its gravitational pull, is one-sixth that of Earth.*

WHAT IS GRAVITY?

Gravity is usually thought of as the force that pulls objects down towards Earth's surface. So, if you throw a ball in the air, gravity is the force that makes it fall back to Earth – and keeps your feet planted firmly on the ground. But, in fact, all objects exert a gravitational pull on each other – including, in this example, you and the ball. The gravitational pull of an object depends on its mass, however, and can usually only be measured where an object has a very large mass, like Earth or the Moon.

WHAT'S THE DIFFERENCE BETWEEN MASS AND WEIGHT?

Weight is the force experienced by an object under the effect of gravity. Though your weight is always the same on Earth, it would be one-sixth that weight if you were on the Moon, due to the Moon's gravity being one-sixth that of Earth's. Mass, on the other hand, is the amount of matter an object contains, independent of the force of gravity – in other words, your mass is the same on Earth and on the Moon. Scientists measure mass using grams, kilograms and tonnes (or, in the imperial system, ounces, pounds and tons), and force in newtons (or in the imperial system, pound-force). In daily life we can use the same measurement for mass and weight because they are virtually the same everywhere on Earth.

APPLE MASS *A 1 kg (2 lb) bag of apples has a mass of 1 kg (2 lb). Scientists would record its weight in newtons as 9.8 N. On the Moon, the bag would still have a mass of 1 kg (2 lb), but its weight would be 1.6 N.*

fast fact

In a vacuum, where there is no air resistance, a falling ping-pong ball accelerates at the same rate as a huge boulder.

WHAT IS INERTIA?

Inertia is the tendency of an object to resist any change in its stationary state or steady motion. The greater the mass of an object, the greater its inertia. So it takes a strong push to get a heavy object, such as a broken-down car, to move. Once it is going, the car's inertia will tend to keep it moving in a straight line.

WHAT IS FRICTION?

Friction is the force that slows the motion of a solid body moving across another surface. The rougher the surface and the greater the area of the solid body in contact with the surface, the greater the force of friction. Air resistance is friction between moving objects and air molecules.

LEAST RESISTANCE *Slippery surfaces, such as snow and ice, generate little friction, so bobsleds move at high speed, unpowered.*

WHAT IS MOMENTUM?

Momentum is an object's mass multiplied by its velocity (speed in a particular direction). So, the more massive an object is, and the faster it is moving, the greater its momentum and the greater the force required to halt it. When you are travelling in a car at speed, the car and you (and any other objects in the car) have momentum. If the car stops suddenly, your momentum will still propel you forwards rapidly. Seat belts apply the force required to bring you safely to a halt.

FORCE TRANSFER *When two objects collide, momentum is transferred. On a pool table, for example, if one ball hits another and the first one stops, the other absorbs all the momentum. If both balls continue to move, they have shared the momentum.*

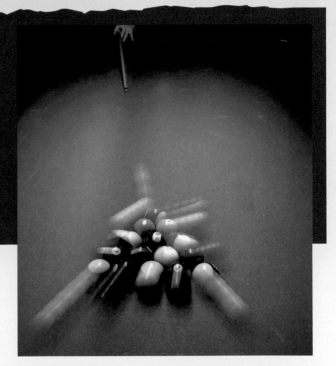

HOW DO FORCES AFFECT US?

Riding a bike is a good way to experience and learn about forces, as they constantly affect your progress. For instance, you are constantly experiencing friction – between the ground and your tyres, between parts of the bike, and in the form of air resistance.

AGAINST GRAVITY *Going uphill you have to pedal hard to counteract the effects of gravity and friction.*

HELPING HAND *Going downhill, gravity makes you go faster. You keep speeding up until friction matches the pull of gravity.*

STANDING START *On a level surface you have to push hard on the pedals to overcome the bike's inertia and get it going.*

TO A HALT *On flat ground, even if you don't brake, friction and air resistance will eventually bring you to a halt.*

ENERGY

Energy is the capacity to do work – or, in other words, to make things happen. There are many forms of energy, including light, heat, sound and electricity. All energy derives originally from the Big Bang (▶8), the immense burst of energy that created the Universe. This energy is still around because when we use energy it is not used up or destroyed but simply changed into another form. For example, when we turn on a light we change electrical energy to light energy, and when we run a car we convert chemical energy stored in the fuel into movement, noise and heat.

HOW HOT OR COLD CAN THINGS BECOME?

There is no limit to how hot things can become, but if something becomes extremely cold, its atoms stop moving. It cannot get any colder. Scientists have come close to reaching this temperature, called absolute zero, at –273.15°C (–459.67°F). Near absolute zero, matter starts to behave in strange ways. Some gases turn into metals, and some metals become 'superconductors'. This means that electricity (▶198) can flow through them for ever, without needing any energy from outside.

HOT AND COLD *Certain temperatures trigger changes of energy or state.*

4 trillion°C (7.2 trillion°F)	Hottest temperature ever generated
15 million°C (27 million°F)	Centre of the Sun
30,000°C (54,000°F)	Inside a lightning bolt
5500°C (9930°F)	Surface of the Sun
5000°C (9000°F)	Hottest flame
1535°C (2795°F)	Iron melts
184°C (363°F)	Paper catches fire
100°C (212°F)	Water boils
37°C (98.6°F)	Human body temperature
0°C (32°F)	Water freezes
–89.2°C (–128.6°F)	Lowest temperature ever recorded on Earth
–200°C (–328°F)	Air becomes liquid
–273.15°C (–459.67°F)	Absolute zero

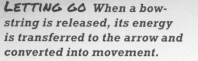

LETTING GO *When a bowstring is released, its energy is transferred to the arrow and converted into movement.*

WHAT IS POTENTIAL ENERGY?

Potential energy is energy stored in an object because of the object's position or shape – for example, a weight raised off the ground, a car sitting at the top of a hill, a compressed spring or a pulled bowstring. When released, potential energy converts into kinetic energy, the energy of movement.

fast fact

The hottest temperature ever created in a laboratory, of 4 trillion°C (7.2 trillion°F), was achieved at the Brookhaven National Laboratory near New York in 2010 by smashing subatomic particles together.

WHAT IS HEAT?

An object's temperature is related to the kinetic energy of its atoms and molecules (▶186). The hotter an object gets, the faster its atoms or molecules move. Heat is the transfer of energy from a hotter to a colder object. Things feel hot when some of their energy enters your skin; they feel cold when energy flows from you to them. Heat energy can be used to do work. In a car engine, for example, heat causes gases to expand, pushing on pistons that ultimately turn the wheels.

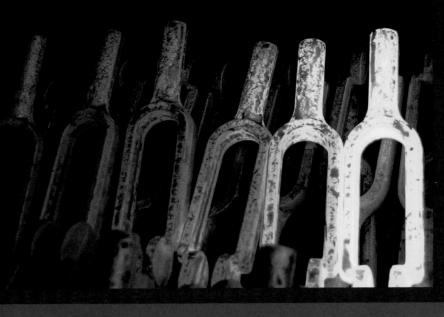

HEAT TO LIGHT *When atoms are very hot they give out light, converting their kinetic energy to light energy. First they glow dull red then bright orange, yellow, white and, finally, blue.*

IN WHAT OTHER FORMS DOES ENERGY EXIST?

Light is a visible form of electromagnetic energy (▶192). Sound energy takes the form of alternating waves of high and low pressure (▶196). Chemical energy is the energy stored in chemical compounds, such as the fuel in an aircraft's tanks. Electrical energy derives from the forces between electric charges, while nuclear energy is locked in the nuclei of atoms and released as heat and electromagnetic energy by nuclear reactions (▶241).

JET FUEL *Burning fuel in a jet engine converts the energy into heat, which is in turn converted by the aircraft's engine into kinetic energy, light and sound.*

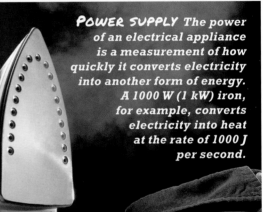

POWER SUPPLY *The power of an electrical appliance is a measurement of how quickly it converts electricity into another form of energy. A 1000 W (1 kW) iron, for example, converts electricity into heat at the rate of 1000 J per second.*

HOW DO WE MEASURE ENERGY?

Energy is measured in units called joules (J) and kilojoules (kJ). The latter unit is also used to quantify the energy content of foods (▶172). Gas and electricity bills often measure usage in kilowatt hours (kWh) – 1 kWh is the equivalent of 3.6 million joules. The work done by energy is also measured in joules and kilojoules. Power is a measurement of how quickly work is done – in other words, the rate at which energy is converted into another form. It is measured in watts (W), with 1 W being the conversion of 1 J in one second. So power equals the amount of work (J) divided by the number of seconds.

LIGHT AND COLOUR

Light is the only kind of energy that we can see, and it is what allows us to see our world.

Light moves about a million times faster than sound, and can travel through a vacuum (empty space). It moves in straight lines, but many things reflect it, causing it to change course and move in different directions. As it passes through certain materials, light may bend, or refract, and even be split into its constituent colours – what we call the spectrum.

WHAT IS LIGHT MADE OF?

Light is a form of electromagnetic radiation that forms waves or vibrations in space. We can't touch it or pick it up, but we can see it. White light is made up of a range of colours, each of which has a slightly different rate of vibration (frequency) and wavelength. Different objects and materials reflect light in different ways and at different wavelengths; the colour sensors in the retinas in our eyes interpret these signals and produce the huge range of colours we see in our brain (▶154).

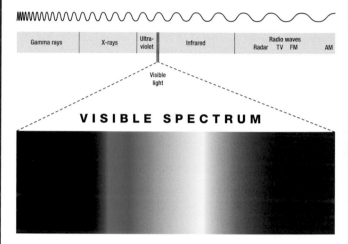

VISIBLE WAVES *Light is part of the electromagnetic spectrum, a whole family of waves that includes X-rays, microwaves and radio waves (▶200).*

WHAT SURFACES REFLECT LIGHT BEST?

Pale-coloured surfaces reflect light more than dark ones. Rough surfaces scatter light in all directions, while flat polished surfaces reflect light rays more directly and evenly, thereby creating a mirror image. Transparent objects such as glass let light shine through them, while opaque ones block the light and cast a shadow.

MIRROR IMAGE *Metals reflect light particularly well. So modern mirrors usually consist of a dark backing, a thin film of a highly reflective metal, such as silver or aluminium, and a sheet of glass to protect the metal without distorting its reflection.*

HOW FAST DOES LIGHT TRAVEL?

Nothing moves faster than light, which travels at 299,792 km (186,287 miles) per second. That means it can journey from the Sun to Earth in around eight minutes and can cross the average room in about one hundred-millionth of a second.

WHAT MAKES LIGHT BEND?

When light passes from one medium into another – say from air into glass or water – it changes speed. In turn, this causes the light to move at a different angle through the new medium. Known as refraction, this phenomenon explains why a straw in a glass of water or an oar in a river may look bent. Using a triangular piece of glass called a prism, you can refract light in such a way that it splits up into its constituent colours – the colours of the spectrum.

TRUE COLOURS *The two planes of angled glass in a prism cause the different wavelengths, or colours, in light to bend at different angles and emerge separated from each other.*

PRIVATE VISION *To see a rainbow you must be between the Sun and the rain. Because the image varies depending on the precise angle of vision, no two people ever see exactly the same rainbow.*

WHAT CREATES A RAINBOW?

A rainbow forms when sunlight passes through raindrops in the air. Some of the light refracts as it enters the raindrop, then reflects off the back of the raindrop and is refracted once more as it passes out again. Each colour emerges at a slightly different angle and, as the same colour comes out of every raindrop at precisely the same angle, the viewer sees clear bands of colour in the air. Because raindrops are round, the colours are bent into a circular shape; however, the ground usually conceals the bottom half of this circle, and so we normally see a rainbow as an arch.

HOW DO LENSES WORK?

The lenses in your eyes must bend light so that the image you are seeing is the right size and in focus when it reaches the retina at the back of your eye (▶154). If your eyeball is too long, the image will focus in front of the retina and you'll have trouble seeing things in the distance – you'll be short-sighted, in other words. Concave glass lenses bend light out slightly so that the image does not focus until it reaches the retina. If, on the other hand, your eyeball is too short, it will focus beyond the retina and you'll be long-sighted. Convex lenses bend the light sooner so that it comes into focus on the retina. Certain combinations of lenses greatly magnify images and so are used to make binoculars and telescopes (▶194).

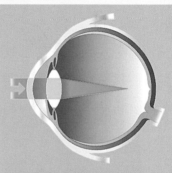

MYOPIA In short-sightedness, images focus in front of the retina, causing distant objects to blur. This is corrected with a divergent (concave) lens.

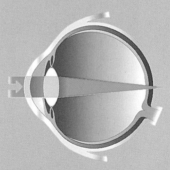

HYPERMETROPIA In long-sightedness, images focus behind the retina, blurring nearby objects. This can be corrected with a convergent (convex) lens.

fast fact
The brain has only three types of colour sensors, which respond to red, green and blue, but it can still perceive about 10 million different colours.

MICROSCOPES AND TELESCOPES

Our knowledge of the world we live in, and the Universe that surrounds us, owes a great deal to microscopes and telescopes. The first microscopes were developed by spectacle makers in the Netherlands in the 1590s and early 1600s. The Italian scientist Galileo Galilei also made microscopes and in 1609 he built one of the first telescopes, which he used to conduct pioneering studies of the Sun, Moon, planets and stars.

HOW POWERFUL ARE STANDARD MICROSCOPES?

With the naked eye, we can see objects as small as a particle of dust, but without any detail. Traditional optical, or light, microscopes usually magnify up to a maximum of about 1000 times. By comparison, the electron microscope, which was invented in 1932 by German physicist Ernst Ruska, can magnify more than a million times.

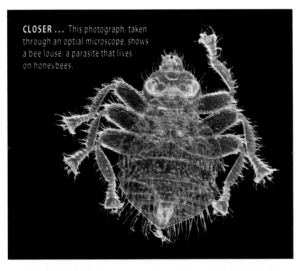

CLOSER ... This photograph, taken through an optial microscope, shows a bee louse, a parasite that lives on honeybees.

... AND CLOSER
A scanning electron microscope image reveals the minuscule features of a tiny spider.

HOW DOES AN OPTICAL MICROSCOPE WORK?

An optical microscope uses a mirror or lamp in its base to shine light through a specimen held on a glass plate. Inside the microscope are two sets of lenses – the objective lens (or lenses) at the bottom and the eyepiece at the top. The objective lens focuses an image of the specimen inside the microscope and the eyepiece then magnifies it again. The objective lens may enlarge by anything between 5 and 100 times, while an eyepiece usually magnifies by between 2 and 10 times. The total magnification is worked out by multiplying the power of the eyepiece by the power of the selected objective lens.

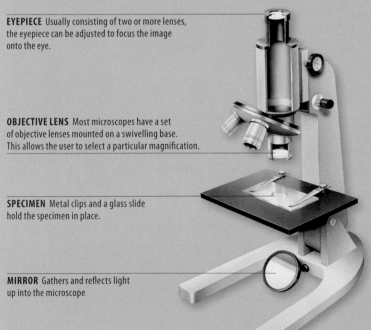

EYEPIECE Usually consisting of two or more lenses, the eyepiece can be adjusted to focus the image onto the eye.

OBJECTIVE LENS Most microscopes have a set of objective lenses mounted on a swivelling base. This allows the user to select a particular magnification.

SPECIMEN Metal clips and a glass slide hold the specimen in place.

MIRROR Gathers and reflects light up into the microscope

fast fact

The most powerful microscope in the world can be found at the University of Victoria in Canada. Known as the STEHM – Scanning Transmission Electron Holography Microscope – it can magnify at up to 20 million times human sight.

How does an electron microscope work?

Instead of light, an electron microscope uses a beam of electrons to scan an object and create an image. An electron gun fires electrons through a series of lenses that focus its beam onto the specimen. Depending on its make-up, the specimen will block electrons, scatter them or allow them to pass through. The resulting pattern of electrons is captured by a detector and translated into an image on a photographic plate or computer screen.

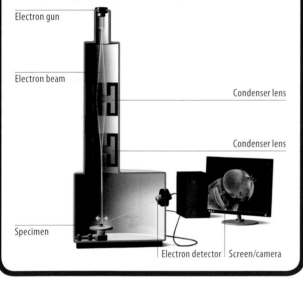

Electron gun

Electron beam

Condenser lens

Condenser lens

Specimen

Electron detector | Screen/camera

What is a reflecting telescope?

In a reflecting telescope, a primary large concave mirror or an array of concave mirrors gathers light and focuses the image onto a secondary mirror. From there the image is reflected and focused through an eyepiece lens or, more usually today, onto electronic sensors. Computers are used to gather images and enhance them, revealing details invisible to the naked eye. Almost all large astronomical telescopes are reflecting telescopes. Radio telescopes use a similar principal to focus radio waves from space, which can be turned into images of distant objects.

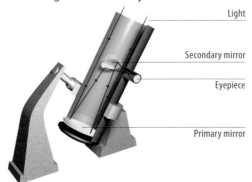

Light

Secondary mirror

Eyepiece

Primary mirror

Path of light

Eyepiece

Objective lens

Mirror

Tripod

How does a telescope work?

The simplest telescope is a refracting telescope; it refracts light, or bends it, down a long tube. At one end is the objective lens, which is pointed at the object you want to study; at the other end is the eyepiece, which you look into to see the magnified image. The bigger the objective lens, the more light it will let in, which helps to make the final image brighter and clearer.

What is the world's most powerful telescope?

The ALMA (Atacama Large Millimeter/Submillimeter Array) telescope in northern Chile consists of 66 radio antennae. Combining the data from these antennae produces images equivalent to those that would be gathered by a reflecting telescope with a diameter of 14 km ($8 2/3$ miles).

KEEN SIGHT *The ALMA telescope can detect radiations of energy outside the spectrum of visible light. By combining its images with those of the Hubble Space Telescope – which captures the clearest possible images of visible light – scientists can generate extraordinary composite images, such as this one, at right, showing the Antennae Galaxies 70 million light years away.*

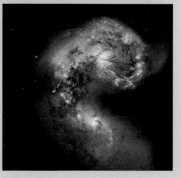

SOUND

Sound is caused by waves of pressure that spread out through the air, making the air molecules squeeze together and then push apart. These waves are started by anything that is vibrating, from a car engine to the strings of a violin. Unlike light, sound cannot travel through a vacuum, so in outer space there is no sound at all.

HOW DO WE MEASURE SOUND?

A sound's pitch is measured in units called hertz (Hz), or waves per second. Humans can normally hear sounds ranging from about 20 Hz to 20,000 Hz (20 kHz). The loudness of a sound is measured in decibels (dB). The softest sound that the human ear can hear has a decibel rating of about 4, while the loudest ones that it can cope with have a rating of over 150 – though permanent damage can be caused to the ears by sounds louder than 100 decibels. The decibel scale works logarithmically. This means that if two sounds differ by 10 decibels, one of them is 10 times more powerful than the other.

HOW DO SOUNDS VARY?

A sound is a wave of high and low pressure made by a vibrating object. More powerful vibrations result in a greater difference between the high and the low pressure – and louder sounds. More frequent vibrations result in more closely spaced waves, and higher-pitched sounds. The graphs below show the changes in air pressure produced by four different vibrating objects over a fraction of a second.

Soft, high-pitched sound

Soft, low-pitched sound

Loud, high-pitched sound

Loud, low-pitched sound

TURNING UP THE VOLUME *A loud rock or pop concert can create noise levels of 100–120 dB and result in temporary deafness among listeners.*

WHISPER QUIET *The sound of someone whispering measures roughly 20–30 dB.*

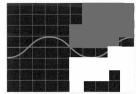

ROCKET LIFT-OFF
150–190 dB

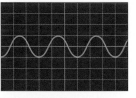

JET TAKE-OFF
120–140 dB

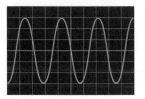

MOTORBIKE
70–90 dB

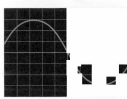

ORCHESTRA
50–70 dB

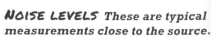

RUSTLING LEAVES
10 dB

NOISE LEVELS *These are typical measurements close to the source.*

BUBBLING UNDER *Sounds reach you faster under water than on land.*

HOW FAST DOES SOUND TRAVEL?

Sounds travel through air at about 340 m (1115 ft) a second. As the waves travel outwards, their energy spreads out over a larger volume and eventually they become too weak to be heard. This is why it is hard to make yourself heard a long way off – even if you shout. Sound moves slightly faster on a warm day than on a cold one, and more slowly at high altitudes. In water, it travels 4.3 times quicker than it does in air.

fast fact

Because sound travels much further under water than in the air, a blue whale can communicate with another whale 160 km (100 miles) away. Studies show whales could once hear messages from 1600 km (1000 miles) away, but have lost this ability due to human noise pollution in the oceans.

WHAT IS THE DIFFERENCE BETWEEN A NOTE AND A NOISE?

A noise consists of a complicated jumble of different soundwaves, while a musical note has just a few waves, all regularly spaced apart. In a pure note, the waves are exactly the same distance from each other.

HOW DOES AN ECHO WORK?

Soundwaves can bounce off solid objects, just as light waves can bounce off mirrors. But because sound travels much more slowly than light, it can take several seconds to reach our ears. When it arrives, we hear it as an echo. Bats and dolphins use high-pitched echoes to find their food (▶109). Echoes are also used in sonar – a way of detecting submarines and mapping the seabed.

WHAT IS A SONIC BOOM?

Most passenger jets move at about two-thirds of the speed of sound. At this speed, a plane keeps catching up to the soundwaves in front of it, and races away from the ones it leaves behind. These trailing waves make a low-pitched rumble as the plane flies away. If, however, a plane flies faster than the speed of sound, air begins to pile up in front of it. When this air slips out of the way, it suddenly expands, making a loud noise called a sonic boom.

BOOM TIME *Sometimes as a plane breaks the sound barrier a circular cloud forms around it, due to a related drop in air pressure.*

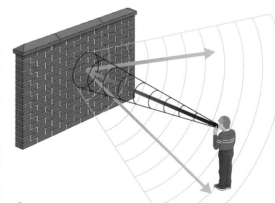

CALLING BACK
If you shout at a wall, the sound will bounce back as an echo. To produce a good echo, the wall needs to be big and at least 25 m (80 ft) away.

ELECTRICITY AND MAGNETISM

The forces of electricity and magnetism are both caused by charged subatomic particles – most importantly, electrons (▶186) – and are therefore closely linked.

Electricity can be generated using magnetism, and a magnetic field can be created with electricity. This close relationship was exploited to develop one of the most useful inventions in history: the electric motor.

WHAT IS ELECTRIC CURRENT?

Electric current is the movement, or flow, of electric charge. In everyday situations, it is usually negatively charged electrons that move – inside circuits made of metal wires, for example – since they can break free from their atoms (▶186). Electrons are made to move by an 'electromotive force' (emf) of voltage. The emf can be caused by the attraction and repulsion resulting from a build-up of charges, as in a battery, or by magnetic forces, as in a generator. Either way, the electrons then repel nearby electrons, which in turn repel others, creating a domino effect.

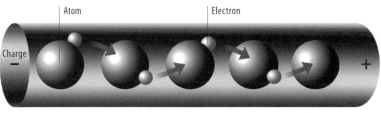

Atom   Electron

Charge   +

Electric current is a flow of charge

CURRENT FLOW *Electric charge is measured in coulombs (C); current is measured in amps (A) – coulombs per second.*

fast fact

As a result of the rotation of its iron-nickel core, planet Earth is a giant magnet, with its poles near the geographical North and South poles (▶30).

CABLE SHIELD *Ceramic or plastic insulators are used where power lines join utility poles.*

WHAT IS A CONDUCTOR?

A conductor is a material through which electricity can flow easily. Its electrons are loosely attached to their atoms, so that they move readily from atom to atom. This is the case with all metals (especially silver and copper) and the nonmetal carbon. Insulators are materials that do not have free electrons and therefore have a high resistance to the flow of current. Semiconductors are materials that can be made to conduct electricity under certain circumstances; an example is silicon. Superconductors are materials that offer no resistance at all to electron movement. Most metals become superconductors at temperatures of close to absolute zero, –273.15°C (–459.67°F).

WHAT IS STATIC ELECTRICITY?

Static electricity – the kind that makes clothes crackle – is produced when electrically charged particles are rubbed off one object onto another. This kind of electricity is described as static because it does not flow. However, a high enough charge may cause a spark (felt as a shock), as electrons jump to a point of lower or opposite charge.

HAIR RAISING *If you pull a woolly hat off your head on a dry day, it can strip negative electrons from the atoms in your hair. The remaining atoms have a positive charge and so repel each other, pushing in opposite directions and causing the hairs to stand on end.*

HOW DOES A BATTERY WORK?

Chemical reactions in a battery create a separation of electric charges – negative at one terminal and positive at the other. When the switch is flicked on, it creates a circuit and the electrons immediately travel along the circuit towards the positive terminal. They continue to circulate until the switch is turned off, breaking the circuit, or the chemical reactions cease.

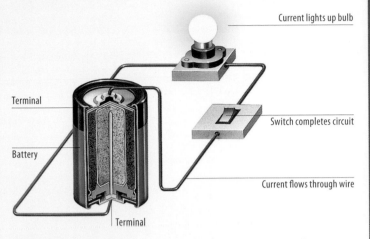

Current lights up bulb

Terminal

Battery

Switch completes circuit

Current flows through wire

Terminal

LIGHTING UP **This circuit consists of a battery linked by wires to a switch and an electric lamp. When the switch is on, electricity passes through a wire filament in the lamp's light bulb, creating heat and, in turn, light.**

WHAT IS MAGNETISM?

Magnetism is a force that attracts or repels other magnetic materials. It is formed by the spinning of electrons inside atoms. All materials are magnetic to some extent, but magnetism is only noticeable in so-called ferromagnetic materials – pieces of metal (usually iron, steel, cobalt or nickel) in which all the electrons are spinning in the same direction, thereby accentuating the force. Every magnet has two poles – north and south – at opposite ends. The invisible area around the magnet that is affected by it is called its magnetic field.

LINES OF FORCE **Iron filings scattered around a magnet reveal its lines of force. The filings cluster around the poles, where the force is strongest.**

HOW DOES AN ELECTRIC MOTOR WORK?

When electricity flows through a wire, it produces a weak magnetic field. This can be intensified by coiling the wire around an iron rod. A coil like this is called an electromagnet (right); its magnetic field disappears as soon as the current is turned off. If an electromagnet is placed on a shaft between two opposing magnetic poles and turned on (below), the forces of attraction and repulsion between it and the magnets cause it to turn. This movement can be used to drive other machines.

ELECTROMAGNET

Magnetic lines of force

Iron rod

Coil of wire

Flow of current

ELECTRIC MOTOR

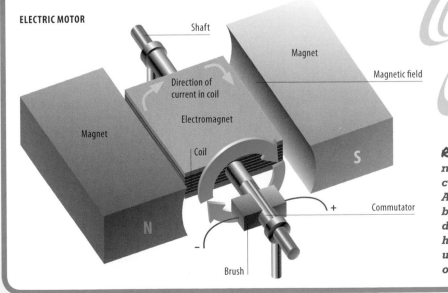

Shaft

Magnet

Direction of current in coil

Electromagnet

Magnetic field

Magnet

Coil

S

N

+

Commutator

−

Brush

ROUND AND ROUND **In most electric motors (left), the current is fed to a coil via carbon blocks called brushes. A device called a commutator links the brushes to the coil. It ensures that the direction of the current reverses every half turn. That way, the coil is pushed up on one side and pulled down on the other, creating continuous rotation.**

GAMMA RAYS

FREQUENCY More than 30 EHz
WAVELENGTH Less than 10⁻¹¹ m (less than 10 billionths of 1 mm)
SOURCES Stars and other cosmic sources, nuclear reactions
USES Checking dense structures for cracks, destroying cancerous cells

X-RAYS

FREQUENCY 300 PHz to 30 EHz
WAVELENGTH 10⁻⁹ to 10⁻¹¹ m (1 millionth to 10 billionths of 1 mm)
SOURCES Sun, outer space, fast electron bombardment of metal target
USES Examining bones and other internal body structures, checking metal joints and welds, destroying cancerous cells

ULTRAVIOLET

FREQUENCY 750 THz to 300 PHz
WAVELENGTH 4 x 10⁻⁷ to 10⁻⁹ m (400 millionths to 1 millionth of 1 mm)
SOURCES Sun and stars and other extremely hot objects, some fluorescent materials, electrical discharge, ultraviolet laser
USES Vision in some insects, optical brighteners in washing powders, sterilisation, fluorescent lamps, sunbeds, forensics

VISIBLE LIGHT

FREQUENCY 430 THz to 750 THz
WAVELENGTH 7 x 10⁻⁷ to 4 x 10⁻⁷ m (700 to 400 millionths of 1 mm)
SOURCES Sun and stars, other hot objects, fluorescent materials, electrical discharge, lasers, chemical reactions
USES Vision, photography, cinematography, TV, bleaching, power generation, communications (fibre optics)

INFRARED

FREQUENCY 3000 GHz to 430 THz
WAVELENGTH 10⁻⁴ to 7 x 10⁻⁷ m (0.1 mm to 700 millionths of 1 mm)
SOURCES Hot and warm objects, lasers
USES Heating, cooking, TV remote controls, night-vision devices, thermal-imaging cameras

MICROWAVES

FREQUENCY 3000 MHz to 3000 GHz
WAVELENGTH More than 10⁻¹ to 10⁻⁴ m (10 cm to 0.1 mm)
SOURCES Outer space, devices such as magnetrons and masers
USES Cooking food, telecommunications, microwave telescopes

RADIO WAVES

FREQUENCY Up to 3000 MHz
WAVELENGTH More than 10⁻¹ m (more than 10 cm)
SOURCES Electric currents, sparks, outer space
USES Radio and TV broadcasting, telecommunications, wireless networks

Electricity and magnetism generate other kinds of energy, which are known collectively as electromagnetic radiation. These types of energy take the form of waves that move through space at the speed of light. Aside from visible light and infrared, or radiant heat, we cannot perceive these forms of energy. All are, however, produced naturally – notably in outer space – and can be detected using specialised equipment.

WHAT ARE THE DIFFERENT KINDS OF ELECTROMAGNETIC RADIATION?

The different kinds of radiation are distinguished by their frequency and wavelength (▶192). The higher the frequency, the shorter the wavelength, and vice versa. The shorter the wavelength, the greater the energy the waves carry. Together these different kinds of waves make up what is known as the electromagnetic spectrum.

HOW DOES A MICROWAVE OVEN WORK?

A magnetron, a device inside a microwave oven, produces microwaves. These waves cause molecules in food to spin, which in turn generates heat and cooks the food. Most kinds of dishes do not absorb microwaves well and therefore remain cool while the food cooks. The inside of the oven is made of metal, which reflects the waves and prevents them escaping.

HOW ARE X-RAY IMAGES CREATED?

X-rays have an extremely short wavelength. This gives them sufficient energy to pass through many materials. When directed at the human body, they pass through flesh but are blocked, to varying degrees, by bones, teeth, organs and some other tissues. The rays that pass through strike a photographic plate behind the body, creating a negative image of the targeted area. X-rays are produced by a machine that uses high voltage to accelerate electrons to an extremely high velocity, which in turn generates the rays.

LOOK INSIDE *As well as being widely used in medicine, X-rays are used by customs officers to examine inside baggage at airports.*

C01A 14-APR-92 10:45:46

HOW DOES RADIO WORK?

Radio waves can be created using a type of current, called an oscillating electric current. Microphones turn sounds into electric signals and combine them with radio waves. Transmitters then send the waves out to repeater stations and satellites, from where they are transmitted onwards to receivers – radio sets – which translate the signals back into the original sounds. Radio signals are broadcast on four main wave bands relating to the wavelength or frequency of the signal: short wave, medium wave, long wave and VHF (very high frequency), also known as FM (frequency modulation).

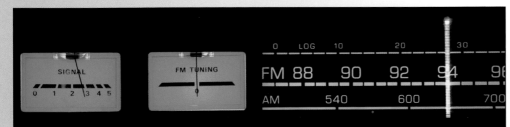

WAVE TYPES *Each radio wave band has its strengths and weaknesses. Long waves, for example, travel well through water and so are used by submarines; short waves can be bounced off the atmosphere to reach far corners of the planet; and VHF, though it loses power quickly, carries a lot of information and is thus used for high-quality broadcasts.*

WHAT IS DIGITAL RADIO?

With digital radio, sounds are converted to digital signals, transmitted on extremely high frequency wave bands and decoded by digital receivers. Not only is the sound quality better and less prone to interference, but users can also receive additional information such as song titles and store and replay programs.

fast fact

During bursts of intense activity called solar flares, the Sun emits tremendously powerful X-rays. These can damage satellites and electrical equipment on Earth.

MAKING LIGHT

Electric lighting became widely available by the end of the nineteenth century. All early lamps were incandescent bulbs. But by the early twenty-first century, compact fluorescent lamps (CFLs) and light-emitting diode (LED) lamps have become more common, because they are more energy-efficient and longer lasting. Another type of electric light, the laser, invented in 1960, produces a very pure light that has a wide range of applications.

WHY ARE FLUORESCENT LAMPS MORE EFFICIENT?

Visible light accounts for only about 4 per cent of the energy output of an incandescent bulb – the rest is heat. Compact fluorescent lamps, or CFLs, produce much less heat for the same intensity of light, which makes them more energy efficient. The light from a CFL is produced by compounds called phosphors that coat the inside of the glass tube. There are red, green and blue phosphors, which together produce white light. An electronic circuit creates an electric discharge inside the tube that produces invisible ultraviolet radiation – and this radiation excites the phosphors to produce light.

NEAT FIT *CFL tubes are shaped to fit the same space as an incandescent bulb.*

HOW DOES AN INCANDESCENT LIGHT BULB WORK?

Very hot objects glow red, yellow or white depending upon their temperature (▶191) – a phenomenon known as incandescence. An incandescent bulb contains a long, thin, coiled filament that heats up when electric current flows through it. The glass bulb is filled with a mixture of inert (unreactive) gases that prevent the filament from burning. At very high temperatures, the filament slowly evaporates, reducing the lamp's lifetime and blackening the inside of the glass. Halogen lamps contain small amounts of bromine and iodine gases to prevent this, allowing them to produce brighter, whiter light and last longer.

HOT LIGHT *The filament in an incandescent bulb is usually made of the metal tungsten.*

WHAT ARE LED LIGHTS?

The light from a light-emitting diode (LED) is produced inside a 'p-n junction', the filling in a sandwich of two types of semiconductor. In the p-n junction, positive and negative charges combine, releasing packets of light (photons) of a particular colour. By combining red, green and blue LEDs in one unit, LEDs produce white light – and since LED lamps are even more efficient and long lasting than compact fluorescent lamps, they are increasingly used in lighting. LEDs have many applications beyond domestic lighting, including torches and traffic lights. LED panels are also used to backlight some televisions (▶214), portable computer screens and mobile phones.

EYE CATCHING *Rows of LED lights are now used in place of single bulbs in car lights.*

HOW DO LASERS WORK?

The word 'laser' comes from the phrase 'Light Amplification by Stimulated Emission of Radiation'. Laser light is produced inside a 'lasing medium', which can be solid, liquid or gas. Inside the lasing medium, photons of light bounce back and forth between two mirrors, stimulating atoms to produce more photons identical to the original ones. One of the mirrors is semitransparent, and it is from here that the sharp, thin beam of pure laser light emerges. The lasers at the heart of consumer products such as laser pointers, DVD players and laser printers are laser diodes – in which the lasing medium is a semiconductor junction like that found in an LED.

LIGHT SHOW *Lasers are used in stage shows to create spectacular effects.*

fast fact

The amount of visible light a lamp produces is measured using a unit called the lumen. A reading lamp produces about 500 lumens.

WHAT ARE FIBRE-OPTIC CABLES?

Lasers and LEDs can be turned on and off extremely rapidly, making them ideal for representing the 0s and 1s of digital information (▶204). Fibre-optic cables contain bundles of thin glass fibres that carry light along their length, guiding it around corners and across large distances. Optical fibres play a crucial role in most modern telecommunications networks, including much of the Internet.

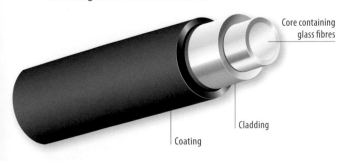

Core containing glass fibres

Cladding

Coating

LIGHT SHIELD *Fibre optic cables have thick outer layers to prevent leakage of light and, therefore, data.*

HOW ARE LASERS USED?

Lasers have many uses besides impressive light displays. Laser light can deliver energy precisely to a very small region, so is often used in surgery, to cut and to cauterise flesh (▶180). Its straight, thin beams are also ideal for marking straight lines during land surveys and construction. A laser can be directed as a very thin, precise beam, so it is used in computer-controlled etching and cutting. Low-power laser light is also ideal for reading information, as reflections off surfaces. For example, light-sensitive components detect light reflected off the alternating black-and-white lines on a barcode, or off indentations on the underside of a DVD.

READING THE LINES *On a barcode, a laser recognises different shapes of vertical lines as numbers.*

COMPUTERS AND ELECTRONICS

WHAT DOES DIGITAL MEAN?

Most electronic devices represent text, sound and images 'digitally': as sets of numbers. The numbers are binary, using only two digits (0 and 1) – not 10 digits (0 to 9) – because it is very easy for the electronic circuits inside computers to store and manipulate 'off' (0) and 'on' (1) signals. So, pressing a key on a computer keyboard sends a set of on-and-off pulses of electricity to the computer's processing unit. Sounds can be 'digitised' by assigning numbers to measurements of the intensity of a soundwave thousands of times every second; images, by breaking them into millions of picture elements, or pixels (▶211), and representing the colour and brightness of each pixel as numbers. Digital representations can be copied across many different media without losing quality.

Pixels

DIGITAL IMAGE *Each pixel in a digital image is assigned a number. In turn, that value is converted into a binary number for ease of transmission.*

The electronic devices that feature in our everyday lives – radios, televisions, cameras, mobile phones and computers – all rely on complicated electric circuits to achieve tasks such as controlling machines or processing sound and video. Most of today's electronic devices are digital, and most digital devices are computers, which store and process information.

WHAT IS A MICROCHIP?

Most modern electronic devices contain integrated circuits, sometimes called microchips. They are entire, complicated circuits created on the surface of a small piece of semiconductor material, normally silicon. At the heart of every computer is the central processing unit (CPU), a single chip, also known as a microprocessor, that carries out millions of mathematical operations every second. Many other electronic devices contain microprocessors

– including digital cameras and even most washing machines. These devices are computers too, although they can only carry out a specific set of tasks, while general-purpose computers can be programmed for almost any task.

WHAT ARE HARDWARE AND SOFTWARE?

Hardware is any physical part of a computer system, such as the mouse, keyboard, trackpad, monitor, disk drive, processor and so on. Software is the sets of instructions that make the computer work. There are three main types of software: 'firmware' enables the processor to communicate with the hardware; the 'operating system' is responsible for the computer's basic functions; and the 'applications', or programs, enable the computer to

carry out specific tasks, such as accessing the Internet, playing music or manipulating digital photos and video.

DESK TOP *A normal computer set-up has a central processor, keyboard, screen and mouse.*

HOW DOES A COMPUTER STORE INFORMATION?

Computers store information in microchips called ROM and RAM, and on hard drives and flash drives. ROM (read-only memory) holds the firmware, which is rarely changed. RAM (random-access memory) is working memory, which holds the operating system and any active data and programs; its contents constantly change and are lost when the computer is shut down. The operating system and applications are stored on hard drives. Most hard drives contain spinning magnetic disks, but some have solid-state 'flash' memory, which is made of microchips containing millions of tiny transistors. Flash memory is also present in removable USB or memory 'sticks'.

DISK DRIVE *In hard disks, binary data is stored as changes in the direction of disk magnetisation.*

fast fact

The basic electronic component of a microprocessor is the transistor. A typical computer processor contains more than a billion transistors on a piece of silicon the size of a postage stamp.

HOW DO TOUCHSCREENS WORK?

Tablets and smartphones receive most of their input via a user's touch – from fingers or a stylus – on the device's screen. Some desktop and laptop computers also have touchscreens. There are two main types of touchscreen: resistive and capacitive. In each case, the sensor is laid over the display itself. A resistive touchscreen consists of two thin grids that conduct electricity, separated by a small gap. Pressing on the screen causes the grids to make contact at that point, sending information to the processor. A capacitive screen works by sensing the presence of a finger or special stylus, and requires only a light touch. Trackpads are touchscreens without a display.

WHAT'S A SUPERCOMPUTER?

A supercomputer has hundreds or thousands of processors all working in parallel. It is able to process data – carry out calculations – much, much more quickly than desktop or laptop computers. Computing power is normally expressed in 'FLOPS' (floating-point operations per second) – a measure of the speed at which a computer can carry out mathematical calculations. The most powerful supercomputers achieve thousands of trillions of FLOPS – about 10,000 times as many as a high-end office computer. Supercomputers have a wide range of scientific applications – including, for example, climate modelling.

FAST THINKING *France's Tera-10 supercomputer can carry out 50 billion operations per second.*

THE INTERNET

Billions of people access the Internet every day. They use it to communicate via email or instant messaging, to access information and entertainment on the World Wide Web, to shop, work and do their banking. Not only computers, but also smartphones, computer printers, cameras, games consoles, televisions and even some refrigerators can connect to the Internet.

WHAT IS THE INTERNET?

To exchange information, devices connected to a computer network must present it in the same format, or 'protocol'. The Internet is a global super-network of computer networks – and every connected device uses a standard set of protocols called the Internet Protocol (IP) suite. Users at home are typically connected to 'wide area networks' operated by Internet Service Providers (ISPs), which connect directly to Internet infrastructure. Using the IP protocols, computers divide information into fragments, called packets. Every connected device has an IP address, and source and destination addresses are attached to each packet; though packets may travel separately, they are reassembled when they reach the destination device. IP addresses are complicated sets of numbers, but the range of available numbers is divided up and assigned to 'domains' that can be identified by words like 'wikipedia.org'.

HOW DO YOU MAKE A WEBSITE?

Webpages are composed using a computer code called HTML (hypertext markup language). It describes all the elements on the page and tells the computer how to display them. The code and any related files are stored on specialised computers, called web servers, and given an address, or URL (uniform resource locator), which includes the server's Internet address. When an Internet user requests the webpage, by entering the URL in their web-browser software, their computer downloads the HTML code and displays the page according to the instructions. People with little or no understanding of HTML can still create webpages by using one of many services that now offer simplified templates: all the user has to do is enter their text and upload their images.

HOW DOES EMAIL WORK?

Several hundred billion emails are sent and received every day worldwide. An email message begins with a 'header' that contains the email address of the recipient and sender. Email addresses are made up of a user name, then an @ symbol, then the address of a specialised computer that stores emails: a mail server. Writing emails requires software called a mail client, which can be a stand-alone application or run in a web browser. The mail client communicates with the mail server: sending an email transfers the message to the sender's mail server, which forwards it on to the recipient's mail server. The recipient's mail client picks up the message when it checks for new messages.

HOW DOES WIRELESS NETWORKING WORK?

The most commonly used wireless connection inside buildings is Wi-Fi. In a typical home set-up, a device called a wireless router connects to an Internet Service Provider that acts as a gateway to the Internet; the router then acts as a hub for the home's 'wireless local area network', or WLAN. Computers, smartphones, andeven printers and digital cameras can connect wirelessly to the router, giving them easy access to each other and to the Internet. Mobile phone companies also offer connection to their networks, and so to the Internet, via 3G (third generation) or 4G (fourth generation) mobile data connections.

HOME HUB Via a router, a laptop, tablet and phone can access the Web and stored data.

Tablet
World Wide Web
Router
Storage
Smartphone
Laptop

WHAT IS SOCIAL MEDIA?

Internet users can form 'virtual communities' online, by signing up to social networks – the best known of which are Twitter and Facebook. These companies offer users a chance to share information quickly and easily. On Twitter, a user posts messages called 'tweets'; these can be read by anyone who chooses to 'follow' that user. Tweets can have a maximum of 140 characters; typically they contain brief news and links to webpages. Facebook is aimed at friends and family, and posts often consist of personal pictures or videos, as well as links to web content. Companies are increasingly using both these networks as marketing tools.

fast fact

Estimates suggest that by 2050, more than 50 billion devices will be connected to the Internet.

WHAT IS CLOUD COMPUTING?

A computer traditionally stores applications and data 'locally', on its hard drive. However, many people now depend upon remote, Internet-based server computers to run some or all of their applications and to store much of their data. This is called 'cloud computing'. With access to the Internet now being so fast and readily available, the difference between the traditional and cloud-based approaches is barely noticeable. Cloud computing has many benefits. For example, it makes it possible to access your documents, photographs and music from any computer or tablet, anywhere in the world, and to share them with others and even collaborate with others in real time.

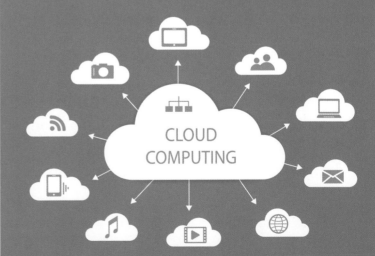

CLOUD COMPUTING

UP IN THE CLOUD Devices in different parts of the world can access the same data stored on a cloud server.

TELECOMMUNICATIONS

The term telecommunications refers to any method of communication over long distances. This includes radio and television broadcasting, but is most often used to refer to person-to-person voice communications over networks such as the telephone network and the Internet.

HOW DOES A LANDLINE WORK?

A landline or 'fixed-line' telephone contains a microphone that converts the sound of your voice into an electric signal, and has buttons that generate signals representing the touch-tone numbers. These signals travel along a pair of copper wires to a box somewhere nearby, where equipment digitises them. The digital signals are then sent along either metal or fibre optic cables to your local exchange, where computerised switchgear works out the best route to reach the desired recipient's phone across the local, national or international telephone network. Along the way, the signal may be carried along fibre optic cables or by radio waves between fixed relay stations, or even via satellite. Eventually, the signal reaches a box near to the receiving end, which converts the digital signal into an analogue signal, which the receiving telephone converts back into sound.

fast fact
The number of mobile phones has been greater than the number of fixed-line phones since 2003.

HOW DOES A MOBILE PHONE WORK?

A mobile phone uses radio waves instead of cables to connect to the telephone network, so it has a radio antenna built in. The area covered by a mobile-phone network is divided into overlapping 'cells'; at the centre of each is a powerful mast antenna. Each mobile phone has a subscriber identification module (SIM card); the phone sends information contained on the SIM card to the antenna, so that the account owner can be charged correctly. As a person moves around – between calls or even during a call – the phone connects to the nearest mast, so that it can always make, receive or maintain a call.

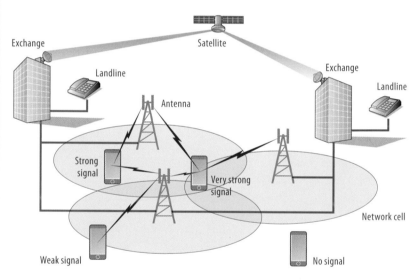

Exchange · Satellite · Landline · Exchange · Landline · Antenna · Strong signal · Very strong signal · Network cell · Weak signal · No signal

WELL CONNECTED *Mobile and landline networks are connected to provide seamless links between the different handset types.*

WHAT IS A SMARTPHONE?

A smartphone is essentially a mobile telephone and a small computer combined. So it can be used not only to make and receive calls, but also to browse the Web and send emails, to record and view photographs and videos, record sound and play games. The controls are mostly accessible via a touchscreen (▸205). Most smartphones can also be used as navigational aids, because they are able to detect their location via satellite navigation systems, such as GPS (the Global Positioning System), and display that position on on-screen maps; they can even guide a driver on a journey by announcing turns.

WHAT IS A SATELLITE PHONE?

A satellite phone, or satphone, functions just like a mobile phone, but communicates directly with satellites in orbit around Earth, rather than with mast antennas on the ground. Satphones are particularly useful in remote areas, or out at sea, where there is no standard mobile-phone network coverage. Relief workers and journalists working in disaster or war zones rely on this technology, as do explorers and some trekkers.

LIVE LINK *A satellite phone can allow a journalist to report from the front line of battle.*

VIRTUAL PRESENCE *Video-conferencing enables organisations to make major savings in money and time spent travelling.*

CAN YOU TELEPHONE SOMEONE USING THE INTERNET?

Since the Internet carries digital information, it can be used to send, or 'stream', sound. As a result, using any computer, smartphone or tablet with a microphone and speaker, it is possible to hold conversations with anyone else similarly connected to the Internet anywhere in the world, free of charge. The technology involved is called VOIP, or Voice Over Internet Protocol. Furthermore, if a computer, tablet or smartphone also has a video camera, it is possible to make video calls using the same principles, so that you also see the person you are talking to. Businesses can thus hold 'video conferences' – meetings in which the participants meet face-to-face but may be separated by hundreds or even thousands of kilometres.

HOW DO PEOPLE TAP PHONES?

Because the signals travelling across regular telecommunications networks are simply radio waves, light (in optical fibres) or electric currents (in cables), it is possible to intercept them and 'listen in' on the messages. At the same time, because nearly all modern communications are digital, and therefore expressed as streams of numbers, they can be kept secret by applying 'encryption codes' to the numbers, thereby rendering the signal meaningless to anyone except those involved in the communication. Nevertheless, hackers are sometimes able to break the codes or find other vulnerabilities in mobile-phone operating systems that allow them to hear and even record conversations.

PHOTOGRAPHY AND VIDEO

A camera works very much like your eye. Rays of light come in through a small hole at the front, pass through the darkness inside and form a picture at the back. In a camera, however, tiny, light-sensitive electric cells register the image and convert it to digital data, ready for storing.

HOW DOES A DIGITAL CAMERA WORK?

Inside the body of a digital camera, the image forms on the surface of a device called an 'active pixel sensor'. It contains an array of light-sensitive elements that produce an electric charge when light falls on them – the more intense the light, the greater the charge. A filter of red, green and blue squares is laid over the sensor, enabling the sensor to capture a full-colour image. The signals forming the picture are stored in the form of digital computer code, first on a memory chip while the camera is in operation, then on a removable SD (secure digital) card inside the camera.

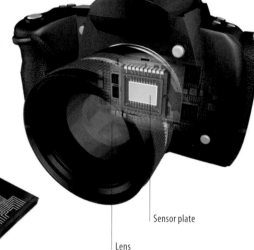

LIGHT SENSOR *In front of the sensor is an array of tiny lenses and an array of red, green and blue filters that allow the camera to produce a full-colour image.*

Sensor

Colour filters

Image

Sensor plate

Sensor plate

Lens

HOW DOES A FILM CAMERA WORK?

Before the advent of digital cameras, photography relied on images being captured on lightweight film. Camera film consists of a strip of plastic coated with chemicals that change their appearance when exposed to light. Silver salts register variations in light and dark, while the colours are produced by three layers of dyes, which are sensitive to, respectively, blue, green and red. Combinations of these colours can reproduce all the colours that we can see.

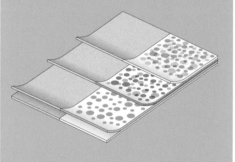

COLOUR FILM *Three layers of dyes produce colour in film. Each is transparent, so you can see the other layers through it.*

HOW DO CAMERAS FOCUS AUTOMATICALLY?

Automatic focusing works by scanning objects in front of the lens with an invisible beam. Some cameras send out a beam of infrared light (▸200), while others use ultrasound (▸176) – soundwaves that can't be heard. If the beam hits an object, it will bounce back at the camera, telling it how far away that object is. The camera then adjusts its lens, so that the object will be in focus when the picture is taken.

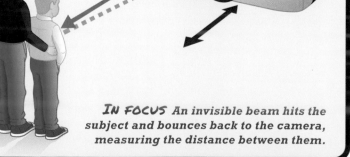

IN FOCUS *An invisible beam hits the subject and bounces back to the camera, measuring the distance between them.*

WHAT ARE EXPOSURE AND APERTURE?

All cameras need to control the amount of light falling onto their sensors. This is done in two ways – by adjusting the speed of the shutter that opens to expose a sensor to the light, and by altering the size of the opening (or aperture) through which the light passes. A dull day needs a slow shutter speed and a big aperture; bright sunshine needs a high shutter speed and a small aperture. Modern digital cameras measure light levels and work out the appropriate exposure and aperture automatically.

EXPOSURE *Capturing a clear image at night-time or on a dull day requires a slow shutter speed to extend exposure and a big aperture to take in more light.*

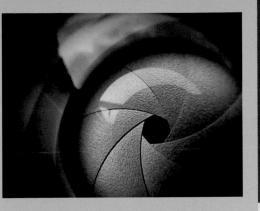

APERTURE *Like the pupil in the human eye, the aperture on a camera opens and closes to let in more light in dark conditions and less in bright conditions.*

WHAT ARE PIXELS?

On a computer or TV screen or digital display, pixels are the many thousands of tiny elements that make up an image – pixel is short for 'picture element'. In a colour display, each pixel is made up of three smaller subpanels: one red, one green and one blue. Digital data received by the unit is translated into electric currents that make the red, green or blue subpixels glow at different levels of intensity. The combination of the brightness and colour of all the pixels makes up the overall image. Because the pixels are too small to be seen by the human eye, they merge into each other, creating a continuous image (▶204). In a camera, on the other hand, the so-called pixels are actually the tiny sensors that register the image. If a camera has an arrangement of 3264 x 2448 sensors, it has 7,990,272 pixels. A million sensors, or pixels, is known as a megapixel (MP), so such a camera is said to be an 8 MP camera.

HOW DO YOU MANIPULATE DIGITAL IMAGES?

Storing image information in digital form allows it to be manipulated in a number of ways. This is usually achieved by using specialized image-manipulation software on a computer, through many different techniques. With such software colours can be altered, images blended and subjects retouched.

BEST LIGHT *The retouching of images is frequently carried out in fashion photography (above). The original sunflowers image (top right) has been manipulated to give it a more richly coloured, retro appearance (bottom right).*

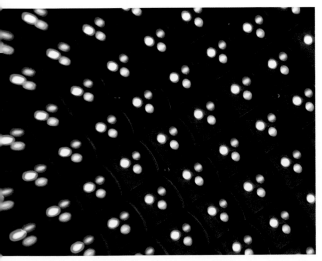

COLOUR PATTERN *This close-up of an LED screen shows the red, green and blue subpixels.*

SOUND RECORDING

The first device that could record and play back sound, the phonograph, was invented in 1879. It produced an analogue, or direct copy, of the soundwaves it recorded. The main recording media of the 1900s, gramophone records and magnetic tape, were also analog devices. By the start of the twenty-first century, however, these had been superseded by digital audio, first in the form of compact discs (CDs), then mp3 files.

HOW ARE SOUNDS RECORDED?

Sound is produced by vibrating objects, and spreads out through the air as waves of varying pressure (▶196). Inside a microphone is a thin membrane, called a diaphragm, which vibrates in sympathy with the pressure variations created by sounds. There are two main types of microphone: in a condenser microphone, the diaphragm is attached to one side of an electronic component called a condenser; in a dynamic microphone, it is attached to a small coil of wire that sits in a magnetic field. In both cases, the result is a tiny electric current, called an audio signal, that is a direct representation (analog) of the original soundwave. In order to digitise the sound, an electronic circuit, called an analog-to-digital converter (ADC), measures the intensity of the signal thousands of times every second and represents each sample as a number.

LIVE ON AIR *High-quality microphones are essential for live radio broadcasts.*

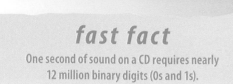

ONE TAKE *A producer and engineer monitor the performances of a guitarist and vocalist.*

WHAT HAPPENS IN A RECORDING STUDIO?

In a recording studio, microphones capture the sounds produced by musical performers in soundproofed rooms or booths; similar devices, called pickups, capture sounds from guitars. The audio signals are routed to a control room, where a sound engineer records them on computers, putting each voice and instrument on a separate track. Keyboard instruments often use a technology called MIDI (Musical Instrument Digital Interface) that records only which keys are pressed, and when and how hard. Using computer software, an engineer can then apply different sounds and effects to those keystrokes, without them having to be played again.

WHAT DO 'PRODUCING' AND 'MIXING' MEAN?

In professional recording, a producer oversees the whole process – much as a producer does in a film production. He or she guides the sound engineer to adjust, or mix, the levels and effects, such as reverb, on each track to produce the desired overall sound. Today, it is possible to compose, produce and mix music using personal computers and even some tablet computers, so that a nonprofessional can be a performer, producer and sound engineer and make high-quality music at very low cost.

fast fact
One second of sound on a CD requires nearly 12 million binary digits (0s and 1s).

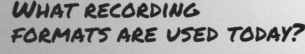

1920–90 Gramophone or vinyl record   **1965–88** Eight-track tape   **1963–2006** Compact cassette   **1982–** Compact disc   **1992–2013** MiniDisc   **1995–** Digital

HOW DOES A DIGITAL AUDIO PLAYER WORK?

The fact that digitised music exists as computer files makes it conveniently portable. A digital audio player or even a smartphone can hold thousands of tracks of music, stored on a hard drive or flash memory (▶205). The compressed audio files also contain information about the track, such as the artist and composer; these 'tags' make it easy for the player's software to organise the tracks, and for the listener to find what they want to hear. The fact that the digital audio is compressed dramatically increases the number of tracks a player can hold.

ON THE GO
Digital audio offers a degree of portability far beyond other formats.

WHAT RECORDING FORMATS ARE USED TODAY?

Since modern sound production is digital, the resulting recordings are computer files, which are ideally suited to delivery over the Internet. Most Internet-based audio is 'compressed': computer programs remove parts of the sound the ear cannot usually hear, dramatically reducing the file size. The most common compressed format is 'mp3' (short for Moving Pictures Expert Group Audio Layer III), but a similar approach creates mp4 and AAC (Advanced Audio Coding) files. These formats result in a loss of quality compared to CD audio; a newer format, called FLAC (Free Lossless Audio Codec) compresses the file in a different way, with no reduction of quality. The very act of digitising audio compromises quality for many people, some of whom still prefer to listen to analog recordings in the form of vinyl records.

'Tweeter' speaker for high-frequency sounds

HIGH AND LOW *Many speaker cabinets contain two or more speakers. Circuits separate high- and low-frequency signals and send each to a different speaker.*

Paper cone

Vibrating cone produces sound

'Woofer' speaker for low-frequency sounds

Speaker coil oscillates in magnetic field

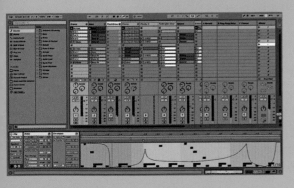

SOUND BOARD *Sequencer software allows users to record and edit music.*

HOW DO SPEAKERS WORK?

For us to hear recorded sounds, the signals must be fed to a loudspeaker. Digital recordings are first converted to an analog signal by a digital-to-analog converter. An amplifier increases the power of the signal's alternating electric current. The amplified current then flows through a coil of wire in the speaker, creating an oscillating magnetic field that varies with the signal. The speaker also contains a strong magnet, so the coil moves rapidly to-and-fro within the magnetic field. Attached to the coil is a paper cone, which vibrates, reproducing the signal as an audible sound.

TELEVISION AND HOME CINEMA

In addition to programs that TV stations broadcast from large antennas, by satellite or over cable networks, many people routinely watch programs supplied 'on-demand' via the Internet. As a result, some people watch television programs on computer screens or tablets. But in most homes, the television set is still the focus of home entertainment.

HOW DOES A TV CAMERA WORK?

TV cameras contain sensors with a grid that corresponds to the pixels of a television picture. The sensors produce electric signals that represent the pattern of light that falls on them. Most 'broadcast-quality' cameras contain a prism that splits the incoming light, producing three separate images. Each image falls on a separate sensor: one with a red filter over it, one with green and one blue. Electronic circuits combine and digitise the signals and output the result as a TV signal that may be recorded or broadcast live. Increasingly, some TV content is being produced using digital SLR cameras that can also shoot broadcast-quality video.

❶ **CAMERA LENS**

❷ **MONITOR**

❸ **CAMERA TUBE** Focuses and scans a primary-colour image and converts it into an electrical signal

❹ **COLOUR SIGNALS**

❺ **AUDIO ENCODER**

❻ **CAMERA ENCODER** Combines digital images from red, blue and green sensors to produce an image in full colour

❼ **TRANSMITTER** Combines audio and video signals in a single high-definition signal that can be broadcast live or recorded on tape or hard disks for editing

A typical television studio

HOW DOES TELEVISION WORK?

The apparently moving pictures on television screens are actually many still pictures displayed in rapid succession – typically 50 or 60 frames every second. Each still picture is made up of hundreds of thousands or even millions of picture elements, or pixels (▸211). Every pixel is represented by numbers that tell the television how much red, green and blue light to produce to recreate that tiny portion of the image correctly. The numbers are carried by radio waves in the case of terrestrial and satellite TV, and by electric signals in the case of cable TV. A high-definition (HD) television has to be able to display images of either 1280 pixels wide by 720 high ('HD Ready') or 1920 by 1080 ('Full HD').

WHAT'S THE DIFFERENCE BETWEEN PLASMA, LCD AND LED SCREENS?

In a plasma display, each pixel is created by a tiny chamber that is coated with red, green or blue phosphors. When electric current is applied to the chamber, a gas inside produces a burst of ultraviolet radiation, which causes the phosphors to produce light. An LCD (liquid crystal display) screen has a bright white backlight, often an LED (light emitting diode) panel. An array of tiny liquid crystals in front

WHAT IS A SMART TV?

TV screens can display any video signal – from games consoles and video cameras, as well as computers or tablets connected via cables or Wi-Fi. There is a range of set-top boxes available that receive and decode content from the Internet and connect to a television to display the content. So-called smart TVs have the necessary electronics built in, and thus enable viewers to access a wide range of content directly, using the television remote control.

WHAT IS SURROUND SOUND?

Modern films and many television programs are accompanied by 'surround sound', in which the sound is delivered on several separate tracks. Each track is played by a different loudspeaker, and the speakers are positioned in the room to give an experience much richer than ordinary mono or stereo sound reproduction.

ALL AROUND Speakers positioned on all sides of the viewer create a three-dimensional soundscape.

HOW DOES 3D TV WORK?

Televisions that display three-dimensional (3D) images produce two pictures at the same time – one for each eye. There are several ways to achieve this, the most common being to use polarising filters in the screen, and corresponding filters in glasses the viewer wears when watching. Each filter in the glasses blocks one of the pictures. An autostereoscopic television displays 3D pictures that can be viewed without glasses. It achieves this by dividing each picture into thin vertical strips and interlacing the two pictures. A set of thin vertical lenses laid over the screen diverts each picture slightly to the left or right, so that each eye sees only one of the pictures.

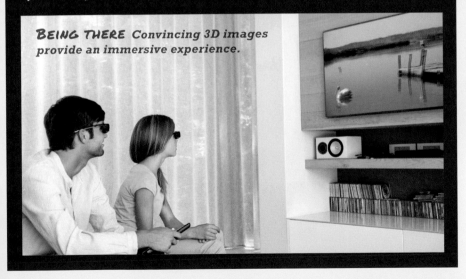

BEING THERE Convincing 3D images provide an immersive experience.

fast fact

Each frame displayed on a 'Full HD' television is made up of 2,073,600 (1920 x 1080) pixels (dots).

of the backlight allows more or less light through, depending on the strength of an electric field applied to them – and a pattern of tiny red, green and blue filters on top of the array ensures that the correct colours are displayed in the right locations. Some newer televisions have so-called organic LED, or OLED, screens. These consist of two electric grids (at least one of which is transparent), separated by a thin layer of synthetic polymers. When current flows through the grids, the polymers emit red, green or blue light. Such screens can be very thin, as they do not require a backlight; they also use less power than LCD screens and in the near future could become much cheaper to make.

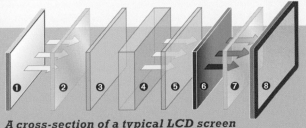

A cross-section of a typical LCD screen

❶ Backlight
❷ Polarising filter
❸ Transparent electrode
❹ Liquid crystal panel
❺ Transparent electrode
❻ Colour filter plate
❼ Polarising filter
❽ Screen

PRINTING AND PUBLISHING

The first forms of printing – using carved wooden blocks to print on paper and cloth – date back to ancient China and Egypt. But it was the invention of metal type in the mid-fifteenth century that revolutionised Western civilisation, allowing multiple copies of books to be made and, in turn, speeding up the flow of knowledge and ideas. In recent times, modern digital technology has transformed the printing process and the distribution of the printed word.

METAL MIX *Gutenberg cast type from a mix of lead, tin and antimony.*

WHAT IS TYPE?

Originally, type was a rectangular piece of wood or metal bearing the carved, reversed shape of a letter. In the mid-1400s, Johannes Gutenberg devised a system for making metal type, arranging it in a frame and printing it onto paper using a wooden press (▶257). His invention spread rapidly, then evolved steadily over the next 500 years. Today, type is usually selected and arranged using computer software, and pages of text are saved as a file or document. This file can be printed on a desktop printer at home, or it can be sent to a printing house to create high-quality books, magazines and other publications.

Early wooden printing press

HOW DOES AN INKJET PRINTER WORK?

As its name suggests, an inkjet printer works by firing dots of ink onto paper. The main printing unit in such printers is called the print head and it is covered in tiny nozzles or holes; behind it are the ink or toner cartridges. Electric charges prompted by the computer software propel tiny drops of ink out through the nozzles and onto the paper in rapid succession. As the print head tracks back and forth across the paper and the paper moves through the printer, the dots build up to create an image. When the paper emerges from the printer, the inks are still damp, but they dry soon after.

HOW DOES A LASER PRINTER WORK?

A laser printer contains a revolving cylinder, or 'drum', that is given a negative electric charge. A laser scans the drum, removing or leaving charges as it rapidly turns on and off, building up a mirror image of the text and pictures. The drum rolls through fine black or coloured powder, called toner. It has a negative charge and so it only sticks to the uncharged areas, creating the image. This image is pressed onto paper and the ink is then dried as the paper passes through a heating unit, called a fuser. (In some types of laser printer, the charges are reversed.)

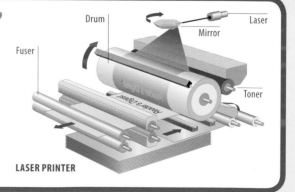

Drum
Laser
Mirror
Fuser
Toner

LASER PRINTER

HOW ARE BOOKS PRINTED?

Most books, magazines and newspapers are printed using a system called offset lithography. Lithography relies on the principle that oil and water will not mix. The page layouts are output by a computer directly onto a flat metal printing plate. The plate is then treated so that only the image areas will attract the greasy ink. In offset lithography, the ink is transferred again, or offset, to a rubber roller, or 'blanket', and then to the paper. This produces a clearer, sharper result than printing directly from the plate.

Cyan

Magenta

Yellow

Black

Most printing uses the four process colours: cyan, magenta, yellow and black.

Printed colours are built up of overlapping dots of the four process colours.

Printing press

PRINT COLOURS *To enable colours to be adjusted, printing software splits a multicoloured image into separate single-colour images. These are combined during printing to recreate the original tones.*

fast fact

When it was released in 2007, JK Rowling's *Harry Potter and the Deathly Hallows* had the biggest first print run of any book ever: 12 million copies.

HOW DO YOU MAKE AN E-BOOK?

An e-book, or electronic book, is a book in the form of digital data, which can be read by a computer, tablet or other electronic device using 'e-reader' software. To create an e-book, you typeset or code the text on a computer then convert it to a format that can be read by e-readers. This may be a PDF, which can be read by all computers; the EPUB format used by many e-readers; or proprietary formats used by particular retailers. E-books can be purchased online and downloaded instantly.

PAGE TURNER *E-reader software normally allows the user to view text as a single page or a two-page spread, turn pages, enlarge type, search the text and bookmark pages.*

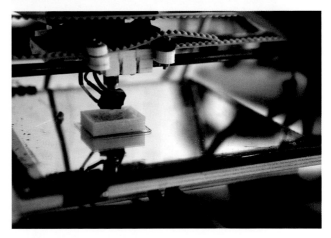

WHAT IS 3D PRINTING?

A 3D printer is a machine that makes a solid, three-dimensional object by building up thin layers of a material, such as a plastic or a metal alloy, and then fusing them together. As with two-dimensional printing, instructions are provided by a computer program. The main use of 3D printers is to create models and prototypes of industrial products, for review and testing. However, they are increasingly being used to create finished parts and products, ranging from clothing and customised shoes to foods and prosthetic body parts (▶181).

ARTIFICIAL INTELLIGENCE

Just like the human brain, computers can make intelligent decisions based on input from the world around them. They can even be programmed to learn and improve their decision-making capabilities. This artificial intelligence (AI) is put to use in a wide range of situations, including in autonomous or semi-autonomous robots as well as games and other consumer products.

TIGHT BOND *Robots have been shown to improve the quality of car welding and, thereby, vehicle safety.*

GOOD COMPANY? *Japan's NEC corporation developed the PaPeRo, a robot designed to interact with humans*

HOW ARE ROBOTS USED IN INDUSTRY?

Semi-intelligent robots are used extensively in manufacturing to perform repetitive tasks with high precision. In a car factory, for example, they weld, paint, and fit windows, seats and doors. Most factory robots have strong, dextrous arms, and video cameras provide them with visual feedback of the pieces they are manipulating. However, these industrial robots cannot adapt themselves to new tasks, but instead have to be reprogrammed.

DO ROBOTS HAVE MEDICAL USES?

Robots are sometimes used in surgery, but such robots are not very intelligent – they do not make decisions about where and what to cut, for example. Instead, they are very sophisticated manipulators that are controlled by a surgeon, who may be on the other side of the operating theatre or even in a distant location. Somewhat more intelligent, autonomous robots are used in rehabilitation, helping people to gain muscle strength or regain abilities lost after a stroke, for example, while also helping to document the patients' progress on doctors' computers. Some hospitals employ semi-autonomous mobile robots with video cameras and infrared and sonar sensors to deliver medicines and bed linen.

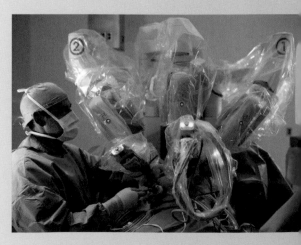

FINER CUT *Surgical robots help improve the efficiency and accuracy of medical procedures.*

CAN ROBOTS HELP IN THE HOME?

Several robots are already available that are designed to help around the home. There are robot vacuum cleaners that clean the floor while the homeowner is out; robots that keep gutters clear from blockages; solar-powered lawnmowing robots and swimming-pool-cleaning robots. Each of these devices has sensors that help it function autonomously and effectively – but they only work well in limited environments; they require assistance from a human being if anything unforeseen occurs. Even so, with artificial intelligence and computer power advancing rapidly, an all-round home help may one day become a reality.

CAN A ROBOT REALLY THINK FOR ITSELF?

Much of the research into AI aims to model human intelligence. However, no one knows when, if ever, robots with human-like intelligence will become a reality. There are several competitions to encourage advances towards greater intelligence and sophistication in robots – one is the RoboCup, whose aim is to produce by the middle of the twenty-first century a team of robots that can beat the human soccer World Cup-winning team. The creation of truly intelligent, perhaps even conscious, robots would raise many ethical issues, and some fear that such robots would be living things that could demand rights and present a threat to humans. For now, however, such questions remain in the realm of philosophy.

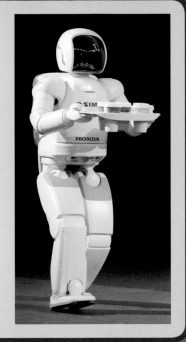

MOBILE HELPER *ASIMO, a humanoid robot, can identify different voices and respond to commands.*

REMOTE VIEW *Military drones can safely scout areas inaccessible to ground forces.*

WHAT IS A DRONE?

Semi-autonomous, uncrewed aerial vehicles, or UAVs, are already in use in conflict zones – flying reconnaissance or even bombing missions, for example – and above crowds, looking for potential trouble or unlawful behaviour. While they are normally remotely controlled by ground-based pilots, some do have intelligence built in that makes them able to navigate and achieve some of their goals without direct input from humans.

fast fact

The word 'robot' was coined by Czech playwright Karel Capek, in his 1920 play *R.U.R.* The initials in the name of the play stand for Rosumovi Umelí Roboti (Rossum's Artificial Robots).

HOW ELSE IS ARTIFICIAL INTELLIGENCE USED TODAY?

AI is used in web-based software that helps present people with online content suited to their interests or 'virtual assistants' that can give reasonable, useful answers to questions entered on business websites or spoken into a smartphone. Some computer games incorporate AI to produce virtual opponents or make software-generated game characters behave in a more realistic way. Sophisticated engine control units in some car engines use AI to help improve performance or fuel economy by monitoring the car's systems and its speed as well as environmental variables, such as temperature. Self-driving cars, with powerful intelligent computers onboard, have been the subject of extensive development and testing, and will become widely available in the near future.

TRIPLE CHALLENGE *A Russian-built robot plays chess against three grandmasters during a demonstration game in Moscow.*

SATELLITES IN SPACE

Artificial satellites are devices that have been launched into orbit around our planet to gather and send information to scientists or to enhance communications on Earth. Though they operate automatically, they include space stations visited by astronauts. Since the first satellite went into orbit in 1957, more than 6000 have been launched and it is estimated that around 3600 are still in orbit. Some are low enough to be visible to the naked eye, appearing like stars moving steadily across the night sky.

BALANCING ACT *A communications satellite, or comsat. Like most satellites, it is powered by solar panels and travels at just the right speed for it to remain in orbit rather than falling to Earth.*

WHAT ARE SATELLITES USED FOR TODAY?

There are two main kinds of satellites: observational and communications satellites. Observational satellites gather images from space and transmit them to Earth; these include images of outer space from orbiting telescopes, such as the Hubble Space Telescope, which are much clearer than those obtained from Earth, and pictures of Earth's atmosphere and surface, which can be used for weather forecasting (▶43) and mapping. Communications satellites relay radio waves (including telephone and television signals) transmitted from one point on Earth back to another, often thousands of kilometres away, greatly speeding up global communications.

WHICH WERE THE FIRST SATELLITES?

The first satellite was *Sputnik I*, which was sent into orbit aboard a rocket by the Soviet Union in October 1957. After 57 days in orbit, sending out steady *beep-beep* signals relayed by media around the world, it burned up in the atmosphere. Eager to compete in what was then known as the 'Space Race', the United States followed suit in January 1958, with *Explorer I*. The first real scientific satellite, it remained in orbit until 1970 and has since been succeeded by more than 90 other *Explorer* satellites.

HITCHING A RIDE *Satellites are carried aloft on rockets and launched once they reach the correct altitude.*

fast fact

Launched in 1958, the *Vanguard I* satellite maintained communication with Earth for almost seven years before becoming inoperative. Nevertheless, it remains in orbit today, the oldest artificial satellite in space.

EYE IN THE SKY *Since the early 1970s, NASA's Landsat satellites have helped map terrain and environmental changes.*

Space stations, telescopes and other observational satellites orbit in a band approximately 300–800 km (190–500 miles) above Earth's surface, often providing detailed images of the planet's surface. Navigational satellites follow a so-called semi-synchronous orbit at about 20,000 km (12,400 miles) from

Earth – that means they circle Earth every 12 hours, or twice a day. The majority of communications satellites orbit at around 36,000 km (22,000 miles), at the same rate as Earth turns, so that they remain in a fixed position above a point on Earth's surface – a so-called geostationary orbit.

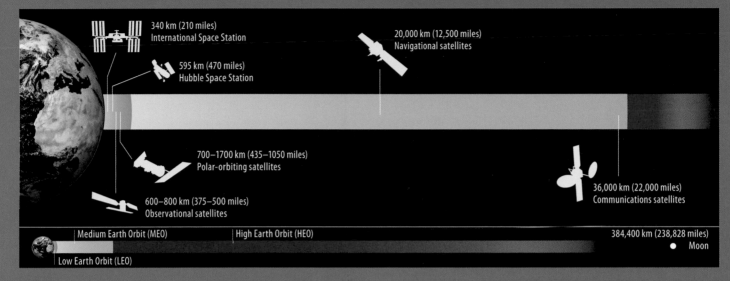

340 km (210 miles)
International Space Station

595 km (470 miles)
Hubble Space Station

700–1700 km (435–1050 miles)
Polar-orbiting satellites

600–800 km (375–500 miles)
Observational satellites

20,000 km (12,500 miles)
Navigational satellites

36,000 km (22,000 miles)
Communications satellites

Medium Earth Orbit (MEO)   High Earth Orbit (HEO)   384,400 km (238,828 miles)
● Moon

Low Earth Orbit (LEO)

RUBBISH DUMP *This simulated illustration shows all the recordable objects orbiting Earth at up to 2000 km (1200 miles).*

IS SPACE CLUTTERED WITH OLD SATELLITES?

If a satellite can't be repaired, or is decommissioned, it may be deorbited by bringing it down into Earth's atmosphere, where it will burn up; left in its current orbit; set adrift; or moved to what is known as a graveyard orbit, out of the way of active satellites. Large numbers of old satellites are part of the vast array of 'space junk' that orbits Earth, including jettisoned parts of rockets, old fuel tanks, tools and debris from explosions. Scientists estimate there are at least 10,000 pieces of junk more than 10 cm (4 in) long and 100,000 pieces between 1 cm (½ in) and 10 cm (4 in) long. At orbiting velocities of up to 50,000 km/h (30,000 mph), even a tiny piece of metal can punch a hole through the pressure hull of a spacecraft.

HOW DOES SATELLITE NAVIGATION WORK?

A satellite navigation system allows a ground-based device to work out its exact location on Earth using signals from a group of satellites. Each satellite transmits highly precise time signals. The navigational unit on Earth compares the time signals from at least three of the satellites to work out its exact distance from each satellite. This allows the unit to calculate its position on Earth, and thereby display the user's position on a map and plot routes.

LOCATION FINDER *The most widely used satellite navigation system is the GPS (Global Positioning System), developed by the US Army.*

CARS, BICYCLES AND MOTORCYCLES

Prior to the invention of cars and bicycles, people relied mainly on horses or horse-drawn carriages to travel overland. The first bicycles allowed people to travel quickly using their own power, thus providing unprecedented freedom of movement. But it was the introduction of the motor car that revolutionised road transport, bringing mobility to millions and creating a range of new industries.

WHEN WERE BICYCLES INVENTED?

In 1818, German inventor Baron Karl von Drais patented a design for a two-wheeled wooden vehicle with a seat and steerable front wheel, the draisine. In the 1860s, the French Michaux family began producing versions of the draisine with pedals and cranks; these became known as velocipedes. The large front wheel of the 'high bicycle' or 'penny-farthing', which appeared in the 1870s, provided greater speed but was less stable. In 1885, John Kemp Starley introduced the 'safety bicycle', with a chain-driven rear wheel. Two further improvements were John Dunlop's pneumatic (air-filled) rubber tyres (1888), and gears developed by the British firm of Sturmey-Archer (1901–06). Today, carbon-fibre materials and designs that reduce air resistance have made bikes lighter and faster than ever.

WHEN WAS THE FIRST MOTORBIKE INVENTED?

The first motorbike was built by Gottlieb Daimler in 1885. It consisted of a petrol-powered internal-combustion engine on a wooden-framed bicycle.

CYCLE STORY *The basic design of the bicycle has been refined over 200 years.*

1818 Draisine, Karl von Drais, Germany

1860s Velocipede, Michaux family, France

1870s Penny-farthing, Eugene Meyer, France, and James Starley, England

1885 Safety bicycle, John Kemp Starley, England

1970s Mountain bike, USA

Today Racing bicycle

HOW DID THE MOTOR CAR DEVELOP?

The key developments in the history of the motor car were the invention of the compact petrol-fuelled internal-combustion engine and the creation of the pneumatic (air-filled) tyre. These took place in Europe and were first brought together in Germany and France. The United States then took the lead in manufacturing in the early 1900s. The number of cars on the road worldwide rose steadily, from just 20,000 in 1900 to more than 1 billion in 2010.

ON THE ROAD *Ever-changing technologies and needs repeatedly altered the form of the motor car.*

HORSELESS CARRIAGE Following the invention of the internal-combustion engine in the 1860s, several engineers used it to power road vehicles. German engineer Gottlieb Daimler's adapted carriage of 1886 (above) was the first four-wheeled motor car.

MASS PRODUCTION Problems with wind and dust soon led to the introduction of windscreens. In the early 1900s, the Americans pioneered the mass production of cars, most notably Henry Ford's Model T (above), introduced in 1908.

HOW DOES A CONVENTIONAL CAR ENGINE WORK?

Conventional cars are powered by an internal-combustion engine. A spray of petrol and air is drawn into each of the car's four cylinders, and compressed and ignited. The explosion drives down a piston, which turns a crankshaft connected to the car's wheels. Burned gas is then forced out via the exhaust valve. The ignitions are timed so that each piston fires in turn.

PISTON POWER *Each piston in an engine goes through the four-stage cycle shown at right. This is the source of the term 'four-stroke engine'.*

1. As the piston moves downwards, fuel is sucked into the cylinder.

2. As the piston moves back up, it compresses the fuel, which ignites.

3. As the fuel explodes, the piston is pushed down once again.

4. Moving up again, the piston forces gas through the exhaust valve.

WHAT OTHER FUELS CAN POWER A CAR?

Some cars are adapted to run on liquid petroleum gas, or LPG, a by-product of the petroleum industry, which is cheaper, more efficient and more abundant than conventional fuel; it is, however, still a fossil fuel, with finite reserves (▶240). Other vehicles run on biofuels, such as ethanol, a renewable fuel made from maize and other crops. Fully electric cars are becoming more widely available and the expansion of networks of recharging centres is making them increasingly attractive to consumers. However, the engine of the future is likely to be powered by a fuel cell that generates electricity by combining hydrogen released through the electrolysis of water with oxygen in the air. The technology for this already exists, but remains expensive.

TOPPING UP *In the United States, electric car recharging stations now permit widespread travel.*

fast fact

In 1997, a British-built supersonic car, the Thrust SSC, became the first car to break the sound barrier and also established the current world land-speed record of 1228 km/h (763 mph).

HOW DOES A HYBRID CAR WORK?

Hybrid cars usually have two power sources: a large, powerful electric motor and a small, fuel-efficient internal-combustion engine. The electric motor aids ignition and acceleration but once the car reaches set cruising speed, the internal-combustion engine takes over. At higher steady speeds it will run much more efficiently than it does at lower, frequently changing speeds. While the car is stationary or decelerating, the electric battery recharges.

GAS GUZZLER Increasing affluence in postwar America and the ready availability of cheap petrol led to the massive, fuel-hungry US cars of the 1950s, distinguished by their tail-fins and sparkling chrome details.

SCALING DOWN In the early 1960s, the Mini Minor, designed by Alec Issigonis and first built in England, sparked a trend for front-wheel-drive compact cars – a trend given further impetus by widespread petroleum shortages in the 1970s.

ALTERNATIVE POWER Increasing concerns in the 1990s regarding the rising costs and diminishing reserves of oil, as well as the impact of fossil fuels on global warming, led to the development of highly fuel-efficient petrol-electric, or hybrid, cars.

TRAIN TRAVEL

The train was the first form of large-scale mechanised transport.

The first railway opened in 1830 and many hundreds of thousands of kilometres of track were built through the remainder of the nineteenth century. Despite stiff competition from road and air transport, railways still thrive – hauling heavy freight, transporting millions of commuters and linking cities separated by long distances.

WHICH WAS THE FIRST TRAIN?

Trains were first developed between 1800 and 1830 in England, mainly for carrying coal and iron. The steam locomotive was invented by the Cornish engineer Richard Trevithick in 1803, and the first steam passenger train was built by another English engineer, George Stephenson, in 1825. It carried 450 passengers the 13 km (8 miles) from Stockton to Darlington in Yorkshire, England, at 24 km/h (15 mph). The first scheduled rail service, on the Liverpool and Manchester railway, began operating in 1830.

ROCKET POWER George Stephenson's 'Rocket', built in 1829, was the fastest and most powerful locomotive of its day, reaching speeds of 46 km/h (36 mph).

HOW DO TRAINS WORK?

The age of steam trains is long gone. Today most trains run on electricity, or a combination of electric power and diesel fuel. Other innovations, including the use of magnetic fields in place of wheels, are steadily increasing the speed and efficiency of trains.

STEAMING AHEAD In a steam locomotive, a coal fire boils water, producing steam, which pushes a piston up and down in a cylinder. The piston is linked to the driving wheels by a connecting rod.

Steam train, Cumbria, England

Acela Express, Washington DC, USA

EXTRA CHARGE Electric trains pick up electricity from overhead cables or a third rail. This drives a motor that turns the wheels. Diesel locomotives are also driven by electricity; however, they use diesel-fuelled engines to generate the power.

FAST AS A BULLET Modern high-speed trains, such as the French TGV and Japanese Shinkansen (or 'bullet train'), have a powerful electric engine at each end. Some high-speed trains are designed to tilt as they round bends – a tilting train can take bends 25–40 per cent faster.

TGV Euroduplex, France

Shanghai Maglev Train, China

EXTRA LIFT On a Maglev (magnetic-levitation) track, magnetic fields generated by electric coils in the track alternately repel and attract similar coils in the cars, making the train float just above the track. This allows it to move at great speed and with very little friction.

What safety systems prevent trains colliding?

Railways still use red, yellow and green signals – much like traffic lights – to keep trains on separate sections of track. But other automatic safety systems are now in use. With the Automatic Warning System (AWS), if a driver passes a red or yellow signal the system triggers a buzzer in the cab and applies the brakes if there is no response from the driver. A similar system, called the Train Protection and Warning System (TPWS), applies the brakes if a driver is going too fast or passes a red signal; it cannot be overridden by the driver. And a yet more advanced system, called Automatic Train Protection (ATP), monitors train speed and transmits a safe speed to the driver's display panel; if the driver exceeds this, the brakes go on automatically.

N700 SERIES This train can reach 270 km/h (170 mph) in three minutes.

Which are the world's fastest trains?

In recent times, speed records for conventional trains have been repeatedly claimed by France's TGV trains, the latest world record being established by a TGV POS train in 2007, when it reached a speed of 574.8 km/h (357 mph) in tests. However, this is less than a Japanese SCMaglev train, which reached 581 km/h (361 mph) in a 2003 test. The maximum speeds achieved by trains in commercial service are around 300 km/h (200 mph) for the TGV and Japan's bullet trains, and 431 km/h (268 mph) for the Shanghai Maglev Train.

DRIVER'S SEAT In the cab of a German Intercity-Express (ICE) train, the driver monitors the controls.

fast fact

The world's longest railway line is the Trans-Siberian Railway, which runs from Moscow in western Russia to Vladivostok, on the country's east coast, covering a distance of 9289 km (5772 miles).

How will train travel change in the future?

Researchers are investigating the potential of vacuum tube trains, or vactrains. These Maglev trains would run underground through airless tunnels (a vacuum, in other words). With no air resistance, such trains could, in theory, reach speeds of up to 8000 km/h (5000 mph) and make the journey between New York and Beijing in two hours. A similar proposed system, the Hyperloop, suggests pod-like trains could travel through a partial-vacuum tube on cushions of air, at up to 1200 km/h (750 mph).

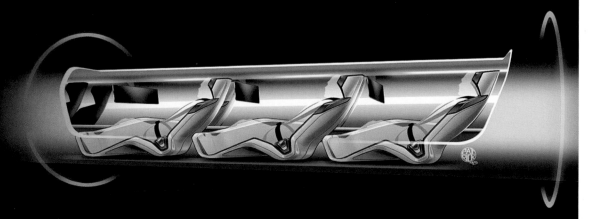

TRAVEL POD This cutaway shows the passenger capsule inside the proposed Hyperloop transportation system.

SHIPS AND SUBMARINES

From the earliest times, humans built boats to cross otherwise unpassable waterways, such as rivers, lakes and seas. The invention and evolution of sails led to the first large seagoing craft, which in turn resulted in the expansion of trade and the creation of maritime empires. Even today, in the era of mass air travel, shipping still carries the bulk of the world's cargo, powerful navies continue to patrol the seas, and ever-larger ships carry thousands of holidaymakers on cruises.

WHEN WERE SAILS FIRST USED?

The first known sails, used on Egyptian vessels more than 5000 years ago, were rectangular and hung from a horizontal spar. Such a 'square rig' yields good speed if the wind is coming from behind, but the boat cannot sail into the wind. This problem was solved in the Roman Empire during the second century AD with the lateen sail. A triangular sail hanging from an angled spar, it deflected the wind so that the boat could sail into it at an angle. From then on the history of sailing was largely a matter of refining these two systems.

LATEEN RIG In the fifth century AD, Arab shipbuilders refined the lateen sail in small ships known as dhows.

PORTUGUESE CARAVEL This ship's enlarged version of the lateen rig made it highly manoeuvrable. It was on such ships that European mariners first reached Africa, India and the Americas.

WHEN DID ENGINES REPLACE SAILS?

Large sailing ships continued to evolve up to the late nineteenth century, reaching a pinnacle of efficiency with three-, four- and five-masted clipper ships. From around 1870, these gave way to steam-powered and then diesel-powered vessels. The first mechanically operated submarines also appeared in the late 1800s and soon proved highly effective in warfare. Modern innovations in shipping include nuclear-powered warships, giant supertankers and multistorey cruise ships.

CRUISE SHIP Today's towering cruise ships have facilities such as gyms, tennis courts, swimming pools, theatres, restaurants, bars, hairdressers and shops.

TEA CLIPPER Among the fastest sailing ships ever built, square-rigged clippers carried cargo swiftly over long distances.

CHINESE JUNK For hundreds of years until the nineteenth century, junks were the biggest, safest and most efficient ships in the world.

UNDER WATER Second World War submarines like this German U-boat used diesel engines on the surface and battery-powered electric motors (which do not use up air) when under water.

HOW DO METAL SHIPS FLOAT?

Anything that is less dense than water will float. Most metals are denser than water, but if you make a hollow metal container, the air inside it means that the whole thing is lighter than the same volume of water, so it floats. The heavier the load, however, the lower the ship will sink, so lines, known as Plimsoll lines, are marked on a ship's hull to indicate the maximum safe load in different kinds of seas.

TOP LINE *The maximum safe load indicated by a Plimsoll line varies for sea or fresh water, winter or summer, and tropical or high-latitude seas.*

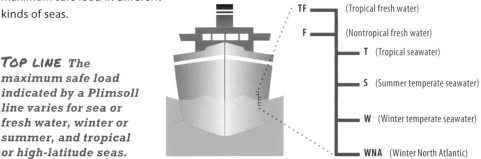

TF — (Tropical fresh water)
F — (Nontropical fresh water)
T — (Tropical seawater)
S — (Summer temperate seawater)
W — (Winter temperate seawater)
WNA — (Winter North Atlantic)

HOW DO SUBMARINES GO UP AND DOWN?

A submarine has special tanks, known as ballast tanks. It dives by flooding these with seawater and tilting downwards. To surface, compressed air is blown into the ballast tanks, which pushes the water out of them, lightening and refloating the submarine.

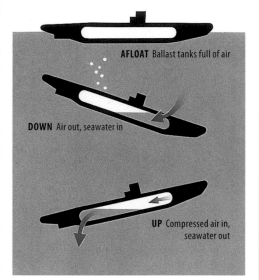

AFLOAT Ballast tanks full of air

DOWN Air out, seawater in

UP Compressed air in, seawater out

STEADY DESCENT *A submarine's individual ballast tanks can be flooded one at a time for greater control.*

HOW DO SHIPS' CAPTAINS KNOW WHERE THEY ARE?

Along with traditional instruments, such as a compass and detailed maps, today's navigators use satellite navigation systems (▶221) to plot and monitor their course. When deep underwater, submarines cannot pick up satellite signals, however; so their crews then rely on their compass, maps of ocean currents, motion sensors and computers to work out how far their vessel has travelled and in what direction.

WHAT IS A SUBMERSIBLE?

Submersibles are small diving machines launched from a mother ship. Used for deep-sea exploration, making repairs to oil rigs and undersea cables, and in scientific research, they usually have a crew of two or three people, though some are remote-controlled. Submersibles are heavily reinforced to withstand the intense pressure under the sea – 400 times greater at a depth of 4000 m (13,000 ft) than at sea level – and are usually equipped with spotlights, video cameras and robotic arms.

fast fact

A modern nuclear-powered submarine can carry sufficient fuel to run for 30 years and stay under water for weeks on end. Its diving duration is limited only by the need to replenish food stores for its crew.

INTO THE DEEP *Two researchers and a pilot venture below the Sea of Cortez in a DeepSea submersible, which can reach depths of 450 m (1500 ft). The view through the 10 cm (4 in) thick acrylic sphere is crystal clear underwater.*

BALLOONS AND AIRSHIPS

The first human flights were achieved in hot-air balloons, in the 1780s, when French adventurers launched balloons filled with hot air and hydrogen, drawing huge, excited crowds. The craze for ballooning continued into the 1800s and in the early twentieth century massive airships were built to carry passengers. Though these airships ceased operation in the 1930s, balloons and airships are still used today for research, recreation and exploration.

HEATING THE AIR The burners are positioned above the capsule. Different sets are used for different altitudes.

CONTROL CENTRE Instruments inside the capsule allow the pilots to monitor altitude, speed, fuel levels and other vital data.

FUEL TANKS Fuel tanks are attached to the outside of the capsule so that they can be released into the sea when empty.

UP AND AWAY A modern, high-altitude hot-air balloon is made of strong, synthetic materials and incorporates a range of safety features.

HOW DOES A BALLOON WORK?

Balloons are based on the principle that hot air rises: warm the air in a balloon and it will lift any attached basket or capsule upwards. A modern hot-air balloon has an 'envelope' of tough nylon, with stainless-steel cables to support the burners and the basket or capsule. The air in the outer envelope is normally heated by burning liquid propane gas. Some balloons also have a separate cell containing highly buoyant helium gas.

HOW DO YOU CONTROL A HOT-AIR BALLOON?

To make a balloon rise, the balloonist heats the air inside it with the burners. When the burners are turned off, the air cools and the balloon descends. A quick blast of flame about once a minute keeps the balloon level. This is the only control the balloonist has. There is no steering, and the balloon is blown along by the wind, which varies in speed and direction, so the pilot has to anticipate and monitor wind strength and direction.

FIRING UP Long-distance balloons have an inner cell of helium. A burner heats the air in the outer cell, making the balloon rise.

LIGHTENING THE LOAD As the balloon rises, the pilot may throw ballast overboard to lighten it further.

GAS RELEASE To descend more quickly, the pilot opens the valve at the top of the helium sphere, releasing some of the gas.

LIMITED CONTROL Balloonists have close control of their aircraft's altitude but not of its direction.

BASKET WITH A VIEW Hot-air balloons are commonly used for sightseeing flights.

WHEN WERE AIRSHIPS INVENTED?

The first airship, filled with hydrogen and powered by a steam engine, was flown by Frenchman Henri Giffard in 1853. In 1900, German inventor Count Ferdinand von Zeppelin launched the first of his vast, cigar-shaped airships, or zeppelins, which were used for reconnaissance and bombing raids during the First World War. After the war, zeppelins provided passenger services, including luxury transatlantic trips beginning in 1928. The biggest airships were huge. The *Hindenburg*, for example, was three times the size of a jumbo jet, with double cabins for its 72 passengers, a dining room, lounge and bar with grand piano, as well as an open promenade deck. But the increasing viability of aeroplane travel and a series of accidents brought this glamorous form of travel to an end.

UP IN FLAMES *The* **Hindenburg** *caught fire as it was landing at Lakehurst, New Jersey, USA, on 6 May 1937, killing 36 people and fatally denting confidence in airship travel.*

HOW DO AIRSHIPS FLY?

Modern airships are filled with helium gas. They fly at about 160 km/h (100 mph), using two propellers driven by engines. The pilot steers with rudders and flaps, called elevators, which can be tilted up or down. The propellers can also be tilted to allow the airship to take off and land vertically.

HOLDING UP *Airships are still used today, mainly where the craft's ability to stay aloft in one spot for a long period is a benefit – as with advertising, filming and scientific observation.*

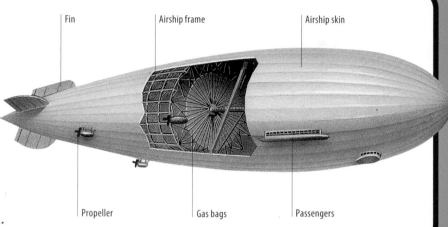

Fin | Airship frame | Airship skin

Propeller | Gas bags | Passengers

HOW FAR CAN BALLOONS FLY?

In theory balloons can fly great distances, but due to their limited steering controls and fragility in extreme weather, they often come to grief. In the late twentieth century, several teams of balloonists competed to become the first to fly around the world nonstop. A number of the attempts ended with crashes, but in 1999 Bertrand Piccard from Switzerland and Englishman Brian Jones flew their *Breitling Orbiter 3* balloon right round the world, touching down in Egypt on 21 March after a nonstop flight of 19 days, 21 hours and 55 minutes.

fast fact

In 2012, Austrian skydiver Felix Baumgartner used a helium balloon to travel 39 km (24 miles) into the stratosphere before making the highest ever skydive, during which he reached a freefall speed of 1357.6 km/h (844 mph).

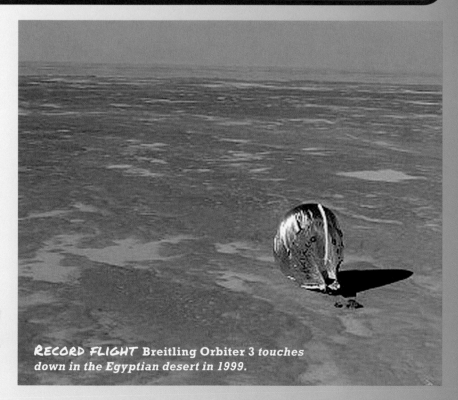

RECORD FLIGHT Breitling Orbiter 3 *touches down in the Egyptian desert in 1999.*

AEROPLANES AND HELICOPTERS

Little more than a century ago, humans first achieved powered flight in an aeroplane. Today, highly sophisticated airliners carry millions of people around the world daily, with some major airports handling more than a thousand flights every 24 hours.

HOW DOES A HEAVY AEROPLANE STAY UP IN THE SKY?

The secret of flying lies in a force called 'lift'. To achieve lift, you need a forward speed of around 80 km/h (50 mph) for a light aircraft and about 160–240 km/h (100–150 mph) for a heavier plane. You also need wings of the right shape. Most plane wings have a 'half teardrop' shape – they are curved above and flatter below, tapering towards the back. This shape makes the air flow much faster over the top than underneath. The pressure of fast-flowing air above the wing is lower than that of the slower-moving air beneath it, and this pushes the wing upwards as it moves through the air.

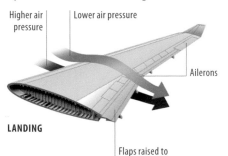

Higher air pressure

Lower air pressure

Ailerons

LANDING

Flaps raised to reduce drag

IN FLIGHT The shape of the wing creates lift. Panels called ailerons can be moved up on one wing and down on another to bank (tilt) the plane. The tail has an adjustable rudder for steering from side to side and horizontal tailplanes (elevators) that move the nose up and down and prevent the plane from rocking.

WHICH WERE THE FIRST PLANES TO FLY?

After balloonists, the first people to fly did so in gliders – aircraft without engines. They included a German, Otto Lilienthal, and a Frenchman, Octave Chanute, in the 1890s. In 1900, two American bicycle-makers from Dayton, Ohio, made a wind tunnel and used it to study how glider wings work. They were the Wright brothers, Wilbur and Orville, who then built their own plane, the *Flyer* and added an engine and propeller to it. On 17 December 1903, they made the first four powered flights ever in the *Flyer* – the longest lasting 50 seconds and covering 260 m (852 ft). The age of aviation had begun.

The Wright brothers' Flyer

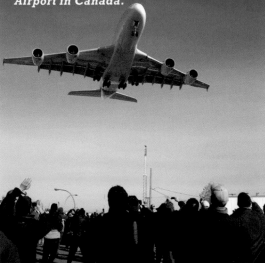

TOUCH DOWN A four-engined Airbus 340 comes in to land at Montreal Airport in Canada.

HOW DOES A PLANE TAKE OFF AND LAND?

To take off, a plane speeds along a runway on full power until it reaches the required speed to gain lift. At that point the pilot raises elevators on the tail to lift the nose, and lowers the flaps on the wings to increase lift. When landing, the pilot again raises the elevators on the tail to bring the nose up and puts the engines into reverse thrust to slow the plane down. At the same time the pilot raises spoilers on the wings to act as air brakes, and lowers the wing flaps to increase airflow and maintain lift at low speed.

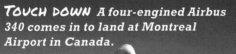

LANDING

Spoilers raised to act as brakes

Flaps lowered to provide lift

Flaps lowered to maintain lift at slow speed

TAKE-OFF

WHAT HAPPENS ON THE FLIGHT DECK?

The pilot and copilot of a passenger aircraft spend most of their time watching the plane's instruments to check that everything is going smoothly. Because modern aircraft are computerised, the pilots no longer need to keep their hands on the controls. The whole flight is followed closely by radar and radio contact from the ground. All pilots have to make a flight plan, which they give to the air traffic controllers before leaving. This tells the controllers where the plane is going, so that they can keep that part of the sky clear of other planes.

WHAT ARE SUPERSONIC PLANES?

Supersonic planes are those that can fly faster than the speed of sound, 1234 km/h (767 mph). Most such aircraft are military planes, but two supersonic airliners were at one time in service as passenger planes, the Soviet Tupolev Tu-144 and Concorde. The former carried passengers for only a year before being withdrawn in 1978 following a series of accidents. Concorde was in service as an airliner for 27 years from 1976, flying transatlantic flights in half the time of conventional airliners, but was decommissioned after a crash in 2003.

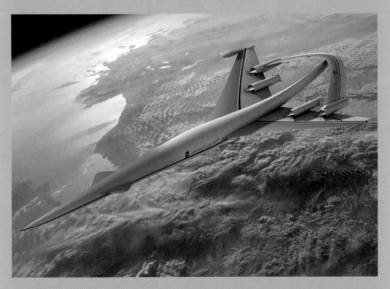

READY FOR REVIVAL *Supersonic airliners could yet make a comeback. This design for a supersonic 'green machine' was produced by Lockheed Martin for NASA in the United States.*

HOW DOES A HELICOPTER WORK?

A helicopter's main rotor blades are, in fact, long thin wings, and by spinning very quickly through the air they create lift just like wings on an aircraft do. A complex gearing mechanism allows the rotors to be tilted forwards, backwards or to the side. This provides horizontal thrust, allowing the helicopter to move in any direction. Most helicopters also have a tail rotor that holds the helicopter steady – without this, the helicopter would spin in the opposite direction to the main rotor. Twin-rotor helicopters, however, have two horizontal rotors turning in opposite directions, whose turning forces cancel each other out, and therefore don't require a tail rotor.

FORWARDS The pilot can tilt the main rotor so that the blades in front are set flat, and the ones behind are set steeply. This lifts the tail and pulls the helicopter forwards.

UP The blades are set at a steep pitch or angle, giving plenty of lift.

DOWN The blades are set almost flat, giving very little lift.

DUAL LIFT *Twin-rotor designs are typically used on transport helicopters.*

fast fact

The fastest speed ever reached by a piloted aircraft is 3530 km/h (2193 mph), achieved on 26 July 1976 by a Lockheed SR-71 Blackbird fighter, piloted by Eldon W Joersz and George T Morgan over California, USA.

SPACE EXPLORATION

For centuries, people studied the heavens and dreamed of travelling into space. In the late twentieth century, this finally became a reality with the first orbits of Earth in spacecraft and the first Moon landings. Though lunar expeditions lasted only a few years, astronauts have continued to travel into space, with some undertaking extended stays on space stations. Meanwhile, space probes are voyaging immense distances across the Solar System, gathering information on our small corner of the Universe.

HOW MANY PEOPLE HAVE STOOD ON THE MOON?

In 1966, the unmanned Soviet space probe *Luna 9* landed on the Moon. Three years later, the first human set foot there, when Neil Armstrong stepped onto the surface from the landing module of America's *Apollo 11*, followed by Buzz Aldrin, on 20 July 1969. Six more *Apollo* missions took place, but just a few years after the first landing the program was scrapped. In total, only 12 people have set foot on the Moon. No one has been there since *Apollo 17* in 1972.

MIRROR IMAGE *Buzz Aldrin on the Moon, in a photograph taken by Neil Armstrong during the Apollo 11 landing*

CARRIED ALOFT *Ariane 5 is a widely used rocket-launching system.*

WHO WERE THE FIRST PEOPLE IN SPACE?

Space travel began after scientists developed large, powerful rockets in the 1950s. The first creature in space was Laika, a dog, which orbited Earth in the Soviet *Sputnik 2* satellite. On 12 April 1961, Soviet cosmonaut Yuri Gagarin became the first person to orbit Earth, aboard the spacecraft *Vostok 1*. His flight lasted 1 hour and 38 minutes before the craft returned to Earth by parachute. The first American in space was Alan Shepherd, on 5 May 1961, and the first American to orbit Earth was John Glenn, on 20 February 1962.

FIRST LADY *Russian cosmonaut Valentina Tereshkova became the first woman in space on 16 June 1963, travelling aboard Vostok 6.*

HOW DO SPACECRAFT GET INTO SPACE?

Powerful rockets provide the thrust necessary to lift a heavy spacecraft above Earth's atmosphere. Most rockets have three 'stages': the first accelerates the payload to speeds of around 9000 km/h (6000 mph). Once its fuel is spent, the first stage falls back to Earth, reducing the overall weight, and a less powerful second-stage rocket takes over. The third stage has smaller rockets still, and propels the payload into orbit.

WHY DO PEOPLE FLOAT IN SPACE?

People and spacecraft in orbit are constantly in 'freefall', hurtling towards Earth, but since they are also travelling at speed around the planet, they do not move closer to the ground. However, because the crew and the spacecraft are both falling together, the crew appear to be 'weightless'.

ZERO GRAVITY *During a steep dive, an aeroplane can create brief bursts of freefall, allowing trainee astronauts to experience the sensation of zero gravity.*

PHASED OUT *The Space Shuttle Atlantis was the second last to be built.*

WHAT WILL REPLACE THE SPACE SHUTTLE?

NASA is currently developing a new spacecraft, the Orion Multi-purpose Crew Vehicle (MPCV), for crewed journeys to the International Space Station (ISS) (▶234), the Moon, asteroids and Mars. The maiden voyage of the Orion is not likely to take place until after 2020, however. In the meantime, NASA has entered into agreements with commercial companies to build uncrewed and crewed spacecraft to service the ISS.

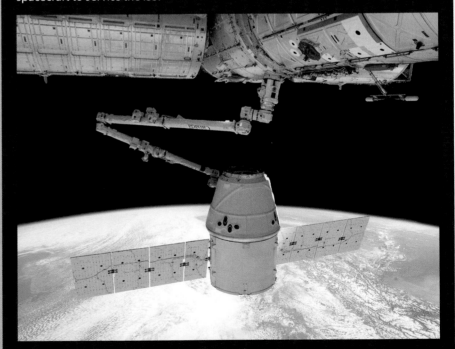

PRIVATE ENTERPRISE *In 2012, the uncrewed SpaceX Dragon became the first commercially built spacecraft to dock at the ISS. A crewed version is currently being developed.*

WHAT WAS THE SPACE SHUTTLE?

First launched in 1981, the Space Shuttle was the first partially reusable spacecraft, operated by NASA (the US National Aeronautics and Space Administration). Known more correctly as the Space Transportation System (STS), it was a cross between a rocket and a glider. Take-off was achieved using its own rockets plus those of attached boosters, and a huge supply of fuel contained in a massive external tank; the boosters and tank were jettisoned shortly before reaching orbit. After re-entering Earth's atmosphere, the shuttle would glide down to Earth. Until 2011, when the Space Shuttle was retired, five such craft were used to deliver and mend satellites, to research the effects on humans of living in space, and to ferry astronauts to space stations.

SPACE EXPLORATION CONTINUED

WHEN WERE THE FIRST SPACE STATIONS BUILT?

A space station is a craft that is designed to remain in orbit for an extended period of time as a base for astronauts who arrive and depart on other spacecraft. The first space station was the Soviet *Salyut 1*, launched in 1971, which was followed by another five *Salyut* stations before 1986. The United States launched its first space station, *Skylab*, in 1973, which remained in orbit for six years. More recently, Russia maintained the successful *Mir* space station, from 1986 to 1998, and 15 countries collaborated to build the International Space Station (ISS), launched in 1998 and still aloft. And in 2011 China launched the first of a series of *Tiangong* space stations.

FIERY DEMISE *Skylab was deorbited in 1979 – and crash-landed in Australia.*

SPACE TOUR *Due to take to the air by 2015, Virgin Galactic's SpaceShip Two will carry passengers in suborbital flights.*

CAN ORDINARY PEOPLE TRAVEL TO SPACE?

Yes. Since 2001 the Russian Space Agency has made places aboard its *Soyuz* spacecraft on trips to the ISS available to space tourists. The minimum fee for a place is US$20 million and the prospective space tourist has to be prepared to undertake several months of training. Many commercial companies are now planning space tourism ventures, including journeys to the Moon and even to hotels on proposed space stations, as well as suborbital flights – flights at an altitude of about 110 km (68 miles) – during which passengers will experience several minutes of weightlessness and obtain a view of Earth and the stars.

WHAT DO PEOPLE DO ON THE INTERNATIONAL SPACE STATION?

Since November 2000, the ISS has been continuously occupied by astronauts and scientists. Being on a space station allows scientists to conduct research into the effects of space on human biology, as well as into physics, astronomy and (by observing Earth's atmosphere from above) climate and weather. In particular, experiments on board space stations may help scientists plan and prepare for longer journeys in space. Negative effects of being in space include motion sickness, muscle atrophy due to weightlessness, and greater exposure to solar radiation, which can increase the risk of developing cancers and cataracts.

POWER SUPPLY *Massive arrays of solar panels provide power to the ISS.*

MARS SCENE *An artist's impression of a US expedition to Mars*

WHAT STOPS US FLYING TO MARS?

An obvious problem is the distance. Mars is an average of 220 million km (135 million miles) away and the journey would take at least six to seven months using available technology. Even then the launch would have to take place when Earth and Mars were suitably aligned, and the astronauts would possibly have to wait on Mars up to 18 months for Earth to be in a suitable position for the return flight. Such a trip would consequently entail major risks. If there were a medical emergency, for example, it would be impossible to return to Earth. The travellers would also have to take all supplies with them for the entire trip. But the greatest danger would be prolonged exposure to the Sun's radiation, due to Mars having a much weaker magnetic field than Earth, which would provide little protection.

WHERE HAVE SPACE PROBES TRAVELLED?

Numerous unpiloted space probes and landers have been sent to other planets in our Solar System – and beyond. Early probes launched in the 1960s and 1970s, such as the Russian *Venera* and the US *Mariner* series, focused on our closest neighbours, Venus, Mercury and Mars. Since then, several

STILL IN TOUCH *In space since 1977, Voyager 1 is expected to maintain communication with Earth until 2025.*

probes have orbited and landed on Mars, revealing much about its surface and atmosphere (▶17). The first probes to reach Jupiter and Saturn were, respectively, the *Pioneer 10* (1973) and *Pioneer 11* (1979) probes. *Voyager 2*, launched in 1977, was the first probe to pass Uranus (1986) and Neptune (1989). It is now at the edge of the Solar System and still sending data back to Earth, as is *Voyager 1*, also launched in 1977 and now even further afield, in interstellar space, more than 19 billion km (12 billion miles) away.

FUTURE FLYER *Antimatter spaceships, which use the colossal energy released by the collision of matter and antimatter, could move at close to the speed of light.*

HOW LONG WOULD IT TAKE TO JOURNEY TO THE STARS?

Current technology permits travel at about one-hundredth of the speed of light. At that velocity it would take several centuries to reach the nearest stars. Of course, if it ever becomes possible to fly at close to the speed of light, such journeys would be much shorter. An astronaut aboard a spacecraft travelling at 99.9 per cent of the speed of light could reach a star 100 light years away in four and a half years. For everyone left at home, however, 100 years would pass, and the astronaut would return to find a world quite different to the one he or she had left 200 years earlier.

fast fact

The longest space flight ever undertaken was made by Russia's Valeri Polyakov in 1994–95. He stayed aboard the *Mir* space station for 14 months (437 days and 18 hours).

BRIDGES, DAMS AND TUNNELS

Roads, railways, bridges, canals, dams, tunnels and harbours are challenging to build. They have to be strong enough to stand up to enormous stresses, both from extreme weather and heavy use, over many years. Given this and the huge expenditure involved, designs and plans have to be drawn up with the utmost care.

HOW ARE MODERN ROADS MADE?

When building a road, first the earth is levelled and pressed down until it is hard. Then a foundation bed of crushed rock or stones is laid on top of the earth, crisscrossed with drainage pipes. On urban roads, another layer of small stones is placed on top of this then surfaced with a mix of asphalt and small stones, whereas on some motorways a stronger concrete mix is used for the top layer. A road surface is usually curved, or cambered, so that water runs off it, and drainage ditches are built on either side of it. Grass verges – or raised pavements in cities – stop the sides from washing away.

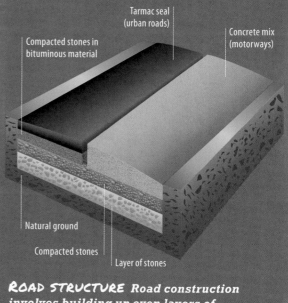

Tarmac seal (urban roads)

Concrete mix (motorways)

Compacted stones in bituminous material

Natural ground

Compacted stones

Layer of stones

ROAD STRUCTURE *Road construction involves building up even layers of different materials.*

INTER CITY *The 42.5-km (26½-mile) Jiaozhou Bay Bridge links the Chinese cities of Qingdao and Huangdao. Built to withstand earthquakes and typhoons, it is the world's longest bridge over water.*

HOW ARE BRIDGES BUILT?

Most bridges rest on pillars, known as piers. Sometimes these piers have to be built in water. As building underwater is impractical, a dry area has to be created. To do this in shallow water, interlocking sheets of steel are driven into the riverbed to form a waterproof circle. The water is then pumped out of the enclosure, and a pier is built inside on foundations resting on rock below the riverbed. In deeper water, a giant concrete tube is used for each pier instead.

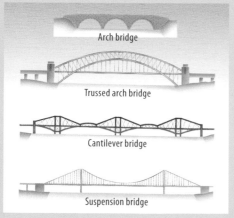

Arch bridge

Trussed arch bridge

Cantilever bridge

Suspension bridge

WHAT ARE THE MAIN TYPES OF BRIDGES?

The simplest bridge is a beam bridge, in which a horizontal deck rests on piers at either end. In an arch bridge, the deck rests on one or more curved arches. More complex forms of arched bridges include the bowstring arch, in which the deck hangs from arches that rise above it, and the trussed arch bridge, in which the deck is supported by a framework of bars that are arranged in a crisscross pattern for rigidity. A more complex version of a trussed bridge is a cantilevered bridge, which usually has at least two lozenge-shaped rigid trusses, each with a central pier and anchored to the shore at one end. A suspension bridge is often used to span very wide crossings. Its piers are extended upwards to form towers. Heavy, multistrand suspension cables, anchored firmly to the banks and passing over the tops of the towers, support the deck via vertical hangers.

HOW ARE TUNNELS MADE?

First, geologists carry out a survey to find out what kinds of rock or soil lie in the area of the tunnel; then the best route is chosen. Some hard rock may be blasted out with explosives, but most tunnels are now cut by a giant tunnel-boring machine, which is like a giant drill with a rotating cutter head and hard tungsten-carbide teeth. Other types of automatic equipment follow behind, removing the spoil (broken rock) and installing supports and tunnel lining (usually made of reinforced concrete).

UNDER PASS *This massive bore was used to dig the 57-km (35-mile) Gotthard Base Tunnel, in Switzerland, the world's longest railway tunnel.*

HOW ARE DAMS DESIGNED?

When designing a dam, engineers must carefully calculate the required width and height, and the pressure likely to be exerted by the river or lake at different times of the year. All dams are given deep foundations to prevent water from flowing under them, and to anchor them against the weight of the water. Dams may be built of earth and loose stone, or concrete, often reinforced with steel rods or cables. Some dams have buttresses on the downstream side.

GRAND DESIGNS *There are three main kinds of dams.*

EMBANKMENT DAM Wider dams, such as the Aswan Dam in Egypt, are often embankment dams, colossal banks of earth, rock and sand with a less permeable clay core.

GRAVITY DAM A gravity dam, such as the Grand Coulee Dam in the United States, is usually straight and made of concrete. It depends entirely on its own weight to block the water.

CURVED DAM In a narrow canyon, the structure is curved outwards on the upstream side, as at the Xiaowan Dam, China. This shifts much of the water pressure off the dam and onto the canyon walls.

fast fact

China has more than 87,000 dams, including the world's tallest, the Jinping-I dam, which rises 305 m (1000 ft), as well as the world's largest hydroelectric power project, the Three Gorges Dam.

HOMES AND OTHER BUILDINGS

The earliest homes and buildings were constructed with readily available natural materials, such as timber, mud and stone. In ancient times, the introduction of handmade bricks, terracotta and – in the Roman era – durable cement and concrete enabled builders to become far more ambitious and inventive. In the modern age, the development of even stronger materials, such as iron, steel and reinforced concrete, has allowed buildings to rise ever taller, while other innovations have made structures more sustainable.

WHAT IS THE WORLD'S TALLEST BUILDING?

Opened on 4 January 2010, the Burj Khalifa in Dubai is the world's tallest building, at almost 828 m (2716½ ft), as well as being the world's tallest freestanding structure. It has more than 160 storeys and, on the 124th floor, the world's highest open-air observation deck.

HOW DO YOU BUILD A SKYSCRAPER?

Skyscrapers stand on huge reinforced concrete rafts, which are supported by piles that go deep underground to rest on solid rock. Most skyscrapers have a rigid frame made out of steel girders, or steel and concrete, which supports the weight of the building; diagonal cross-bracing girders or trusses may be used to provide extra rigidity and resistance to wind. The floors and so-called curtain walls are attached to this frame but need only support their own weight, which means they do not need to be massive (they can even be glass). A significant development in skyscraper design took place in the 1960s with the introduction of the 'bundled-tube' design, which involves joining together a group of steel-framed columnar units to provide even greater rigidity. This allowed architects to not only build higher but also vary designs through the use of tubes of different heights.

CONCRETE CORE *A skyscraper under construction in Shanghai, China*

TUBE CLUSTER *Chicago's Willis Tower, formerly known as the Sears Tower, is a classic example of bundled-tube design. Completed in 1974 and standing 442 m (1450 ft) high, it was the tallest building in the world until 1996.*

WHAT IS AN ECO-HOUSE?

An eco-house is a home that has been designed to use as little energy and as many natural, recycled and nontoxic materials as possible. Such designs usually incorporate solar energy for heating and hot water; efficient insulation to keep buildings warm in winter and cool in summer; low-energy light bulbs and the use of sunlight instead of electricity for daytime lighting; recycling of water; and the use of environmentally friendly materials, such as straw, mud-brick and recycled wood and glass.

GREEN DESIGN *Homes can be designed to exploit sunlight and natural heating and counter wind and cold.*

❶ Louvred windows allow air to circulate

❷ Skylight lets out heat, lets in light

❸ Underfloor insulation

❹ Walls and floors absorb then later reradiate heat

❺ Large windows let in low winter sun

❻ Wide eaves and trees provide shade in summer

HOW DO YOU MAKE BUILDINGS EARTHQUAKE-PROOF?

Stone and brick (masonry) buildings are the most vulnerable to earthquake damage because they are heavy and have no way of bending. So in quake-prone zones, wood-framed and steel-framed buildings are preferred because they will flex in response to ground movement without collapsing. Large modern buildings in earthquake zones also incorporate a range of protective features. Base isolators – feet made of layers of rubber and steel – allow a building to move independently of the ground. A shear core, consisting of internal walls around lift shafts and stairwells, strengthens its centre. Walls are made of reinforced concrete and braced with diagonal beams, and windows are fitted with strengthened, shatterproof glass.

EARTHQUAKE PROTECTION

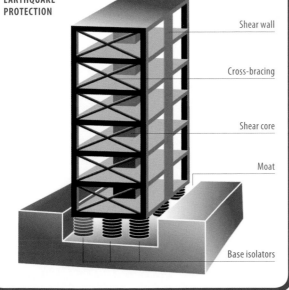

Shear wall

Cross-bracing

Shear core

Moat

Base isolators

HOW CAN SKYSCRAPERS BE MORE EFFICIENT?

Like eco-homes, skyscrapers can make use of solar power, water recycling and effective insulation. Some now have their own power-generation systems fuelled by environmentally friendly energy sources. Many large modern buildings are designed with systems that channel natural light into their interior. One sophisticated method for doing this is a heliostat, a computer-controlled set of mirrors that tracks the Sun and reflects its light to where it is required.

HARNESSING NATURAL LIGHT *One Central Park in Sydney, Australia, incorporates a 33-storey tower and a 16-storey tower. Mirrors on top of the smaller tower reflect sunlight up to a heliostat on a massive cantilever, which in turn uses an array of angled mirrors to direct the light to different parts of the complex.*

fast fact

Currently under construction and due to open in 2019, the Kingdom Tower in Jeddah, Saudi Arabia, will rise more than 1 km (3280 ft) in height – 50 storeys taller than the Burj Khalifa.

SOURCES OF ENERGY

Most of the world's energy is obtained by burning fossil fuels – oil, coal and gas (▶72).

These fuels are, however, finite and will run out: oil supplies, for example, are likely to dwindle later this century. Furthermore, the carbon dioxide released by burning fossil fuels has been shown to contribute significantly to global warming. Consequently, many countries are now adopting alternative methods for producing energy, including renewable sources such as solar and wind power.

WHAT IS OIL USED FOR?

Oil as it comes out of the ground is called crude oil, or petroleum. Through a process known as refining, it is turned into a range of fuels and other products, including plastics and pharmaceuticals.

OIL REFINING *When heated, crude oil separates into different chemical components, or fractions. At a refinery, crude oil is boiled and then fed into the bottom of a distillation tower. The oil vapour rises up the tower and condenses into a different substance at each level as it cools.*

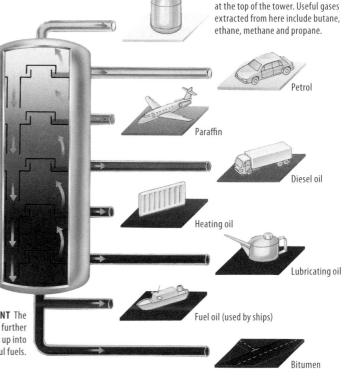

ON TOP Some vapour remains as gas at the top of the tower. Useful gases extracted from here include butane, ethane, methane and propane.

Petrol

Paraffin

Diesel oil

Heating oil

Lubricating oil

Fuel oil (used by ships)

Bitumen

ON THE RISE Vapour rises through perforated condensation trays placed at different heights.

RAW RESOURCE En route to the distillation tower, the crude oil is heated to 400°C (750°F).

FURTHER TREATMENT The heaviest fractions require further treatment to break them up into lighter, more useful fuels.

fast fact

About 95 per cent of the world's oil has come from 5 per cent of its oil fields. The countries with the largest reserves are Venezuela (18 per cent of the world's total) and Saudi Arabia (16 per cent).

WHERE DOES MOST ELECTRICITY COME FROM?

Most of our electricity is provided by large power stations. To create electricity, you need a generator and turbines. Inside the generator, where the electricity is made, a coil of wire spins at high speed between the two poles of a magnet. Turbines spin the coil. In most power stations, the turbines are fan-like machines with blades that turn when hot gases, or steam, are passed through them at high pressure. Steam is made by heating water using gas, coal, oil or nuclear energy. Around three-quarters of the world's electricity is made like this.

DRIVING FORCE *A massive steam turbine lies stationary while under repair at a power station.*

HOW DOES POWER REACH OUR HOMES?

Electricity is generated in power stations and then sent all over a region or country through a network of cables, called a grid. The energy supply is measured in volts.

POWER STATION

In power stations such as this one, coal or gas is burned to produce steam, which is in turn used to drive another generator. Electricity is usually output to the grid at a strength of about 25,000 volts, then substations boost the power so that it can travel across country.

CROSS COUNTRY Pylons or underground cables carry high-voltage lines across the region or country.

DOMESTIC POWER Substations also reduce the voltage before the electricity is fed into factories and homes via local power lines.

HOW DOES NUCLEAR POWER WORK?

Nuclear power is generated by fission, the splitting apart of the nuclei of atoms of uranium or plutonium. This is achieved by bombarding the atoms with neutrons inside a reactor. Neutrons released by the atoms are captured and used to bombard further atoms, continuing the process in a chain reaction. Using small amounts of raw materials, fission produces huge amounts of energy as heat and radioactivity.

NUCLEAR REACTOR The most common type of nuclear reactor is a pressurised water reactor, which uses high-pressure water as a coolant. The coolant removes heat from the reactor's core and channels it into a heat exchanger, which produces steam. The steam is then used to drive turbines to generate electricity.

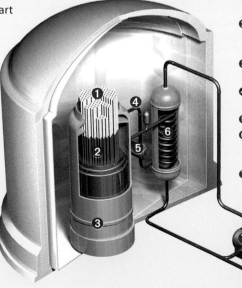

❶ **FUEL RODS** The fuel – usually uranium oxide – is held in rods and placed at the centre of the reactor.

❷ **CONTROL RODS** Rods of cadmium or boron, which both absorb neutrons and therefore slow fission, are moved in and out of the reactor to control the reaction speed.

❸ **PRESSURE VESSEL** A heavy steel container surrounds the reactor.

❹ **COOLANT** Water or a gas passes through the reactor and draws off heat energy.

❺ **PUMP** Coolant is circulated through the reactor.

❻ **HEAT EXCHANGER** Heat from the coolant is transferred to water in a secondary circuit, turning it into superheated steam.

❼ **TURBINES** The superheated steam drives the turbines. As the steam condenses, the resulting water is pumped back to the reactor.

❽ **GENERATOR** The turbines drive a generator, which produces electricity.

SOURCES OF ENERGY CONTINUED

HOW DOES A DAM MAKE ELECTRICITY?

A flowing river contains enormous energy in its thousands of tonnes of water constantly on the move. A dam traps that energy then converts it into electricity by channelling the water through pipes to spin turbines that power generators. This type of energy production is known as hydroelectric power. Although it doesn't produce any harmful emissions and running costs are low, the construction of a dam may flood large areas of a valley, forcing people to move and altering the region's ecological balance.

HYDROELECTRIC POWER STATION *A dam's power-generating plant is usually housed below the dam wall.*

fast fact

Fossil fuels still supply more than 80 per cent of the world's energy, with oil providing almost one-third, coal more than a quarter and natural gas just over a fifth. Just over 13 per cent of energy comes from biomass, hydroelectric and other renewable sources.

HOW DOES SOLAR POWER WORK?

There are two main forms of solar power. With solar thermal power, large arrays of mirrors focus sunlight onto a heat collector in a power station, which uses the heat to create steam to drive turbines. Solar electric technology exploits the principle that combinations of certain dissimilar materials, such as silicon and boron, create an electric charge when exposed to light. This photoelectric effect is the basis of solar panels.

SUN TRAP *Ivanpah Solar Power Facility in the Mojave Desert, USA, is the world's largest solar power plant. It has 173,500 heliostats, each with two mirrors, focusing on three towers.*

HOW DO WIND TURBINES WORK?

Wind turbines catch the power of moving air. The wind spins a rotor shaped like an aeroplane propeller, and this drives a shaft connected to a generator. The rotor has a rudder at the back, which keeps the rotor facing into the wind. Wind turbines are placed on high ground, where the wind blows faster. About 2.5 per cent of the world's electricity is currently generated by wind power, but this figure is likely to grow rapidly as more and more countries adopt the technology.

AIR CURRENT *Wind power now produces over one-fifth of Spain's electricity.*

WAVE POWER *Barrages in front of the port of Mutriku, Spain, house wave turbines.*

CAN THE SEA GENERATE ELECTRICITY?

Technologies have been designed to harness the energy of both waves and tides. Some coastal power plants can use the constant movement of waves to compress air inside metal chambers, which in turn drives turbines. Dams built across river estuaries channel the incoming tide through reversible turbines; at high tide the water is trapped then released in a steady flow back through the turbine.

CAN WE TURN WASTE INTO ENERGY?

Yes, organic matter such as plants, wood, straw and manure – known as biomass – can be burned for cooking and heating. Biomass can also be 'digested' by microbes, which produce methane, a useful fuel. Methane is also made in landfill sites, and at some, the gas is collected. Allowing plant matter with high sugar content to ferment produces ethanol, which can be blended with petrol in suitably modified vehicles. Waste vegetable oil can be made into biodiesel, which can be used in diesel vehicles. There are even power stations that rely on the heat generated by burning domestic waste.

WASTE NOT *Millions of Indians now have domestic biogas plants. Using waste, they produce enough energy to power their lighting and cooking.*

WHICH COUNTRIES USE THE MOST ENERGY?

The United States uses 19 per cent – almost one-fifth – of the world's energy, but has only 4.44 per cent of the world's people. However, fast-developing China, which has one-fifth of the world's population, has now overtaken the United States as the largest energy user, and its energy use is expected to more than double between 2010 and 2040.

STEAM HEAT *Iceland produces 84 per cent of its energy from renewable sources, with 66 per cent coming from geothermal power.*

HOW DOES GEOTHERMAL POWER WORK?

In regions of high volcanic activity, large amounts of heat and steam are generated underground. Steam can be drawn up to the surface via pipes and used to produce power. Holes are also drilled down to hot rocks and water is run across them to generate more steam. Major producers of geothermal power include the United States, the Philippines, Iceland and New Zealand.

WHAT OTHER ENERGY SOURCES COULD WE USE IN THE FUTURE?

Two potential sources of energy that are currently being investigated are hydrogen fuel cells – devices that combine hydrogen and oxygen to produce electrical energy (▶223) – and nuclear fusion, or fusion power. Nuclear fusion is how the Sun generates its power: by fusing together the nuclei of different elements (▶70), a process that generates a large amount of energy, mainly as heat. This heat could potentially be used to drive a steam turbine hooked to a generator. But while nuclear fusion has been achieved in laboratory experiments, it is still many years from becoming a practical source energy.

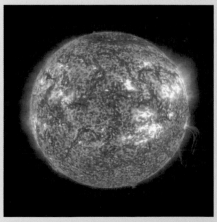

TIMELINE OF DISCOVERY AND INVENTION

Our far-distant ancestors learned how to grow crops rather than just gather them, and how to use metal rather than stone for their tools and weapons.

In recent times, we have put men on the Moon. The human race's journey of discovery continues, and is still transforming our lives.

2.5 million years ago Hominins begin to use tools.

c. 800,000 BC First clear evidence of human use of fire, though it is likely that cooking food began much earlier.

c. 10,000 BC People begin **farming** in China and, by 8000 BC, South-West Asia. The subsequent creation of food surpluses results in the formation of the first towns.

c. 6000 BC Metalworking, using copper and gold, begins in south-eastern Europe and soon after in South-West Asia. It is first used to make artefacts displaying status.

c. 5000 BC Bronze, an alloy of copper and tin, is smelted at several sites along the lower Danube River, in south-east Europe. It is first used to make small items such as foils, awls, rings and needles.

c. 4500 BC Animal-driven ploughs, which increase the area of land that can be cultivated, appear in South-West Asia and eastern Europe.

c. 3200 BC Sailing boats are in use in Egypt and South-East Asia.

c. 3100 BC The Sumerians, living in present-day Iraq, devise the first system of writing, based on pictograms.

It develops into **cuneiform script**, formed of wedge-shaped marks.

c. 3000 BC People in Egypt and the Middle East discover how to make arches out of stone, which in turn permits the construction of stone bridges and wide roofs.

c. 2800 BC Egyptians devise one of the world's first calendars and use it to

anticipate the annual flood of the Nile River, which covered their fields with fertile mud.

c. 2500 BC People in South-West Asia and Egypt develop iron smelting.

c. 400 BC A Greek philosopher called Democritus suggests that everything is made up of tiny particles called atoms. Over 2000 years later, scientists will discover he was right.

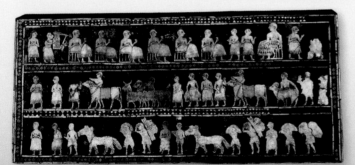

c. 10,000 BC FARMING Images of farming appear on this ancient Sumerian artefact called the Standard of Ur.

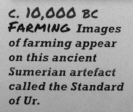

c. 3100 BC CUNEIFORM SCRIPT The first form of writing, it was often imprinted on soft-clay tablets.

c. 350 BC ARISTOTLE The writings of Aristotle influenced scientists for centuries after his death.

ARISTOTELI. STAGIRITAE

c. 220 AD
PRINTING IN CHINA
Dating from 868 AD, this Chinese copy of the Diamond Sutra is the oldest known printed book.

c. 1090 AD
MAGNETIC COMPASS
The Chinese steadily refined the design of the compass.

c. 350 BC Greek philosopher **Aristotle** decides that Earth is round, not flat as most people then think. One piece of evidence that convinces him is that distant ships seem to sink below the horizon.

c. 270 BC Ctesibius, a Greek inventor then living in Egypt, designs a water-operated clock.

c. 240 BC Eratosthenes, a Greek mathematician, correctly works out that Earth is about 40,000 km (25,000 miles) in circumference.

c. 85 BC In Greece, water wheels are first used to drive millstones for grinding corn.

c. 50 AD Hero of Alexandria invents the first steam engine, a hollow metal ball that spins when water inside it is boiled. The invention is ingenious, but has no practical use.

c. 220 Carved woodblocks are first used for **printing in China**.

c. 650 Windmills are in use in Persia.

808 First evidence of the use of gunpowder, in China.

c. 810 Muhammad Al-Khwarizmi, an Arab mathematician, becomes the first to use the number zero in calculations – before this, there was no mathematical symbol for 'nothing'.

c. 1090 The **magnetic compass** is first used for navigation, in China, where magnetised needles may have been used for ritual purposes as early as the third century.

c. 1280 Italian glassmakers make **spectacles**, perhaps copying inventions made by the Chinese.

1455 In Germany, Johannes Gutenberg produces Europe's first printed book – a copy of the Bible – using movable type and a new machine for pressing the type onto paper, called the **printing press**.

1504 The first pocket watch is made in Germany. Unlike other clocks of the time, it is powered by a wind-up spring.

1543 Polish astronomer Nicolaus Copernicus publishes a book claiming that Earth orbits the Sun. At the time, most people believe the Sun orbits Earth and Copernicus's ideas cause a storm of protest.

1590s The first microscopes are invented by spectacle-makers in the Netherlands.

1592 Galileo Galilei makes the first thermometer. It contains air sealed in a tube by water; the air expands as it warms, moving the water level.

c. 1280 AD
SPECTACLES
A priest wears spectacles in an Italian painting dating from 1352.

1455 AD
PRINTING PRESS
Printer Johannes Gutenberg studies a typeset page in his workshop.

TIMELINE OF DISCOVERY AND INVENTION CONTINUED

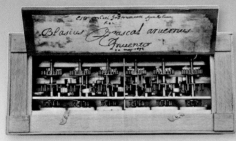

1642 MECHANICAL CALCULATOR *Pascal's machine could subtract, add, multiply and divide.*

1676 EARLY MICROSCOPE *Dutchman Antony van Leeuwenhoek's microscope had a bead-like lens at the centre of a brass plate.*

1608 A Dutch spectacle-maker called Hans Lippershey is the first to patent a design for the telescope.

1609 Galileo builds his own telescope and uses it to study the night sky. This leads to him discovering Jupiter's moons, and sunspots.

1625 The first submarine is launched on the River Thames near London. Made of wood and waterproofed with animal fat, it is powered by men pulling oars.

1628 William Harvey, an English doctor, publishes a book in which he correctly explains how blood circulates.

1642 Blaise Pascal, a French mathematician, invents a **mechanical calculator**. It does not catch on.

1643 Evangelista Torricelli, Galileo's assistant, invents the world's first barometer.

1658 Using a microscope, Jan Swammerdam, a Dutch scientist, becomes the first person to see red blood cells.

1666 Using a glass prism, English mathematician and physicist Isaac Newton splits a beam of sunlight into its constituent colours – those of the rainbow.

1675 Olaus Roemer, a Danish astronomer, becomes the first person to calculate the speed of light. He estimates it at about 227,000 km (141,000 miles) per second – only about 20 per cent less than the true figure.

1676 Using an **early microscope**, Dutchman Antony van Leeuwenhoek becomes the first person to see microorganisms, in a sample of pond water.

1698 Thomas Savery makes the first steam-powered pump. Used to pump water out of mines, it becomes known as 'the Miner's Friend'.

1751 US politician, author and scientist **Benjamin Franklin** does experiments that show that lightning is a kind of electricity. This in turn leads him to invent the lightning conductor.

1769 English inventor Richard Arkwright builds the 'spinning frame' – a machine for making cotton thread.

1783 Joseph and Étienne Montgolfier make the world's first **hot-air balloon flight** outside Paris.

1790 In France, scientists devise a new system of measurements, now known as the metric system.

1796 English doctor Edward Jenner demonstrates the efficacy of vaccinations against many infectious diseases.

1783 HOT-AIR BALLOON FLIGHT *The first balloon flights caught the imagination of the public and drew huge crowds.*

1751 BENJAMIN FRANKLIN *Franklin famously used a kite to study lightning.*

1821 MICHAEL FARADAY The inventor of the electric motor is seen here, at right, in his laboratory.

1800 FIRST BATTERY In Volta's battery, the electric charge passed through layers of discs of moistened card separated by copper and zinc discs.

1800 An Italian physicist, Alessandro Volta, makes the **first battery**, using plates of copper and zinc. William Herschel, a British astronomer, discovers that light contains invisible heat rays – now known as infrared rays.

1803 English mining engineer Richard Trevithick demonstrates the first steam engine to run on rails, at an ironworks in South Wales.

1816 René Laennec, a French doctor, invents the stethoscope.

1820 In Europe, several physicists discover that when electricity flows through a wire it produces a magnetic field.

1821 **Michael Faraday**, a British scientist, invents the electric motor.

1827 Joseph-Nicéphore Niépce takes the world's first photograph – a view from the window of his workshop in France – by focusing daylight onto a metal plate covered with bitumen (tar).

1837 English mathematician Charles Babbage starts to build his **Analytical Engine** – a mechanical general-purpose computer designed to be programmed with punched cards. He never completes this, the first mechanical computer.

1855 Alexander Parkes, a British chemist, makes a flexible material called Parkesine from chloroform and caster oil, a discovery that will lead to the production of the first plastics.

1859 English naturalist Charles Darwin publishes *On the Origin of Species*, in which he sets out his theory of evolution. The Belgian inventor Étienne Lenoir builds the first internal-combustion engine, powered by gas.

1862 Louis Pasteur, a leading French biologist, demonstrates that infectious diseases are caused by germs and other microorganisms.

1865 An Austrian monk called Gregor Mendel works out the basic rules of genetics, but his work goes unnoticed for the next 35 years.

1866 Swedish chemist Alfred Nobel invents a new explosive called dynamite.

1876 Scottish-born American scientist Alexander Graham Bell makes the world's first phone call. Robert Koch, a German biologist, discovers a way of growing bacteria in the laboratory, enabling him to test methods of fighting disease.

1879 American Thomas Edison invents the first reliable electric light bulb.

1884 Gottlieb Daimler constructs the first lightweight petrol engine. A year later, he tests it out on a motorbike.

1885 In Germany Karl Benz produces one of the world's earliest motor cars.

1888 American Herman Hollerith invents a punched-card tabulating machine. His company becomes the International Business Machines (IBM) Corporation.

1895 **Guglielmo Marconi** makes one of the world's first radio transmitters. Wilhelm Röntgen, a German physicist, discovers X-rays.

1837 ANALYTICAL ENGINE A section of Babbage's proposed machine was built by his son, Henry, in 1910.

1895 GUGLIELMO MARCONI In the early 1900s, Marconi managed to send radio messages across the Atlantic Ocean.

TIMELINE OF DISCOVERY AND INVENTION CONTINUED

1908 GEIGER COUNTER This example dates from 1932.

1946 ENIAC The construction of this giant computer took three years.

1900 Karl Landsteiner, an Austrian doctor, establishes that all people belong to one of four blood groups. His finding makes blood transfusions safe for the first time.

1903 On 17 December, Americans Orville and Wilbur Wright make the world's first powered plane flights.

1908 The German physicist William Geiger invents a device that detects radioactivity. It becomes known as a **Geiger counter**, because it counts the number of radioactive particles that it picks up.

1916 Physicist Albert Einstein completes his general theory of relativity – a new explanation of the way space and time are related. The Trans-Siberian Railway, the world's longest railway, is completed.

1926 Scotsman John Logie Baird demonstrates his newly invented television set.

1928 Scottish scientist Alexander Fleming discovers penicillin, which will lead to the world's first antibiotic.

1929 By examining light coming from distant galaxies, US astronomer Edwin Hubble discovers that the Universe is expanding.

1942 Italian physicist Enrico Fermi builds the world's first nuclear reactor – in a squash court at the University of Chicago, USA.

1943 French diver and naturalist Jacques Cousteau invents the aqualung – a portable breathing device that revolutionises the exploration of the oceans.

1945 The US Army conducts the first ever detonation of a nuclear weapon – an event codenamed Trinity – in the desert of New Mexico, USA. Later that year, two **atomic bombs** are dropped on Japan.

1946 One of the world's first computers is built in the USA. Called **ENIAC** (short for Electronic Numerical Integrator And Calculator), it fills an entire room, and uses enough electricity to power 100 homes.

1948 In the USA, William Shockley, John Bardeen and Walter Brattain invent the transistor, an electronic device that makes electric signals stronger, or 'amplifies' them.

1949 German V2 rocket pioneer Wernher von Braun creates the first two-stage rocket in the USA.

1953 US biologist James Watson and English physicist Francis Crick successfully uncover the structure of DNA – the chemical that makes up genes.

1957 The Soviet Union launches the world's first artificial satellite, *Sputnik*.

1958 Americans Jack Kirby of Texas Instruments and Robert Noyce of Fairchild create the first integrated circuits by placing two transistors on a single piece of silicon.

1960 America launches the first communications satellite, *Echo 1*. Swiss oceanographer Jacques Piccard and American Donald Walsh achieve the deepest ever dive, descending 11,000 m (36,000 ft) into the Pacific Ocean's Mariana Trench in the bathyscaphe *Trieste*.

1945 ATOMIC BOMB The Japanese city of Nagasaki was struck on 9 August 1945.

1961 YURI GAGARIN Gagarin was the first human to travel in outer space.

16 GB – 64 GB Flash storage

1961 Soviet cosmonaut **Yuri Gagarin** becomes the first person to orbit Earth – just once. A few months later another Russian cosmonaut, Gherman Titov, circles Earth 17 times.

1962 Astronaut John Glenn becomes the first American in space.

1964 US scientists Arno Penzias and Robert Wilson discover cosmic background radiation, convincing evidence that the Big Bang was the beginning of the Universe.

1973 MOBILE PHONE *The DynaTAC 8000x by Motorola was the first mobile phone on the market.*

1967 At Cape Town in South Africa, Dr Christiaan Barnard carries out the world's first heart transplant operation.

1969 Two US astronauts, Neil Armstrong and Buzz Aldrin, become the first human beings to land on the Moon.

1971 The Soviet Union launches the first space station, *Salyut 1*.

1973 US scientists Herbert Boyer and Stanley Cohen transfer DNA from one organism to another – the beginning of genetic engineering. US company Motorola sells the first handheld **mobile phone**.

1975 The first microchips go into mass production and the first personal computer, the Altair 8800, is launched.

1978 On 25 July Louise Brown, the first 'test tube baby', is born. She is the first person to be conceived by in vitro fertilisation (IVF).

1979 The first cellular mobile phones are introduced in Japan. The *Voyager 1* and *2* space probes are launched. Today they are still travelling, far beyond the edge of the Solar System.

1981 The Space Shuttle, the first partially reusable spacecraft, is launched. IBM introduces its first personal computer.

1982 US surgeon Robert Jarvik carries out an operation to give a patient an artificial heart. The patient survives for nearly four months.

1984 The **Apple Macintosh** becomes the first successful personal computer with a graphical interface.

1986 Scientists begin work on the Human Genome Project, an international scientific collaboration that aims to map all the genes in human beings.

1990 English scientist Tim Berners-Lee devises the World Wide Web and its URL, HTML and HTTP standards. The Hubble Space Telescope is launched into orbit.

1997 Ian Wilmut, Keith Campbell and their team at the Roslin Institute in Scotland achieve the first successful cloning of a mammal from an adult cell with the birth of a sheep dubbed **Dolly**.

1998 The International Space Station is assembled in orbit above Earth. Scientists Gerson Goldhaber and Saul Perlmutter discover that the expansion of the Universe since the Big Bang is accelerating.

2001 The first draft of the human genome is completed. Apple introduces the iPod music player.

2003 Toyota launches its Prius hybrid motor car, which pairs a small internal-combustion engine with an electric motor to achieve greater fuel efficiency.

1997 DOLLY *The world's first cloned animal lived for six and a half years.*

2010 Apple launches the **iPad**.

2012 Scientists discover the Higgs boson particle, whose existence had been first theorised by British physicist Peter Higgs and five other physicists in 1964. In the widely accepted 'Standard Model' of particle physics, the Higgs boson, colloquially known as the 'God particle', is the key to explaining why all particles have mass and how matter holds together.

HISTORY AND CULTURE

THE ORIGINS OF HUMANS

We humans are animals, and our closest relations are the great apes. After our first distinctively human ancestors appeared between 5 and 7 million years ago, a range of species evolved. Our species, *Homo sapiens*, emerged only 200,000 years ago – but came to dominate the planet.

HOW ARE HUMANS RELATED TO OTHER APES?

Humans belong to the primates, a large group, or order, of mammals with 10 fingers and toes, and fingernails and toenails instead of claws. Other modern primates include monkeys, lemurs and chimpanzees. The oldest primate fossils date from about 55 million years ago, though primates may have formed a distinct group as early as 85 million years ago. Gradually primates diverged to form smaller groups, including, about 15–20 million years ago, the hominids, or 'great apes', consisting of humans, chimpanzees, gorillas and orangutans.

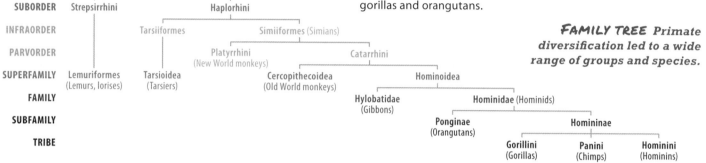

FAMILY TREE *Primate diversification led to a wide range of groups and species.*

ORDER	PRIMATES	
SUBORDER	Strepsirrhini	Haplorhini
INFRAORDER		Tarsiiformes / Simiiformes (Simians)
PARVORDER		Platyrrhini (New World monkeys) / Catarrhini
SUPERFAMILY	Lemuriformes (Lemurs, lorises)	Tarsioidea (Tarsiers) / Cercopithecoidea (Old World monkeys) / Hominoidea
FAMILY		Hylobatidae (Gibbons) / Hominidae (Hominids)
SUBFAMILY		Ponginae (Orangutans) / Homininae
TRIBE		Gorillini (Gorillas) / Panini (Chimps) / Hominini (Hominins)

WHEN DID HUMAN-LIKE CREATURES FIRST APPEAR?

Hominids diverged further and between 5 and 7 million years ago, in Africa, human-like creatures split from their closest relatives, chimpanzees, to form a distinct tribe, the hominins. More than 4 million years ago, several kinds of hominins known as australopithecines (southern apes) began walking on two legs. Early australopithecines were about 1.2–1.5 m (4–5 ft) tall, with a large jaw, a low forehead and a brain less than half the size of that of modern humans. Gradually, however, larger species of hominins emerged.

OUT OF AFRICA *A model of 'Lucy', an australopithecine whose 3-million-year-old bones were found in Ethiopia.*

HANDY MAN *Homo habilis tools. Although similar in height and shape to other australopithecines,* Homo habilis *had a larger brain.*

SHARPER EDGE Homo ergaster *tools.* Homo ergaster *had a bigger brain than* Homo habilis *and grew to 180 cm (6 ft).*

ADVANTAGE HUMANS *Skills that advantaged Homo sapiens may have included complex speech, food preservation and sewing clothes.*

DID EARLY HUMANS SPREAD TO OTHER CONTINENTS?

Around 1.8 million years ago, a species called *Homo ergaster* began spreading from Africa into Europe and Asia and evolving into *Homo erectus*. About 600,000 years ago, another species, *Homo heidelbergensis*, emerged in Africa and also migrated to Europe. It was as tall as and had a larger brain than *Homo erectus*, and showed even greater skill with tools and language. By about 250,000 years ago, another species called *Homo neanderthalensis* was living in Europe. These Neanderthals, as they are known, hunted in groups, used fire for heating and possibly cooking, wore clothes, conducted rituals and created art. Our species, *Homo sapiens*, or modern humans, evolved in Africa more than 200,000 years ago and began moving into Europe about 100,000 years later.

Neanderthal

WHAT HAPPENED TO THE OTHER EARLY HUMANS?

Six hundred thousand years ago, Earth's climate started to fluctuate dramatically, resulting in a series of ice ages. Ultimately, only the most adaptable species survived, notably *Homo neanderthalensis* and *Homo sapiens*. Recent evidence suggests these two species lived alongside each other in Europe and even interbred. But about 30,000 years ago the Neanderthals disappeared, most likely because *Homo sapiens* was more adaptable and had acquired additional skills.

WHEN DID OUR ANCESTORS FIRST USE TOOLS?

Australopithecines are thought to have been using stones and bones as tools by about 2.6 million years ago and possibly as early as 3.4 million years ago. Around 2.5 million years ago, a new genus (group of species), *Homo*, split off from the australopithecines. Among the first species in this new genus was *Homo habilis*, or 'handy man', named for the wide range of stone tools found near its fossil remains, including sharp-edged stone flakes for cutting. Another larger, more upright species named *Homo ergaster*, or 'working person', was present from about 1.9 million years ago. It produced more sophisticated tools including scrapers, axes and cleavers. *Homo ergaster* may have used fire, eaten more meat than its predecessors, had less body hair and been capable of rudimentary speech.

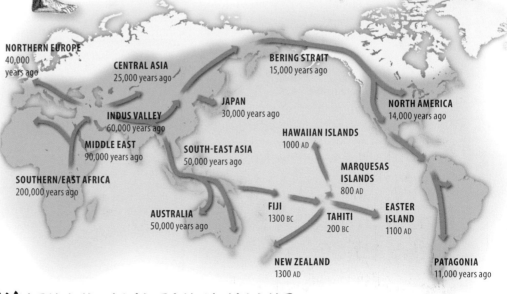

NORTHERN EUROPE
40,000
years ago

CENTRAL ASIA
25,000 years ago

BERING STRAIT
15,000 years ago

JAPAN
30,000 years ago

NORTH AMERICA
14,000 years ago

INDUS VALLEY
60,000 years ago

HAWAIIAN ISLANDS
1000 AD

MIDDLE EAST
90,000 years ago

SOUTH-EAST ASIA
50,000 years ago

MARQUESAS
ISLANDS
800 AD

SOUTHERN/EAST AFRICA
200,000 years ago

AUSTRALIA
50,000 years ago

FIJI
1300 BC

TAHITI
200 BC

EASTER
ISLAND
1100 AD

NEW ZEALAND
1300 AD

PATAGONIA
11,000 years ago

WHEN DID MODERN HUMANS REACH OTHER CONTINENTS?

After migrating out of Africa about 100,000 years ago, *Homo sapiens* subsequently spread around the world. With much of the world's water locked up in icecaps and glaciers during the ice ages, sea levels were lower than today. Land bridges linked many South-East Asian islands, which helped modern humans cross into Australia around 50,000 years ago, and connected Siberia to Alaska, which allowed humans to reach North America at least 14,000 years ago.

THE FIRST CIVILISATIONS

For a long time, prehistoric humans lived by hunting and gathering. This necessitated a nomadic existence, following prey animals as they migrated or moving to areas where plants were fruiting. But then, about 8500 BC, people began to cultivate a range of plants. This resulted in momentous changes to human lifestyles, and the emergence of the first civilisations.

WHO WERE THE FIRST FARMERS?

The first farmers were people who grew millet in northern China and rice in southern China over 12,000 years ago. About 10,000 years ago the inhabitants of the Fertile Crescent region of South-West Asia (shown above), started cultivating the wild ancestors of wheat and barley and gradually domesticated them. They also domesticated sheep and cattle, probably through the selection of tamer offspring over many generations. Farming developed in parts of Africa, Central America and Papua New Guinea at about the same time, and brought taro, bananas, sugarcane, maize, pigs and chickens into common use.

FARM STOCK *This Sumerian grave object, known as the Standard of Ur, shows early farmers and their animals.*

HOW DID AGRICULTURE CHANGE SOCIETY?

Collecting food gave rise to semipermanent villages as early as 10,000 years ago, and growing food then led to the gradual development of towns and, eventually, cities. Crop production yields far more food than hunting and gathering, so communities soon began to have surpluses of food, which meant not everyone had to work the land. People began to take up specialist occupations, becoming, for example, bakers, potters and architects, and this led to new inventions and technologies. As settlements grew larger, small groups of people were appointed (or appointed themselves) to run them, which gave rise to ruling elites. Other members of the community were employed by these elites to construct buildings, keep order or protect the settlement – or wage war on others (▶258).

FRUITS OF LEISURE *This Syrian bowl dates from the sixth millennium BC.*

WHICH WERE THE FIRST CITIES?

Cities are more than just big towns. They need a complex society, large buildings, central records and a dominating religion. In the Fertile Crescent, large towns such as Jericho (10,000 years ago) and Çatal Hüyük (8500 years ago) existed well before true cities such as Ur, Eridu and Uruk, which had developed by about 5500 years ago in the Tigris–Euphrates lowlands. These cities formed part of the Sumerian civilisation, which depended on long-distance exchange for vital resources, such as stone and minerals.

HIGH–DENSITY LIVING *Çatal Hüyük's dwellings abutted each other and were accessed via openings in their rooftops.*

WHY DID PEOPLE BUILD PYRAMIDS?

As building skills developed, people created monumental architecture to celebrate their gods and kings. The pyramid became a popular form for such buildings, perhaps because it resulted in a very stable structure. Large, stepped pyramids, known as ziggurats, were built as temples in South-West Asia from the fourth millennium BC onwards; among the oldest is the ziggurat of Ur in Sumer, Mesopotamia. The pyramids of ancient Egypt were built to house the tombs of kings and to ease their journey into the afterlife. Other civilisations that built temple pyramids were the Mayans (fourth to ninth century AD) and the Aztecs (fourteenth to fifteenth century AD) of Central America.

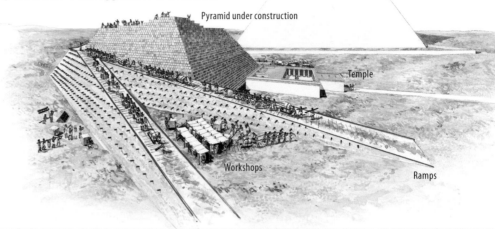

Pyramid under construction

Temple

Workshops

Ramps

BUILDING BIG *Egypt's largest pyramid, the Great Pyramid at Giza, was built in the twenty-sixth century BC to house the tomb of a king, or pharaoh, called Khufu.*

HOW DID EARLY PEOPLES GET ABOUT?

People relied on their own two feet until horses were domesticated. That may have taken place as early as 6000 years ago in Central Asia, and by 3000 years ago horses were in widespread use in South-West Asia. Wheeled carts were introduced around 3500 BC, in Mesopotamia, the Indus Valley and Central Europe. At first they had solid wooden wheels but by 2000 BC lighter, spoked wheels had been invented for use on war chariots, which led in turn to speedier domestic vehicles. River and sea transport was also common. The oldest known canoes date to about 9000 years ago, but some island settlements are much older.

HOW DID DAILY LIFE CHANGE IN CITIES?

Settlements gradually became grander and more sophisticated. Fine palaces were built and some, notably in the early Minoan civilisation of ancient Greece (around 2000 BC), even had plumbing. By Roman times, noble families lived in villas with marble floors and furniture made of bronze, ivory or wood, while poorer people occupied multistorey apartments.

ANCIENT STREETSCAPE *Following the example of the Greeks, the Romans adorned city buildings with stylised decorations, such as carved pillars, statues, fountains and elaborate murals.*

THE WRITTEN WORD

One of the most important developments in history was the introduction of writing.
This took place in Mesopotamia, more than 5000 years ago. Other civilisations then took up the idea and developed a wide array of symbols and alphabets. The dissemination of written texts and, thereby, the spread of knowledge and ideas accelerated rapidly following the invention of printing in the fifteenth century.

KEEPING COUNT *Sumerian tablets incorporate a range of counting and notation systems to tally animals.*

WHO INVENTED WRITING?

The earliest known form of writing developed in Sumer, southern Mesopotamia, around 3100 BC, among priests and merchants who wanted to keep records of harvests or areas of land sold. The writing initially took the form of picture symbols, or pictograms – simplified representations of objects or people – pressed into wet clay tablets using reed tips. By about 2500 BC, these pictures had become simpler still, so that the writer could use wedge-shaped marks to represent each object and action. This script is known as 'cuneiform', from the Latin *cuneus*, meaning 'wedge'.

PICTURE TO SYMBOL *This series of illustrations shows how the pictogram for 'cow' was steadily simplified to an abstract symbol.*

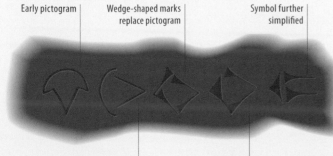

Early pictogram | Wedge-shaped marks replace pictogram | Symbol further simplified

Simplified pictogram | Simplified symbol

DOES ALL WRITING RUN FROM LEFT TO RIGHT?

When writing systems first emerged, there were no common rules about the direction in which words or symbols should be arranged. Chinese, Japanese and Korean are traditionally written in columns, proceeding from top to bottom and from right to left – probably because the earliest such writing was made on vertical strips of bamboo. The Western custom of writing from left to right down the page became fixed by the ancient Greeks around 1000 BC. Arabic script runs from right to left, so Arab newspaper readers begin on what would be the back page of a Western paper.

NEWS PRINT *Arabic-language newspapers on sale at a kiosk*

HOW DID EARLY WRITING SYSTEMS DEVELOP?

The Sumerian pictogram system spread to the Indus Valley and to Egypt, where scholars developed a system of around 2500 symbols, or hieroglyphs, which would remain in use for the next 3600 years. From around 1500 BC, the Chinese created their own system of pictograms, which gave rise to modern Chinese characters. The early Greek culture in Cyprus developed a semi-hieroglyphic script, called Linear A, about 1750 BC. By about 1450 BC this had evolved into Linear B, a system of syllabic symbols, representing groups of sounds.

Egyptian hieroglyphs

WHEN WAS THE FIRST ALPHABET INVENTED?

In an alphabet, each letter represents a single sound. The first such systems appeared in Egypt around 1800 BC, but the first complete alphabet, of 22 letters, was created by the Phoenician people of the eastern Mediterranean, around 1300 BC. The Phoenicians were successful traders and they carried their alphabet around the Mediterranean. It was adapted by the ancient Greeks and then by the Etruscans of central Italy, before being adopted by the Romans, who slightly reshaped the letters to create the alphabet we use today.

A FOR ALPHABET *The word alphabet derives from the first two letters of the Greek alphabet,* **alpha** *and* **beta***.*

Phoenician   Early Greek   Etruscan   Roman

WHEN WERE THE FIRST BOOKS MADE?

The world's oldest known book comes from Italy. Consisting of six sheets of 24-carat gold bound together with gold rings and written in Etruscan, it is 2600 years old. Among other early books to have been discovered are Egyptian texts written on papyrus about 1700 years ago, and a Latin gospel on vellum (animal skin) dating to 700 AD. The oldest printed book is a Buddhist scripture, the *Diamond Sutra*, which was printed on grey paper and dates to 868 AD.

ILLUMINATED LETTER *When medieval monks copied books by hand, they decorated the pages with ornate letters and patterns.*

fast fact
Chinese has tens of thousands of different symbols, or characters. But only about 4000 are required for literacy.

DIFFERENT STROKES *Writing systems evolved differently across ancient civilisations.*

Early Chinese characters

Linear B

WHO INVENTED THE PRINTING PRESS?

In the 1440s, German goldsmith Johannes Gutenberg invented the first mechanical printing press. It was based on an old wine press, and he gradually refined it. The machine held lines of movable type made up of individual metal letters. Ink was dabbed onto the metal letters by hand, and the press applied the pressure needed to transfer the inked text onto a sheet of paper.

LETTER PRESS *Gutenberg's printing press meant that books could be mass produced for the first time.*

WARFARE

Following the founding of the first cities, people started forming armies so they could protect their settlements and, increasingly, acquire new territories. This led to a ceaseless quest for military superiority through the development of ever-more advanced weapons and sophisticated battle strategies. Warfare has since repeatedly reshaped our world, through the dispersal and unification of peoples, and the forging and destruction of nations and empires.

CAREER SOLDIERS *Roman infantry were thoroughly drilled, protected by armour and carried a javelin and short sword.*

WHICH WERE THE FIRST ARMIES?

The founding of sedentary societies in South-West Asia from 8500 BC onwards (▶254) provided sufficient manpower for rulers to create armies. In the same era, the refinement of metalworking techniques resulted in more effective and lethal weaponry, including bronze swords and spears, as well as the first types of armour. These developments enabled Mesopotamian city-states to establish the first large armies and the first true empires, beginning with Sumer (2370–2000 BC).

VICTORY PARADE *This Sumerian carving from 2500 BC depicts the return of a triumphant army.*

WHEN DID PEOPLE START BUILDING FORTS AND CASTLES?

People fortified major settlements from ancient times. But in the Middle Ages the practice took a new turn. Powerful landowners, including minor nobility, set themselves up as lords and protectors and recruited their own armies, headed by mounted knights. This led to more frequent warfare on a smaller scale.

As a result, small towns and even private residences were heavily fortified with thick walls, towers and moats, turning them into castles. In response, armies refined the design and use of siege machines, including catapults, battering rams and scaling towers.

Battering ram | Scaling tower

Catapult

UNDER SIEGE *This artist's impression shows an assault on a medieval castle.*

WHICH WERE THE ANCIENT WORLD'S MOST SUCCESSFUL ARMIES?

Early armies tended to be temporary formations: soldiers returned to farming or other occupations between campaigns. It was the Spartans of ancient Greece who created the first full-time army, by enrolling all males from the age of seven onwards. Through the period 600–300 BC their force was widely feared. After gaining overseas territories during the Punic Wars (264–201 BC), the Romans formed a professional standing army, which attracted an increasing number of volunteers willing to sign up for long periods. It was thus able to hone its training and tactics until it became the world's most formidable fighting force, which underpinned the vast Roman Empire (27 BC–476 AD). The core of the army was the infantry, organised in legions of 5000 men each, which was bolstered by foreign auxiliaries.

WHEN WERE GUNS INVENTED?

Gunpowder is made by mixing saltpetre (potassium nitrate) with sulfur and powdered charcoal. A formula was published in 1044 AD in the Chinese *Complete Compendium of Military Classics*. In the twelfth century, the Arabs acquired knowledge of gunpowder and began using it to fire arrows from guns. Meanwhile, the Mongols carried gunpowder and firearms on their campaigns in Europe, where the new weapons were soon adopted too. The first record of cannon being used in Europe dates from 1326.

FIRE POWER *In this Chinese painting, curious onlookers watch a group of men experimenting with gunpowder.*

HOW DID WARFARE CHANGE IN THE MODERN AGE?

British Mark V tank

The increasing use of firearms made armour redundant. Nevertheless, cavalry remained the most effective form of attacking force for some time. That changed when US engineer Hiram Maxim invented the machine gun in 1884: thereafter, a single, well-positioned gunner could mow down cavalry and infantry in droves. Combined with the introduction of powerful artillery, as well as poison gases and mortars, this resulted in the mass slaughters of the First World War. Also introduced during that conflict, tanks and military aircraft played a central role in the Second World War. Bombers laid waste to entire cities and vast tracts of countryside, culminating in the dropping of atom bombs on Hiroshima and Nagasaki in Japan, in 1945. More recent advances in technology have yielded supersonic fighters with computerised weapons systems, and remote-controlled missiles, or drones (▶ 219).

ATTACK FORCE *The F4 Phantom is a widely used supersonic fighter.*

fast fact

During the Cold War arms race of the twentieth century, the Soviet Union and the United States each amassed more than 30,000 nuclear warheads.

WHICH WERE THE MOST DESTRUCTIVE WARS IN HISTORY?

Modern technology made weapons far more destructive, and the Second World War saw the greatest loss of life in a single conflict in history. However, many of the deadliest wars took place hundreds of years ago and affected a higher percentage of the population at the time. For instance, the Mongol invasions of Central and Western Asia between the early thirteenth and mid-fourteenth centuries are thought to have killed 30 million people (7.5 per cent of the world population). And several wars and uprisings in China have resulted in massive death tolls, including the An Lushan Rebellion of the eighth century, which killed between 13 and 36 million people, and the Taiping Rebellion of 1851–64, for which estimates of fatalities range from 20 to 50 million.

TAIPING TERROR *Led by Hong Xiuquan, who claimed to be Jesus's younger brother, the Taiping Rebellion was a widespread but unsuccessful peasant uprising against the Chinese Ming dynasty.*

EXPLORING THE WORLD

Though humans became more sedentary after the advent of farming and cities, people still continued to move from place to place. As the centuries passed, the accounts of travellers and explorers increasingly helped humans map and understand their world.

WHY DID PEOPLE GO EXPLORING?

Sometimes people travelled because they were forced to move by invading armies or had to go in search of new food sources. Trading peoples went looking for new markets, and adventurers were lured to other lands by the promise of wealth, including fabled cities of gold. But from ancient times, some travellers wandered simply because they were curious and wanted to learn more about the world.

WHO WERE THE FIRST EXPLORERS?

Greek and Phoenician sailors explored Africa's coastline around 600 BC and soon learned they could sail round its southern tip to the Indian Ocean. One of the earliest individual explorers was a Greek scholar, Pytheas, who lived in what is now Marseilles in France, then a Greek colony. Around 320 BC, he travelled north, crossed to Britain and sailed to Iceland, which he named Thule. He returned home via Scandinavia, and wrote accounts of his journeys. In Asia, pioneering travellers included Buddhist monks, such as Xuanzang, who set out from China in 629 AD in search of sacred writings. Over the next 16 years he wandered around Central Asia and India, before returning home loaded with artefacts, plant specimens, religious relics – and 644 sacred texts.

TRAVEL GUIDE *England as shown in a 1540 edition of Ptolemy's Geographia. Compiled in the second century AD, it remained a major source of geographical information through the Middle Ages.*

HEAVY LOAD *Buddhist traveller Xuanzang returning home in 645 AD. The relics he brought back were housed in a specially built pagoda in Chang'an, modern-day Xi'an in northern China.*

WHEN DID EUROPEANS FIRST REACH THE AMERICAS?

For centuries, people believed that Christopher Columbus (▶262) was the first European to reach the Americas. More recently it has been shown that he was beaten to it – by almost 500 years – by the Vikings of Scandinavia. Beginning in the late eighth century, they spread out around mainland Europe and to Iceland. From there, the Viking adventurer Erik the Red sailed west to Greenland, where he founded a settlement in 982. Around 1000, his son Leif Eriksson ventured across what is now the Labrador Sea to establish a colony on Newfoundland. But the colony was abandoned in 1012, and knowledge of North America all but lost.

NORSE COLONY *A reconstructed Viking village at L'Anse aux Meadows, Newfoundland, Canada.*

WHICH EARLY TRAVELLERS MADE THE LONGEST OVERLAND JOURNEYS?

The most famous overland traveller of the Middle Ages was an Italian, Marco Polo. After setting off with his father and uncle from Venice in 1271 on a trading expedition to China, where they arrived 4 years later, Marco entered the service of the Mongol ruler, Kublai Khan, and spent 17 years roaming the East as a diplomat. On his return to Italy, he published an account of his travels that became the era's most widely read travel book. Around the same time, a Chinese Christian cleric, Rabban bar Sauma, made a similar journey in the opposite direction, initially setting off on a pilgrimage to the Holy Land and then, in the 1280s, detouring to Rome and Paris as an envoy of the Persian Empire. In the early 1300s, a Muslim scholar from Tangier, called Ibn Battuta, undertook a pilgrimage to Mecca, and from there set off to visit centres all over Asia and North Africa, a journey that lasted 29 years.

UNDER SAIL *The departure of the Polos from Venice in 1271 is recorded in this Italian painting. At that time Venice was already a major trading centre.*

fast fact
Muslim traveller Ibn Battuta's journeys of 1325–54 took in the lands of 44 modern countries and covered more than 120,000 km (75,000 miles).

HOW DID NAVIGATORS FIND THEIR WAY?

PATH FINDER *This Spanish mariner's astrolabe dates from the 1500s.*

The magnetic compass was invented in China, first used for navigation in the eleventh century, and reached Europe in the twelfth century. Sea charts and several early navigational devices were steadily refined by Chinese, Arab and European mariners, including the cross-staff, which was lined up with the midday Sun, or another star, in order to work out its height above the horizon and, thereby, the user's latitude; in the sixteenth century it was replaced by the more efficient mariner's astrolabe. Measuring longitude at sea depended on knowing the precise time at two different locations and this was not possible until the invention of a sufficiently accurate and portable timepiece, the marine chronometer, in the 1760s.

EXPLORING THE WORLD CONTINUED

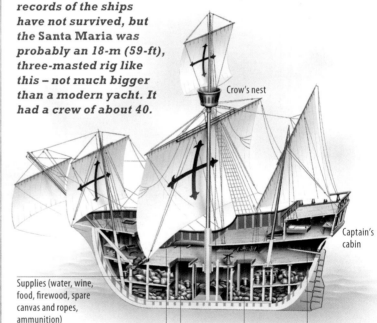

FLEET AHOY *The Chinese treasure fleet would have been an astonishing sight.*

WHAT WERE THE CHINESE 'TREASURE SHIPS'?

At the beginning of the fifteenth century, China's Ming dynasty constructed one of the largest sailing fleets the world had ever seen, including some of the biggest wooden ships ever built. These so-called treasure ships were up to 120 m (400 ft) long and 50 m (150 ft) wide and carried hundreds of sailors and vast supplies of food and trading goods. From 1403 to 1433, a Muslim admiral, Zheng He, led this fleet on a series of epic trading and exploratory voyages from China to India, Arabia and the east coast of Africa. Soon after this, however, China abandoned ocean-going exploration on such a large scale.

fast fact

During the first successful traverse of the Northwest Passage between Canada and the Arctic in 1903–06, Roald Amundsen, his ship and his crew spent almost two years trapped in ice near King William Island. When they became trapped a second time, off Alaska, Amundsen travelled 800 km (500 miles) by sled to raise the alarm.

DID COLUMBUS KNOW THE AMERICAS WERE THERE?

In the late 1400s, most Europeans believed that the eastern part of Asia lay far to the west, across the Atlantic Ocean, then known as the Ocean Sea. When Italian mariner Christopher Columbus, sponsored by the Spanish rulers Ferdinand and Isabella, set off in 1492 to sail west to Asia, he had no expectation of finding any other landmass en route. He reached what we now call the West Indies in October of that year and returned on three more voyages. To the end of his days he remained convinced that what he had discovered was part of Asia.

PIONEERING CRAFT *On his first voyage, Columbus sailed in the Santa Maria, which was accompanied by two smaller vessels, the Pinta and the Niña. Detailed records of the ships have not survived, but the Santa Maria was probably an 18-m (59-ft), three-masted rig like this – not much bigger than a modern yacht. It had a crew of about 40.*

Crow's nest

Captain's cabin

Supplies (water, wine, food, firewood, spare canvas and ropes, ammunition)

Anchor   Rowing boat   Cookbox   Tiller

CUT DOWN *An artist's impression of the death of Magellan*

WHO WAS THE FIRST PERSON TO SAIL AROUND THE WORLD?

Sailing on behalf of the Spanish crown, Portuguese mariner Ferdinand Magellan resolved to follow up on Columbus's discoveries and pioneer a western route to the Spice Islands (now part of Indonesia) and back to Europe. Heading a fleet of five ships, he sailed south in 1519 around the southern tip of South America and across the Pacific Ocean to what is now the Philippines. There, in 1521, he was killed in a skirmish with native people and it was left to one of his deputies, Juan Sebastián Elcano, to lead the last surviving ship back to Portugal the following year, thereby completing the first circumnavigation of Earth.

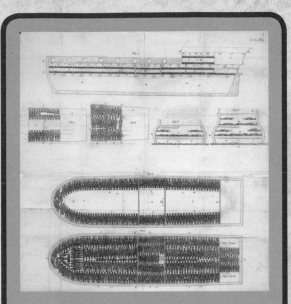

HOW DID EXPLORATION EXPAND THE SLAVE TRADE?

Slavery existed all over the world long before Europeans reached other continents. But with the arrival of the Portuguese in Africa and the creation of European colonies in the Americas, the practice proliferated. Because the American colonists required labour, they began buying huge numbers of slaves from Africa – more than 12 million would eventually be transported to the New World.

WHEN DID EUROPEANS DISCOVER AUSTRALIA AND NEW ZEALAND?

In 1600, the region now known as Australasia remained a great blank on mariners' maps, though it was surmised it must contain a large continent, known as the Great Southern Land. A number of Dutch mariners making their way to trading posts in South-East Asia made landfall on formerly uncharted coastline in the south – including Willem Janszoon in 1606 and Dirk Hartog in 1616. Two voyages by their compatriot Abel Tasman, in 1642 and 1644, charted this coastline further. Tasman named the landmass Nova Hollandia (New Holland) after the Dutch province of Holland, and dubbed another, far to the south-east, Nova Zeelandia (New Zealand), after another Dutch province. But it was not until the epic voyages of James Cook in the 1770s that the outlines of Australia and New Zealand were more fully mapped.

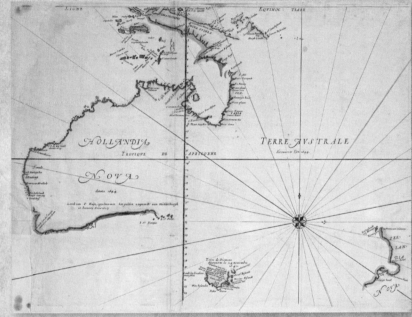

TAKING SHAPE *The Thevenot map of the mid-1600s combines the findings of Abel Tasman with those of earlier Dutch navigators.*

WHICH WERE THE LAST PARTS OF THE WORLD TO BE EXPLORED?

Cook's journeys took him south towards Antarctica and his reports piqued interest in both polar realms. Numerous expeditions scouted the Arctic and Antarctica in the 1800s, but it was not until the early 1900s that explorers attempted to reach the poles over the ice. In a famous race to the South Pole, Norwegian Roald Amundsen and his team beat a British expedition, led by Robert Scott, to reach Earth's southernmost point on 11 December 1911; Scott and his men perished on the return journey. Americans Robert Peary and Frederick Cook claimed, separately, to have reached the North Pole in 1909; but their stories are now doubted and the first confirmed over-ice journey to the North Pole was achieved only in 1969, by Englishman Wally Herbert.

ICE BREAKER *Norwegian explorer Roald Amundsen travelled to Antarctica aboard a specially reinforced ship, the* **Fram**.

FOCAL POINT *Initially, the Industrial Revolution was concentrated in the north of England. From there it spread through Britain and then to Western Europe and the United States.*

In Britain, from the early 1700s, new inventions began to transform the way that goods were produced. People used machines more and more to do work once done by hand. Factories were built to house the machines and manufacturing towns grew up, connected at first by canals and later by railways.

WHICH TECHNOLOGICAL CHANGES SPURRED THE INDUSTRIAL REVOLUTION?

STEAM POWER
Newcomen's steam engine pumped water out of flooded mines.

In 1709, ironmaster Abraham Darby developed a process of making iron using coke instead of expensive and scarce charcoal. This in turn permitted much greater quantities of iron to be produced for making machinery and building. In the textile industry, the invention of the flying shuttle, by John Kay in 1733, increased the speed of broadloom weaving. The hand-operated spinning jenny, created by James Hargreaves around 1764, spun eight threads at a time, while Samuel Crompton's spinning mule, devised in 1779, enabled one worker to operate 1000 spindles. A key development was the invention of steam-driven machinery. In 1712, Englishman Thomas Newcomen invented a steam-powered engine for pumping water. From the 1760s, it was steadily refined by Scotsman James Watt, who in 1781 added a gearing system so that the steam engine could power other machines.

WHY DID THE INDUSTRIAL REVOLUTION BEGIN IN BRITAIN?

Industrial development began in Britain partly because it was then one of the world's richest nations, with a highly productive agricultural sector and large supplies of iron and coal. Its population was then growing rapidly, creating strong demand for food and other goods, which in turn gave producers an incentive to become more efficient. Britain's large overseas empire also provided new markets for exports. Furthermore, the creation of the Bank of England in 1694 enabled businessmen to borrow money to finance new enterprises, and rapid scientific progress in Britain during the Enlightenment resulted in a spate of technological innovations.

IMPROVED INFRASTRUCTURE *In the 1790s Britain embarked on a major canal-building program. Soon after the canals were eclipsed by railways and by 1850 trains were Britain's main form of transport.*

WHAT WERE THE DOWNSIDES OF INDUSTRIALISATION?

Industrialisation brought problems too. In the coal mines there were accidents from cave-ins and gas explosions. Families who had once worked side by side in the countryside were broken up as thousands moved to the cities in search of work. There, people often ended up living in inadequate, overcrowded housing and crime proliferated. Smoke and soot from new coal-powered industries filled city air. And factory workers, including young children, were made to work long hours amid hazardous fumes and dangerous machinery.

HARD WORK *Many mill workers were women and children because they had small, nimble fingers for working threads and were cheaper to employ than men. Often they worked 12–16 hours a day, under the watchful eye of sometimes brutal overseers.*

Overseer
Quality controller
Loom
Machine operators
Young worker

PIECE BY PIECE *Workers on the assembly line in an early Ford car factory*

WHEN DID MASS PRODUCTION BEGIN?

Factory output increased considerably when manufacturers adopted mass production methods. The motor magnate Henry Ford pioneered this system in the United States. Instead of using skilled craftsmen to make a car from start to finish, he employed teams of workers to put together standardised parts. Each worker did the same one or two simple jobs on every car as the vehicles came past on a moving assembly line. The Model T Ford was launched in 1908, and 15 million were made in the next 19 years. Mass production meant that the 'Tin Lizzie', as the Model T was called, became cheap enough for even ordinary families to afford. There was little variety in design, though. Ford said that the customer could have any colour, so long as it was black!

HOW DID DAILY LIFE CHANGE FOR THE BETTER?

The Industrial Revolution brought many benefits. Advances were made in iron production, leading to the cheap manufacture of everything from iron bridges to iron frying pans, and to the machines and engines used in textile mills and railway travel. Bumper harvests were achieved with the assistance of new farm machinery, and transport by railways and steamships meant that food could be imported from other countries, giving people a more varied diet.

RAIL LINK *Opened in 1890, the Forth Bridge in Scotland was a major engineering achievement.*

fast fact

As a result of industrialisation, the population of Manchester, England, grew tenfold in the last quarter of the eighteenth century, transforming it from a small town to a city of more than 75,000 people.

TIMELINE OF WORLD HISTORY

Europe

Americas

Asia

Africa

Oceania

The history of humankind is the story of nations rising and falling; of great empires that triumph over all around them for a while, before fading and being replaced by others. It is also the story of how humanity has come to dominate Earth, and even threaten its continued existence.

The Stone Age
50,000 BC
By 50,000 years ago, *Homo sapiens* (▶253) had migrated out of Africa and spread across much of the world. Early modern humans had a hunter-fisher-gatherer lifestyle, foraging for fruit, berries, nuts and small animals and pursuing game. They built shelters and sometimes used caves. Their tools were made of wood, stone and bone.

The first farms and cities
Worldwide, c. 8000 BC
Crop cultivation developed in several parts of the world between 12,000 and 6000 years ago. Some permanent settlements took shape even earlier, but large settlements and cities required the food surplus created by well-organised farming. Such cities first arose in Mesopotamia, about 7500 BC (▶254). Efficient farming could support specialists, who were not food producers, such as priests, craftsmen and warriors.

ANCIENT EGYPT
The Great Sphinx of Giza and the Pyramid of Khufu

The dawn of history
Mesopotamia, c. 3100 BC
Strictly speaking, history begins with the invention of writing. It is generally agreed that this took place around 3100 BC in Mesopotamia, among the people of the city-states of Sumer (▶254). The Sumerians were also among the first people known to use wheeled vehicles (▶255).

Ancient Egypt
Egypt, 3100–1780 BC
For food, the cultures of ancient Egypt depended on the annual flooding of the River Nile, which deposited rich silt that crops could be grown on. To predict the best time to sow, priests created perhaps the first 365-day calendar. Egyptians believed strongly in an afterlife, so they preserved the bodies of important people and entombed them, along with treasured belongings, inside massive pyramids, thus allowing them to continue to the next world.

The monument builders
Western Europe, 2510–1500 BC
The early peoples of Western Europe built monuments of enduring mystery and astonishing size. Four thousand years ago, at Carnac in Brittany, France, more than 3000 standing stones were set in lines more than 1 km (½ mile) long. Some 500 years earlier, at Stonehenge in England, people constructed a circle of gigantic upright stones capped by stone lintels. Its likely purpose was to honour the dead.

Cities of the Indus
Indus Valley, 2500–1900 BC
More than 4000 years ago, people of the Indus Valley, in what is now Pakistan, were living in cities that had streets laid out in a grid pattern, as well as baths and drains. The citizens of Harappa and Mohenjo-Daro grew wheat, barley, rice and cotton, and traded as far away as Mesopotamia. The cities were abandoned around 1900 BC.

The Minoan civilisation
Crete, 2000–1400 BC
Named after King Minos, the Minoan civilisation grew rich on commerce – its wine and olive oil were traded for such luxuries as gold and pearls from Egypt, and ivory from Syria – and constructed grand palaces, including that found at Knossos. It came to a rapid end after an immense volcanic eruption on a nearby island, and an invasion by a warrior race from mainland Greece, the Mycenaeans.

STONE MONUMENT Stonehenge in England was likely built as a site of rituals for the dead.

SUMERIAN ART This pendant was made in Sumer in the third millennium BC.

MINOAN ART These frescoes adorn the walls of the Minoan Palace of Knossos in Crete.

MISSING MARVEL No trace of the Hanging Gardens of Babylon has ever been found, even though they were described by many ancient authors.

The birth of the caste system
Indus Valley, 1900 BC

The Aryans, fierce invaders on horseback, swarmed into the Indus Valley, bringing with them a tradition of dividing society into priests, warriors, farmers and semiskilled or unskilled labourers; considered beneath these four classes were those who did the most menial jobs. This was the origin of Southern Asia's rigid caste system, in which, to this day, members of the fifth group are called 'Untouchables'.

Mythical battles
Troy, 1200 BC

The Mycenaeans, rulers of Greece and Crete after the collapse of the Minoan civilisation, were the most fearsome warriors of the era. Their conflict with the city of Troy, which controlled trade from the Black Sea, inspired one of the world's most powerful stories, *The Iliad*. Composed about 400 years later by the poet Homer, it describes the Greeks' 10-year war on Troy and how they finally penetrated its defences by hiding warriors inside a huge wooden horse.

Empires in collision
Middle East, 1200–612 BC

Social order broke down along the eastern coasts of the Mediterranean as a group of refugees, pirates and bandits known as the Sea Peoples caused havoc. Only Egypt stood firm. In Mesopotamia, the Assyrians built the most powerful empire that the world had yet seen. In 612 BC, it was brought to an end when an alliance of Medes and Babylonians captured the Assyrian capital, Nineveh.

The first money
Lydia, eighth century BC

The first coins, made of a mixture of gold and silver, appeared in Lydia, in eastern Turkey, and in China. Later, in the sixth century BC, Lydia's King Croesus ruled that his coins should have a set weight and be worth a fixed amount. Croesus became widely renowned for his wealth and the phrase 'as rich as Croesus' is still used today.

Wonder of the world
Mesopotamia, 630–562 BC

The rule of King Nebuchadnezzar II saw Babylon become the world's most splendid city. Its massive gates were 15 m (50 ft) high, set in a wall 17 km (10½ miles) long, and its hanging gardens became renowned as one of the Seven Wonders of the World. Under Nebuchadnezzar, Babylon captured Jerusalem and, in 586 BC, took the Jews back to Babylon as slaves.

King of kings
Persia, 539–486 BC

In 539 BC Babylon fell to a surprise attack by Cyrus, King of Persia, who allowed the captive Jews to return to Jerusalem. Under a later king, Darius the Great, Persia's empire stretched from the Mediterranean to India. In letters carved on a cliff face he boasted: 'I am Darius, king of kings.' He died in 486 BC.

The vision of the Buddha
India, 528 BC

Becoming aware of human suffering, a young prince, Gautama Siddhartha, turned his back on luxury and sought spiritual consolation. Meditating one day under a fig tree, he found the spiritual knowledge he was looking for, and became the Buddha ('Enlightened One'). He taught that human suffering would end only when people were freed from selfish desires and that the way we each live determines our next life. These ideas gave rise to Buddhism, one of the world's major religions.

Chinese wisdom
China, late sixth century BC

Isolated from other lands by mountains, deserts, seas and huge distance, the Chinese developed a civilisation based on respect for tradition and authority. The philosopher Confucius (551–479 BC) taught that children should obey their parents, people should know their place in society, and those in authority should behave justly. His ideas still influence Chinese society today.

TROJAN HORSE This modern replica can be found in Çanakkale, Turkey.

SIGN OF WEALTH Coins issued by Croesus of Lydia are still found today.

TREE OF KNOWLEDGE Gautama Siddhartha found enlightenment while meditating under a fig tree.

TIMELINE OF WORLD HISTORY CONTINUED

ROUTE MAP *Alexander's journey through Asia*

GREEK CITADEL *Major monuments crown the Acropolis in Athens.*

The rise of Athens
Greece, sixth to fifth century BC
Greek-speaking Dorians from the north, who had begun moving into southern Greece about 1200 BC, gradually built up a dazzling civilisation, based on individual, isolated city-states. The most significant was Athens, where democracy had its beginnings in 508 BC, when every adult male was given the right to vote, and where philosophy and the arts flourished.

The Greco–Persian Wars
Greece, 490–480 BC
King Darius of Persia sent an army to invade Greece in 490 BC, but was defeated at Marathon. Tradition says that the Greek Pheidippides ran the first marathon – nearly 42 km (26 miles) – to bring news of the victory to Athens, then fell dead. Darius's son, Xerxes, invaded again in 480 BC and took Athens before being definitively repelled.

Alexander the Great
Persia and India, 336–323 BC
After coming to the throne of Macedonia aged just 20, Alexander began one of the most extraordinary campaigns of conquest in history. Backed by an army of more than 50,000 men, he overwhelmed Phoenician Mediterranean ports, Egypt, Persia and much of Central Asia, halting in northern India only because his troops refused to go any further. Heading home, he died in Babylon, aged just 33.

An empire built on peace
India, 269–238 BC
An uprising broke out in India soon after the departure of Alexander the Great. Its leader, Chandragupta Maurya, went on to establish India's first empire, which reached its height under his grandson, Asoka. Though he initially waged violent campaigns, around 263 BC Asoka renounced war, became a Buddhist and sent out missionaries, who carried the Buddha's message of peace as far as Greece.

China's first emperor
China, 221–206 BC
King of the state of Qin, Qin Shi Huang conquered the whole of China in 221 BC and declared himself emperor the next year. He tolerated no opposition, even burning books that displeased him and executing more than 400 scholars. Using the forced labour of 700,000 troops and peasants, he started building China's Great Wall. When he died, an army of life-sized terracotta warriors was buried with him.

Hannibal crosses the Alps
Italy, 218 BC
In one of the most astonishing feats of military history, Hannibal, a general from Carthage in North Africa, led about 50,000 men and 38 elephants across the Alps from France into Italy to wage war on Rome for the next 14 years. Two years after that Hannibal was defeated, at Zama in North Africa. But it wasn't until 146 BC that Rome gained complete victory over Carthage and control of the Mediterranean.

The murder of Julius Caesar
Rome, 44 BC
From its beginnings as a village on the Tiber River, Rome grew into a mighty empire. The city started as a republic, ruled by a senate and elected consuls. Its tough legions expanded its borders and Julius Caesar was made dictator for life to honour his overseas conquests. But many saw him as a threat, and in 44 BC a group of plotters in the Senate, led by Brutus, stabbed Caesar to death.

CRUCIAL BATTLE *A Greek victory at Salamis in 480 BC ended the war with Persia.*

NATIONAL DEFENCE *A series of walls, the Great Wall of China extends for 8000 km (5000 miles).*

Rome's first emperor
Rome, 27 BC–63 AD

After the murder of Julius Caesar, his adopted son Octavius allied himself with Mark Antony and Marcus Aemilius Lepidus to defeat Caesar's assassins. The three allies ruled as a triumvirate but then turned on each other. Octavius emerged victorious and in 27 BC he was proclaimed Augustus ('Revered One'), making him emperor in all but name.

The Crucifixion
Jerusalem, 33 AD

A young prophet emerged in Palestine, preaching a philosophy of love and forgiveness, reportedly performing miracles and claiming to speak with God's authority. Jesus Christ's growing band of followers, or disciples, believed he was the Messiah, come to lead the Jews to freedom. But Jewish leaders regarded him as a troublemaker and in 33 AD colluded with the Romans to have him arrested and executed.

Last stand at Masada
Palestine, 73 AD

Rome had first taken control of Judaea in 63 BC, when the consul Pompey captured Jerusalem. In 66 AD a major Jewish rebellion took place against Roman rule. After it was brutally put down by the Roman general Vespasian, the last remaining rebels, members of a sect called the Zealots, took refuge in the fortress of Masada. There they committed suicide rather than fall into Roman hands.

Hadrian's Wall
Britain, 122–383

Wherever the legions of Rome marched, Roman builders followed, constructing roads, defences, aqueducts, drains and houses. In Britain, the emperor Hadrian had a 117-km (73-mile) wall built to mark and protect Rome's north-west frontier. It had watchtowers, forts stood along its length, and troops were stationed in 'mile-castles' every Roman mile (1480 m/4855 ft).

A new Rome in the East
Turkey, 330

In the third century, the emperor Diocletian divided the vast Roman Empire into four parts to make it easier to rule. Under Constantine (306–337), Rome became Christian and the city of Byzantium, initially renamed 'New Rome', was established as its capital. After the death in 395 of Theodosius, the last emperor to rule the whole empire, Rome was divided definitively into two separate realms, the Western Empire and the Eastern Empire.

The 'Barbarian Invasions'
Europe, fourth and fifth centuries

Beginning around 376, the arrival of the Huns, a tribe from Central Asia, pushed other peoples westward. The Goths spilled into the Eastern Roman Empire and killed the emperor, Valens. Western Goths, or Visigoths, under Alaric, sacked the city of Rome in 410, before moving on to Spain. Rome was threatened again in 453, by the Huns under Attila, and sacked once more by the Vandals, in 455. After the last Roman emperor, Romulus Augustus, was deposed in 476, Italy fell to the Ostrogoths, or eastern Goths, under Theodoric.

Works of the saints
Europe, 435–529

Despite the fall of Rome, many of the empire's institutions and much of its infrastructure were retained by its successors, most of whom also converted to Christianity. The religion was disseminated by pioneering monks, who founded monasteries and religious orders all over the continent. Notable among them were St Patrick, who took Christianity to Ireland and slowly won converts in Britain, and St Benedict, who was the founder of the influential Benedictine order in Italy in the early sixth century.

The rise of Islam
Arabia, 610–750

In 610, after experiencing a series of divine revelations, a prophet called Muhammad founded a new religion based on faith in a single god, clear social rules and the promise of an afterlife. His ideas were documented in the holy book The Koran. By 750 his followers had established a vast Islamic kingdom, stretching from Spain in the west through North Africa and South-West Asia to the Indus Valley.

TIMELINE OF WORLD HISTORY CONTINUED

Europe

Americas

Asia

Africa

Oceania

OCEAN GOING
A Polynesian double-hulled canoe

Viking expansion
Scandinavia, eighth to tenth centuries

Late in the eighth century, the Vikings burst out of their homelands in Scandinavia and commenced a series of raids that brought terror to Europe. Sailing across oceans and up rivers, they seized control of lands throughout Britain and Ireland, founded the Duchy of Normandy in France, and established colonies in Russia, Iceland and even North America (▶261).

The empire of Charlemagne
Western Europe, 800–814

From the late fifth century, the Germanic kingdom of the Franks had taken shape in what is now Belgium and northern Germany and steadily expanded south through modern-day France. Under Charlemagne, the Franks conquered heathen peoples, such as the Saxons and Avars, and established a Christian realm spanning much of western Europe. In recognition of this achievement, Pope Leo II crowned Charlemagne as Holy Roman Emperor on Christmas Day 800.

The Norman Conquest
England, 1066–71

In 1066, William, Duke of Normandy in northern France, pursuing a claim to the English throne, invaded England and defeated the Anglo-Saxons under Harold Godwinson at the Battle of Hastings. Brutally quashing rebellions, William swiftly transferred ownership of much of England to his Norman barons. To take stock of these new holdings, he commissioned the remarkable Domesday Book, a survey of every property in the country.

The power of the Papacy
Italy, 1077

Following a bitter dispute over who had the authority to appoint bishops, Holy Roman Emperor Henry IV renounced Pope Gregory VII. In response, Gregory excommunicated Henry. This prompted German princes to rebel against Henry, who was then forced to back down. As a penance, he walked barefoot across the Alps in winter, wearing only a hairshirt, to Gregory's residence at Canossa, Italy. There he was made to wait in the snow for three days before being received and officially forgiven.

The Crusades
Palestine, 1095–1291

The Crusades began in 1095, when Pope Urban II called on Christians to drive the Muslim Turks from the Holy Land. Jerusalem fell to the Crusaders in 1099, and both Muslims and Jews were massacred. Eight other crusades followed over the next two centuries, with control of the holy city of Jerusalem repeatedly changing hands, but by 1291 the Christians had been definitively repelled.

The Mongol Conquests
Central Asia and eastern Europe, 1206–81

Emerging from the steppe grasslands of Central Asia, the Mongols, led by their fearsome leader Genghis Khan, cut a swathe through western Asia, overrunning city after city and killing millions (▶259). They came close to conquering Europe in 1241 and Egypt in 1259, but after losing the Battle of Ain Jalut in 1260 retreated east to consolidate their control of China.

HOLY ROMAN EMPEROR
Charlemagne established his imperial capital at Aachen, now in Germany.

STITCHES IN TIME The *Bayeux Tapestry depicts the Norman invasion of Britain.*

A watershed for liberty
England, 1215
When King John I of England came into conflict with his barons over taxes, they rebelled and forced him to sign the Magna Carta ('Great Charter'). By doing so, he agreed he could no longer impose taxes without the consent of his council. The document came to be seen as a milestone in the evolution of human rights, as it forced rulers to accept they were accountable under a nation's law.

A divine wind saves Japan
Japan, 1281
In the thirteenth century, Japan was under the control of a military dictator, the Shogun, and society was dominated by samurai warriors. In 1281, the Mongol emperor of China, Kublai Khan, sent an army of 140,000 men to invade Japan. The battle raged for seven days, but then a powerful wind, known as the kamikaze, or 'divine wind', wrecked the Mongol fleet and Japan was saved.

Peopling the Pacific
New Zealand, c. 1300
Polynesian voyagers reached New Zealand in open, double-hulled canoes around 1300. They were completing an exploration that had begun about 3300 years ago in island South-East Asia and New Guinea, when people speaking Austronesian languages migrated beyond the Solomon Islands. They voyaged to New Caledonia, Vanuatu and Fiji within a few hundred years. From there, Polynesian people migrated east to Tahiti (200 BC), Easter Island (1100 AD) and Hawaii (1000 AD), and south to New Zealand.

Kingdoms of gold
Nigeria and Zimbabwe, thirteenth to fifteenth centuries
Trade in gold and other resources, including copper, tin, salt and cattle, gave rise to powerful kingdoms in West Africa, notably Mali, Songhay and the rainforest realm of Benin. In southern Africa, another successful trading people, the Shona of Great Zimbabwe, built imposing stone palaces and walled compounds.

The Aztec Empire
Mexico, fourteenth and fifteenth centuries
In 1325, the Mexica people established a settlement they named Tenochtitlán, on the central plateau of what is now Mexico. From 1428, under Iztcoátl, they rapidly expanded their realm, creating the Aztec Empire and turning Tenochtitlán into one of the world's great cities. The Aztecs' priests believed they had to feed their god of war, Huitzilopochtli, with human blood, and so they sacrificed thousands of prisoners in their temples.

The Hundred Years' War
France, 1337–1453
After a dispute over succession to the French crown, England and France fought a century of battles. England scored early victories at Crécy (1346), Poitiers (1356) and Agincourt (1415). But inspired by 17-year-old Joan of Arc, who claimed to have had a vision telling her she would drive out the English, France won a momentous victory at Orléans (1429). Though Joan was captured and burned at the stake in 1431, by 1453 only Calais remained in English hands.

The Black Death
Europe, 1347–52
Carried by the fleas of rats and transported westward along trade routes from China, the bubonic plague, or Black Death as it became known, reached Italy aboard merchant ships in 1347. During the next two years, it spread all over western Europe, wiping out between one-third and a half of the entire population and leaving the survivors with a huge labour shortage.

Peasants in revolt
France and England, 1358–81
Disease, famine, war and taxes made life a misery for peasants after the Black Death. In France, a revolt called the Jacquerie (which came from a nickname for peasants) was crushed in 1358, with the loss of 20,000 lives. In England, 60,000 men from Kent and Essex, led by Wat Tyler, marched on London in 1381 to protest against taxes. The rebellion was soon put down by the army of the young King Richard II.

Building the Forbidden City
China, 1406–20
In China, a Buddhist monk led a rebellion against Mongol rule in 1368 and became the first ruler of the so-called Ming dynasty, the Hongwu Emperor. The third ruler, the Yongle Emperor, initiated major construction projects, including China's Grand Canal and a vast imperial palace, the Forbidden City in Beijing. Completed in 1420, it remained closed to all but the emperor and his official household for the next 500 years.

TIMELINE OF WORLD HISTORY CONTINUED

MOORISH GEM *The magnificent Alhambra was the palace of southern Spain's Muslim rulers.*

The Renaissance
Italy, fifteenth and sixteenth centuries
Powerful dynasties in Italy, including the Medici in Florence and the Borgias in Rome, supported a flourishing of the arts, much of it inspired by the rediscovery of the glories of ancient Greece and Rome. Leading lights of the era included the artists Leonardo da Vinci, Raphael and Michelangelo, and the writers Francesco Petrarch, Giovanni Boccaccio and Niccolò Machiavelli.

RENAISSANCE HUB
Florence's Cathedral, or Duomo, designed by Filippo Brunelleschi

The cities of the Incas
South America, 1438–1533
From the city of Cuzco in the Peruvian Andes, the Incas, under their emperor Pachacuti, began extending their territory around 1438. In less than 100 years they ruled a vast empire and had palaces crammed with treasure. They had no wheeled transport and no writing, but built remarkable stone roads, walls and buildings.

The fall of Constantinople
Europe, 1453
From 330 AD, Constantinople had been the seat of the Eastern Roman Empire – later referred to as the Byzantine Empire – and the gateway to Christian Europe. As such, it had suffered repeated attacks by invading forces from the east, most notably the Ottoman Turks. In 1453, they finally conquered the city, whose great churches, including the cathedral of Hagia Sophia, then became mosques.

The Christian reconquest of Spain
Spain, 1492
Through the early 1200s, Christian kings gradually reclaimed most of the Iberian Peninsula from its Muslim rulers, and after 1248 the only remaining outpost of Islam in Spain was the southern city of Granada. It remained a centre of Arab culture until 1492, when the Spanish rulers Ferdinand and Isabella decreed it too should be retaken and its inhabitants convert to Christianity or be expelled from Spain.

Columbus finds a new world
West Indies, 1492
The voyages of Portuguese sailors in the early fifteenth century initiated the so-called Age of Discovery and opened trade routes to South-East Asia. In the late 1400s, Italian navigator Christopher Columbus had the daring idea of reaching the Far East by sailing west.

Sponsored by Spain's rulers, Ferdinand and Isabella, he crossed the Atlantic with three ships, reaching the West Indies and returning on two further expeditions (▶262).

The battle for Italy
Italy, 1494–1529
The wealth and the military weakness of its city-states made Italy a rich and alluring prize for its powerful northern neighbours. In 1494, France invaded Naples, partly to prevent Charles V, the Holy Roman Emperor and ruler of Spain, Austria and the Netherlands, from extending his empire south into Italy. But Charles V defeated the French at Pavia in 1525 and by 1529 had forced them out of Italy.

The Reformation
Germany, 1517
The German monk Martin Luther started the Reformation when he nailed 95 theses (statements) to a church door, protesting against the authority of the Pope. He was especially angered by the way Indulgences (pardons for sin) were being sold to pay the Pope's debts. Luther's belief that salvation lay in faith alone, not through obedience to the Church, spread rapidly through northern Europe, where by 1570 so-called Protestantism held sway.

CROWNING GLORY *The imposing Inca citadel of Macchu Picchu*

REFORMER *Martin Luther, instigator of Protestantism*

SPANISH ARMADA *A dramatic rendering of a decisive naval battle*

The Spanish conquest of the Americas
Mexico and Peru, 1519–33
Hungry for gold, Spanish conquistadors invaded Central and South America. Their guns and horses terrified the native peoples and allowed them to overcome vastly superior forces. Backed by a small Spanish army and Indian allies, Hernán Cortés took the Aztec capital of Tenochtitlán in 1521. With an even smaller force – just 180 men – his distant cousin Francisco Pizarro seized control of the Inca Empire in 1533.

Ivan the Terrible
Russia, 1533–84
Through the 1400s, the grand princes of Moscow steadily expanded their realm. Ivan IV acceded to the throne in 1533, at just three years of age. As an adult he became the first Russian ruler to take on the title of tsar and vastly extended Russian control of Central Asia and Siberia. His brutal suppression of all opposition to his rule gained him the nickname of Ivan the Terrible.

The Counter-Reformation
Europe, 1545–63
At the Council of Trent, held over 25 sessions between 1545 and 1563, the Catholic Church responded to the Reformation. It set out a clear and complete statement of Catholic doctrine and identified what it saw as heresies in Protestant teachings. New religious orders, most notably the Society of Jesus, or Jesuits, founded in 1534 by St Ignatius Loyola, did much to help reassert Catholic doctrines and halt the spread of Protestantism.

The Dutch Revolt
The Netherlands, 1568–1648
King Philip II of Spain, a devout Catholic, could not tolerate the fact that the Protestant faith had been taken up by his subjects in the Netherlands. In 1567 he sent the Duke of Alba to bring them under control, but Alba's brutality and high taxes caused a full-scale revolt. By 1609, seven northern provinces had won their freedom, though it was not recognised by Spain until 1648.

The St Bartholomew's Day Massacre
Paris, 1572
Wars between French Catholics and Protestants, or Huguenots, were supposed to be brought to an end by the marriage in Paris of the Huguenot Henry of Navarre to Margaret, sister of the French king, Charles IX, a Catholic. But some Catholics saw it as a chance to end the Protestant threat, and turned on the Huguenots, slaughtering them. Henry, however, escaped, and in 1589 brought the wars to an end when he became King Henry IV of France.

The Spanish Armada
England, 1588
After Henry VIII made England a Protestant country, his successor, daughter Mary, tried to bring her country back to Catholicism. Mary married King Philip II of Spain, but after she died childless, her half-sister Elizabeth restored Protestantism. Furious, Philip sent a mighty Armada of 130 ships and over 19,000 soldiers to invade England. But it was blocked by the English navy under Francis Drake, then scattered by violent storms.

French colonies in Canada
Quebec, 1608
French explorer Jacques Cartier had sailed up the St Lawrence River in 1534 while searching for the Northwest Passage, an Arctic sea route to China. Following in his path, the explorer and fur trader Samuel de Champlain constructed a fort on the St Lawrence in 1608, which would grow to become the city of Quebec, the centre of French power in Canada.

The Thirty Years' War
Europe, 1618–48
The war began when Protestants in Prague, in revolt against their Habsburg rulers, hurled two governors out of a window. Both men lived, and the rebellion was crushed, but the struggle sparked a war between the Catholic Habsburg Empire and a predominantly Protestant alliance formed by Denmark, Sweden, the Netherlands and France. Its conclusion left France the strongest power in Europe, the Holy Roman Empire in tatters and Germany devastated by violence.

ROUGH JUSTICE *Many Aztecs were burned by the Spanish for refusing to convert to Christianity.*

TIMELINE OF WORLD HISTORY CONTINUED

Europe
Americas
Africa
Asia
Oceania

DISPLAY OF WEALTH The French court at Versailles was the epitome of opulence.

PIONEERING VOYAGE The *Mayflower* endured fierce storms in the Atlantic.

The voyage of the *Mayflower*
North America, 1620
Crowded aboard the *Mayflower*, a ship less than 28 m (92 ft) long, 102 passengers set sail from England in 1620 for a new life in America. Among them were 35 people, later called the Pilgrims, who were seeking the freedom to worship in their own way. The first winter was so harsh that nearly half of them died.

The Sun King
France, 1643–1715
Nobody believed more fervently that kings were appointed to rule by God than Louis XIV of France. He was called the Sun King because the affairs of the nation revolved around him like planets. 'I am the State,' he declared. Living lavishly, he built a great palace at Versailles, outside Paris, with 1400 fountains, roofs covered in gold leaf, and rooms full of mirrors to fill them with light.

The Manchu take over China
China, 1644–45
In 1644, facing two major rebellions, the last Ming emperor, Chongzen, committed suicide in Beijing. Ming commander Wu Sangui joined forces with the Manchu, long-term opponents of the Ming from beyond China's north-eastern frontier, to defeat the rebels. But the Manchu then seized control of China and founded the Qing dynasty, which would rule for nearly 300 years.

The English Civil War
England, 1642–60
King Charles I made himself unpopular with his ministers and his people by repeatedly clashing with elected members of parliament. This led to uprisings and, in 1642, a civil war between 'Parliamentarians' (named 'Roundheads' for their close-cropped hair) and 'Royalists' (called 'Cavaliers'). Charles's forces were defeated in battle;

he was executed for treason in 1649. Puritan leader Oliver Cromwell then became the country's 'Lord Protector' (1653–58), but after his death the monarchy was restored under Charles II.

Peter the Great
Russia, 1682–1725
When Peter I became Tsar of Russia aged 10, it was a backward country with a mass of hard-working serfs (peasants) at the bottom, and princes and boyars (nobles) living in idleness and luxury at the top. Peter earned the title 'The Great' by his tireless campaign to modernise his country. He also extended its territory, creating a vast empire that extended from the Baltic and Black seas to the Pacific Ocean.

The Ottoman siege of Vienna
Austria, 1683
After capturing Constantinople in 1453, the Ottoman Turks remained a threat to Christian Europe for the next 200 years. In 1683 an Ottoman force of 300,000 besieged Vienna, capital of the Austrian Empire and gateway to the west. German states rallied to help, as did the Polish king, John III Sobieski and his 25,000 cavalry. On 12 September, Sobieski and his horsemen put the Turks to flight, saving the day – and Europe.

An era of change
Western Europe, eighteenth century
In Europe, the eighteenth century was an era of rapid and profound developments in technology, society and thought. The Industrial Revolution (▶264) transformed farming and manufacturing and boosted the growth of urban areas as people left the land to work in factories. Meanwhile, the new ideas of the Enlightenment, as it was called, overturned conventional beliefs, with philosophers such as Voltaire and Denis Diderot promoting reason and science over tradition and superstition, and questioning the right of hereditary rulers to limit the freedoms of individuals.

LORD PROTECTOR Oliver Cromwell, in a portrait by Emanuel Gottlieb Leutze

- Austrian Habsburgs
- Spanish Habsburgs
- France
- Great Britain
- Russia
- Ottoman Empire
- Non-aligned states
- Papal States
- Poland
- Sweden
- Dutch Republic
- Prussia

SOUTHERN LAND *James Cook's voyages revealed new realms.*

The Black Hole of Calcutta

India, 1757

In 1756, the nawab (ruler) of Bengal, Siraj ud-Daulah, attacked a British East India Company fort in Calcutta and put 146 British prisoners into its dungeon, known as the Black Hole, in 1757. A story reached Britain that most of the prisoners then died. In retaliation, a British force under Robert Clive defeated Siraj at the Battle of Plassey. The victory gave the East India Company control of Bengal and laid the foundations of Britain's Empire in India.

Wolfe takes Quebec and Canada

Canada, 1759

In the 1750s, Britain and France fought a war for control of Canada. At Quebec, the French, fighting under the Marquis Louis-Joseph de Montcalm, constructed an imposing fortress atop high cliffs – an impregnable base, they believed. However, the British general, James Wolfe, surprised them by having his troops scale the cliffs. The battle that followed lasted only 10 minutes but won both Quebec and Canada for Britain – and cost the lives of both Wolfe and Montcalm.

America's War of Independence

North America, 1775–83

In the 1760s and 1770s, British colonists in North America grew dissatisfied about paying heavy taxes without having a say in how their government was run. In 1775, violent clashes in Massachusetts between colonial militia, known as the Minutemen, and British troops triggered a war. Led by George Washington and aided by the French, the rebels won a series of remarkable victories. The British surrendered at Yorktown in 1781 and in 1783 signed the Treaty of Paris, recognising American independence.

The colonisation of Australia

Australia, 1788

During three voyages to the Pacific between 1768 and 1779, James Cook claimed the east coast of Australia for Britain. His glowing reports prompted Britain to plan a penal colony in Australia. The 11 ships of the First Fleet arrived at what would become Sydney in 1788, carrying more than 1200 prisoners, soldiers and sailors. Drawing increasing numbers of free settlers, the colony grew steadily, forming the nucleus of what would become Australia.

The French Revolution

France, 1789–94

For years, the ordinary people of France had suffered under a crushing burden of taxes. In 1789 their anger erupted, and an enraged crowd stormed the Bastille, a hated royal prison in Paris. King Louis XVI and his queen were guillotined in 1793, the monarchy was abolished and the revolution's guiding principles of 'liberty, equality and fraternity' were widely proclaimed and celebrated. But disputes between factions soon led to violence, civil war and mass executions.

The liberators of Latin America

Central and South America, 1791–1821

The ideas unleashed by the French Revolution quickly spread beyond France. In 1791, a slave revolt led by Toussaint l'Ouverture paved the way for Haiti to achieve independence from France in 1804. In 1816, Argentina threw off Spanish rule. Soon after, Simón Bolívar, 'The Liberator', drove the Spanish out of Colombia, Venezuela, Ecuador, Peru and Bolivia, while Chile was liberated by Bernardo O'Higgins and José de San Martín, who also helped to free Peru in 1821.

The rise and fall of Napoleon

Western Europe, 1795–1815

In 1795, General Napoleon Bonaparte helped put down an uprising in Paris, thereby gaining favour and fame. In 1799, after a series of hugely successful overseas campaigns, he returned home a hero and was declared First Consul, ruler of France. He continued to win dazzling victories abroad but over-reached himself in Russia, from where he was forced to make a long, costly retreat. An alliance of opposing nations, led by the Duke of Wellington and Marshal von Blücher, finally defeated him in 1815 at Waterloo.

The Congress of Vienna

Vienna, 1815

The allies who defeated Napoleon sought to reverse the advances of revolution and nationalism and restore the old order when, at the Congress of Vienna, they redrew the map of Europe. What would later be Belgium was given to Holland; Norway went to Sweden; Austria kept Lombardy and Venetia in Italy; and most of Poland fell under Russian control. These actions provoked anger among nationalists in many countries, which would later boil over as revolution.

MAN OF INFLUENCE *At the height of his power, Napoleon held sway over almost half of Europe.*

TIMELINE OF WORLD HISTORY CONTINUED

Europe
Americas
Asia
Africa
Oceania

NAVAL FORCE *British ships attack China during the Opium Wars.*

The fight against slavery
British Empire, 1833
More than 15 million people were sold as slaves during the 400 years of the African slave trade (▶263). From the seventeenth century religious groups opposed the practice, and Enlightenment thinkers later declared it an affront to the 'rights of man'. A more practical and vigorous anti-slavery campaign mounted in England by a group led by William Wilberforce from the late 1700s finally achieved success in 1833, when slavery was abolished within the British Empire.

The Great Trek
South Africa, 1835–40
From the day that Britain seized the Cape Colony in southern Africa in 1806, the local Boers (Dutch farmers) began to fear that their future was under threat. From 1835 to 1840, 14,000 of them packed their belongings and their Bibles into ox-drawn wagons and moved north to find new farmland, fighting battles along the way. At Blood River, in 1838, 468 Boers faced and defeated more than 10,000 Zulus.

The Opium Wars
China, 1839–60
To keep foreigners out of China, the Manchu emperors ruled that trade with the West should be limited to one port – Canton. But British traders used the port to smuggle in opium from India, and millions of Chinese became addicts. When Chinese officials seized 20,000 chests of the drug, Britain sent gunboats. Two Opium Wars forced China to open more ports to Western trade, and to cede Hong Kong to Britain.

The Year of Revolutions
Europe, 1848
Growing nationalist sentiment and dissatisfaction with widespread unemployment triggered a series of revolutions in 1848. The impetus came from France, where crowds stormed the Palais Royal and forced the king to abdicate. In Vienna, rebels compelled the government to extend the right to vote. Meanwhile nationalist uprisings in Hungary, Italy and Germany were violently suppressed.

The California Gold Rush
United States, 1849
The discovery of gold in the Sacramento Valley in 1849 sparked one of history's major gold rushes. American clerks and cowboys, salesmen and barkeepers deserted their jobs and headed for California, while other hopeful 'Forty-Niners' came from as far away as Australia and China – more than 300,000 people in all. The influx not only boosted the region's population but also led to the rapid development of shipping and railways, services and towns and cities.

The Taiping Rebellion
China, 1850–64
Around 1850, a Chinese student called Hong Xiuquan had a series of religious visions and proclaimed himself the brother of Jesus Christ. Seeking to establish a new era of 'Great Peace' (*taiping* in Chinese), he led a peasant revolt against the Qing dynasty. War spread across China. By the time the Qing, with Western aid, finally quashed the rebellion in 1864, more than 20 million, and possibly as many as 50 million people, had died.

GOLD STANDARD *A US gold coin, of a type issued throughout the 1800s*

The Crimean War
The Crimea, 1854–56
Forty years of peace in Europe came to an end in 1853, when Russia attacked Turkey. Britain and France, anxious to prevent Russia from becoming too powerful, sent armies to the Crimea. These allied forces spent a year besieging the Russian stronghold of Sevastopol before the Russians abandoned it, finally suing for peace in early 1856. About 250,000 people died on each side, many from disease.

Uniting Italy
Italy, 1859
Inspired by nationalist politicians, such as Giuseppe Mazzini, Italians began to push for liberation from foreign control. Directed by statesman Camillo Cavour and benefiting from French support, northern Italian forces drove Austrian troops out of Lombardy. In the south, Giuseppe Garibaldi led his 'Redshirts' – just over 1000 volunteers – against armies of twice their size to free Sicily and Naples from Spanish Bourbon rule. A united Italy was proclaimed in 1861, though unification would not be completed until 1871.

AFRICAN RIVARLY *The Great Trek marked the start of a long conflict between the Boers and the British in southern Africa.*

LADY WITH THE LAMP Pioneering nurse Florence Nightingale first gained fame for her heroic work during the Crimean War.

UNDER GUARD German soldiers and Chinese allies guard a Boxer prisoner (centre), 1900.

Crossing the outback
Australia, 1860–72

In 1860, Robert O'Hara Burke, William Wills, Charles Gray and John King became the first explorers to cross Australia from south to north. However, only King made it back alive. A more successful journey, via a similar route, was made by John McDouall Stuart two years later, and this paved the way for the construction of the Overland Telegraph Line. Completed in 1872 and connected via submarine cable to Java, Indonesia, it provided the first rapid communications link between Australia and the rest of the world.

The US Civil War
USA, 1861–65

In 1861, the year Abraham Lincoln became President of the United States, slavery was forbidden in the North, but there were 4 million black slaves in the South. Fearing that they might lose their 'right' to their slaves, a group of Southern states broke away from the Union and formed their own rebel nation – the Confederacy. Civil war then broke out. Backed by more men, more industries and more money, the North triumphed, accepting the surrender of the South on 9 April 1865.

The unification of Germany
Germany, 1864–71

In the late 1860s, Count Otto von Bismarck, prime minister of Prussia, set out to unite the different states of Germany into a single nation. First, he made war against Denmark, with Austria as an ally; then he turned against Austria. In 1870, he provoked the French emperor, Napoleon III, into declaring war. The French were defeated at Sadowa, and Paris was starved into submission. In 1871, Wilhelm I of Prussia was crowned Emperor of Germany.

The Scramble for Africa
Europe and Africa, 1880–1900

The 'Scramble for Africa' was a feverish competition between European nations to establish or extend their holdings in Africa. Plundering its treasures and enslaving its peoples made fortunes for the likes of King Leopold of Belgium, who ruled a vast territory in the Congo. Other colonisers and missionaries, however, genuinely believed they were bringing 'civilisation' to what they regarded as the 'Dark Continent'.

The Boxer Rebellion
China, 1899–1900

Western missionaries, diplomats and trading companies began moving into China after the Opium Wars. But the humiliation of those wars had produced strong anti-Western feelings. In 1899 a semi-religious secret society dubbed the Boxers (their full name was the 'Righteous and Harmonious Fists') started killing Western missionaries and Chinese Christian converts and attacking foreign embassies. Only with the arrival of an international relief force was the rebellion suppressed.

The Anglo-Boer War
South Africa, 1899–1902

Seeking greater control over the Boer South African Republic's gold mines, Britain sent troops to the region, provoking a war. The Boers scored early victories, but, bolstered by reinforcements, British forces under Lord Kitchener slowly gained the upper hand. Kitchener responded to guerilla attacks by burning the Boers' farms and herding their women and children into the world's first concentration camps. In 1902 the Boers capitulated.

Russia's first revolution
Russia, 1905

In St Petersburg on Sunday 2 January 1905, 200,000 people marched on the palace of the tsar, Nicholas II. With wages low, factories on strike and no political freedom, they were appealing to him for help. Suddenly, the army opened fire and soon 500 marchers lay dead in the snow. As a result, riots and unrest spread to many other cities. Though the tsar survived, he was forced to establish a parliament, the Duma, and introduce a new constitution.

VITAL LINK Alice Springs Telegraph Station, central Australia, built in 1872

FOR THE CAUSE Sailors on the battleship *Potemkin* joined the 1905 uprising.

Europe

Americas

Asia

Africa

Oceania

CROWD CONTROL A vast audience awaits the Führer, Adolf Hitler, in Germany, 1937.

REBEL LEADER General Francisco 'Pancho' Villa, photographed in 1913

The Mexican Revolution
Mexico, 1910–20

Three centuries of Spanish rule left Mexico with a huge gap between rich and poor. The lengthy, corrupt and repressive rule of Porfirio Díaz (president from 1877–80 and 1884–1911) did little to improve that inequality. Resentment erupted in 1910 in regional uprisings, led by the likes of Emiliano Zapata, a fierce champion of the indigenous people, and Pancho Villa, a former bandit. The US supervised the creation of a new constitution in 1917, which improved workers' rights and saw dissent begin to diminish.

China's last emperor
China, 1912

With the power of the Manchu emperors crumbling and regional warlords causing chaos, a revolution broke out in China in 1911. Its leader was a doctor called Sun Yat-sen, and he became president of the new Chinese Republic. The six-year-old emperor, Puyi, abdicated in February 1912, but was allowed to continue living in Beijing's Forbidden City on a generous pension until 1924.

The First World War
Worldwide, 1914–18

Nationalism increased rivalries over trade and colonies, in turn fuelling an arms race. The assassination of the heir to the Austro-Hungarian throne in Bosnia led Austria to declare war on Serbia; within weeks Germany and Austria were at war with France, Russia and Britain. Both sides expected a quick victory. Instead, forces became bogged down in trench warfare on the Western Front and millions died in futile attacks and counterattacks. The tide turned when America entered the war in 1917. On 11 November 1918, the Germans surrendered.

The Easter Rising
Ireland, 1916

On Easter Monday, 1916, Irish patriots led by James Connolly seized the central post office in Dublin, and declared an end to centuries of British rule. They gave up after a five-day bombardment, and 15 rebels were shot by firing squads. Further fighting between rebels and British forces ended in 1921 with the Anglo-Irish Treaty, under which the Catholic south became self-governing while the Protestant north opted to remain part of the United Kingdom.

The Bolshevik Revolution
Russia, 1917–22

There were two revolutions in Russia in 1917. The first, in February, led by liberals and the moderate socialist Alexander Kerensky, overthrew the tsar. The second, in November, led by Vladimir Lenin, drove out Kerensky and brought the communist Bolsheviks to power. In an ensuing civil war, they were opposed by the anti-Bolshevik White Russians. Lenin and the Bolshevik Red Army eventually triumphed and founded the Soviet Union in 1922.

SOVIET PROPAGANDA A poster commemorating the Bolshevik Revolution of 1917

Rise of the dictators
Europe, 1920s and 1930s

Three ruthless dictators rose to power in the 1920s and 1930s. In Italy, Benito Mussolini and his National Fascist Party seized power in a coup in 1922 and gradually eliminated all opposition to their rule. In the Soviet Union, communist dictator Joseph Stalin seized land, livestock and crops from peasants, causing a famine in 1932–33, in which 7 million people died; opponents were shot or sent to remote prison camps. Nazi Party leader Adolf Hitler was elected as Chancellor of Germany in 1933; after becoming dictator, he began annexing territories in neighbouring countries and persecuting Jews.

The Wall Street Crash
New York, 1929

Americans went on a share-buying spree during the 'Roaring Twenties', borrowing large amounts of money to invest in the markets. In October 1929, share values fell sharply and huge fortunes were lost almost instantly. Banks called in loans, factories shut down and workers lost their jobs. The Crash triggered a worldwide financial crisis, the Depression. Soon unemployment reached 3 million in Britain, and nearly 6 million in Germany.

CHAIRMAN MAO *For 27 years, Mao Zedong headed the People's Republic of China.*

The Long March
China, 1934–35

Civil war raged in China until the Nationalist Republican Party under Chiang Kai-shek seized power in 1927. But its persecution of Marxist groups led to another war against the Communists, headed by Mao Zedong. In 1934, Mao led his troops on a retreat from central China to the west, then north to Yan'an, covering 9000 km (5600 miles) in around 370 days. Only 7000 of the 90,000 who began the journey survived, but the retreat allowed the Communists to restart their campaign to seize power.

The Spanish Civil War
Spain, 1936–39

In 1936, General Francisco Franco led the Spanish Army in a nationalist revolt against the elected Republican government. Help for the Republicans came from Stalin and from various International Brigades – groups of left-wing volunteers, mainly from France, Britain and America. Franco triumphed after three years of savage war, helped by troops, weapons and planes supplied by Mussolini and Hitler.

The Second World War
Worldwide, 1939–45

In September 1939, Germany invaded Poland, prompting France and Britain to declare war. Germany then overran the Netherlands and much of France, attempted to invade Britain and attacked Russia. Entering the war on Germany's side, Japan bombed Pearl Harbor in Hawaii in 1941, drawing the United States into the war. Germany was overrun, and surrendered in May 1945, while the dropping of two atom bombs by US planes on Hiroshima and Nagasaki in August forced Japan to sue for peace in September that year.

The beginning of the Cold War
Worldwide, 1945–61

In the words of Britain's wartime leader, Winston Churchill, an 'Iron Curtain' fell across Europe after the Second World War. The Soviet Union was in control of countries captured by the Red Army, and did all it could to separate them from the rest of Europe. Meanwhile, the United States and its allies sought to stem communist influence worldwide. The Berlin Wall, built in 1961 to divide the city into Western and communist sectors, became a potent symbol of the divisions created by this 'Cold War'.

Independence and partition
India, 1947

Over many years the Indian Congress Party, led by Mahatma Gandhi and Jawaharlal Nehru, had spearheaded a campaign for independence from British rule. In 1947, victory was in sight; however, India's Muslims, led by Muhammad Ali Jinnah, feared that they might be swamped by Hindus and so insisted on the creation of a separate Muslim nation, Pakistan. India and Pakistan became sovereign states on 14 August. Tragically, Gandhi was assassinated in 1948 by a Hindu fanatic, for being 'too tolerant' to Muslims.

The Arab–Israeli conflict
Palestine, 1948

Both Jews and Palestinian Arabs regard Palestine as their homeland. Increasing Jewish emigration to the region during the twentieth century, especially following the Second World War, fuelled conflict between the two peoples, and in 1948 the United Nations' decision to divide Palestine and create a Jewish state sparked the first Arab–Israeli War. Israel's victory allowed it to consolidate its territory, while hundreds of thousands of Palestinian Arabs fled abroad.

The People's Republic of China
China, 1949

During the Second World War, the Communist Party under Mao Zedong extended its influence and, with Soviet backing, scored victory after victory over the Nationalists. On 1 October 1949, Mao declared the founding of the People's Republic of China. Women were given the vote, education was offered to all, and peasants were provided with land; at the same time, however, strict state control was applied to all economic activities.

Towards unity in Europe
Europe, 1951–57

Europe's move towards unity began in 1951, when France, West Germany, Italy, Belgium, the Netherlands and Luxembourg combined their iron and steel resources. In 1957, these countries, known as 'the Six', set up the European Economic Community, or 'Common Market'. This was the precursor to the European Union, which was founded in 1993 and now includes 28 states.

HARD TIMES *Making a living in the 1930s could require desperate measures.*

BANNER OF UNITY *The official flag of the European Union*

TIMELINE OF WORLD HISTORY CONTINUED

Europe

Americas

Asia

Africa

Oceania

PEACE PROTEST US students campaigning against the Vietnam War

SUEZ CANAL Opened in 1896, the canal is a vital link between Europe and Asia.

The Suez Crisis
Egypt, 1956
President Gamal Abdul Nasser made himself wildly popular in Egypt when he nationalised the Suez Canal and declared that its profits would no longer go to shareholders in Britain and France. Both of those countries believed that control of the canal was vital to protect their oil supplies, so they sent troops on the pretext of keeping Israeli and Egyptian forces apart. This strategy caused a global outcry, and the invaders had to withdraw.

The Hungarian Revolution
Hungary, 1956
Soviet leader Nikita Khrushchev's denunciation of Stalin's tyranny released a pent-up demand for freedom in Eastern Europe. Riots in Hungary brought Imre Nagy to power. He promised free elections and to withdraw from the Warsaw Pact, a military alliance of communist states. In response, Khrushchev sent Red Army tanks into Budapest. Nagy was executed and about 190,000 Hungarians fled to the West.

The Wind of Change
Africa, 1957–74
Through the 1950s, independence movements in Africa gained momentum; in 1960 British Prime Minister Harold Macmillan described them as a 'wind of change'. Most African nations became sovereign states in the early 1960s, sometimes peacefully and sometimes in the wake of violent conflict. Attempts to retain its colonies saw Portugal mired in wars against separatists, notably in Angola and Mozambique, until 1974.

The Cuban Missile Crisis
United States, 1962
Under President John F Kennedy, America sought to undermine Soviet influence in Cuba, even sponsoring an unsuccessful attack on the island by anti-communist Cuban exiles in 1961, the so-called Bay of Pigs invasion. In October 1962, the US discovery that the Soviets had installed missiles in Cuba brought about a tense stand-off, which many feared would lead to nuclear war. But an agreement was reached behind the scenes and disaster averted.

US forces in Vietnam
Vietnam, 1965–75
In 1954, communist forces led by Ho Chi Minh gained control of the northern half of what is now Vietnam. America sent aid to the South, to prevent a communist takeover, and was gradually dragged deeper into a savage war. The first US ground troops arrived in 1965. From then on the numbers of US combat deaths steadily soared while public opinion turned against the campaign. America withdrew in 1975, leaving behind a devastated land.

The Moon landing
The Moon, 1969
The US astronaut Neil Armstrong set foot on the Moon on 20 July 1969 and declared: 'That's one small step for [a] man, one giant leap for mankind.' America had won the space race, which had begun in 1957 when the Soviet Union launched *Sputnik 1*, the first artificial satellite to orbit Earth (▶232). Armstrong was joined on the Moon by Edwin (Buzz) Aldrin, while Michael Collins orbited above them.

The Iranian Revolution
Iran, 1979
With Western backing, Shah Reza Pahlavi instituted a campaign of modernisation in Iran in the postwar period. But his subjects became increasingly dismayed by his extravagant lifestyle, disregard for Islam and violent suppression of any opposition. Islamicists led a revolutionary movement advocating a return to traditional Muslim law. In 1979 the shah fled Iran and a new republic was declared, under the religious leader Ayatollah Ruhollah Khomeini.

LOST LEADER US President Kennedy, shot dead in 1963

The Fall of Communism
Eastern Europe, 1989
In 1989, a series of mainly nonviolent revolutions resulted in the collapse of communist governments in Poland, Hungary, East Germany, Bulgaria, Czechoslovakia and Romania. The most potent symbol of change was the destruction of the Berlin Wall by the inhabitants of the divided city, which began on 9 November 1989. In turn, these uprisings would trigger the dissolution of the Soviet Union itself, in 1991, and the abandonment of communism in several other countries around the world.

BERLIN WALL
Berliners celebrate the breaching of the wall in 1989.

CREDIT WOES
Traders at the New York Stock Exchange, November 2007

The end of apartheid
South Africa, 1990
Apartheid, the racist system that kept a white government In power in South Africa, vanished with remarkable speed after anti-apartheid campaigner Nelson Mandela was freed from jail. Mandela, who in 1964 had been given a life sentence for treason, went on to win the first elections in which black South Africans were allowed to vote and became President of South Africa from 1994 to 1999.

The Gulf War
Iraq, 1990–91
Saddam Hussein, President of Iraq, threatened Western oil supplies when he invaded the tiny neighbouring state of Kuwait in 1990. An American-led coalition of 29 nations defeated Saddam's forces in Operation 'Desert Storm', but did not succeed in toppling him. Instead, Iraq was subjected to crippling economic sanctions.

The break-up of Yugoslavia
The Balkans, 1991–95
Following the death in 1980 of Marshal Tito, the communist leader of Yugoslavia, the country began to fragment. In 1991 Croatia, Slovenia and Macedonia declared their independence. Muslim-dominated Bosnia attempted to do the same, but its Serbian minority objected and initiated a brutal civil war, only ended by NATO intervention in 1995. Four years later, NATO was also forced to intervene in the region of Kosovo to protect its Albanian population against Serb attacks. Kosovo eventually declared independence in 2008.

9/11
United States, 2001
Al-Qaeda terrorists seized four US passenger jets over the north-eastern United States. They crashed two into the World Trade Center in New York and one into the Pentagon in Virginia; the fourth was presumed to be heading towards the White House in Washington DC when it was forced to the ground by a group of passengers. More than 3000 people died in the attacks. The United States and its allies responded by launching attacks on Al-Qaeda bases in Afghanistan, which then led to the ousting of the country's Islamic Taliban government.

The Iraq War
Iraq, 2003–11
Claiming that Iraq's ruler Saddam Hussein had links with Al-Qaeda and had developed weapons of mass destruction, the United States invaded Iraq in March 2003. This led to a new government being installed and Hussein being tried and executed for crimes against humanity. However, various Iraqi insurgent groups launched a violent campaign of opposition to the occupation and the new government, and, despite a US withdrawal in 2011, the civil war continues.

The Global Financial Crisis
Worldwide, 2007–08
The widespread sale of complex and misleading financial products in the early 2000s led to misguided investment in housing and construction throughout the Western world. When the US housing market collapsed, financial institutions worldwide were left with massive debts; many became bankrupt while others were bailed out by their national governments.

Stockmarkets plummeted and credit dried up, causing businesses to fail and homes to be repossessed. Many regarded it as the worst financial crisis since the Depression.

The Arab Spring
North Africa and the Middle East, 2010–
A series of uprisings broke out across the Arab World against what were seen as oppressive or corrupt rulers. This led to the formation of new governments in Tunisia, Egypt, Libya and Yemen, and reforms in Morocco, Jordan, Kuwait, Lebanon and Oman. In Syria, rebellions sparked a violent civil war between the Ba'ath government, headed by Bashar al-Assad, and its opponents.

DUAL STRIKE
The attack on the World Trade Center, 9 September 2001

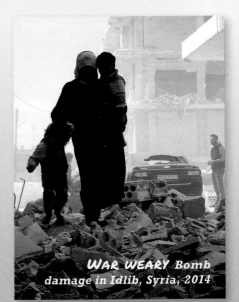

WAR WEARY *Bomb damage in Idlib, Syria, 2014*

LANGUAGE

Animals communicate with each other through a range of about 30 vocal signals, but human language is vastly more complex. An adult human knows hundreds of thousands of words, and can arrange and rearrange those words in countless numbers of sentences. Language has played a key role in the evolution of human ideas and technology. Nothing comparable exists among animals.

HOW DO WE LEARN TO SPEAK A LANGUAGE?

Children learn to speak by imitating adults and older children. First they learn to speak simple words of recognition, such as 'mum' and 'dad', and use single-word statements, such as 'there' or 'gone'. Before they are two, they have started to link words together; then they feel their way into more complex grammar. Children usually acquire all the language skills they'll need by the age of five. The process is much the same and takes the same amount of time, whether the language is French, Chinese or English. However, acquiring a second language is often a different and more difficult task, which requires a more systematic study of the language's grammar and vocabulary.

WHY ARE THERE SO MANY DIFFERENT LANGUAGES?

IN ISOLATION In rugged lands, such as the New Guinea highlands, peoples isolated in deep valleys developed their own languages.

Speech may first have emerged among early humans of the species *Homo erectus*, present from about 1.8 million years ago (▶252). At the end of the last ice age, more than 12,000 years ago, the rise in sea levels cut off many groups of people from each other. This resulted in each group developing its own language, and subsequent separations and migrations led to further diversification over millennia. It is thought that tens of thousands of languages have existed; more than 6000 have been identified.

WHY ARE THERE FAMILIES OF LANGUAGES?

Languages that are historically related are grouped into families. All those in the same family are thought to have evolved out of a single original, or proto, language. Languages in the same family tend to have similar words. For example, the Latin for father, *pater*, sounds like the equivalent word in many other languages – such as *padre* in Italian and Spanish, *père* in French and *fader* in old German – suggesting they have a common origin. The language family with by far the most speakers – almost half the world's population – is the Indo-European family, which includes most European and many Asian languages.

FAMILIES LARGE AND SMALL
This map shows the distribution of the world's major language families.

- Indo-European
- Altaic
- Uralic
- Dravidian
- Sino-Tibetan
- Japanese and Korean
- Austro-Asiatic
- Austronesian
- Afro-Asiatic
- Niger-Congo
- Nilo-Saharan
- Khoisan
- Others

WHICH LANGUAGES HAVE THE MOST SPEAKERS?

Of the more than 6000 languages spoken today, about 200 have more than 1 million speakers and just 23 have more than 50 million speakers. Mandarin is the language with the greatest number of speakers, but English is spoken more widely and is the principal language of international communication.

MANDARIN	848 million
SPANISH	414 million
ENGLISH	335 million
HINDI	260 million
ARABIC	237 million
PORTUGUESE	203 million
BENGALI	193 million
RUSSIAN	167 million
JAPANESE	122 million
JAVANESE	84.3 million

FIRST LANGUAGES The graph shows the top 10 languages according to the number of people who speak each as a first language. At many international assemblies, interpreters (below) provide simultaneous translations.

HOW DO LANGUAGES CHANGE?

Languages never stay the same: new words are continuously being coined, often in response to new developments in technology. Existing words change their meaning – silly, for example, at one time meant 'blessed'. And words regularly pass from one language to another. This is particularly the case today with English words being taken up by other languages – for instance, 'computer', 'Internet' and so on. But foreign words have also entered the English language over the centuries: originally a Persian word for loose-fitting robes, the word 'pyjamas' was imported into the English-speaking world and came to refer to nightclothes. Languages also die out, usually as a result of speakers of a minority language gradually switching to another, more widespread language.

IN DANGER More than 900 languages (about 13 per cent of all languages) are currently regarded as 'dying', meaning that only a few, usually elderly, people still speak the language. They include a number of Australian Aboriginal languages.

IN WHAT OTHER WAYS CAN PEOPLE COMMUNICATE?

People have developed several other systems for communicating, though none of these is as efficient as language. For example, deaf people can use hand signals – commonly known as sign languages – to communicate. A system called semaphore, based on flags that represent letters, is used by sailors and railway workers. And telegraph communications were usually sent as Morse Code – a representation of letters as dots and dashes.

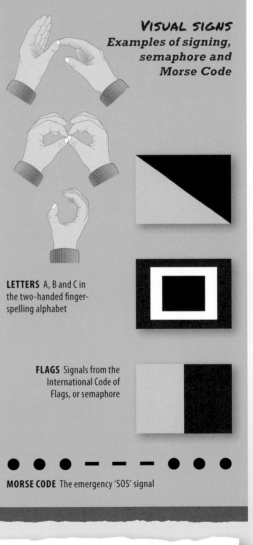

VISUAL SIGNS Examples of signing, semaphore and Morse Code

LETTERS A, B and C in the two-handed finger-spelling alphabet

FLAGS Signals from the International Code of Flags, or semaphore

MORSE CODE The emergency 'SOS' signal

fast fact
The island of New Guinea has more than 800 different languages, making it the most linguistically diverse place in the world.

MYTHS AND LEGENDS

Myths and legends are more than playful inventions. Ancient myths and folk tales expressed people's beliefs and fears and their sense of right and wrong. Legends often incorporated ancient memories of real heroes from the past and offered people models of courage and nobility. All cultures have a store of myths and legends, but for a variety of reasons some are much better known today than others.

WHAT ARE THE ANCIENT GREEK MYTHS ABOUT?

Greek mythology focuses primarily on the activities of 12 'sky gods', who were believed to live on top of Mount Olympus, the country's highest mountain. Ancient Greeks worshipped these and a variety of other, often older, deities. When the Romans conquered Greece in the second century BC, they adopted Greek mythology but gave the gods Latin names. This, and the fact that many of the stories were written down, meant that Greek mythology endured and became widely known.

THE SKY GODS *The Greeks' supreme god, Zeus, fathered lesser deities with his sister, Hera, and with other goddesses and mortals. (Roman names are given in brackets.)*

POSEIDON (NEPTUNE)
Brother of Zeus; ruler of the seas

HESTIA (VESTA)
Sister of Zeus; goddess of hearth and home

ZEUS (JUPITER)
King of the gods; lord of wind and thunder

=

HERA (JUNO)
Sister and wife of Zeus; goddess of marriage and motherhood

HADES (PLUTO)
Brother of Zeus; ruler of the underworld

HEPHAESTUS (VULCAN)
Blacksmith and patron of industry

ARES (MARS)
God of war, highly revered by the Romans

HERMES (MERCURY)
Quick-witted messenger god

ATHENA (MINERVA)
Goddess of wisdom and patron of architects and sculptors

ARTEMIS (DIANA)
Twin of Apollo and goddess of hunting

APOLLO
God of medicine, poetry and science

APHRODITE (VENUS)
Goddess of love

Zeus

Athena

Poseidon

WHAT IS THE MOST COMMON MYTH?

Of all the world's myths, the most widespread is that of a great flood. The story of an angry god destroying much of humankind in a deluge is told in the Biblical story of Noah, and in the earlier *Epic of Gilgamesh* of the Sumerians in Mesopotamia. Flood stories were also told among the Aztecs of Mexico and Vikings of Scandinavia. Some people believe that these myths go back to the end of the last ice age, around 10,000 BC, when the melting ice caps caused worldwide flooding.

FLOOD TABLET *The section of the* Epic of Gilgamesh *featuring the story of a catastrophic flood and the building of a giant ship,* The Preserver of Life, *is inscribed on this tablet, which dates from the seventh century BC.*

fast fact

Vampire myths may have been inspired by a rare disease, *Erythropoietic protoporphyria*, which causes skin to bleed when exposed to light. Medieval doctors told sufferers to go out only at night and drink blood to replace the lost liquid.

RIDE OF THE VALKYRIES *Gold-haired warrior maidens, the Valkyries brought victory to heroes chosen by Odin and carried fallen heroes to Valhalla, the gods' hall of immortality.*

WHO WERE THE MAJOR NORSE GODS?

The Norse and Germanic Norse peoples of the fifth to ninth centuries shared a common mythology. According to this, the creator of the world was Odin (Wotan in the Germanic version), who presided over the Vanir, a group of gods of land, water and fertility. Odin's wife, Frigga, was associated with marriage and childbearing, while Freya was the main goddess of love and fertility. The god of thunder, Thor, used his powerful hammer, Mjolinir, to smash opponents. A trickster and thief, Loki was a malevolent joker god, seen as the creator of chaos.

NOBLE QUEST *In some of the Arthurian legends, the Knights of the Round Table are tasked with finding the Holy Grail, the cup used by Christ at the Last Supper.*

WHICH GODS DID THE AZTECS WORSHIP?

Among the best-known myths of the Americas are those of Mexico and Central America. Successive waves of invaders occupied these lands, each absorbing earlier myths. Last and bloodiest of all were the Aztecs, who dominated the region from the fourteenth to sixteenth centuries. They sacrificed tens of thousands of victims to their gods, among the most prominent of whom were Huitzilopochtli, a ferocious war god, and Tezcatlipoca, the sun god, who was later ousted by Quetzalcoatl, known to the Mayan people of Central America as Kukulcàn.

WAR GOD *In Aztec mythology, blood sacrifices were needed to nourish Huitzilopochtli and ensure that the Sun continued to shine.*

IN ABORIGINAL CULTURE, WHAT IS THE DREAMTIME?

For Australian Aboriginal people, the Dreamtime is the period during which ancestor spirits created landforms, plants and animals, and established relationships among groups of humans and animals. The ancestors then changed into animals, stars or features of the landscape, remaining spiritually alive. Each tribe has its own Dreaming, a collection of stories of the Dreamtime that has been passed down through the generations. These stories are remembered and affirmed through song, dance and painting. Some Dreamtime stories may date back 10,000 years and therefore be among the world's oldest belief systems.

SHAPING THE LAND *Aboriginal people in many parts of Australia share a belief in a creator being called the Rainbow Serpent. As it travelled during the Dreamtime, it moulded mountains, rivers, valleys and lakes.*

WHERE DID THE LEGEND OF KING ARTHUR COME FROM?

The famous legend of King Arthur and the Knights of the Round Table is associated with medieval England. But it has its origins in early Celtic and Breton accounts of a heroic leader, which from the seventh century appeared in Welsh literature. Geoffrey of Monmouth included some of the stories in his *History of the Kings of Britain*, published in 1135–39 and translated into French soon after. The French writer Chrétien de Troyes drew on the history to create a series of romantic poems about Arthur. Hugely popular, these poems influenced and were imitated by other writers across Europe and have since inspired countless poems, stories, paintings, operas and movies.

THE WORLD'S RELIGIONS

The power of the world's many religions lies in the way that they seek to answer the great questions of human existence. How should we live our lives? Does our existence have any meaning or purpose? What happens after death? In a world full of uncertainty, religion can also offer the reassurance of age-old ceremonies and beliefs.

ARE SOME RELIGIONS RELATED?

Most religions can be placed in family groups, as they share common roots. Christianity and Islam emerged out of Judaism; all three revere Abraham as a key figure, albeit for different reasons. Likewise, Buddhism and Jainism spring from the teachings of elders steeped in the traditions of Hinduism. Some faiths, such as Confucianism, Taoism and Shintoism, have developed independently but display strong similarities, probably because they are closely linked to Asian folklore. All three are practised alongside Buddhism in their countries of origin.

WHAT ARE THE WORLD'S MAJOR RELIGIONS?

Almost a third of people worldwide profess to be Christians, while nearly a quarter are adherents of Islam. Hinduism is followed by about 15 per cent of the world population, and Buddhism by 7 per cent; they are the third and fourth largest religions. About 6 per cent of people subscribe to various folk religions, while more than 16 per cent profess no religious affiliation.

WHO WORSHIPS WHAT *This map shows the distribution of major religions around the globe.*

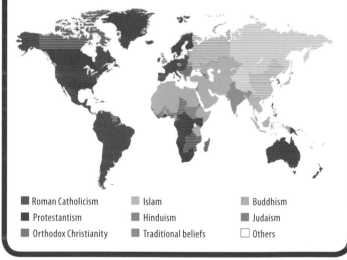

- Roman Catholicism
- Protestantism
- Orthodox Christianity
- Islam
- Hinduism
- Traditional beliefs
- Buddhism
- Judaism
- Others

COMMON ORIGINS
The diagram shows the relationships between major religions.

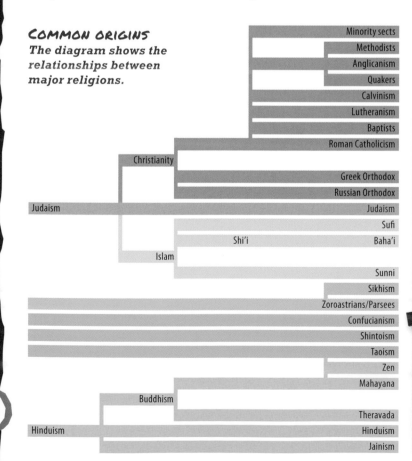

Minority sects
Methodists
Anglicanism
Quakers
Calvinism
Lutheranism
Baptists
Roman Catholicism
Christianity
Greek Orthodox
Russian Orthodox
Judaism
Judaism
Sufi
Shi'i — Baha'i
Islam
Sunni
Sikhism
Zoroastrians/Parsees
Confucianism
Shintoism
Taoism
Zen
Mahayana
Buddhism
Theravada
Hinduism
Hinduism
Jainism

WHY ARE THERE DIFFERENT KINDS OF CHRISTIANITY?

After the crucifixion of Jesus, his followers, the Apostles, spread his creed far and wide. St Peter became first Bishop of Rome – the first pope, in other words – and adherents of the Roman Catholic Church still acknowledge the pope as God's representative on Earth. Challenges to papal authority from the Eastern or Orthodox Church, in Constantinople, culminated in it breaking away in 1054. In 1517, a German monk, Martin Luther, questioned the legitimacy of Catholic priests selling indulgences – pardons that would reduce time in Purgatory. This brought about a new type of Christianity, Protestantism, which stresses a more direct relationship with God, and gave rise to other Protestant sects, such as Calvinists, Baptists and Methodists.

Where and when did Islam originate?

Islam, meaning 'submission to God', originated in 622 AD, when the prophet Muhammad experienced a series of divine revelations. When his preaching aroused hostility in his home town of Mecca (in present-day Saudi Arabia), he led his followers to Medina, an event known as the Hegira. Following his death, the religion spread rapidly (▶269). Muslims regard this world as preparation for the next. They believe in the oneness and omnipotence of God (Allah) and see Abraham, Moses and Jesus as the precursors of Muhammad.

ACT OF DEVOTION *Every Muslim is expected to make a pilgrimage to Mecca's Grand Mosque at least once.*

DIVINE IMAGE *A giant reclining gold Buddha in Thailand*

Do Buddhists have a god?

Buddhism has no omnipotent god, but its followers revere the Boddhisattvas, saint-like historical figures who turned their backs on the world to help others achieve enlightenment. The first of these and founder of Buddhism was Gautama, also known as the Buddha or Enlightened One. Buddhists seek enlightenment through the snuffing out of attachment and wrong desire (*tanha*). This leads in turn to nirvana, the escape from the cycle of death and rebirth (*samsara*). Different forms of Buddhism hold sway in different parts of Asia, each with its own rituals.

Who do Hindus worship?

Hindus worship a wide range of gods and goddesses, the most prominent of which are Brahma, the Creator; Vishnu, the Preserver; Shiva, the Destroyer; and Kali, the goddess of death. They believe that each person has an eternal soul that is born and reborn many times in different forms. All the gods represent Brahman, the supreme reality, and at the core of every human, buried beneath layers of egotism, lies the divine spark, Atman. The aim of worship is to unite Atman and Brahman and thereby escape the repeating cycle of life, death and rebirth (*samsara*) through spiritual liberation (*moksha*).

ANCIENT FAITH *Hinduism originated in India 4000 years ago, and by the eleventh century AD had become the region's dominant religion.*

fast fact

Christian hermits isolate themselves to focus on worship. Simeon Stylites (c. 390–459) spent 37 years living on top of a high column, near Aleppo, Syria.

Do all religions have a holy book?

All of the world's major religions have sacred texts containing early accounts of the founder's visions and teachings. The Old Testament, revered by Jews and Christians, covers 4000 years of Jewish history, while the New Testament recounts the life and teachings of Jesus Christ. The holy book of Islam, The Koran is believed to be the word of God revealed to the Prophet Muhammad; it contains 114 chapters, or suras, providing detailed rules on every aspect of life. Written around 1500 BC, the Vedas are the basic Hindu scriptures, containing hymns and prayers. Hindus also revere the Ramayana, a series of epic poems; the Mahabharata, a long account of Krishna, god of love; and the Upanishads, a collection of historical writings. The different types of Buddhism each have their own sacred texts, or canons.

SACRED TEXT *Usually transcribed onto scrolls, the Torah is the main holy book of the Jewish faith.*

HOME LIFE

Though prehistoric peoples often lived in caves, they also made tents from animal skins stretched over frames of wood or bone. Building in brick and stone came later, as did the idea of dividing the home into separate rooms. The modern home took shape as the result of a succession of inventions, including the chimney, glass-paned window and electric light and heating.

WHAT IS A LONG HOUSE?

A long house is a large communal dwelling. The Vikings used a long house as a home for several families, along with their thralls (slaves) and livestock. Even today, some traditional peoples build similar structures, notably those who live in clans rather than individual families. The long houses of Borneo, for example, are large wooden structures, usually raised off the ground and with a long covered veranda along one side.

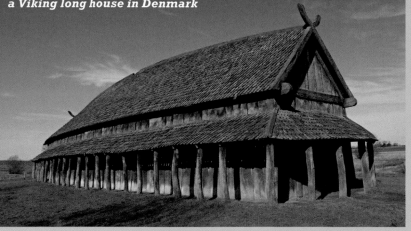

NORSE HOME *A reconstruction of a Viking long house in Denmark*

HOW DID EARLY PEOPLES LIGHT AND HEAT THEIR HOMES?

LIGHT SOURCE *This Roman oil lamp dates from the second century BC.*

HOW DID NOMADIC PEOPLES MAKE TENTS AND TEPEES?

Nomadic hunters and herders need movable homes, and one of the most portable and easily erected and dismantled dwellings is a tent. The peoples of the Great Plains of North America devised a form of tent known as a tepee (from the Dakota word *tipi*, meaning dwelling). It was made from buffalo hides stretched over a dozen or more long poles and it had a skin curtain hanging across the entrance hole, which always faced the rising Sun. Ventilation flaps at the top could be opened to let out smoke and closed to keep out cold or rain. When people moved to a new site, they took down the tepee and packed up the buffalo skin. The poles were attached to packhorses and trailed behind them, forming a platform (or travois) on which goods could be carried.

BUFFALO HIDE *Prepared buffalo hides are stretched over poles that slant towards the centre, and are pegged out around the bottom.*

ROUND HOUSE *Nomadic Mongolian herders traditionally use a type of portable home called a yurt. Strips of wood form a circular framework, which is covered with animal skins, felt or woven textiles.*

A simple lamp can be made with a container of fuel and a wick. When lit, the fuel-soaked wick feeds the flame, which provides light. In ancient times, oil or melted animal fat provided the fuel, and the wick was often no more than a piece of twisted dried moss. Adapting this principle, the Romans made candles using a wick surrounded by solid beeswax and tallow (refined animal fat). Gas lighting was first used in 1799 in France; the first electric light bulb (▶202), the invention of a Scottish schoolmaster called James Bowman Lindsay, appeared in 1835. Electric fires were first produced later that century and today many homes are warmed by gas, electric, oil-fuelled or even solar-powered heating.

ALPINE HOUSES *Strong, broad, steeply sloping roofs support the weight of heavy snow while also allowing it to slide off easily.*

WHY ARE SOME ROOFS SLOPING AND SOME FLAT?

The design of houses around the world is influenced by the local climate. In places where there is rain and snow, houses have sloping roofs to allow water and snow to drain off quickly. In hot countries, stifling heat is the problem, and houses often have thick walls to keep out the heat, and flat roofs. A flat rooftop can also provide an open-air living room; people can also cook out on the roof and avoid making the house hot and smoky, or sleep under the stars on hot nights.

CAN A HOUSE HAVE PAPER WALLS?

Traditional Japanese houses have internal walls made of paper, with sliding screens instead of doors. These wood-framed buildings are not designed to last for more than about 40 years – but they can be rebuilt quickly in the event of earthquakes, which occur frequently in Japan.

PAPER-THIN *This traditional Japanese sitting room has sliding paper-covered panels.*

HOW HAVE WESTERN HOMES CHANGED OVER THE CENTURIES?

Primitive dwellings around the world had one dark, smoky room with a central cooking fire. In European homes, brick-built chimneys and glazed windows arrived towards the end of the Middle Ages, letting in more light and air. Living space was shared and privacy was limited. Eventually, separate living rooms, kitchens and dining rooms appeared.

20,000 BC *People in eastern Europe used mammoth bones to make their tents. They cooked, made tools, prepared animal hides and slept in the one living space.*

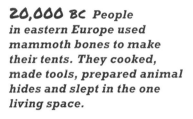

EARLY 1400s *Houses had one main room, the hall, where the family and servants all lived and ate. A central fire was used for cooking and heating. Shuttered windows let in light and air.*

MID-1700s *Houses were divided into a number of separate rooms for different activities. Chimneys allowed rooms to be heated by fires set into walls. Large glass windows let in light.*

EARLY 2000s *Today many people live in small households, in compact homes. Homes can be warmed by central heating and cooled by air conditioning.*

CLOTHES AND FASHION

Prehistoric peoples learned to sew skins together using needles made from bone. The first farmers discovered how to extract linen thread from the flax plant, and how to spin wool from their sheep, weaving it into fabric for clothing. By ancient Egyptian times, noblemen and women adorned themselves with fine pleated tunics and dresses, elaborate hairstyles, jewellery and cosmetics. For centuries, fashion was created by the rich for the rich. But in the late twentieth century, increased wealth and mass production allowed a much wider range of people to participate.

❶ ❷ ❸ ❹ ❺

FASHION PARADE
This line-up shows British clothing styles of different eras.

WHY DO WE WEAR CLOTHES?

The answer might seem simple: to keep warm. But there are other reasons for wearing clothes, such as modesty and display – clothing is used to attract the attention of the opposite sex. In traditional societies, magic provides another motive: leopard skins and sharks' teeth charms supposedly give the wearer the strength of those creatures. Some clothes are worn to show a person's position in society, whether it's a medieval monarch's crown or a police officer's uniform.

A CUT ABOVE *Feathers, furs and beads adorn the clothes of these shamans from Russia's Tuva region.*

HOW HAVE FASHIONS CHANGED THROUGH THE AGES?

In the past, kings, queens and courtiers set the fashions, which were often more complex and ornate than ordinary people could hope to match. Twentieth-century trends have moved towards more casual and relaxed styles.

❶ **MIDDLE AGES (1000–1485)** People wore fabrics dyed rich colours. Pointed shoes for men were fashionable for a time.

❷ **TUDOR PERIOD (1485–1603)** Men and women in England wore exaggerated shapes and elaborately decorated fabrics.

❸ **1700s** Men wore knee breeches and women voluminous dresses. By 1810, styles had become straighter and simpler.

❹ **VICTORIAN ERA (1837–1901)** English women wore large hooped petticoats, called crinolines, to make their skirts stand out.

❺ **POSTWAR AUSTERITY** A shortage of fabrics following the Second World War meant that fashions were plain. Styles were for the most part fairly formal.

❻ **1960s AND 1970s** Fashion designers produced simpler, more colourful clothes for women. Late 1960s hippie culture encouraged men to also wear colourful attire and grow their hair long.

❼ **EARLY TWENTY-FIRST CENTURY** Tailored clothes gave way to looser, less structured outfits, with a continuation of the late 1990s fashion of clothing influenced by military and sportswear.

fast fact

Jeans were first produced using a material called *jene fustian*, which came from, and was named after, the Italian city of Genoa (*Gênes* in French). This gave us the English name 'jeans'. Later, another material was more commonly used, known as *serge de Nîmes* – literally 'serge from (the French city of) Nîmes', which provided the word 'denim'.

WHY DO FASHIONS CHANGE?

In 1380, a writer complained, 'To be a good tailor yesterday is no good today. Cut and fashions change too quickly.' Styles change because fashionable people want to stand out in a crowd. As soon as everyone copies an outfit, it ceases to cause a stir and designers have to think up something new. Other factors also influence changes. Hemlines rose in the Second World War because fabrics were in short supply. They rose again with the 'miniskirt' in the 1960s, when it was acceptable for women to show almost the whole length of their legs.

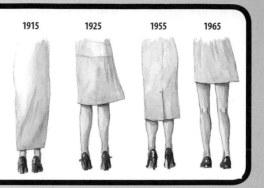

1915 1925 1955 1965

WHY DO PEOPLE WEAR MAKE-UP?

Cosmetics are used to cleanse skin, hide blemishes and draw attention to attractive features, such as the eyes and mouth. In ancient times, cosmetics also had magical significance. The Egyptians used a black eye paint called *kohl* not only to make their eyes more beautiful but also to ward off danger. Ideas of beauty have changed. In sixteenth-century Europe, pale skin was thought attractive and women whitened their faces with a poisonous powder made from lead. In the twentieth century, having a suntan became fashionable – before it was realised that exposure to the Sun can cause skin cancer.

⑦ HOW DO HAIRSTYLES COMPLEMENT FASHION?

Hairstyles have always mirrored fashion in clothes. In the late 1700s, a fashion for enormous wigs reached its peak at the French court, where Marie-Antoinette was said to have had doors raised to allow her lofty hairstyles to pass through. In the mid-1800s, men's hair was short, with sideburns being the only decorative touch, while women's hair was long but usually worn pinned up. After the First World War, short hair became a new symbol of women's independence. In the mid-1900s, women returned to longer, more wavy styles created with curlers, but in the 1960s their daughters adopted short, asymmetric cuts to complement the clean, straight lines of the latest fashions, such as the miniskirt. From the late 1970s, the desire of youth to shock was often expressed through outlandish hairstyles. At the end of the twentieth century it became fashionable for men to crop hair very short or even shave it all off.

YOUTH OF TODAY In Japan, Tokyo's Harajuku district is renowned as a centre of youth culture and cutting-edge fashion.

WHEN DID TROUSERS BECOME POPULAR?

The idea that men should wear trousers is relatively new. In the civilisations of ancient Egypt, Greece and Rome, men wore loose-fitting tunics and togas well suited to the warm climate of southern Europe and South-West Asia. Trousers originated among the tribes of the chilly Asian steppe. During the Dark Ages, when these tribesmen overran much of Europe, trousers became more widespread. In later centuries, fashion-conscious noblemen preferred to wear knee breeches. At the start of the nineteenth century, long trousers were associated with the ordinary people of Paris who overthrew the nobles during the French Revolution. As a result, trousers came to be seen as modern, democratic garments.

WOMEN TOO Trousers grew in popularity among women as casual wear during the 1940s and 1950s. The next decade saw the appearance of more formal styles and the acceptance of trousers as everyday fashion wear.

FOOD CULTURE

From ancient times onwards, food evolved into something far beyond its fundamental function of sustaining life. The cooking and eating of food became rituals that promoted social cohesion. And the types of food consumed and the way they were eaten came to define particular social groups and express religious and moral beliefs.

HOW DO PEOPLE EAT?

Early peoples would have eaten with their hands and many cultures still do this. Forks were first used in South-West Asia in the seventh century AD, but did not catch on in Europe until 1589, when they were adopted at the French royal court. Most people, however, continued eating with their fingers until the Industrial Revolution gave rise to cheap metal cutlery. In East Asia, chopsticks are used in many countries. Traditionally made of wood, bamboo, bone or ivory, they originated in China, possibly as far back as the second millennium BC and are now the standard eating utensil there as well as in Japan, Korea and Vietnam.

LATE SITTING *Meal times vary even in Western nations: in Hispanic countries lunch is taken between 2 pm and 4 pm and dinner may be eaten at 11 pm.*

WHEN DO PEOPLE EAT?

In Western countries most people eat three meals a day. But in other cultures and at other times in history, different practices have prevailed. The Romans, for example, ate only one meal a day, at noon. And until the Middle Ages, most people ate their main meal – called 'dinner' in English – in the middle of the day. Only with industrialisation, from the late 1700s, did people start to eat an early meal to give them energy at work (breakfast), grab a quick, light 'lunch' to save time, and then eat a larger meal in the evening, 'dinner'.

STRICT ON STICKS
Strict etiquette applies to the use of chopsticks. In Japan, for example, crossing chopsticks on a plate or table is considered offensive because it is a symbol of death.

WHAT DO PEOPLE EAT?

Regional cuisines are distinguished by particular foods and flavours, as well as distinctive eating habits. This is just a selection.

North America
Indigenous ingredients include maize (corn), but there are few truly native dishes. Instead, immigrants have created a cuisine blending Central American, European and Hispanic influences.

Central and South America The cuisines of Spain, Portugal and other European nations are combined with local ingredients, such as beans, maize (corn), chilli peppers and plantains. Beef and lamb are popular in the south.

fast fact
The sandwich is said to have been invented by English aristocrat John Montagu, the fourth Earl of Sandwich. He asked his servant to bring him meat between two pieces of bread so that he wouldn't miss a turn at a gaming table. Soon others were copying the idea.

WHAT IS THE MOST EATEN FOOD?

Foods that form the basis of a regular diet are known as staple foods. These tend to be inexpensive cereals, such as maize (corn), rice and wheat, or root plants, notably potatoes, which are rich in energy-giving starch. The world's most commonly eaten staple food is rice, which feeds more than half the world's population and provides a fifth of their annual kilojoule (calorie) intake.

MAJOR CROPS *Although more maize (corn) is grown annually, much of the crop is used to feed animals. Rice and wheat, which is used in breads, pastries, pastas and cereals, are more important for humans.*

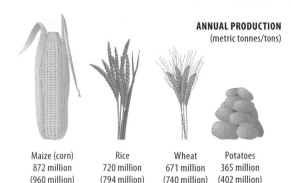

ANNUAL PRODUCTION
(metric tonnes/tons)

Maize (corn)	Rice	Wheat	Potatoes
872 million	720 million	671 million	365 million
(960 million)	(794 million)	(740 million)	(402 million)

HOW HAVE FOODS SPREAD AROUND THE WORLD?

CUCUMBERS First grown in Mesopotamia 4000 years ago

From the earliest times, travellers, explorers and conquering armies exported and imported foods. Alexander the Great, for example, introduced apricots to Greece from Asia around 300 BC. The Romans brought orange trees from India to North Africa and then Arabs from North Africa introduced them to Spain in the eighth century. Columbus took maize (corn), pineapples and beans from the Americas to Europe, while the Spanish conquistadors learned from the Aztecs how to make chocolate. Some foods made two-way journeys: after explorers brought tomatoes and potatoes back from Central and South America in the sixteenth century, Europeans introduced them to North America in the 1700s.

PEAS Cultivated by the Greeks and Romans. Frozen peas were first sold by Clarence Birdseye in the 1930s.

BEANS Many kinds of beans were introduced to Europe from Central America. Tinned 'baked beans' were first marketed by HJ Heinz in 1901.

COFFEE First drunk in Arabia in the 1400s and imported to Europe by the Turks in the early 1600s

CHOCOLATE Made as a drink by the Aztecs of Mexico, using cocoa beans; first grown in South America 3000 years ago

TOMATOES First domesticated in Mexico and taken to Europe by the Spanish in the early 1500s

POTATOES Grown in South America since at least 5000 BC and taken to Europe by the Spanish in the 1500s

COLA Invented by American John Pemberton in 1886; first made with coca leaf and kola nuts

Europe The use of olive oil distinguishes southern cuisines while northerners tend to use butter and other animal fats. Root vegetables are favoured in the north, tomatoes and garlic in the south.

East Asia Rice and noodles are staples, usually accompanied by vegetables and some kind of meat or, especially in Japan, fish. Flavourings such as ginger and lemongrass are widely used in South-East Asia.

Middle East and North Africa This cuisine is much influenced by Ottoman culture. Lamb dishes predominate and are accompanied by olives, nuts, couscous and rice. Sweet pastries such as halva are popular.

Southern Asia Spices are employed to create a wide range of flavours. Chicken and lamb are often added, but religious beliefs restrict meat eating: strict Buddhists and many Hindus eat no meat; Muslims do not eat pork.

PREPARING AND PRESERVING FOOD

WHY DO WE COOK FOOD?

The process of heating food can kill some of the bacteria that cause food poisoning, and can make food easier to digest. In prehistoric times, humans learned to cook over fire. Early people also discovered that smoking, drying or pickling food with natural preservatives, such as salt and vinegar, could prevent it from spoiling. These processes also created new flavours.

SMOKEHOUSE *Smoking fish involves soaking them in brine, allowing them to dry and then hanging them over a smouldering pile of wood shavings. Smoking prevents the growth of bacteria.*

All food goes 'off' unless something is done to preserve it. For thousands of years people have known that you can keep fruits by drying them; fish and meat by smoking, pickling or salting them; and milk by turning it into yogurt or cheese. In more recent times, the use of refrigeration, chemical preservatives and other technologies has greatly extended the shelf life of many foods.

HOW DO REFRIGERATION AND FREEZING WORK?

The warmer it is, the faster bacteria will develop and multiply in food. By reducing the air temperature around food, refrigeration dramatically slows the rate at which it spoils, from, roughly, a day or two to a week or two. Freezing food halts bacterial action altogether and has little impact on taste or consistency, so it can be used to preserve food almost indefinitely, as long as the subzero temperature is maintained.

COOL IT *The first domestic refrigerator, powered by a steam pump, was invented by German engineer Karl von Linde in 1879. The first electric model, the Electrolux, was made by Swedish engineers Carl Munters and Balzer von Platen in 1923.*

HOW DO CANS KEEP FOOD FRESH?

Cans are airtight and therefore keep microbes out of the food as long as they remain sealed; in this way, they can preserve food for many years. To prevent any bacteria entering the container during canning, a range of techniques is used to sterilise the food, including boiling, pressurising, freezing and drying. The use of airtight containers for food was introduced in France during the Napoleonic era, after the French army offered a prize of 12,000 francs to anyone who could come up with a method to preserve food in an easily portable form. Chef and confectioner Nicolas Appert's idea of using airtight jars won him the prize in 1810. Inspired by this, English merchant Peter Durand patented a similar process using tin cans before the end of that year. Of course, canned foods were not especially convenient prior to the invention of the can opener, by Englishman Robert Yeates, in 1855.

IN THE CAN *At this Californian factory, tomatoes can be peeled and canned within eight hours of being picked.*

HOW DO CHEMICAL PRESERVATIVES WORK?

Among the chemical preservatives that are commonly added to food, some, such as sorbic acid, benzoic acid and sodium nitrite, are antimicrobial; that is, they inhibit the development of bacteria and moulds. Others, including butylated hydroxytoluene (BHT) and butylated hydroxyanisole (BHA), are anti-oxidants, meaning that they slow the oxidisation of fats in foods – the process that turns them rancid. Although preservatives are tested to check that they are generally safe for consumption, concerns have been raised that they may contribute to or exacerbate some illnesses.

GOOD COLOUR *Some chemical preservatives are also used to improve the presentation of certain foods. Sodium nitrite, for example, gives bacon, salamies and other cured meats their bright red hue.*

HOW ARE FIZZY DRINKS MADE?

Drinks are usually made fizzy by pumping carbon dioxide gas into them. Carbon dioxide dissolves easily in water, especially when it is under pressure in a bottle or can. The gas stays dissolved in the drink until someone opens the container. Then there is a hiss as the pressure is released and the gas comes out in the form of bubbles. As the drink warms up, more carbon dioxide is released.

POPPING THE CORK. *In champagne, fermenting yeast and sugar produce carbon dioxide naturally inside the bottle. When the cork is popped, the liquid often bursts out of the bottle.*

WHAT OTHER TECHNIQUES ARE USED TO PRESERVE FOOD?

Food irradiation exposes food to ionising radiation, which strips away electrons, thereby killing off any microorganisms present. It can also delay the ripening of fruits and vegetables, allowing time for transportation and extending their shelf life. No radioactive energy is left behind in the food, however. Freeze-drying involves freezing food very quickly in a vacuum, then quickly heating it. Any liquid in the food is turned into ice during the freezing then escapes as steam when the food is heated; the steam is sucked out by vacuum pumps. The absence of water in freeze-dried food greatly limits the development of bacteria, so it can be stored, without refrigeration, for years; such food is also said to retain its taste and nutritional value.

SPACE FOOD *Light and compact, freeze-dried food is used by astronauts on space flights, as well as explorers and soldiers on manoeuvres.*

FARMING

About half of Earth's people work on the land, growing crops and raising livestock to provide food and drink, as well as raw materials, such as wool and cotton. Modern industrialised farming methods are remarkably efficient. However, their reliance on chemical fertilisers has raised health concerns and led many farmers to adopt organic production methods.

WHAT IS CROP ROTATION?

All crops absorb minerals from the soil in order to grow. However, different plants absorb different minerals, and some also return minerals to the soil. By planting different crops in rotation, farmers can help the soil to maintain a healthy balance of minerals. The best-known and most widely used system of crop rotation in the West is the so-called Norfolk 'four-course' rotation system, which was first introduced in Norfolk, England, in the 1700s. It rotates wheat, root vegetables, barley and clover.

FOUR-YEAR CYCLE This illustration shows the Norfolk rotation system.

YEAR 1 Wheat is sown.

YEAR 2 Root vegetables, such as turnips, are grown to provide winter food for livestock.

YEAR 4 The clover and rye are left for grazing. The clover adds nitrogen to the soil and droppings from the grazing animals further enrich it.

YEAR 3 Using manure from the livestock to fertilise the soil, spring barley or wheat is sown, with an undersowing of clover and rye.

HOW DO FARMING METHODS VARY AROUND THE WORLD?

There are big differences in the way that farmers operate across the world. In affluent Western countries, most food is produced using heavy machinery and mass production methods, in contrast to the developing world, where most farming is still done by hand. Organic farmers are those who use traditional methods to control pests and fertilise the soil.

WAY TO GROW Methods of farming depend on resources and farmers' objectives.

SOWING BY HAND Following age-old methods in a remote part of the world, a farmer and his family dig furrows by hand. The seeds are sown and then lightly covered with soil. The furrows are dug in straight lines in order to make weeding easier.

GREEN FARMING Organic methods have been developed by modern farmers who prefer not to use chemicals. Instead, they use vegetable compost and animal manure as fertiliser. The plastic covering, or polytunnel, shown here helps to trap heat from sunshine.

MASS PRODUCTION A combine harvester sweeps the vast wheatfields of a large modern farm. The machine cuts the crop and separates the grain from the chaff (husks), combining the jobs of reaping and threshing, which were once performed by a whole village. It then pours the grain into the tractor-drawn trailer running alongside it.

WHAT ARE GENETICALLY MODIFIED (GM) CROPS?

Advances in biotechnology have made it possible to transfer genes from one organism to another. That means that a gene that gives a bacterium resistance to a particular disease or pest can be inserted into a species of food plant to create a modified, or GM, form of the plant that gains immunity to the same disease or pest. This in turn reduces the need for pesticides and results in a more abundant crop. Plants can also be modified to increase their levels of nutrients and thereby provide health benefits to consumers. For example, a GM rice called golden rice has been created with enhanced levels of beta-carotone, which the human body converts to vitamin A; researchers say that bolstering disease resistance this way could save the lives of up to 1 million children a year, mainly in developing countries. So GM crops could improve global health and help feed Earth's burgeoning population. At the same time, many observers have concerns about the long-term effects of GM crops on humans and biodiversity.

NEW PLANTS *Flasks of genetically engineered seedlings in a laboratory*

A STEP UP Rice terraces are today a distinctive feature of many East and South-East Asian landscapes.

HOW DO YOU CULTIVATE STEEP SLOPES?

Growing crops on steep hillsides presents major challenges. The soil and plants can subside or be washed away by rain. A solution, used since ancient times in many places, is to cut terraces into hillsides to form narrow fields. Some of the first agricultural terraces were created about 3000 years ago in South America, and the practice was widely used by the Incas. Terraces are especially suited to cultivating plants that need abundant watering, such as rice.

fast fact

Approximately 2500 litres (660 gallons) of water are required to produce 1 kg (2 lb) of rice. To produce 1 kg (2 lb) of beef takes more than 15,000 litres (4000 gallons) of water, while making 1 kg (2 lb) of chocolate uses 17,000 litres (4500 gallons) of water.

HOW CAN COMPUTER TECHNOLOGY HELP FARMERS?

Many aspects of a busy modern farm can be computerised. For example, automated systems can monitor crops, determine when they need to be fertilised, sprayed with weedkiller or watered, and distribute the correct amounts at the right times. Similar systems can supply appropriate amounts of feed to livestock automatically. Farmers are increasingly using satellite data to monitor the condition of farmland and in the near future may also be able to use GPS (▶221) to operate remote-controlled tractors. Robots have even been developed that can identify and remove weeds and gather snails and slugs.

ELECTRONIC FARMER *This computerised watering system meets the daily needs of plants.*

FISHING

As with farming, fishing has grown from supplying local needs into a major economic activity. Globally, around 55 million people make their living from fishing, and for many countries trade in fish and fish products is vital to the economy. Overfishing of many regions has, however, depleted fish stocks and placed some regional industries at risk.

HOW DO PEOPLE CATCH FISH?

A rod and line will catch barely enough fish for personal consumption. Fishing on a larger scale involves the use of various kinds of boats, large nets and sophisticated tracking devices, including aerial surveillance and computer-controlled satellites and sonar.

❶ DRIFT NETTING *Long curtain-like nets of plastic webbing are hung vertically across an area of ocean, either drifting freely or weighted to the seafloor. They catch anything that swims into them. Dolphins and turtles often die after becoming entangled in drift nets, as a result of which some types have been banned.*

❸ PURSE SEINING *Wire ropes pass through rings attached to the edge of a circular purse-sein net. The net is towed around a shoal of fish then pulled shut to trap them. Most of the world's annual fish yield is caught this way.*

❹ TRAWLING *A huge, cone-shaped net is dragged through the ocean or along the bottom, collecting everything in its path. Factory trawlers carry facilities for processing, freezing and even packaging the fish immediately after they are caught, thereby allowing their crews to stay at sea for long periods.*

❷ LONG LINING *Long lines attached to hundreds of shorter lines carrying baited hooks are allowed to drift in the ocean to catch surface fish, such as tuna and salmon, or spread on the seafloor to catch groundfish, including cod and halibut.*

298

fast fact

Scientists estimate that as wild fisheries decline, fish farms will provide a much larger proportion of food fish – close to two-thirds by 2030.

WHICH COUNTRIES FISH THE MOST?

About 4.36 million fishing vessels operate around the world. China is now the largest producer of fish, with 35 per cent of the world total (compared to 7 per cent in 1961), 14 million of its people working in the industry and about 675,000 fishing vessels in its fleet.

OCEAN'S BOUNTY *A fresh catch offloaded in a harbour in China*

ON THE MARKET *Tuna ready for auction at a market in Tokyo, Japan*

WHICH FISH ARE MOST IN DEMAND?

The most widely traded fishery product is prawns, which accounts for 15 per cent of internationally traded fishery products. Salmon and trout make up 14 per cent, while bottom-dwelling fish (including cod and hake) account for 10 per cent. Tuna is also much in demand, partly for canning and, in Japan, for sashimi and sushi; about 8 per cent of all fishery exports are tuna.

WHAT IS FISH FARMING?

Fish farming, or aquaculture, is the intensive cultivation of fish in controlled environments. Fish eggs are placed in warm-water tanks until they hatch into fry, then reared in seawater or freshwater tanks or cages. Fish farming has long been practised in Asia, notably to raise carp. First farmed in Scotland and Norway, trout and salmon are today reared in many parts of the world, including Chile and Canada, which are both major producers for the European market. In North Africa and Asia, the farming of tilapia, a group of perch-like species, has become a major industry.

FARM FRESH *Many of Chile's fish farms are located in its remote southern region of Patagonia.*

WHAT CAN WE DO ABOUT OVERFISHING?

Overfishing is the harvesting of fish populations to the point where their depleted numbers affect the environmental balance or their numbers cannot recover. Decades of overfishing have led to declining or static fish stocks in most of the world's oceans – it is now estimated that over 85 per cent of the world's fish stocks are either overfished or fished to full capacity. This is the result of a combination of factors, including rising demand for fish, the rapid growth of fishing fleets, improvements in fishing technology and the widespread use of large factory trawlers. Strategies being adopted to help reverse the decline of fish stocks include the protection of important habitats, the imposition of fish quotas, controlling net-hole size to limit the capture of young fish, outright bans on fishing, and fish farming.

CONTROLLED CATCH *To maintain sustainable populations, strict limits have been imposed on catches in the highly productive Bering Sea fishery.*

THE HISTORY OF ART

Throughout history, artists have made paintings and sculptures to record the world around them, to tell stories, explain religious beliefs, and to provide objects of beauty. Art is often an expression of the artist's own personality, and the spirit of his or her age, and even an abstract arrangement of colours or shapes can communicate a message that may be passionate, mysterious, calm or playful.

HOW DO ARTISTS EXPRESS MEANING?

Artists include many clues to what is going on in a painting. Settings and costumes can be real, historical, mythological or dream-like, telling us what type of story it is. Weather and lighting may suggest a mood. People's gestures and the expressions on their faces also provide hints. In portraits, objects are often included that tell us about the sitter – his or her background or profession, interests and character.

WHAT ARE PAINTS MADE OF?

Prehistoric peoples often created art using charcoal and ochre, a natural pigment found in earth and rocks that contain iron oxide and hence have a red or orange hue. In ancient times, artists discovered other sources of natural pigments, including minerals and plants. Sometimes egg yolk was mixed with the pigment to cause it to set hard. Oil paints, made by combining pigments with linseed oil, came into use in the Middle Ages. Watercolour paints, in which pigments are mixed with a water-soluble gum, have a long tradition of use in South-East Asia but only became popular in Western art from the 1700s on. Many modern artists use synthetic paints, called acrylics, which can be easily cleaned off brushes but are water-resistant once dry.

PRECIOUS BLUE *In medieval times, one of the most sought-after pigments was made from the mineral lapis lazuli.*

fast fact

In the past, a paint colour called Indian yellow was made from the urine of cows fed on mango leaves. Another, carmine red, came from juice made with the powdered bodies of a South American insect.

HOW HAVE ART STYLES CHANGED?

The way artists paint depends on the techniques and materials they use, the way they percieve the world, and the ideas of their time. Early artists tended to design flat shapes on a plain background, ignoring the relative proportions of figures and objects, so that their works, though striking, look unrealistic to the modern eye. An awareness of proportion and perspective developed among ancient Greek and Roman artists, but it was not until the Renaissance that the mathematical principles of perspective were worked out by Italian artists, such as Filippo Brunelleschi. From that period on, artworks, especially paintings, became increasingly realistic, particularly as artists also refined techniques for rendering light and shade. In the late 1800s and early 1900s artists developed these ideas in different ways, some attempting to render fleeting impressions, others multiple perspectives. In the mid-1900s, many artists abandoned the idea of realistic representation altogether to focus on the formal qualities of line, colour and canvas, resulting in art that was entirely abstract.

WHAT NEW FORMS OF ART HAVE EMERGED?

In the 1900s, art came to encompass much more than just painting and sculpture. A group of artists called the Dadaists pioneered the use of collages, photomontage and so-called 'ready-mades' – everyday objects that were modified by the artist and then presented as artworks. Later sculptors continued to experiment with 'found' objects, such as driftwood and scraps of metal, and from the late 1960s a group of artists known as 'land artists' began making large-scale, often temporary, artworks out of natural materials, including rocks, earth, ice and even sunlight. More recently, many cutting-edge artists have combined performance, costume, sound, video and computer graphics to create multimedia artworks that may be projected in galleries and even involve viewer interaction.

Egyptian wall painting
The figures are usually idealised – made to look as perfect and beautiful as possible. Often their relative sizes relate more to their social standing than to their physical reality.

Realist painting In the late sixteenth century, artists were admired for their skill in painting solid-looking objects in realistic settings. Italian artist Caravaggio used high-contrast light and shade to achieve a high degree of realism.

Impressionist painting
The Impressionist artists, based chiefly in late-nineteenth-century France, used vivid colours and bold brushwork to depict the effects of changing light.

Cubist painting
The Paris-based painters known as the Cubists, active in the early 1900s, combined multiple viewpoints to draw attention to the structures of subjects and how we perceive them.

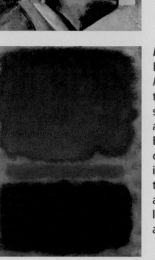

Abstract Expressionism
Artists belonging to the New York school known as Abstract Expressionism created powerful images through the careful arrangement of lines, patterns and shapes.

MOVING IMAGES *Video art developed from the 1960s as video technology became more available.*

OUT THERE *Modern artists have repeatedly reassessed what constitutes art. In 1917, Marcel Duchamp presented a urinal as a 'found' artwork, Fountain (left). Contemporary UK artist Andy Goldsworthy works with natural materials, often outdoors (far left).*

HOW ARE SCULPTURES MADE?

Sculptures can be either two-dimensional forms, known as bas-reliefs, or three-dimensional works – statues. They may be carved using sharp implements, such as chisels, from a hard material, such as wood, stone or glass, or they may be worked or moulded into shape using a soft material, such as clay, which then either hardens naturally or is baked hard. A combination of these techniques can also be used to create hollow moulds, with which numerous copies of a work can be made.

CIRE PERDUE *With the 'lost wax', or cire perdue, technique, sculptures can be cast in metal, usually in bronze.*

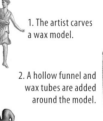

1. The artist carves a wax model.

2. A hollow funnel and wax tubes are added around the model.

3. Clay is packed around the figure and allowed to harden. The wax is then melted and runs out.

4. Molten metal is poured through the funnel and tubes to completely fill the mould.

5. The bronze sets and the mould is removed.

6. The tubes are removed and the figure is finished by hand.

DECORATIVE ARTS AND CRAFTS

HOW IS CLOTH WOVEN?

At least 5000 years ago, the skill of weaving provided an alternative to animal skins for clothing and blankets. Wool was probably the first fibre used. Then, as now, cloth was woven on a loom, which was basically no more than a square-sided wooden frame. Weaving uses two sets of yarn, called the warp and the weft. Warp threads run along the length of the cloth. Weft threads are woven across the warp threads, passing over one and under the next.

HAND WOVEN *A woman weaves a patterned rug in Cappadocia, Turkey.*

MODERN SPIN *Traditional methods are used worldwide to make colourful crafts.*

Craftworks, such as ceramics and jewellery, represent a mix of art and technology that dates back to the earliest civilisations. The ancient Egyptians, Greeks and Romans were all familiar with the arts of the potter, glass-maker, weaver, jeweller, woodworker, metalworker and leatherworker, and ceramic techniques were perfected in medieval China. The Industrial Revolution introduced new materials and methods, and the potential to mass-produce such items.

WHEN DID WOODWORKING BEGIN?

Prehistoric peoples undoubtedly fashioned wood into a wide range of objects, including weapons, vessels, coffins and furniture, but few prehistoric wooden artefacts survive due to wood's tendency to perish. Much clearer evidence of competent woodworking comes from ancient Egypt, in the form of well-preserved objects from tombs, and artworks depicting craftsmen at work. Around 1300 BC, the Egyptians also developed the first forms of wood-turning. Wood-carving reached a pinnacle during the fifteenth century in the magnificent carved doors, choir stalls and retables of many Gothic cathedrals.

HIGH ART *The magnificent wooden altarpiece in Schleswig Cathedral, northern Germany, was carved by Hans Brüggemann in 1514–21.*

HOW IS POTTERY MADE?

Around 9000 years ago, people discovered that a container could be made by scooping out a hole in a lump of wet clay and waiting for it to dry. Then people began shaping pots, or building up coils of clay. Later, pots were made by hollowing out a ball of clay on the middle of a spinning, or potter's, wheel. Experimentation with different types of clay eventually resulted in a range of ceramics, including earthenware, stoneware, porcelain and china.

FIRING AND DECORATING The pot is fired in a kiln to dry out the clay and harden it. Then it is decorated and covered with a glaze, a transparent liquid that makes the pot waterproof. The pot is then fired again.

ON THE WHEEL As the clay spins, the potter hollows out the centre and shapes the object. The potter must keep the clay centred on the wheel or the pot will become crooked.

FINISHING OFF Glazes are made from ingredients that change colour when heated, so the second firing brings out the colours in the glaze and sets, or hardens, it.

MING VASE *This glazed, decorated vase was made in Ming-dynasty China, around 1644.*

HOW DO YOU MAKE GLASS?

Glass is made by heating a mixture of silica-rich material – usually sand – and an alkaline material, such as soda or potash. The combination melts and vitrifies (turns glassy) at about 1100°C (2012°F). Extra ingredients can be added to give the glass particular colours or properties. The glass is usually shaped while hot. Often this is achieved by blowing into the molten glass through a metal pipe. After the glass has cooled it may be decorated, cut or inscribed.

HOT WORK *Glass-blowers shape an object by turning the molten glass as they blow and by teasing out the soft material with pliers.*

WHAT MAKES JEWELLERY VALUABLE?

Since ancient times, jewellery has been worn for personal adornment but also as a sign of power or status, or for religious or magical purposes. The most prestigious jewellery has long been made with precious metals and gems (▶68) and therefore has been available only to the wealthy. While cheaper, imitation materials were introduced following the Industrial Revolution and low-cost 'costume jewellery' became popular in the 1900s, prestige jewellery remains fabulously expensive today. This is not only due to the materials used – gold, diamonds, pearls and so on – but also the intricate, exclusive designs of leading jewellery houses, such as Cartier, Tiffany & Co. and Van Cleef & Arpels.

PRECIOUS EMBLEM
Commissioned by actor Tyrone Power, Fulco di Verdura's Wrapped-Heart Brooch (1941) combines gold, rubies and diamonds.

fast fact
A Cartier 'panther' bracelet formerly owned by the Duchess of Windsor was sold in 2010 for US$7 million, making it the most expensive bracelet of all time.

WHAT ARE NETSUKE?

Netsuke are small, carved objects, usually made out of ivory, bone or wood, which were used in Japan from the 1600s onwards to attach a pouch or box to the belt of a traditional robe. Often depicting animals or figures from folklore, these miniature sculptures became increasingly intricate and, eventually, valuable and collectable.

ARCHITECTURAL STYLES

Highly visible and usually durable, buildings reveal much about the cultures in which they are produced. The style of a building usually relates to the technical advances and limitations of a particular age, but it may also reflect the ideals and fashions of an era, as well as the taste and beliefs of an architect or wider art movement.

WHY DO WE NEED ARCHITECTS?

As well as design skills and a sense of aesthetics, architects possess detailed knowledge of construction and the forces that affect buildings, including gravity and wind shear. They understand the strengths and appropriate uses of a wide range of materials, and they know how to incorporate services, such as plumbing, electricity and lifts. Architects must also plan for the provision of natural light through the orientation of the building and placement of windows, and be able to incorporate a range of safety features, from fire exits to sprinklers. An architect specifies all these elements in detailed two-dimensional plans. He or she may also use CAD (computer-aided design) software to create a three-dimensional 'walk-through' rendering of the proposed design.

COMPUTER AID *Specialised software permits continuous adjustment and refinement of architectural plans.*

WHAT ARE THE CLASSICAL ORDERS OF ARCHITECTURE?

Ancient Greek and Roman architects established standard relationships between various architectural elements, most notably a building's base, structural supports (columns) and entablature (roof beams). This resulted in fixed styles, known as orders, which also included rules for decoration and other elements. The Greeks devised three major styles – Doric, Ionic and Corinthian – and to these the Romans added two more, Tuscan and Composite.

Doric   Ionic   Corinthian   Tuscan   Composite

SET IN STONE *The distinctive column styles of the five classical orders*

HOW ARE DOMES BUILT?

People first discovered how to make arches – by wedging specially shaped stones together to hold each other in place – about 5000 years ago in the Middle East and Egypt. The Romans made prominent use of the form in numerous grand structures, from enormous aqueducts to massive stadiums, such as the Colosseum. By extending an arch horizontally, ancient peoples also devised the barrel vault, and by overlapping a series of arches around a central point they created the dome. Partly due to their invention of the first form of concrete, made with light but strong volcanic stone, the Romans were able to create astonishingly large domes, as epitomised by the Pantheon, a giant simple dome. Other forms of dome were subsequently developed, including compound domes and convoluted, or pumpkin, domes.

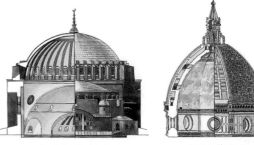

Hagia Sophia, Istanbul   Duomo, Florence

DOME SHAPES *The basic structure can be adapted to produce domes that are shallow or high.*

HOW HAVE BUILDING STYLES CHANGED?

The size, shape and style of new buildings have changed through the ages, depending on their intended use, the materials and amount of space available, and contemporary technology, as well as the builders' ideas about what looks beautiful.

MODERN WORKPLACE *The Lloyd's Building in London is constructed from glass and steel. Lifts and staircases are housed in towers attached to the outside of the building to provide as much open space as possible inside.*

GOTHIC CHURCH *The Gothic style of architecture flourished in the late medieval period. Pointed windows, pinnacles and spires all directed the eye upwards. The use of stone meant that architects could build stronger, taller structures.*

ANGLO-SAXON LONG HOUSE *In the early Middle Ages, domestic buildings were simple structures, even when large, like this long house. Made as a home for an extended family, it was built of wood and had a raised floor and thatched roof.*

WHY ARE GLASS BUILDINGS SAFE?

The glass in modern 'glass-box' high-rises does not support weight; it hangs from a load-bearing framework of concrete or steel, forming a so-called curtain wall (▶238). Curtain-wall skyscrapers first appeared in Chicago, USA, in the late 1800s and were developed by a number of pioneering architects throughout the early 1900s. The glass in modern curtain-wall buildings is specially strengthened, either by using heat to toughen it or by a process known as lamination, which involves interleaving sheets of glass with layers of plastic.

GLASS BOX *The Seagram Building in New York (1958), designed by Ludwig Mies van der Rohe, is a classic curtain-wall building.*

(▶238)

WHAT ARE THE LATEST TRENDS IN ARCHITECTURE?

The ongoing development of high-tech materials has allowed architects to move beyond regular box shapes and build spectacularly irregular, organic structures. Pioneering designs of this kind include those of Frank Gehry, Santiago Calatrava and Zaha Hadid. Architects have also become more focused on improving the sustainability of buildings by, for example, using passive solar design principles (▶239), incorporating recycled materials and utilising renewable energy sources.

(▶239)

GREEN BUILDING *One Angel Square in Manchester, England, is considered one of Europe's most sustainable large buildings. It has its own renewable power supply, uses low-energy lighting and recycles most of its water.*

DESIGN WITH A TWIST *Spanish architect Santiago Calatrava's Turning Torso tower in Malmo, Sweden (2005)*

fast fact
Completed in 126 AD, the Pantheon was the world's largest dome until Filippo Brunelleschi built the Duomo, in Florence, in 1436.

INDUSTRIAL DESIGN

Even the simplest mass-produced objects have been carefully designed by someone.

Industrial design involves using design, technology and engineering to create objects that not only look good and work well, but are also easy and enjoyable to use.

WHAT ARE THE CHALLENGES OF INDUSTRIAL DESIGN?

When designing a new product, an industrial designer has to consider the interests of everyone involved in producing, selling and using the item. Manufacturers require an item that is economical to make and easy to repair. Retailers want something that stands out in a crowded marketplace. Customers demand a product that meets their needs, works well and is pleasing to the eye. Additionally, an ambitious designer will aspire to create something that is original and bears his or her own distinctive stamp.

STARTING POINT *Most new designs begin as a series of sketches.*

TRUE ORIGINAL *The anglepoise lamp is a design that has remained virtually unchanged since it was devised in 1932 by English automotive engineer George Carwardine.*

WHAT MAKES A DESIGN SUCCESSFUL?

Designs do not need to be complicated to be successful. Some classic designs are very simple but function so well that they hardly ever change – or people keep returning to them. Pop-up electric toasters, for example, were first made in the 1920s and have altered little over the years. The ballpoint pen has also been very successful, probably because it is so simple and works so well, and the classic design of the electric kettle almost never goes out of fashion.

fast fact

The safety pin was invented in 1849 by US mechanic Walter Hunt. In order to pay a personal debt of $15, he sold his patent to chemical company WR Grace and Co for $400. The company went on to make millions from his design.

HOW DO YOU REINVENT AN OBJECT?

Everyday objects are constantly being redesigned, sometimes successfully, sometimes not. New designs often reflect the influence of fashion or particular art movements, but may also be based on the availability of new materials or technologies that could improve functionality or comfort.

SHAKER CHAIR

RED AND BLUE CHAIR

TULIP CHAIR

INFLATABLE CHAIR

ENDLESS VARIATIONS *The chair is a good example of an everyday object that has been repeatedly redesigned over the centuries.*

SHAKER CHAIR The Shakers are an American religious group who reject worldliness in favour of a life of austerity. Their ladder-backed chairs, produced by US Shaker communities from the 1860s on, embody this, being spare and functional but exquisitely crafted.

RED AND BLUE CHAIR Gerrit Thomas Rietveld, a member of the Dutch De Stijl art movement, designed this chair in 1918–21 to reflect the group's interest in arrangements of simple shapes and bold colours.

TULIP CHAIR Created in the late 1950s by Finnish designer Eero Saarinen, the Tulip Chair made effective use of the latest mouldable plastics to create a fluid, organic shape that was also distinctively modern.

INFLATABLE CHAIR Designed by the Italian company Zanotta in 1967, 'Blow' was the first widely distributed piece of inflatable furniture. Made out of transparent PVC, it reflected the 1960s counterculture's rejection of traditional values of solidity and permanence.

ARE COLOURS AND PATTERNS IMPORTANT IN DESIGN?

Colour and pattern play an important part in an object's design, but tastes have changed over time. In the nineteenth century, designers favoured rich, strong colours and ornate patterns, which many people today consider over-fussy. Modern taste has been strongly influenced by Modernism and especially the Bauhaus school of design, which flourished in Germany from 1919 to 1933. Bauhaus designers stressed simplicity in everything, from architecture to furniture and tableware. Consequently, many late-twentieth-century designs eschewed patterns for sombre tones and plain finishes.

Early twentieth-century tea service

Late-twentieth-century coffee set

POINTING THE WAY
The minimalist designs of Dieter Rams (left), chief designer for the German Braun electrical company, as exemplified by this portable radio (above), have been highly influential.

Graves kettle and sugar bowl

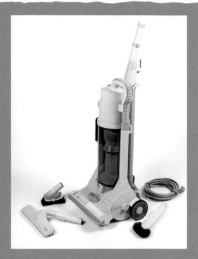

Early Dyson vacuum cleaner

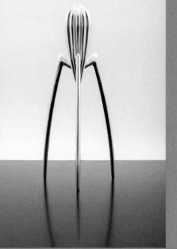

Juicy Salif lemon squeezer

First-generation iPod

WHICH ARE THE MOST ICONIC MODERN DESIGNS?

In the late twentieth and early twenty-first centuries, a number of designers and design houses applied their talents to restyling classic items and a number of playful redesigns achieved iconic status, including the Graves Kettle, designed by Michael Graves in 1984, and French designer Philippe Starck's Juicy Salif lemon squeezer of 1989, both produced by the Italian company Alessi. In 1990, English inventor James Dyson radically overhauled the design of the vacuum cleaner, which had remained unchanged since its introduction in 1907. Dispensing with the dust bag, he created a new mechanism whereby heavier-than-air dust particles are spun out into a collection bin while still allowing the air to flow through the machine. Another famous recent example of innovative and influential industrial design is the Apple iPod, created by Englishman Jonathan Ive. It not only fulfilled a new need for a portable digital music player and appeared ground-breaking and stylish in its design but was also simple to use. Like many influential designs, it was quickly imitated.

THE WORLD OF LITERATURE

Shaped with passion and skill, words have the power to excite a reader's imagination. Yet literature offers more than entertainment. Whether true to life or exploring realms of fantasy, good writing helps people to understand themselves and the world around them.

SPOKEN WORD Bestselling author JK Rowling reads from one of her Harry Potter books.

WHY DO PEOPLE TELL STORIES?

Stories give shape and meaning to human fears and desires. Some stories grew from simple tribal tales to become epics – long narratives dealing with heroes and heroic deeds. Examples include the *Odyssey* of ancient Greece and the Indian *Ramayana*. The novels of some nineteenth-century writers, such as *Oliver Twist* and *Great Expectations* by Charles Dickens, and *War and Peace* by the Russian writer Leo Tolstoy, also have an epic quality, as they mirror the life and dreams of entire societies.

fast fact

Some writers have produced a vast number of stories. Victorian novelist Anthony Trollope regularly reeled off 3000 words before breakfast. Frank Richards, creator of the Billy Bunter stories, wrote up to 80,000 words a week for boys' comics. And bestselling romance novelist Barbara Cartland has produced more than 700 books, often writing more than 20 a year.

WHAT ARE THE MAIN FORMS OF LITERATURE?

The main forms of literature are poetry, drama and prose. Many of the earliest works of literature were long poems, often recounting founding myths. Examples include Homer's *Iliad* and *Odyssey*, Roman poet Virgil's *Aeneid* and *Beowulf* from Anglo-Saxon England. In ancient Greece, public performance of such works evolved into the first plays. The Greeks also produced some of the first historical works and scientific texts. However, the novel, as we know it today, did not evolve until much later. Long, fictional prose works first appeared in China, Japan and Arabia in the Middle Ages. In Europe, such works emerged out of the tradition of the medieval romance epics – accounts in verse or prose of the exploits of kings and warriors – and the Italian early Renaissance interest in the prose short story, or *novella*, as exemplified by Giovanni Boccaccio's *Decameron* (1354). The first modern European novel is widely considered to be *Don Quixote* by Miguel de Cervantes, published in 1609 in Spain, but it wasn't until the 1700s that the novel became a widely read form in the West.

FIRST NOVEL An engraving from an early edition of Cervantes's Don Quixote

WHY WRITE IN VERSE?

Before books were made, tales were passed on by word of mouth. Storytellers used a foot-tapping beat to remember the words. Rhyme and rhythm in songs have also influenced poetry. Poems achieve their effects through combinations of features, such as striking, expressive language and sound patterns. Some poems tell a story, but many explore the meaning of an event, sensation or experience.

PATTERN POEM In concrete poetry, such as Guillaume Apollinaire's Calligrammes (1918), the typographical layout of the work helps reinforce the poem's meaning.

WHICH WERE THE FIRST CHILDREN'S BOOKS?

Books written specifically for children did not appear until the 1700s and it was only in the mid-1800s that modern children's genres began to take shape. Among the first 'boys'-own' adventure stories were FR Marryat's *Masterman Ready* (1841) and RM Ballantyne's *The Coral Island* (1857). Louisa May Alcott's *Little Women* (1868) was an early example of the family saga, while Anna Sewell's *Black Beauty* (1877) provided a model for animal stories. In the early 1900s several illustrated books for younger readers quickly gained classic status, including Kenneth Grahame's *The Wind in the Willows* (1908), AA Milne's *Winnie the Pooh* (1926) and the stories of Beatrix Potter (1902–30). Drawing on medieval myths, works such as CS Lewis's *Chronicles of Narnia* series (1950–56) and JRR Tolkien's *Lord of the Rings* series (1954) established the now hugely popular fantasy genre, which spawned JK Rowling's phenomenally successful *Harry Potter* books.

FICTIONAL HOME *The Sherlock Holmes Museum is modelled on a late 1800s apartment.*

CAN FICTION BECOME REALITY?

Some fictional characters have become so well known that people have sometimes thought that they were real. Many of Scottish author Sir Arthur Conan Doyle's readers came to believe that his fictional detective Sherlock Holmes was an actual person. An apartment at 221B Baker Street in London – the address at which Holmes lived in the stories – was even turned into a re-creation of his home and is now the Sherlock Holmes Museum. Doyle in fact modelled his famous character on a real person, his friend and Edinburgh surgeon Dr Joseph Bell.

WHAT MAKES A POPULAR CLASSIC?

Some books remain popular long after they were written. The quality of the writing is part of their success. Suspense – keeping the reader guessing about what is going to happen next – is important, and not only in adventures and mysteries. Not all favourite books are action-packed, though – the appeal of Jane Austen's novels lies in her insight into human affairs as they unfold in outwardly uneventful situations. Character is, however, vital. Colourful heroes and heroines are essential, but a villain – such as the thief-master Fagin in Dickens's *Oliver Twist* or Long John Silver in Robert Louis Stevenson's *Treasure Island* – may prove even more memorable.

ENDURING NONSENSE *Published in 1865,* Alice's Adventures in Wonderland, *and its sequel,* Through the Looking-Glass *(1871), popularised a genre sometimes referred to as nonsense literature.*

MAKING MUSIC

Bone flutes and whistles have been found in prehistoric caves, along with rattles and castanets made from mammoths' jawbones. From such basic elements as clapping hands and tapping sticks on a log, the entire musical heritage of the world has grown.

SOUND OF STRINGS
This 1800s engraving depicts a Greek muse playing the lyre.

WHAT WERE THE FIRST INSTRUMENTS?

The earliest instruments were probably simple percussion instruments, such as drums and rattles. Flutes and other wind instruments have been traced back to more than 30,000 years ago. Small, stringed, harp-like instruments gained favour in ancient Egypt and Mesopotamia almost 5000 years ago, and the lyre was much revered in ancient Greece. The Arabs introduced the four-string oud to Spain in the eighth century and by the twelfth century an instrument called the *guitarra* was widely played in Spain. From this evolved the modern six-string guitar.

HOW DO INSTRUMENTS PRODUCE SOUNDS?

IN UNISON *Playing several instruments together creates a rich, full sound.*

All musical sound, whether from string, reed or cymbal, is created by vibrations. These travel as pressure waves in the air. Fast vibrations produce high-pitched notes; slower vibrations produce low-pitched notes. When the rate of vibrations changes, so does the note. Different instruments create vibrations in different ways to produce a different range of notes.

❶ KEYBOARD In a traditional keyboard, such as the piano, the keys move hammers that strike steel strings, producing vibrations. In electronic keyboards, pressing the key completes an electric circuit, triggering a note.

❷ GUITAR The player plucks or strums the strings, causing them to vibrate and resonate inside an open sound hole. The notes and chords are altered by holding combinations of strings down with the other hand.

❸ VIOLIN Sound is produced by drawing a bow, consisting of a wooden rod along which is strung a ribbon of horsehair (or synthetic fibres). The pitch and notes are controlled by pressing on the strings with the left hand.

❹ BANJO The banjo works in a similar way to the guitar, but the sound resonates inside a circular wooden frame covered by a membrane (either animal skin or a synthetic equivalent).

❺ PERCUSSION Drumskins and metal cymbals vibrate to create different textures (patterns) of sound.

❻ DOUBLE BASS Like a violin, it has four strings and f-shaped sound holes. It can be played with a bow or by plucking the strings.

HOW DO WE SING?

Singing is produced by air making the vocal cords vibrate as the singer breathes out. The higher, louder and longer the note being sung, the more breath is needed. The pitch of the voice is varied by tensing and relaxing muscles in the throat. In Western classical music, singing voices are classified in seven types based on the range of notes the voice can comfortably cover.

VOICE TYPE	FEMALE	MALE
Higher	Soprano	Countertenor
Lower	Mezzo-soprano	Tenor
	Contralto	Baritone
		Bass

FULL SONG *Opera is a form of musical theatre in which performers act out a story while singing their lines. It emerged about 400 years ago in Italy and reached a pinnacle of popularity in the late 1800s, notably with the works of Giuseppe Verdi and Richard Wagner.*

fast fact

German composer Georg Philipp Telemann (1681–1767) was possibly the most prolific composer in history, producing more than 3000 works.

How do we write music down?

We write music down using musical notation, a system devised by an Italian Benedictine monk, Guido d'Arezzo, in the early eleventh century. It works by showing notes as symbols on a five-line stave, or staff. The pitch of a note is indicated by its position on the stave, and its duration is represented by the form of the note, as well as other annotations, including dots and ties. A stave begins with a clef, which shows the position of one note on the stave as a guide. The start of the stave may also show a key signature, which alters the tone of the piece by requiring that some notes are played flat (half a step lower) or sharp (half a step higher).

SEMIBREVE Whole note (four counts)

= **TWO MINIMS** Half note

= **FOUR CROTCHETS** Quarter note

= **EIGHT QUAVERS** Eighth note

= **SIXTEEN SEMIQUAVERS** Sixteenth note

♭ **FLAT** Half-step lower

♯ **SHARP** Half-step higher

TREBLE CLEF   **BASS CLEF**   **KEY SIGNATURE**

What is classical music?

Classical music is the Western tradition of composing complex musical works (as distinguished from simpler 'popular' music). It arose out of medieval church music and Renaissance songs and instrumental works. In the so-called Early Baroque period of the 1600s, a variety of forms emerged, including the sonata (for solo instruments), the cantata (for voice and instruments) and the concerto (for a solo instrument with orchestra). Compositions became increasingly complex in the Late Baroque period of the late 1600s and early 1700s, notably in the works of Johann Sebastian Bach and George Frideric Handel, and the system of notation, key changes and scales became formalised and consistent. The so-called Classical period of the later 1700s and early 1800s – the era of Mozart and Haydn – saw the emergence of the symphony, which became a powerful form of expression for later 'Romantic' composers, such as Ludwig van Beethoven. Modernist composers, such as Arnold Schoenberg, pushed music into new realms, rejecting traditional rhythms and adopting unconventional, 'atonal' scales.

Symphony orchestra *The United Nations Orchestra rehearses under the direction of conductor Antoine Marguier, in the ornate Victoria Hall in Geneva, Switzerland.*

Fab four *The Beatles provoked hysteria among teenage fans.*

WHAT IS POPULAR MUSIC?

The term 'popular music' encompasses a wide range of styles. Late 1800s forms included light opera, or operetta, and songs written for music hall entertainments (known as vaudeville in the United States). A syncopated style called ragtime became hugely popular around 1900 – songwriters included Scott Joplin and Irving Berlin. Meanwhile, African-American musicians blended African rhythms with blues and ragtime to create jazz, which soon spread worldwide. Country music became popular with late 1920s radio audiences, and in the 1940s a mix of jazz and blues resulted in a style called rhythm and blues, which in turn inspired rock 'n' roll. The 1960s saw a revival of folk singing and the flowering of melodic 'pop' epitomised by the Beatles. Rock and pop have since evolved into diverse subgenres ranging from punk and heavy metal to disco, techno and grunge.

THE ART OF DANCE

Dance has always been important as a social activity, as entertainment and as a means of self-expression. In ancient times, people danced to make magic, to tell sacred stories or to bind themselves together as a tribe. Since then, different forms of dance have developed their own languages and conventions.

HOW CAN DANCES TELL STORIES?

Indian dance and traditional Western ballet both use a highly developed language of steps, movements and gestures. Series of movements are linked together in different combinations to tell a story or create a mood. Many years of intensive training are needed to master the intricate steps and movements and develop the necessary suppleness and strength.

EXPRESSION In traditional Indian dance, movement, hand gestures and facial expressions are often used to tell stories of the gods. Set movements can be combined to create decorative patterns.

HOW DID DANCING BEGIN?

The dances of our ancestors were group activities and provided a way of rejoicing and sharing an experience of togetherness. Many celebrated times of importance to the group, such as the completion of a harvest, success in a battle or hunt, a wedding or a birth. But people also danced as an act of devotion to their gods.

TRIBAL DANCE Young Masai men dance in a traditional ceremony.

ROUND THE POLE The maypole dance, in which people circle around a tall pole hung with garlands and ribbons, survives from times when people danced around a tree to ask for their crops to grow.

WHEN DID BALLET BEGIN?

The first performances resembling modern ballet were held in Italian Renaissance courts – in 1489, the Duke of Milan was entertained by the story of Jason and the Argonauts enacted in dance and mime. In 1661, King Louis XIV, an avid dancer himself, set up the French Royal Academy of Dance, which in turn led to the founding of the Paris Opera Ballet, the world's first national ballet company. French companies shaped many of the conventions of modern ballet, but Russian companies created many of its most enduring works, such as *The Nutcracker* (1892) and *Swan Lake* (1895), as well as groundbreaking shows, such as Sergei Diaghilev's *The Firebird* (1910). Pioneers of modern ballet include US-based Russian émigré George Balanchine and US choreographers Twyla Tharp and Mark Morris, who have taken ballet to a wider audience by combining it with contemporary dance.

BALLET PRACTICE Dancers work to develop skill, balance and grace, and to produce a good 'line' – the flowing lines and curves that can be traced through a dancer's body.

❺ **BASIC POSITIONS** Most ballet steps begin and end in one of the five basic positions. This is the fifth position.

❹ **ATTITUDE** One leg is raised and bent.

❸ **ARABESQUE** The dancer creates a long line from the ends of the fingers to the tips of the toes.

❷ **RONDE DE JAMBE** 'Circles of the leg', being done here 'en pointe'.

❶ **PIROUETTE** Turns, or spins, can be done on the spot or travelling across the stage.

WHAT IS BALLROOM DANCING?

Dancing in couples became popular in Europe in the fourteenth century and by the seventeenth century new styles for couples had appeared. The courtly minuet appeared in France in 1663, followed by the lively gavotte in 1696. The waltz evolved in Austria during the 1780s out of traditional peasant dances and became a hugely popular ballroom dance throughout the 1800s. Meanwhile, the three quick steps and a hop of the polka grew out of Bohemian folk dances. In the early 1900s new steps were introduced, including the foxtrot in 1913 (pioneered by US dancer Harry Fox) and the maxixe, a mixture of polka and African-influenced Brazilian dance. Other Latin American styles gained popularity too, including the tango (1913) from Argentina, the swaying Afro-Cuban rumba (1922), and the salsa (1962), which was influenced by jazz and rock.

SCREEN STARS *From the early 1930s, performers such as Fred Astaire and Ginger Rogers showcased tap dancing in a series of hugely popular musical movies.*

WHERE DID TAP DANCING COME FROM?

Tap dancing is thought to have evolved out of the meeting of different kinds of ethnic foot-stomping dances, especially African tribal dances, Irish step dances and English clog dances. African, English and Irish immigrants compared and swapped dance steps, creating a new style of dance that became popular in late 1800s minstrel shows and vaudeville, or music hall, shows. The routines became increasingly complex and frenetic and dancers began to attach hard 'taps' to their heels and toes to accentuate the rhythms. The popularity of tap reached a peak in the 1920s and 1930s.

HOW DO DANCE STYLES BECOME FASHIONABLE?

At various times, particular dances have become fashionable, often in tandem with certain styles of music. In 1900, as jazz was taking off, Afro-Americans created a satirical mimicking of white ballroom dancing, called the cakewalk. The 1920s dance known as the Charleston owed its popularity to a hit musical, *Running Wild* (1923), which introduced this black folk dance. In the 1930s and 1940s, African dance also inspired the high lifts and fast footwork of the jitterbug and the jive. Films and TV popularised the Twist in the 1960s, while social media have created modern dance crazes, such as South Korean singer Psy's 'Gangnam Style'.

VIENNESE WALTZ *German artist Wilhelm Gause's painting shows Austrian couples dancing a waltz during the annual Viennese Ball in the late 1800s.*

fast fact

Between the fourteenth and seventeenth centuries, numerous cases were reported across Europe of a dancing mania that afflicted large groups of people without warning. Of uncertain origin, it was sometimes referred to as St John's Dance.

DOING THE TWIST *Originated by US singer Hank Ballard in 1958, the Twist caught on in London in the early 1960s.*

DRAMA AND THEATRE

HIGH DRAMA *Many early Greek plays are still performed at the open-air theatre atop Mount Lycabettus, Athens.*

Since ancient times, humans have acted out stories on stage to entertain, instruct and inspire others, and over the centuries diverse forms of theatre have evolved in different parts of the world.

Whether the setting is a grand theatre house or a simple church hall, plays rely on the cooperation of a willing audience and the skills of the actor to conjure up another, fictional world.

TEN-YEAR RE-ENACTMENT *The Oberammergau Passion Play has been staged in the German village of the same name every 10 years since 1634.*

WHERE WERE PLAYS FIRST PERFORMED?

The first plays to feature individual actors playing different parts were staged by the ancient Greeks. They evolved out of religious festivals at which choruses of masked male actors recited or sang stories about the fortunes of heroes of myth and history. About 550 BC, a Greek poet called Thespis stepped forward from the chorus to recite speeches, becoming the first actor. Greek theatre took three main forms: tragedy, in which a hero is pitted against the forces of fate; satire, which poked fun at public figures; and comedy, in which stock character types representing human follies were set against each other for fun. Plays were also performed in India from the first century AD onwards.

WHAT WERE MEDIEVAL PLAYS BASED ON?

From around 1100, new forms of drama emerged in Europe. Plays based on Bible stories – known as mystery or miracle plays – were performed, either in churches or outdoors. Some were assembled into cycles of plays, such as the York Cycle in England. Other religious performances included re-enactments of the crucifixion, known as passion plays. Alongside these, plays developed in which virtues and vices were embodied by actors in order to instruct the audience, known as morality plays.

WAS SHAKESPEARE POPULAR IN HIS OWN TIME?

Yes, Shakespeare's plays, and theatre in general, were enormously popular in Elizabethan London. A strong theatre tradition had grown there out of renewed interest in classical drama and medieval morality plays, and several playwrights, Shakespeare included, took theatrical performances in new directions. Ben Jonson used satire to attack greed and hypocrisy,while Christopher Marlowe presented plays that probed the inner conflicts of tragic heroes. Shakespeare's blend of poeticism, high drama and, in some plays, comic elements produced highly original entertainments that drew large crowds.

ON STAGE *A Shakespearean performance in London's Globe Theatre*

Which theatrical traditions exist in Asia?

In Japan, a highly stylised form of theatre known as Noh emerged in the fourteenth century. Its subjects were taken from Japanese literature; regular characters in elaborate costumes performed stately dances to the accompaniment of drums and flute. Another stylised form of performance, Kabuki, appeared in the early 1600s. Its stories became increasingly melodramatic and appealing to contemporary audiences. Both forms of drama are still widely performed in Japan. In China, what is known as Chinese Opera has long been the most popular form of theatre. Based around four central characters wearing elaborate traditional costumes and bold make-up, it combines music, dance and acrobatics in a colourful spectacle.

MEN ONLY *Originally all Kabuki parts were played by women, but from 1629, when women were banned from performing, males acted all roles and still do today.*

WAITING IN VAIN *In Samuel Beckett's play* Waiting for Godot, *two characters, Vladimir and Estragon, wait day after day for the arrival of a mysterious character called Godot.*

What happens behind the scenes in a theatre?

Theatrical performances combine scenery, props, lighting, sound, music and costumes, as well as acting. Much of the work of preparing a production goes on unseen, in backstage areas, workshops and rehearsal rooms.

GOING BACKSTAGE *This illustration shows the activities that typically take place in the different parts of a modern theatre.*

❶ **DRESSING ROOMS** Actors put on costumes and make-up in preparation for going on stage.

❷ **CONTROL DESKS** Technicians control the sound and lighting.

❸ **AUDITORIUM** This is the area occupied by the audience.

❹ **ORCHESTRA PIT** The area where the orchestra plays. The orchestra and the performers on the stage can usually see the conductor.

❺ **THE WINGS** The unseen area at the sides of the stage. The scenery is arranged so that the cast can enter and exit.

❻ **THE SET** The stage with its grouping of scenery. Movable pieces of scenery mounted on frames are called 'flats'.

❼ **LIGHTING** Rows of spotlights hang from a gantry or rig. Lights also shine upwards from the front of the stage.

What is the Theatre of the Absurd?

In reaction to the predominance of realism and political satire in the theatre in the early 1900s, a new type of drama developed in Paris in the 1950s, in which motiveless characters and sparse or nonexistent plots were used to highlight life's futility. The leading exponents of this kind of theatre were Irish writer Samuel Beckett and Romanian-born Eugene Ionesco, whose works inspired a generation of dramatists, such as Harold Pinter, Tom Stoppard and Vaclav Havel.

fast fact

The longest dramatic performance ever took place in Belmar, New Jersey, USA, in 2010. A version of Eugene Ionesco's *The Bald Soprano* presented by the 27 O'clock Players, it ran for 23 hours 33 minutes and 54 seconds.

FILM-MAKING

Within 20 years of the invention of the motion picture in the 1890s, the cinema had become an enormous international industry, with Hollywood at its heart.

Today, despite competition from television, video and the Internet, movies and cinema retain mass appeal, and technological and creative innovations keep the medium vital and viable.

WHEN WERE THE FIRST MOVIES MADE?

In the 1870s, photographic pioneer Eadweard Muybridge made animated images by running together a sequence of photographs taken one after another on multiple cameras. In the 1880s, the first motion picture cameras were introduced, which allowed users to capture moving images on a continuous roll of celluloid film. French pioneers Auguste and Louis Lumière made many of the first movies and began showing them in their own cinema in Paris from 1895. One of the earliest narrative films was *The Great Train Robbery*, a 12-minute movie made by US inventor Thomas Edison's company in 1903, but the first feature film is generally agreed to be *The Story of the Kelly Gang*, directed by Charles Tait and released in Australia in 1906.

WHEN WAS SOUND INTRODUCED TO MOVIES?

Though they often had musical accompaniments, all movies before the early 1920s were silent. Experiments with projecting sound and images – which were captured separately – were carried out in the United States and France from the late 1890s. However, synchronising the two media proved problematic until US inventor Lee de Forest perfected a technology known as 'sound on film'. This involved converting the soundtrack into a photographic pattern that appeared on a strip down the side of the projector film and was translated back into sound when the movie was played. The first feature film to incorporate sound was the US movie *The Jazz Singer*, released in 1927 and starring Al Jolson.

THE FIRST TALKIE *The Jazz Singer was the first film to have synchronised speech as well as music and sound effects.*

MOON SHOT *Parisian film-maker Georges Méliès pioneered special effects.*

HOW DOES A MOVIE CAMERA WORK?

A traditional movie camera captures a series of pictures, called frames, at a rate of 24 per second. When the film is projected, light shines through it and throws the pictures onto a screen; the changes from frame to frame occur so fast that the motion appears continuous to the human eye. Although digital video (▶210) is now used for most television programs and some movies, many feature-film makers still favour traditional movie cameras using 35-mm film.

FILM STRIP *Traditional film carries a series of frames. The soundtrack is recorded on the strip down the side.*

POST-PRODUCTION *A director views a rough cut of a film prior to editing*

HOW ARE FILMS PUT TOGETHER?

Making a film can take many years, but it usually proceeds through five main stages. The first, development, involves selecting a story or topic, writing a screenplay and obtaining funding, usually from a movie studio. During pre-production, the next stage, the film's producer recruits a director, actors and crew and refines the budget, while the screenplay is finalised. Then the film enters production: designers create sets, actors learn lines, and the director supervises the filming. In post-production, a film editor assembles and trims the film, the soundtrack is added, and visual effects are incorporated. Finally, distribution involves the end-product being marketed and sent to cinemas.

WHAT DO THEY DO?

BEST BOY	Assisting chief lighting technician (called 'best boy' whether male or female)
BOOM OPERATOR	Person who operates a microphone on a long pole
CLAPPER LOADER	Person who loads film into cameras and operates clapper-board
DOLLY OPERATOR	Operator who moves cameras around on wheeled trolleys (dollies)
FOCUS PULLER	Person who adjusts the focus of the camera during filming
GAFFER	Chief lighting technician
GRIP	Crew member responsible for assembling and maintaining equipment
KEY GRIP	Chief grip, who works closely with the gaffer
PROPS	Person who acquires all the props
SET DRESSER	Crew member who arranges scenery on the set

fast fact

In terms of the number of movies made annually, India has the biggest film industry, producing more than 1200 Bollywood films a year. Second is Nigeria's 'Nollywood', which turns out almost 1000 films, though most are released only on video or DVD.

WHAT DOES A FILM DIRECTOR DO?

The role of the director has evolved over the decades. Most 1920s and 1930s directors were little more than glorified technicians employed by studios to create showcases for stars. But certain pioneering directors – the likes of DW Griffiths and Cecil B DeMille in the United States, Jean Renoir in France and Sergei Eisenstein in Russia – began to take greater control of the whole process, so that the result was more of a personalised work of art. By the late 1950s, the director was seen as the main creative force behind a movie, with his or her own distinctive style. In the 1960s, avant-garde directors, such as France's François Truffaut and Jean-Luc Godard, took this approach further, establishing the idea of the director as the *auteur*, or author, of the movie. The advent of the blockbuster in the 1970s, generally requiring a large team of contributors, took some attention away from the director, but today a director's name still indicates the style of a film and can help ensure a level of success at the box office.

ON SET *English film director Alfred Hitchcock*

HOW HAS COMPUTER TECHNOLOGY CHANGED FILM-MAKING?

Technology has brought a new sophistication and almost limitless scope to film-making. CGI, or computer-generated imagery, can be used to add all sorts of images and effects to scenes, such as spectacular landscapes, duplicated figures forming vast crowds, the seamless visual transformation of characters, and life-like simulations of catastrophes, such as explosions and earthquakes. Computer-animated figures can be inserted into live-action movies, or films can be entirely animated. The first fully computer-animated film, *Toy Story* (1995), has been followed by numerous others of its ilk, all created by vast armies of animators and technicians.

NEW DIMENSIONS *James Cameron's 2009 film Avatar employed cutting-edge technology including stereoscopic cameras to create a highly immersive 3D experience.*

THE MASS MEDIA

The mass media is all the forms of communication that reach large numbers of people. Among the most powerful are books, newspapers and magazines, radio, film and television. With the advent of the Internet, these have been joined by a range of online media, including websites, blogs, RSS feeds, podcasts and social media (▶207).

WHEN DID THE FIRST NEWSPAPERS APPEAR?

From around 59 BC, Roman authorities carved news reports in metal or stone – such as Rome's *Acta Diurna* ('Daily Events') – and hung them in prominent places for people to read. But the first printed pamphlets containing news items appeared in the late 1500s, and what is acknowledged today as the first regular newspaper was produced by Johann Carolus from 1605 in Strasbourg, now in France but then part of the Holy Roman Empire. Printed in German, it was called the *Relation aller Fürnemmen und gedenckwürdigen Historien* (Account of all distinguished and commemorable news). From 1618 the Dutch pioneered weekly newspapers featuring *corantos*, or 'current news', translated into French and English, which were widely distributed through the nation's flourishing trading links. A similar digest of 'weekly news' was published in London from 1621 and is regarded as the first British newspaper.

FIRST WITH THE NEWS The front page of the world's first newspaper, published in Strasbourg in 1605

WHEN DID RADIO BEGIN?

Italian inventor Guglielmo Marconi developed the first radio system in the late 1890s and sent the first transatlantic signals in 1901. Radio was subsequently used widely for communications, and the idea of using it to transmit news and entertainment to the public soon caught on. A Canadian radio station, Montreal's XWA, started broadcasting to the public in 1919 and in August of the following year the Argentina Station began transmitting programs from Buenos Aires. The United States's first licensed radio station, KDKA, was founded in Pittsburgh, Pennsylvania, in October 1920, and within two years there were more than 500 US radio stations. In Britain, the BBC (British Broadcasting Corporation) began transmitting to the nation and its empire in 1922.

WHICH WAS THE FIRST FORM OF MASS MEDIA?

The mass media began with the invention of the printing press in Germany in 1453 (▶257), which allowed multiple copies of the same images or texts to be distributed to large numbers of people. Essential for its success was a significant level of literacy, which was then beginning to be achieved in Europe.

BOOKS FOR LOAN Increased literacy led to the creation of the first lending libraries.

LONG RUN A country music program called The Grand Ole Opry was launched in 1925 on US station WSM; still broadcast today, it's the world's longest-running radio program.

ROYAL SHOW *The coronation of King George VI*

WHAT WAS THE FIRST TELEVISION CHANNEL?

Three years after the first demonstration of television by John Logie Baird in 1925, the US company General Electric began broadcasting the first television programs from a station in Schenectady, New York, known as WGY. However, the first regular public television service was established in London in 1936 by the BBC, which also conducted one of the first major outside broadcasts the following year – the coronation of King George VI.

HOW HAS THE INTERNET AFFECTED MASS MEDIA?

The availability of free online news services has led to a significant decline in sales of printed newspapers. Proprietors of newspapers have tried to counter this by charging fees for access to their online services, with limited success. Most radio services are also available online today, but given that most stations are funded by on-air advertising the change of medium has had less impact on their revenue streams. Many television programs are now available through online 'on-demand' services set up by major broadcasters, whereby the viewer can watch a previously transmitted program (often on a computer rather than a television set) at the time of their choosing. Music, films and television programs are also widely available on Internet 'streaming' services, which offer a wide range of audio and video content in return for a regular subscription. These programs are usually watched as they are downloaded, or 'streamed', to the subscriber's computer but do not remain there afterwards.

PORTABLE MEDIA *Streaming services allow viewers to watch at home and when on the move.*

HOW HAS THE MASS MEDIA BEEN USED FOR ADVERTISING?

The mass media is used not only for disseminating information and entertainment but also to advertise products. The first newspaper advertisements – mainly for books and other publications – appeared in newspapers in the 1700s. More elaborate print-media advertising campaigns were developed in the late 1800s, notably by Thomas J Barratt of London, who made Pears soap one of the first high-profile brand names. Radio advertising grew rapidly in the 1920s, when many programs had commercial sponsors, but it was the advent of television that gave rise to sophisticated marketing campaigns, including memorable USPs, or unique selling propositions, such as the tagline for M&Ms – 'They melt in your mouth, not in your hand' – devised in 1954 by US advertising pioneer Rosser Reeves. Advertising provided a new source of revenue and few TV stations now function without it. New forms of advertising have emerged on the Internet, including banners and 'pop-ups' on websites; the marketing of products via mass emails; promotion via social media (▶207); and search engine marketing (SEM) and search engine optimisation (SEO), which involve tailoring a company's web data so that it appears more often in online searches.

SOAP STARS *An illustration from an early Pears soap ad*

fast fact
Soap operas are so named because the first such multi-episode radio and TV dramas in the United States were sponsored by manufacturers of soap powder.

SPORTS

Sports are leisure activities, usually physical ones, which people undertake for recreation, entertainment or to keep fit. Normally a sport is based on a set of rules, requires certain physical skills and involves a degree of competition between participants or some kind of challenge or target. Some sports have become forms of mass entertainment, and many major sporting competitions now draw vast audiences.

TARGET PRACTICE *A vital component of war in ancient times, archery was also practised for recreation.*

HARD HIT *In the Japanese martial art of kendo, contestants wear protective armour and use bamboo staffs or wooden swords to try to hit specific targets on their opponent's body. Two hits result in a win.*

WHAT ARE MARTIAL ARTS?

The ancient tradition of the martial arts grew out of the self-defence skills of Zen Buddhist monks in medieval China, and involves spiritual philosophy as well as physical training. The term 'kung fu' comes from the Chinese 'gong fu', which simply means 'skill'. Kung fu is a system of unarmed fighting that uses sharp blows struck with the hands and feet. The Japanese combat sport of karate (meaning 'empty hand') came from the kung fu tradition. Another martial art is the Japanese combat sport of kendo (which means 'way of the sword'). Kendo was associated with the sword-fighting skills of the samurai, the warriors of feudal Japan.

WHICH WERE THE FIRST SPORTS?

Some of the world's oldest cave art, found at Lascaux in France and dating from more than 17,000 years ago, is thought to show people running and wrestling; other prehistoric Asian and African cave art from around 9000 years ago clearly depicts wrestling, swimming and archery. Organised sports, many originating as training for war, were practised across the ancient world. They include wrestling and boxing in Mesopotamia about 5000 years ago; wrestling, running, rowing and fishing in Egypt around 4000 years ago; and polo and jousting in Persia more than 2000 years ago.

HOW DID THE OLYMPICS BEGIN?

Sports became popular and prestigious in ancient Greece. The Olympic Games, a festival of sporting events, evolved out of a religious festival and was first staged in 776 BC, then every four years until 393 AD. The main events included contests still held today: running, wrestling, boxing, long jump, and discus- and javelin-throwing. In 1896, France's Baron Pierre de Coubertin revived the Olympics at Athens. They have been held every four years since, except in 1916, 1940 and 1944, when world war intervened. The Winter Olympics began in 1924; initially they were held in the same year as the summer event, but since 1994 they have taken place two years after each Summer Olympics.

THROW-BACK *An enduring symbol of athleticism, the Discobolus of Myron is a Greek sculpture of a discus thrower, from around 450 BC. Only Roman copies now exist.*

WHICH ARE THE MOST POPULAR SPORTS?

Soccer, or football, is by far the most popular sport worldwide, both in terms of participants and spectators: it is played by more than 250 million people from more than 200 countries. Its major international competition, the World Cup, is the most watched sporting event, followed by the Olympic Games. Other internationally popular sports include basketball, which has spread worldwide from the United States, and cricket, whose popularity is concentrated in two nations, India and Pakistan – the 2011 Cricket World Cup semi-final between those nations' teams is said to have been watched by 150 million people. Baseball is another massively popular spectator sport, drawing more than 70 million spectators over the season in the United States and 22 million in Japan. However, in terms of average attendance at games, American football draws the largest crowds – more than 67,000 per game.

GLOBAL AUDIENCE *Around 910 million people are estimated to have watched at least part of the 2010 World Cup Final, played in Johannesburg, South Africa.*

fast fact

In 1969, a dispute during a World Cup soccer match between El Salvador and Honduras led to a five-day war between the two countries.

CAN ATHLETES GO ON BREAKING RECORDS?

Athletes in all sports continue to break records: at the 2012 Olympic Games in London, more than 30 new world records were established. This is partly due to new techniques and equipment, more focused training from an early age and improvements in medicine and treatment, which enable athletes to overcome injuries more quickly and prepare their bodies for competition. Nevertheless, some scientists think that the physical limitations of the human body, such as leg length, oxygen intake and heart pump rate, mean that we will soon reach absolute limits for many events. Current estimates include 1 hour and 58 minutes for the marathon and 9.48 seconds for the men's 100 metres.

BOLT FROM THE BLUE *The rate of record breaking in track races has slowed since the 1990s. Many observers were astonished when Usain Bolt reduced the 100 metres record to 9.58 seconds in Berlin in 2009.*

MONEY AND FINANCE

Money began as a more convenient alternative to bartering goods. While early coins were valued for their precious-metal content, modern currencies are worth little in themselves; however, by government order they are accepted as a means of payment and therefore have a set value. The widespread use of money from the Middle Ages onwards led to the creation of a range of financial institutions, most notably banks and stock exchanges.

WHY DO PEOPLE USE MONEY?

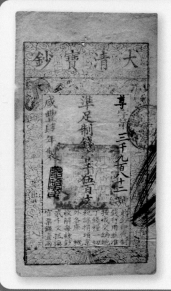

The earliest form of trade was barter, where people exchanged goods of similar usefulness. Later, the idea dawned of selecting one type of object as a measure of value of goods and services. Different communities used different items, ranging from spearheads and shells to beads and metal bars. The first coins with fixed values appeared in Turkey and China in the eighth century BC. Introduced first in China in the seventh century AD, paper notes were essentially a promise to pay the bearer the same amount in coins, but soon became a form of money themselves. Similar promissory notes, also known as bills of exchange, were used in Europe from around 1100. The first banknotes were issued in 1661 by Sweden's private Bank of Stockholm, which collapsed two years later; the Bank of England, founded in 1694, became the first state bank to issue notes, in 1695.

PRICE ON PAPER *China's Song dynasty issued the first official paper money in the tenth century.*

fast fact

In 1920s Germany, over-printing of money caused rapid price rises, or inflation, at one point reaching 332 per cent in a single month. People had to hand over barrowloads of notes to pay for simple commodities.

WHAT DO BANKS DO?

Banks are institutions that hold and provide money. Merchants long ago took to storing their money in banks to avoid carrying cash about. These banks also lent money so that traders could, for example, set up businesses. When someone paid back a loan, the banks charged an additional sum, known as 'interest'; this was how they made a profit. By the end of the Middle Ages, the main features of the modern banking system – such as deposits and loans, accounts against which cheques could be drawn, and exchanging foreign money – had been established. The world's first state-owned, or central, bank was the Bank of Sweden, set up in 1668 after the collapse of the privately owned Bank of Stockholm.

MONEY LENDERS *This illustration from a medieval manuscript shows Italian bankers at work.*

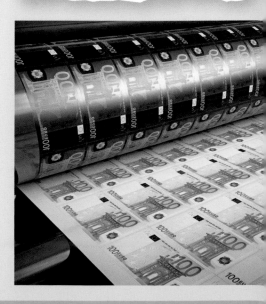

MONEY MARKET *Traders buying and selling stocks on the floor of the New York Stock Exchange*

WHAT IS A STOCK EXCHANGE?

From the Middle Ages, people issued written bills agreeing to assign part ownership of a business in return for a loan or investment. These became known as 'shares', and groups of shares became known as 'stocks'. In the early 1500s, institutions dedicated to managing the buying and selling of stocks and shares were founded. The first such 'stock exchanges' were established in Antwerp in the Netherlands in 1531, in Hamburg, Germany, in 1558, and in Amsterdam in 1611; the London stock exchange opened in 1773, and New York's in 1817. Specialised banks that deal in shares, stocks and bonds are called investment banks.

HOW DO GOVERNMENTS MANAGE MONEY?

A government usually controls the flow of money through its central bank. This bank produces and issues the national currency, sets interest rates, holds reserve stocks of gold and foreign currencies, and provides short-term advances to commercial banks – the private institutions that deal directly with the public – when their funds are low. The main aims of a central bank are to keep employment and production high and stabilise prices. Central banks also sell government bonds – certificates of government debt that will be repaid at a fixed interest rate after a set period – as a form of investment.

PAPER MONEY *Several authorised printing works produce Euro banknotes*

WHEN WERE TAXES INTRODUCED?

Taxes are payments that citizens are required by law to make to the government to pay for state expenses and services, such as schools, hospitals and roads. The first organised systems of taxation were introduced about 5000 years ago in the Middle East and Egypt, where taxes were usually paid in the form of tithes – a proportion (traditionally one-tenth) of any crops or goods produced – or labour. The ancient Greeks and Romans created taxes on the sale or importation of certain goods, and, at times, on property and inheritances. Many rulers, then and later, used taxes as a means to raise funds for wars and lavish building projects. Today, the main form of government taxation is income tax – tax paid on earnings – with the percentage of earnings paid as tax usually increasing as income rises.

DUES PAID *Two Tax Collectors (1540), a painting by Dutch artist Marinus van Reymerswaele*

PHONECO HEADQUARTERS

BANK

Bank provides loan to Phoneco

Phoneco pays interest to bank

Jill buys shares in phone company, Phoneco, and earns dividends

Phoneco uses bank loan to finance factory

Jill puts money in bank and earns interest

Bank provides finance for shopping centre

Phoneco receives profits from phone sales

Shopping centre pays interest to bank on loan

Jill earns money

Jill spends money, gets smartphone

PHONECO FACTORY

Shopping centre pays money to Phoneco for products

Phoneco factory supplies phones to shopping centre

SHOPPING CENTRE

HOW IS MONEY PASSED AROUND?

Most people earn money by working. They use it to pay for essential goods and services. If they then have money left over – so-called disposable income – they can choose to spend that money in different ways, most of which help drive the economy. For example, they can buy more goods and services, thereby supporting businesses; deposit money in a bank and earn interest; or invest money in businesses by buying shares.

GOVERNMENT AND POLITICS

All countries are run by some form of government – usually a group of people who create laws and policies, manage national finances and communicate with other governments. Normally these people are chosen to represent the rest of the community by means of a political process involving the campaigning of rival parties, followed by an election.

DELEGATING POWER *Cyrus the Great of Persia (c. 600–530 BC) was one of the first leaders to appoint regional rulers (satraps) to govern on his behalf.*

WHAT DO GOVERNMENTS DO?

In ancient times, communities were often headed by a chief or king, who usually had a small group of advisers. With the development of agriculture (▶254) and the emergence of larger civilisations, there was an increasing need for regulation and management as major states took shape. Rulers required greater resources to support their armies and began imposing taxes; they also established more complex systems of government, including regional representatives and ranks of government officials to manage state affairs. In modern times, governments still set and impose laws and manage trade and, occasionally, conflict with other nations, but they are equally focused on steering the economy, gathering taxes and providing public services, such as schools and hospitals.

WHAT KINDS OF GOVERNMENT ARE THERE?

Most early civilisations were monarchies; that is, they were headed by an individual ruler with supreme authority, often known as a king or queen. Such a position was usually hereditary, passing to the eldest son on the monarch's death, and many monarchs were regarded, by themselves and their subjects, as having a 'divine right' to rule, as a result of a claimed association with a deity. Some such states evolved into oligarchies, nations run by small, privileged elites, sometimes members of one family or caste. In early modern times, opposition to oligarchies and the idea of the divine right of monarchs to rule led to revolutions, notably the French Revolution of 1789, and the creation of republics – states headed by leaders appointed by other citizens. Many monarchies and republics have since evolved into democracies. However, reactions against democracy led to the foundation of many twentieth-century dictatorships – states headed by individuals or groups (often military) who have seized power by force or other illegal means and maintain control by limiting the freedom of their subjects.

FRENCH REVOLUTION *If a government is especially harsh or unpopular, people may rise up and overthrow it, as the people of France did in 1789.*

WHAT IS DEMOCRACY?

Democracy means rule (*kratos* in Greek) by the people (*demos*). The system originated in Athens, Greece, in the sixth century BC. All free men were entitled to meet and vote on important issues in a general assembly; however, neither women nor slaves were allowed to vote. In the modern world, democracy usually means that all adult citizens have the right to elect representatives to a government, which should make decisions on behalf of everyone. Indeed, democracy today is often defined as 'one person, one vote'.

PUBLIC DEBATE *Renowned orator Demosthenes delivers a speech in the assembly in Athens, in the fourth century BC.*

PARLIAMENTARY DEBATE *UK politicians in the House of Commons*

HOW DOES DEMOCRATIC GOVERNMENT WORK?

Democratic government takes different forms, but it generally has two main branches: the legislature and the executive. The legislature – usually called a parliament, congress or assembly – is made up of elected representatives, who debate what laws should be passed, or measures taken, for the wellbeing of the country. The executive is the branch of government that puts these laws or measures into effect. It is usually headed by a president or prime minister.

MASS RALLY *India is the world's largest democracy.*

HOW DO YOU GET ELECTED TO GOVERNMENT?

In most modern countries, election is the result of a broadly similar process. Political parties, based on different beliefs, select their representatives and present them as candidates for election in state, regional or national ballots. Citizens follow debates at public meetings or in the media, then vote for the person or persons they consider best qualified for the position. Governments may be elected by a 'first-past-the-post' system, whereby the person with the most votes in a particular area wins; a system of 'proportional representation', whereby parties are allocated a number of seats in a parliament or other legislature according to the proportion of the total votes that they have won overall; or a combination of these or other, similar systems.

HOW ARE VOTES COUNTED?

Voters usually mark their vote privately on a ballot paper and then deposit it in a secure box. Even today, votes are often counted manually under the supervision of independent witnesses or observers; however, various automated systems have also been developed. Optical-scan voting systems use a scanner and linked computer to read and count marks on ballot papers, while digital-pen systems rely on pens that contain a tiny camera to record the vote and send it to a computer. The punched-card system, whereby voters use a mechanical punch to make a hole in a card beside the name of their chosen candidate, was introduced in the 1890s and by the 1960s was being widely used in the United States and elsewhere. Other mechanical systems include lever machines, on which voters press a lever or flick a switch to record their vote; these in turn led to modern electronic voting machines, on which people press buttons or icons on touchscreens.

MANUAL COUNT *Electoral officials tally votes during an election in Peru.*

FLICK OF A SWITCH *A voter using a lever machine during a US election*

SIMPLE TOUCH *This touchscreen system incorporates aids for the visually impaired.*

fast fact

Iceland has the world's oldest continuous parliament, the Althing. It was founded by the Vikings in 930 AD.

INTERNATIONAL ORGANISATIONS

WHAT WAS THE LEAGUE OF NATIONS?

The League of Nations was the first international organisation set up to maintain world peace. Established in 1919 in the aftermath of the First World War, it had its headquarters in Geneva and had up to 58 member nations. As well as minimising conflict, it sought to limit arms trading and drug trafficking, improve global health and protect minorities. Although it achieved many notable successes, resolving a number of international disputes through diplomacy and introducing pioneering legislation on social issues, it lacked military might and, critically, the support of the United States. It could therefore do little to prevent the rise of fascism in Europe and the onset of the Second World War. Partly as a result of this failure, it was replaced by the United Nations in 1945.

IN SESSION *The League of Nations assembly, seen here in 1923, was a forum where member states could seek to resolve disputes peacefully.*

fast fact

The world's oldest international organisation is the Central Commission for Navigation on the Rhine, set up in 1815 to ensure security and free passage on the Rhine River, one of Europe's major waterways.

From the 1800s onwards, countries increasingly came to see the benefits of working together.

In the twentieth century, numerous organisations were set up to coordinate international cooperation in areas ranging from security and trade to culture and the environment.

WHAT IS THE UNITED NATIONS?

The United Nations (UN) is the closest thing we have to a world parliament. Founded in 1945, it today counts nearly every country in the world as a member. At its headquarters in New York, it provides a forum where nations can air grievances and concerns and appeal for assistance from other states. It helps maintain peace and avert conflict through diplomacy, arbitration, peacekeeping operations, the imposition of sanctions and, when necessary, direct military intervention. It also works towards solutions to problems that challenge all of humanity, such as poverty, disease and global warming.

THE UN SYSTEM *The UN has six main bodies, five based at its New York headquarters and one, the International Court of Justice, at The Hague in the Netherlands. Specialised agencies within the organisation deal with particular issues, such as food and agriculture, health, refugees and culture.*

SECRETARIAT The UN's administration centre carries out day-to-day work and manages its programs.

INTERNATIONAL COURT OF JUSTICE The UN's main judicial body rules on disputes between states and tries war criminals.

TRUSTEESHIP COUNCIL Set up to manage states defeated in the Second World War, it suspended operations in 1994 but could be reactivated if required.

ECONOMIC AND SOCIAL COUNCIL It coordinates economic and social work, monitoring issues such as human rights, equality and the environment.

GENERAL ASSEMBLY At this forum for discussing global issues, all members are represented, each having one vote.

SECURITY COUNCIL The UN body responsible for maintaining peace. Its five 'permanent' members – the UK, USA, France, Russia and China – have the power of veto (meaning that any one of them can block a motion put forward by the council).

A NEUTRAL FORCE *There is no standing UN peacekeeping force. Instead, units are assembled in response to requests from member states and to meet the needs of a particular situation.*

WHAT DOES THE WORLD BANK DO?

Part of the United Nations, the World Bank aims to reduce global poverty by providing capital to and encouraging international investment in developing countries. Set up in 1944, it consists of two main institutions, the International Bank for Reconstruction and Development (IBRD) and the International Development Association (IDA). The World Bank works closely with another UN organisation, the International Monetary Fund (IMF), which promotes financial cooperation between nations, exchange-rate stability and the expansion of trade.

GLOBAL FUNDING *Based in Washington DC, the World Bank has 188 member states.*

WHICH COUNTRIES ARE PART OF NATO?

NATO, the North Atlantic Treaty Organization, was formed by a treaty signed in 1949 by 12 North American and European nations. The signatories agreed to protect each other in the event of aggression on the part of another nation. At the time, the Soviet Union was seen as the major threat, and Cold War manoeuvring over the next two decades prompted other nations to join the alliance. Today consisting of 28 member states, NATO has in the past 20 years led military interventions in the former Yugoslavia, Afghanistan and Libya.

STRIKE FORCE *US jets participated in NATO interventions in the former Yugoslavia in 1999.*

ONGOING DEBATE *Delegates at a 2013 conference held to discuss the future of the EU*

WHICH REGIONAL ORGANISATIONS HAVE THE MOST INFLUENCE?

Several international organisations promote trade and other forms of cooperation at a regional level. For example, APEC (Asia-Pacific Economic Cooperation), set up in 1989, facilitates economic cooperation between Pacific Rim nations and currently has 21 member states; the Arab League, dating from 1945 and with 22 members, encourages closer ties between its members and coordinates economic, cultural and security policies; and the African Union, founded in 2002, coordinates political, economic and defence policies on behalf of 54 of Africa's 55 nations (Morocco is the only nonmember). The European Union (EU) has become a powerful international body that represents and promotes the interests of its 28 member states. It developed out of the European Coal and Steel Community, set up in 1952 by Belgium, France, Germany, Italy, Luxembourg and the Netherlands. This evolved into the European Economic Community (EEC), which in 1993 became the EU.

WHAT ARE NGOs?

Organisations made up of member nations are known as intergovernmental organisations or international governmental organisations (IGOs). NGOs, or nongovernmental organisations, are international bodies that are not operated by any individual states but manage their own funding and operate across a range of territories. They include many not-for-profit bodies, such as the Red Cross, OXFAM and Médecins Sans Frontières, as well as organisations that campaign on social and environmental issues, such as Greenpeace and the World Wildlife Fund. It is estimated that there are around 40,000 international NGOs and many more national ones – India alone is thought to have as many as 2 million.

MEDICAL AID *Red Cross workers offering free measles vaccinations in Kenya*

INDEX

ACKNOWLEDGEMENTS

All images are copyright of Reader's Digest, except for the following:

Cover: all Shutterstock except r Reader's Digest; **6–7** Shutterstock; **9 t** NASA, ESA and the Planck Collaboration; **9 b** NASA, ESA and The Hubble Heritage Team (STScI/AURA); **11 tr** NASA, ESA, M. Livio and the Hubble Heritage Team (STScI/AURA); **12 tr** NASA, Chandra X-ray Observatory Center; **13 r** NASA/JPL-Caltech/ESA; **14 l, r** Getty Images; **14 b** NASA/JPL/University of Arizona/University of Colorado; **15 b** Shutterstock; **16 t** NASA/JPL/USGS; **16 bl** NASA, JHU/APL, Michael Carroll/Alien Volcanoes by Lopes and Carroll, The Johns Hopkins University Press, 2008; **16 br** NASA/JPL; **17 tl** NASA/Johns Hopkins University Applied Physics Laboratory/Carnegie Institution of Washington; **17 t** Shutterstock; **17 tr** NASA/NOAA/GSFC/Suomi NPP/VIIRS/Norman KuringNASA; **17 tr** NASA/JPL/USGS; **17 r** NASA/JPL-Caltech; **17 b** Getty Images; **18 tr** Shutterstock; **18 b** NASA/JPL; **18 r** NASA/JPL/Space Science Institute; **19 t** Shutterstock; **19 l** NASA/JPL/STScI; **19 r** NASA/JPL; **20 l** NASA, ESA, and M. Showalter (SETI Institute); **20 b** NASA, **20 t** NASA/ESA/J. Parker (Southwest Research Institute), P. Thomas (Cornell University), L. McFadden (University of Maryland, College Park), and M. Mutchler and Z. Levay (STScI); **20 r** NASA; **21 tl** NASA/JPL/DLR; **21 c** NASA/GSFC/Arizona State University; **21 r** NASA/JPL; **21 bl** NASA Apollo; **21 br** NASA/JPL; **22 b** Getty Images; **23 tl** NASA; **23 r** Shutterstock; **24 l, r** Shutterstock; **25 l** NASA, H.E. Bond and E. Nelan (Space Telescope Science Institute, Baltimore, Md.); M. Barstow and M. Burleigh (University of Leicester, U.K.); and J.B. Holberg (University of Arizona); **25 b** ESA/Herschel/PACS/L. Decin et al; **26 t** Christos Kotsiopoulos; **26 b** Shutterstock; **27 tl** NASA; **27 tr, bl** Shutterstock; **27 br** Corbis; **28 b** Corbis; **29 t** Shutterstock; **30 l** Shutterstock; **30 r** Corbis; **31 t** Shutterstock; **31 c** Mohamed Farhadi | Dreamstime.com; **33 t** Jonathan O'Neil/National Science Foundation; **33 l** Shutterstock; **33 c** Wiley/Claudia Rubenstein; **33 b** Science Photo Library; **34 t, b** Corbis; **35 t** Shutterstock; **35 l** iStockphoto; **36 t** Shutterstock; **36 c** iStockphoto; **37 t, b** Shutterstock; **37 r** iStockphoto; **38 l** NASA/NOAA; **38 b** iStockphoto; **39 t** Shutterstock; **39 c** NASA, Ozone Hole Watch; **41 tl** Wikipedia/PiccoloNamek; **41 tr** Shutterstock; **41 l** Wikimedia/Kr-val; **41 bl** Wikipedia/PiccoloNamek; **42 t** Dreamstime; **43 tl** Shutterstock; **43 tr** Getty Images; **43 bl** Wikimedia/William M. Connolley; **43b** Getty Images; **43 br** NASA, Jeff Schmaltz, LANCE/EOSDIS Rapid

Response; **44 l, b** Shutterstock; **45 tl** Shutterstock; **45 tr** Dreamstime; **45 bl, br** iStockphoto; **46 t** Corbis; **47** Shutterstock; **48 t** iStockphoto; **48 l, bl, br** Shutterstock; **49 tl** Getty Images; **49 r, tr, br** iStockphoto; **49 c, bl** Shutterstock; **50 t, b** Shutterstock; **50 l, r** iStockphoto; **51 t** Corbis; **51 r** Getty Images; **51 b** Dreamstime; **52 l** Shutterstock; **52 b** Science Photo Library; **53 t** iStockphoto; **53 b** Shutterstock; **54 l** U.S. Antarctic Program, National Science Foundation; **55 t** Science Photo Library; **55 r** iStockphoto; **55 l, c, bl, br** Getty Images; **56 l** iStockphoto; **57 t, b** iStockphoto; **57 l** Shutterstock; **57 r** Getty Images; **58 l, r** iStockphoto; **59 l, r** Shutterstock; **59 c** Getty Images; **59 b** NASA/JSC; **60 t** Shutterstock; **61 t** NASA; **63 tl, r** Corbis; **63 bl** Science Photo Library; **65 l, r** iStockphoto; **66 t** Getty Images; **66 l** Shutterstock; **66–67 c** Shutterstock; **67 t** Science Photo Library; **67 l, r, bl, br** Shutterstock; **68 l, r** Shutterstock; **68 bl, r** Dreamstime; **68 r** Getty Images; **68 r** Corbis; **69 r** Corbis; **70 l, r** Shutterstock; **70 b** iStockphoto; **71 t** iStockphoto; **71 r** NASA/Martin Lockheed; **71 b** Shutterstock; **72 r** iStockphoto; **73 t** Getty Images; **73 r, l, b** Shutterstock; **74–5** Shutterstock; **76 l** iStockphoto; **76 r** Shutterstock; **77 t** iStockphoto; **78 l** iStockphoto; **78 bl** Corbis; **79 l, r** Alamy; **79 b** iStockphoto; **80 l** Corbis; **81 c, t** Getty Images; **81 r** Shutterstock; **82 c, r** Shutterstock; **82 l** Getty Images; **83 t** Nobu Tamura, spinops.blogspot.com; **83 l, br** Shutterstock; **83 c, r** Corbis; **85** Corbis; **87 b** Shutterstock; **88** Getty Images; **89 t, l, b** iStockphoto; **89 r** Shutterstock; **90 t, c** Shutterstock; **90 b** Corbis; **91 t** Alamy; **91 c, b** Shutterstock; **92 t** Corbis; **92 b** Getty Images; **93 t** Corbis; **93 r** Getty Images; **94 t** Shutterstock; **95 l, c** Getty Images; **95 r** Alamy; **95 b** Corbis; **96 t** Shutterstock; **97 t** Getty Images; **97 b** Corbis; **98 l** Shutterstock; **98 br** Corbis; **99 b** Alamy; **100 b** iStockphoto; **100 t** Shutterstock; **101 br** Corbis; **102 r** Shutterstock; **102 l** Dreamstime; **102 b** Wikipedia/Christian Fischer; **103 t** Corbis; **103 l** iStockphoto; **103 r** Alamy; **105 t, r** Getty Images; **105 l** Corbis; **106 t** Corbis; **107 r** Corbis; **107 c** Shutterstock; **107 b** Science Photo Library; **108 t, bl** Shutterstock; **109 l** Shutterstock; **109 b** Corbis; **110 t** Getty Images; **110 l** Corbis; **111 r** Getty Images; **112 t** Corbis; **113 l, r** iStockphoto; **113 t** Corbis; **114 t** Shutterstock; **115 t, l** Shutterstock; **115 b** Alamy; **115 c, r** iStockphoto; **116 t** Auscape; **116 l** Corbis; **116 b, r** Shutterstock; **117 l** Alamy; **117 b, r** Corbis; **118 l** Shutterstock; **118 r** Corbis; **119 l, b** Getty Images; **120 t** iStockphoto; **121 t** Getty Images; **121 r** Alamy; **123 l** Shutterstock;

READER'S DIGEST ULTIMATE BOOK OF KNOWLEDGE

Consultants Jack Challoner, Robert R Coenraads, Kathy Kramer, Karen McGhee, Margaret McPhee, John O'Byrne, Richard Whitaker, Peter White

Writers Additional text by Jack Challoner, Scott Forbes

Editorial Manager Scott Forbes
Senior Editors Jessica Cox, Bronwyn Sweeney
Project Designer Jacqueline Richards
Cover Designer Mark Thacker of Big Cat Design
Senior Designer Joanne Buckley
Illustrators Ian Faulkner, Stephen Pollitt
Photo Editor Amanda McKittrick
Proofreader Jennifer Taylor
Indexer Jo Rudd
Senior Production Controller Martin Milat

READER'S DIGEST GENERAL BOOKS
Editorial Director Lynn Lewis
Managing Editor Rosemary McDonald
Design Manager Donna Heldon

Reader's Digest Ultimate Book of Knowledge is published by
Reader's Digest (Australia) Pty Limited
80 Bay Street, Ultimo, NSW 2007
www.readersdigest.com.au
www.readersdigest.co.nz
www.rdasia.com

Some of the material in this book originally appeared in *Reader's Digest Book of Amazing Facts* and *Reader's Digest Facts at Your Fingertips*, published by Reader's Digest (Australia) Pty Limited.

® Reader's Digest and The Digest are registered trademarks of The Reader's Digest Association Inc., New York, USA.

National Library of Australia Cataloguing-in-Publication entry:
  Title: Reader's Digest ultimate book of knowledge
  ISBN: 978-1-922085-67-2 (hardback)
  Notes: Includes index.
  Target Audience: For secondary school age.
  Subjects: Handbooks, vade-mecums, etc. —Juvenile literature.
  Natural history—Handbooks, manuals, etc.—Juvenile literature.
  Science—Handbooks, manuals, etc. —Juvenile literature.
  Earth (Planet)—Miscellanea—Juvenile literature.
Dewey Number: 031.02

Prepress by Colourpedia, Sydney
Printed and bound in China by RR Donnelley

Address any comments about *Reader's Digest Ultimate Book of Knowledge* to:
Reader's Digest Association (Canada) ULC
The Book Editor
1100 Rene-Levesque Blvd. West
Montreal, Quebec H3B 5H5
Canada

To order copies of *Reader's Digest Ultimate Book of Knowledge*, call 1-800-465-0780

Visit us on the Web at readersdigest.ca

Concept code: AU 0923/IC

IS THERE LIFE ON OTHER PLANETS?

WHEN WILL WE RUN OUT OF FOSSIL FUELS?

DO BOYS GROW FASTER THAN GIRLS?

HOW ARE X-RAY IMAGES CREATED?

WHO WERE THE FIRST PEOPLE IN SPACE?

...AT ARE SHOOTING STARS? WHICH IS THE...
...STEM? WHAT IS IT LIKE ON THE MOON? JUST HOW...
...D HUMANS APPEAR? WHICH ARE THE OLDEST ROCK...
...HY DOES THE...
...SERTS DRY AND...
...OUNTAINS MADE...
...NTINENT? HOW MANY OCEANS ARE THERE? WHY...
...CKS AND MINERALS? HOW DO YOU CUT A DIAMOND...
...LAND? HOW DO SPECIES CHANGE OVER TIME...
...FIND FOSSILS? HOW CAN WHALES AND DOLPHINS...
...NGUS GROW ON FOOD? DO SOME PLANTS EAT ANIMALS...
...OVE WITHOUT LEGS? DO FLYING SQUIRRELS REALLY FLY...
...D HORNS USED FOR? HOW OFTEN DO ANIMALS...
...AVE POUCHES? WHICH IS THE LONGEST WORM...
...W HEAVY IS THE HEAVIEST FLYING BIRD? WHAT SPEED...
...ANY BONES DO WE HAVE? WHAT...
...USCLES? WHERE DOES BLOOD...
...? WHERE IS OUR SKIN MOST...
...AKE YOU WANT TO GO TO THE TOILET? HOW DOES THE BODY...
...FFERENT COUNTRIES? HOW MUCH DO WE NEED OF EACH...
...HICH BODY PARTS CAN BE REPLACED WITH ARTIFICIAL ONES...
...AN ATOM? HOW DO FORCES AFFECT US...
...BOOM? WHAT IS STATIC ELECTRICITY...
...HOW DO PEOPLE TAP PHONES? WHAT ARE PIXELS? HOW DO SPEAKER...
...ROBOT REALLY THINK FOR ITSELF? IS SPACE CLUTTERED WITH OLD SATELLITES...
...AIRSHIPS FLY? WHAT HAPPENS ON THE FLIGHT...
...LLEST BUILDING? HOW DOES POWER REACH OUR...
...RAMIDS? DOES ALL WRITING RUN FROM LEFT...
...ORLD? WHEN DID MASS PRODUCTION BEGIN? WHY ARE THERE SO MANY DIFFERENT LANGUAGES...
...LIGIONS RELATED? CAN A HOUSE HAVE PAPER WALLS? WHY DO WE WEAR CLOTHES...
...N COMPUTER TECHNOLOGY HELP FARMERS? WHICH COUNTRIES FISH THE MOST...